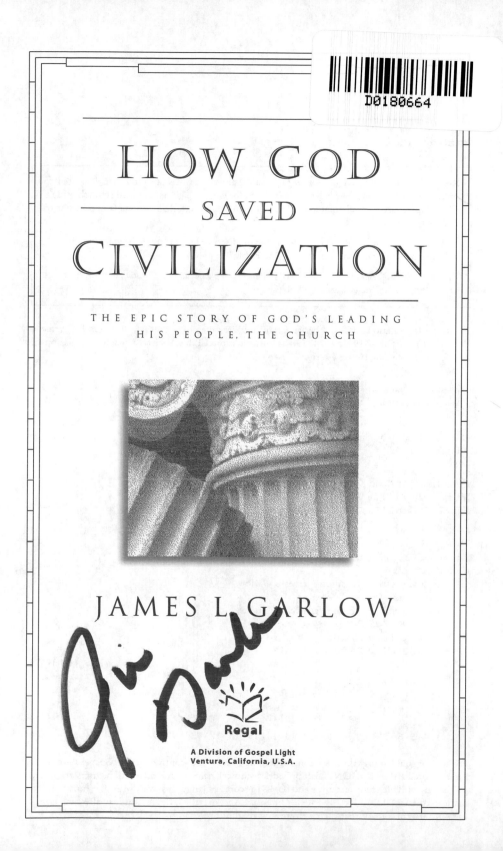

HOW GOD
— SAVED —
CIVILIZATION

THE EPIC STORY OF GOD'S LEADING
HIS PEOPLE, THE CHURCH

JAMES L. GARLOW

Regal

A Division of Gospel Light
Ventura, California, U.S.A.

Published by Regal Books
A Division of Gospel Light
Ventura, California, U.S.A.
Printed in the U.S.A.

Regal Books is a ministry of Gospel Light, an evangelical Christian publisher dedicated to serving the local church. We believe God's vision for Gospel Light is to provide church leaders with biblical, user-friendly materials that will help them evangelize, disciple and minister to children, youth and families.

It is our prayer that this Regal book will help you discover biblical truth for your own life and help you meet the needs of others. May God richly bless you.

For a free catalog of resources from Regal Books/Gospel Light please call your Christian supplier, or contact us at 1-800-4-GOSPEL *or* www.regalbooks.com.

Cover Design by Kevin Keller
Interior Design by Rob Williams
Edited by Rebecca Jones and Wil Simon

Library of Congress Cataloging-in-Publication Data
Garlow, James. L.
    How God saved civilization / James L. Garlow.
       p. cm.
    Includes bibliographical references and index.
    ISBN 0-8307-2525-3
    1. Church history. I. Title.
    BR145.2.G27 2000
    270—dc21   00-037274

1 2 3 4 5 6 7 8 9 10 11 12 13 14 15 16 17 18 19 20 / 05 04 03 02 01 00

Rights for publishing this book in other languages are contracted by Gospel Literature International (GLINT). GLINT also provides technical help for the adaptation, translation and publishing of Bible study resources and books in scores of languages worldwide. For further information, contact GLINT, P.O. Box 4060, Ontario, CA 91761-1003, U.S.A. You may also send e-mail to Glintint@aol.com, or visit their website at www.glint.org.

CONTENTS

ACKNOWLEDGMENTS

I want to express my deep appreciation to:

- Winfred Garlow (1921–), my mother, confidante and constant encourager, for spending several thousand hours typing this manuscript through several editions from muffled cassette voice recordings and several thousand pages of illegible scribbles (always with such patience and excitement) and for continually prodding me forward in this project in such a loving way. Without you, this book would never have come into being.
- *Burtis Garlow* (1915-1998), my father and my best friend, for giving me a deep love for history and a profound respect for those who have gone before us, and for giving me respect for people of other theological streams while at the same time having a strong love and loyalty for our own heritage.

I also want to thank so many wonderful teachers in my life:

- *Ethel Henthorne*, fourth and fifth grade, Hillcrest Elementary
- *Wilbur Rawson*, vocational agriculture instructor; *Lee Tubach*, Spanish; *Jim Douglas*, English (Concordia High School, Kansas)
- *Laverne Atkins*, psychology (Miltonvale Wesleyan High School, Kansas)
- *Merril McHenry*, zoology; *Robert Mattke*, Greek (Bartlesville Wesleyan College, Kansas campus)
- *Richard Howard*, New Testament; *Rob Staples*, theology; *Forrest Ladd*, research; *Loren Greshem*, political science;

Don Owens, cultural anthropology (Southern Nazarene University, Bethany, Oklahoma)

- *Ken Kinghorn,* Church history (gave me my first love for Church history); *Robert Coleman,* evangelism; *Robert Traina,* Bible; *Don Dayton,* mentor and theological big brother (Asbury Theological Seminary, Wilmore, Kentucky)
- *Lefferts Loetscher,* American church history; *Norman V. Hope,* British church history; *Karl Froehlich,* Reformation; *Bruce Metzger,* New Testament mentoring group (Princeton Theological Seminary, Princeton, New Jersey)
- *Russ Richey,* American church history; *Ken Rowe,* Methodist church history (Drew University, Madison, New Jersey)

And to so many other teachers and professors not mentioned here, I say thank you . . . thank you so much. My prayer: "Thank God for teachers!"

And finally, thank you to editors *Rebecca Jones, Wil Simon* and *David Webb;* and special thanks to *Kyle Duncan, Bill Greig II* and *Bill Greig III.*

SEEING THE GOD OF THE AGES

Civilization has no hope. No hope at all, except through God. God alone can preserve a person, a family, a people group, a nation or any part of civilization that's worth preserving. Without God, no one, no nation, no culture can survive. In fact, left to itself, civilization self-destructs.

That's the bad news. But the good news is that God does love the world and preserves it from experiencing its own complete self-destruction. Through the inexplicable gift of His Son, Jesus, God extends His love. And before Jesus left planet Earth, He launched one of God's best ideas: the Church. For some mysterious reason, God chose to accomplish His kingdom through the Church. Through the true Church, He preserves us from inevitable self-destruction. Beginning 2,000 years ago, the Church has preserved and passed on the gospel, praying that people will open their hearts to receive it so that when civilization as we know it *does* end, God's people will all be gathered, ready to receive Him.

The Church is not perfect. In fact, it is the opposite of perfect. It is weak, tainted and blemished. The Church might be described the way Le Corbusier described New York City: "New York is a catastrophe, but a magnificent catastrophe."[1] The Church, as you will discover in the pages that follow, is sometimes a catastrophe. But when viewed as a whole, when viewed in its completeness, it is a *magnificent* catastrophe!

This magnificent catastrophe has an equally magnificent story, but few know it.

As Bruce Shelley stated, "Surely one of the remarkable aspects of Christianity today is how few of these professed believers have ever seriously studied the history of their religion."[2]

Present

The story of the history of the Church is a drama, and I've had two goals in writing this drama in book form: (1) to inform of the past, encourage for the future and inspire for the future, and (2) to make a history book read like a storybook. Whether or not I have achieved my goals is up to the reader, but it remains that Church history is a drama—a spectacular drama.

REASONS FOR STUDYING CHURCH HISTORY

Why study this drama? There are at least 10 good reasons:

1. *It gives you understanding.*
   How did we get the way we are? A study of the drama answers that. The study of history can make you wise without gray hair and wrinkles (though one certainly cannot say the same about the *writing* of that history!).
2. *The study of history introduces you to new friends.*
   How else could you meet Augustine, John of the Cross, Martin Luther, John Wesley or Charles Finney? Only as you investigate the drama can you meet them.
3. *You learn the price that was paid for you!*
4. *You avoid the pitfalls and the land mines of history.*
   It has been said that he who is not a student of history is condemned to repeat it. The study of history is not done to exalt tradition. In fact, tradition can be enslaving. As Richard Halverson noted, "Tradition can be dangerous. It can not only modify the truth; it can replace it altogether."[3] A study of history teaches us which traditions are suffocating and need to be avoided and which are so crucial that they must be preserved at all costs.
5. *Studying history increases your effectiveness.*
   You'll see what worked, what was effective. Mark Shaw said it all

in the title of his book, *Ten Great Ideas from Church History*.[4] You can and should learn from Church history.

6. *History enhances your endurance.*

   When you see what those before you endured, you will be encouraged to persevere.

7. *History will inspire you.*

   Information may guide you, but inspiration keeps you going. A study of history can inspire. Hopefully, this one will.

8. *History makes the dead come to life.*

   My friend Harold Ivan Smith says "no person is dead as long as someone keeps saying their name or telling their stories." By telling this drama, the historical figures live once again.

9. *The study of history humbles you by helping you to understand that there was life before you were born.*

   John Wesley once said to Adam Clarke, "If I were to write my own life, I should begin it before I was born."[5] When I asked a friend why he left a newly formed, independent church to join a church with a long heritage, he answered, "Because I wanted to belong to something that had an existence before 1900!"

10. *A study of history allows you to take a trip without leaving the comfort of your favorite chair.*

    As you read these pages, you are going to visit dozens of nations, many homes, churches, schools and palaces—all without ever leaving your home. Have a wonderful trip.

DISCLAIMERS AND EXPLANATIONS

We can't begin the trip without some disclaimers and explanations. To begin with, this book is not a scholarly treatise. I have the heart of a pastor, not the head of a scholar. Besides, there are many superb scholarly books designed for colleges and graduate schools. This book is especially written for the layperson who will never study history in college or graduate school. I want you to know this powerful drama.

This book is not completely balanced. I gave more attention to Polycarp's death, to John Huss's final moments and to Dwight L. Moody's feelings after the Chicago fire than a normal history book would allow. But this is not a history book; it's a storybook, so some persons and events received extra space and attention because I wanted the reader to linger with me over the passionate and moving moments in the lives of our Christian ancestors.

This book is not exhaustive. For example, an enormous proportion of the believers on Earth today are Eastern Orthodox. They are barely mentioned. It is not because I find them unimportant. On the contrary! But they are not a part of *this* story. Many important persons, movements, events and denominations are left out or barely mentioned. Their stories are equally important. But I could not tell them all in one book.

Some may wonder why I didn't name their favorite Christian leader, denomination, church or movement. They may question why I spent so much time on some individuals (who they may feel are unimportant) while neglecting others (who they feel deserve more attention). For that concern, I have three responses:

1. When doing a broad sweep of 2,000 years of history in a limited number of pages, choices have to be made. Those choices are sometimes admittedly arbitrary, but they nevertheless have to be made .

2. Rob Staples, former professor at Nazarene Theological Seminary, said it well with regard to his own writing: "It's my story. When you write yours, you can write it however you want." Each of us has a story; and, for good or for bad, we tell our stories as we see them. This is the way I see my story.

3. I hope you'll want to interact more with the great personalities and grand themes of Church history. To help you do that I have provided a website (www.jimgarlow.com) located at the end of each chapter. The site offers study questions, charts, diagrams, time lines and links to many other outstanding sites.

It is important to note that writing a broad sweep of history by focusing on some details and having to leave out others may result in caricatures much like a political cartoonist would draw of Richard Nixon (the jaws),

Jimmy Carter (the grin) or Bill Clinton (the chin). In other words, one over-states some aspect of the individual in order to make the point clear and memorable for the reader. My writing of this small book covering 2,000 years of history is much like that—It is filled with caricatures.

This book is written mainly for Americans, though this will not become apparent until the later chapters, since we American Christians share most of our past with Christians the world over. The advance of the gospel in other parts of the world is thrilling, even exhilarating. But in this book I follow the particular thread of Christian history that weaves its way into the United States.

This book is the product of a man with limited perspective and his own biases. I am a Protestant, an Evangelical and, in particular, a Wesleyan/Arminian. And I am heavily influenced by the Third Wave. All of these per-spectives bring certain imbedded biases, for good or for bad.

This book tries to affirm all theological heritages that are within the framework of historic Christianity. For example, as a Protestant I affirm the Roman Catholic church in spite of some obvious differences. It is important to remember that when I discuss the debauchery of Catholic leaders before the Reformation, I discuss my own history. Before the Reformation, we were all part of the Roman Catholic church (unless we're Orthodox). In other words, Christians have a collective history. As a child growing up in a Wesleyan theological tradition, the name Calvin was a negative term. As an adult I still disagree with some of Calvin's fundamental assumptions, yet I make every attempt to affirm his gargantuan contribution to Christianity. As another example, I could not disagree more with Alexander Campbell's fol-lowers (who believe that musical instruments are not to be used in worship), but I still try to put the best possible construction on their motives and the results of their decisions (they learned to sing a cappella and they sang well!).

This book includes more male than female leaders. When I include women, it is not in some attempt to tip my hat to feminism or to include the token woman. I include certain women because they were significant actors in the drama. However you choose to explain it, the Church has been directed mainly by male leadership. However, history is full of unsung heroes—both men and women—who are never mentioned in anyone's histo-ry book. Someday we will hear some very exciting, *untold* stories of God's women and their powerful place in the turns of Christian history. I hope my female readers will not feel as exasperated as Catherine Morland: "But history, real solemn history, I cannot be interested in . . . I read it as little as a duty, but it tells me nothing that does not either vex or weary me. The quarrels of popes and kings, with wars or pestilences, in every page; the men all so good for nothing, and hardly any women at all—it is very tiresome."[6] Anyone could weary of the wars between popes and kings (unavoidable, however!), but there is much more to our drama than that. I invite both male and female readers to see the big picture: God's unending faithfulness to the people called the Church.

TIME PERIODS

To help guide you, I want to introduce you to the time line we will be tracing through history. In the following pages, we will adhere to the following historical time periods:

100-313	The Early Church, Survival
313-590	The Early Church, Supremacy
590-1517	The Middle Ages
1517 and following	The Reformation
1530s and following	The English Reformation
1600s and following	American Christianity[7]

FICTION

One last thing before we begin: You will find at the beginning of each chapter a fictional story. I have tried to help you imagine what an ordinary child, man or woman might have felt during the period treated in each chapter. But I am merely imagining. These initial stories are not recorded history.

Now we are ready. Turn the page. Let the drama begin.

Jim Garlow
San Diego, California
January 2000

Bold in the Face of Death

THE MARTYRS

Dates covered: A.D. 100-313
Key persons: Ignatius, Polycarp, Perpetua, Felicitas

Rostus sat with his chin resting on his bent knees, staring out over the rooftops of Rome, and watched as the moon slid from behind a cloud. He clutched the wooden sword his father had carved for him as a present for his seventh birthday. Between his teeth, Rostus could still taste bits of the honey and almond wafers his mother had prepared. He smiled at the thought of the party with his cousins and his Christian friends. But his smile turned back to a frown as he heard the voices of his father and his uncle mixed in urgent discussion downstairs.

"We've been through this before, Lehue," came the tired voice of Rostus's father, Nascious. "Anyway, it's too late. This morning I refused to go to the stadium. I can't say 'Caesar is Lord' when I know Jesus is Lord."

"Go tomorrow morning! There's still time. The sacrifice is only a ritual. A little powder on a fire. It doesn't mean anything," argued Lehue. "You pay taxes, don't you? So why not declare your allegiance to Rome in a public ceremony? I plan to do it, if I have to. I'm not going to leave my wife and children without anyone to support them. Think of Rostus up there with his birthday presents."

"I would die for my son, Lehue, and you know it. But if I have to die for Jesus before Rostus grows up, at least he will know that Jesus is my Lord. What will I show him if I compromise my faith in Christ by worshiping Emperor Valerian?"

"You'll be torn to shreds. Please, Nascious, promise me you'll go to the authorities tomorrow and tell them you'll do it!"

The voices faded as Nascious and his brother Lehue moved out into the courtyard. Beneath the brilliant moon, Rostus stared at the enormous stadium in the distance. Each day the crowds roared with excitement as ravenous lions devoured prisoners. He rubbed a tear from his cheek. What would happen to him, to mother, to Julia if father were dragged before the city officials? What if they were ever thrown into prison? He clutched his sword tighter to his knees. But what could he do with a wooden sword against the Roman soldiers who marched through the streets outside his window?

Rostus tossed fretfully in his sleep that night. *Surely they won't take Daddy,* he thought. *Daddy's so kind, such a hardworking silversmith. Why would anyone want to kill him just because he loved Jesus?* He fell into a fitful sleep. A loud pounding woke him. Shouts came from the street below. Rostus jumped from his bed and peered through the curtain. Behind him he heard a noise. Turning, he saw his father, out in the hallway, pulling on his linen robe.

"Daddy!" shouted Rostus, as he ran into his father's arms.

"Son," said Nascious quietly as he knelt down. "I love you. You will probably never see me again until we're in heaven. I want you to remember one thing. Jesus is worth everything." He pulled Rostus to his chest and squeezed him tight. A soldier bounded up the steps but stopped, embarrassed. Nascious rose slowly, tenderly said goodbye to his wife and to Julia and, standing tall, followed the soldier down the stairs and out into the night.

It was the last Rostus ever saw of him.

THE PRICE

According to Blaise Pascal, "The last thing that we discover in writing a book, is to know what to put at the beginning."[1] Allow me to cut to the chase. Serving Christ costs. Sometimes it costs one's life. Beginning with the third century and up through the early fourth century, Christian believers were sometimes faced with fierce persecution. By 100, the baby Church was walking on its own, without the direction and oversight of the immediate followers of Jesus. None of the original disciples was living. All had been martyred except for John, who had lived to a very old age—probably 90 or so. Before he died, he wrote the last book in our Bible, Revelation, in approximately A.D. 90 or 95. Our story picks up right where the Bible stops. Now a new story begins—a 1900-year-old story—a glorious story but not an easy one. Immediately, the Early Church was attacked on four fronts: two external and two internal.

EMPEROR LOYALTY

In the centuries of the Early Church many Roman emperors, whose names mean little to us, caused the deaths of thousands of believers who would not conform to the laws of the emperor cult. In an annual event, the government required all to pledge their loyalty to the government by burning some incense and saying "Caesar is lord." Those who refused to comply were accused of being atheistic. Imagine the irony of accusing Christians, who believed in God and specifically in His Son, Jesus Christ, of being atheists simply because they wouldn't announce that "Caesar is lord." But being atheists was one of the accusations made about early believers: These periods of persecution produced new categories of believers: martyrs—who obviously did not survive the persecution; lapsi—who, under the pressure of persecution, had lapsed, or recanted, renouncing their faith in Christ; and confessors—who bore on their bodies the marks of persecution, having survived at a high price.

THE LAPSI

The Church had no difficulty dealing with martyrs or confessors. These were the heroes. But the lapsed posed a problem. One observer, Dionysius of Alexandria, wrote in a letter to Fabius, bishop of Antioch, about Christians who had lapsed, renouncing Christ when the threat of persecution had become evident:

> Immediately, the news spread abroad. The rule that had been more kind to us was changing; now the fear of threatened punishment hung over us. What is more, the edict arrived; it was almost like that which the Lord predicted. It was most terrible so as to cause, if possible, even the elect to stumble. All cowered with fear. A number of the more eminent persons came forward immediately through fear. Others, because of their business and public positions, were compelled to come forward. Others were dragged forward by those around them. Each of those were [sic] called forward by name. They approached the impure and unholy sacrifices, some pale and trembling, as if they were themselves the sacrifices and victims to the idols. The large crowd that stood around heaped mockery upon them. It was evident that they were by nature cowards in everything—cowards both to die and to sacrifice. Others, however, ran eagerly toward the altars, affirming by their forwardness that they had never been Christians. For these, the Lord truly predicted that they shall hardly be saved.[2]

But many did not lapse, and they were either killed or tortured.

WIDESPREAD PERSECUTION

Prior to Emperor Decius, who came to power in 251, the persecution of Christians had been sporadic and localized. However, Decius intensified persecution, which soon became a systematic empirewide elimination of all believers. The 11-year period from 250 to 261 is known as the Decade of Horror.

But Diocletian (284-305) was the harshest of them all. Particularly galling to Diocletian was the fact that many of his slaves and servants, as well as his wife and daughters, were believers. So pervasive was Christianity's expansion that it had moved into the emperor's private dwelling. In an attempt to stymie Christianity's explosive growth, Diocletian issued four edicts. This series of decrees issued in approximately 303 required the destruction of all church buildings (church buildings were a recent phenomenon; the first had been built in about 250). The edict also required the destruction of Christian books and the removal of believers from governmental positions and from the army. All clergy were imprisoned. The next year, Diocletian issued another order insisting that Christians offer sacrifices to pagan deities.

REASONS FOR PERSECUTION

Why were the emperors so set on killing believers? In addition to their refusal to claim Caesar as God, believers did not follow the traditional Roman gods and were considered intolerant of other religions. Their commitment to Christ alone caused them to appear anti-Roman and disloyal. Emperors feared that these people might become subversive because they would yield allegiance only to the One named Jesus. Another bizarre reason given to justify the persecution was that Christianity divided families. The family was the basic unit in Roman culture. When individuals converted to Christ, they would sometimes leave their families; and thus the Christian Church was accused of corrupting society by splitting families.

But Christianity flourished in spite of the persecution. Tertullian (ca. 160-225), an Early Church leader, wrote, "Go on . . . torture, grind us to powder; our numbers increase in proportion as you mow us down. The blood of Christians is their harvest seed."[3] Thus persecution failed to stop the growth of Christianity. Instead, Christianity flourished.

RAPID GROWTH

Why did the Church grow so rapidly during this time? For one thing, the Christian faith was very simple. It was monotheistic, serving only one God.

This seemed attractive to those confused by a complex constellation of Greek and Roman gods. To think that there was only one Lord, one faith and one baptism was appealing. Second, believers lived what they taught. Not only had they developed a rich understanding of life, but they also lived by it so radically that others were intrigued by their power and their love. The Christian faith appealed particularly to slaves and servants. The intimate fellowship of the Church appealed to the homeless and insignificant in Roman society.

The martyrs' attitude toward death was also a tremendously powerful aspect in the spread of the faith. We can be tempted to think of the martyrs as special beings, almost nonpersons, but they were individuals like you and me and were just as afraid of dying. They didn't want to be martyrs. They wanted to live.

It has been said that one person's death is a tragedy, but the death of thousands is a mere statistic. We've spoken about persecution in terms of "thousands." But let's move from the impersonal to the personal and take a look at some of those who died so that you would have faith today.

IGNATIUS

One of the earliest to die for his faith was Ignatius, the bishop of Antioch, (ca. 35-ca. 107) where the disciples were first called Christians (see Acts 11:26). A close friend of the apostle John, Ignatius was the first to describe the Church as "catholic," meaning universal. It was a way of saying that the Church is not merely a collection of individual churches but a universal Church—spread across the world. Ignatius was condemned to die during the reign of Roman Emperor Trajan. After being taken prisoner, he was escorted by 10 soldiers from city to city on his way to Rome.

During this difficult season he wrote seven letters, six of which were addressed to churches: Ephesus, Magnesia, Tralles, Rome, Philadelphia and Smyrna. The seventh was for his good friend Polycarp, bishop at Smyrna. In these amazing letters, Ignatius expresses his deep appreciation to believers who had bidden him farewell as he was forcibly taken on the trip to Rome. He encourages them to be faithful in spite of potential persecution, and he urges his friend Polycarp to "stand firm like an anvil under the hammer."[4] It is little wonder that Christians who shared the incredible fortitude expressed by Ignatius had an impact: "I would rather die for Christ than rule the whole earth. Leave me to the beasts that I may by them be a partaker of God . . . welcome nails and cross, welcome broken bones, bruised body, welcome all diabolic torture, if I may but obtain the Lord Jesus Christ." [5]

Apparently, Ignatius so looked forward to martyrdom that he implored the believers in Rome not to do anything that might delay his impending execution.[6] Ignatius was not disappointed for long. He endured a torture that is almost beyond belief. After having been cast into prison, he was cruelly tormented, for "after being dreadfully scourged, he was compelled to hold fire in his hands, and, at the same time, papers dipped in oil were put to his sides and lighted. His flesh was then torn with hot pincers, and at last he was dispatched by the fury of wild beasts."[7]

POLYCARP

Polycarp (ca. 69-ca. 155), the bishop to whom Ignatius had written, fared no better. He was tortured to death in 155, when he was 86. Polycarp's last moments are described by Eusebius (ca. 260-ca. 339), the court historian of the Christian Roman emperor Constantine, who is also known as the father of Church history:

He stepped forward, and was asked by the proconsul if he really was Polycarp. When he said yes, the proconsul urged him to deny the charge. "Respect your years!" he exclaimed, adding similar appeals regularly made on such occasions: "Swear by Caesar's fortune . . ." But Polycarp, with his face set looked at all the crowd in the stadium . . . and cried: "For eighty-six years . . . I have been His servant, and He has never done me wrong; how can I blaspheme my King who saved me?" "I have wild beasts," said the proconsul. "I shall throw you to them, if you don't change your attitude." "Call them," replied the old man. . . . "If you make light of the beast," retorted the governor, "I'll have you destroyed by fire . . ." Polycarp answered, "The fire you threaten burns for a time and is soon extinguished; there is a fire you know nothing about—the fire of the judgement to come has an eternal punishment, the fire reserved for the ungodly. . . ."

The proconsul was amazed, and sent the crier to stand in the middle of the arena and announce three times; "Polycarp has confessed that he is a Christian. . . ." Then a shout went up from every throat that Polycarp must be burnt alive. . . . The crowds rushed to collect logs. . . . When the pyre (pile of wood for burning Polycarp) was ready . . . Polycarp prayed: "Oh Father of my beloved and blessed Son, Jesus Christ . . . I bless thee for counting me worthy of this day and hour. . . ." The men in charge lit the fire and a great flame shot up.[8]

Although it is tempting to avoid gruesome details, we need to understand the price that was paid for the cause of Christ. John Foxe, in 1563, gave this most unusual account of Polycarp's final moments:

Wood being provided, the holy man earnestly prayed to heaven, after being bound to the stakes; and as the flames grew vehement, the executioners gave way on each side, the heat becoming intolerable. In the meantime the Bishop sang praises to God in the midst of the flames, and remained unconsumed. Determined, however, to put an end to his life, the guards struck spears into his body, when the quantity of blood that issued from the wounds extinguished the flames. After considerable attempts, they put him to death, and burnt his body.[9]

Polycarp is only one of many who were put to death for refusing to recant. The determination of the martyrs helped prevent the extinction of the gospel and preserved it for the next generation.

PERPETUA AND FELICITAS

Not everyone who was persecuted was a well-known bishop, however. One of the most celebrated martyrs was a 26-year-old lady named Perpetua, who, along with Felicitas, was killed in March of 205. Perpetua was married and had an infant. Her father loved her tenderly but became irritated when she refused to renounce her Christian faith. He beat her severely but was unable to convince her to recant, which led to her imprisonment. Her father refused to visit her for some time. She was taken before the proconsul Minutius and commanded to sacrifice to the idols. She refused and was thrown into a dark dungeon without her baby. Finally her father visited her and pleaded with her, this time much more lovingly, to renounce her Christian faith. Perpetua's response to her father was simply, "God's will must be done." The judge at Perpetua's trial begged her to remember her father's tears and the helplessness of her infant. When she refused to recant, she was taken back to prison along with Felicitas. Finally the day of execution came. Perpetua and Felicitas were led into the arena, where wild beasts were released. One beast made his first attack upon Perpetua and stunned her. He then attacked Felicitas and wounded her badly. An executioner stepped forward and brought both of their lives to an end with a sword.[10]

THINK ABOUT IT

It is not my intention to fill your mind with morbid stories. But I do want you to reflect. If I wrote that "thousands were killed because of their faith in Christ," you could easily dismiss martyrdom. But when I show you the faces of these martyrs and you get to know their families, their homes, their joys and fears, you realize that these people are not obscure characters in history. They are our own spiritual family members. Their courage in refusing to recant preserved the faith for us. You have the Christian faith today because there were people willing to stand firm in the face of torture and death.

The story of the Church could have ended after its first 200 years, another failed utopian dream. Many a social movement has burned brightly for a few years, only to fade and grow cold. But Christians would not recant, for Christianity is not a social movement, a hopeless utopia or an inspired fabrication of some dazed apostles' imaginations. Christians were filled with confidence that God had raised Jesus from the dead. On the basis of this reality, ordinary men, women and children faced torture, wild beasts and the flames.

Persecution and the threat of death can never squelch God's promises to His people, His grace to the righteous and unrighteous, and the accomplishment of His ultimate will. The faithful testimony of these Christians perpetuated the faith through many centuries—all the way to you and me. Because of their steadfastness, you and I have the gospel today. That alone is evidence of God's hand through the ages to bless the Church and all the world.

To further assist you in understanding the key individuals and events of chapter 1, study questions, charts, diagrams, time lines and links to biographical websites are available on the Internet at www.jimgarlow.com. Please follow the site links to *How God Saved Civilization*, chapter 1 study helps.

AN APOLOGY DOESN'T ALWAYS MEAN "I'M SORRY"

THE APOLOGISTS

Dates covered: A.D. 100-250
Key persons: Justin Martyr, Aristides, Tertullian, Origen

Athenius peered through the crowded bathhouse. Was it Polarian he could see? He left his seat in the steamy room and got a little closer. Sure enough, there was his childhood friend. What times they used to have together teasing the girls and getting in trouble with their lyceum teachers! Athenius nearly knocked a man into the cold-water bath as he elbowed his way through the crowd. Coming up behind Polarian, he threw his arm around his friend's shoulder.

"Polarian! I thought you were in Gaul!"

Polarian turned and recognized his old friend immediately. After the bear hugs were over and the two had settled into a quiet corner of the baths, they began to chat. By now, each was married and Polarian even had a child. But Athenius noticed a change in his friend. He seemed so much older and calmer, perhaps even a little somber. Remembering the parties they had enjoyed, Athenius asked his old friend, "Why don't you come by Justus's place tonight? You should see the girls he can find! And the wine—it's fabulous—comes from Gaul."

Polarian politely turned him down. "I'm married, now."

"Well, so are a lot of us!" laughed Athenius.

"Polarian, I'm a Christian. It wouldn't please my Lord for me to be at such a party. Besides, I'm a lot happier with Rhoda and my little Marcus than I ever was before I became a Christian."

Athenius's heart sank. "But Pol," he began cautiously. The reunion seemed tiresome now. "Christians don't believe in the gods. They're atheists."

"Not true," said Polarian. "Christians believe in the one true God."

"Well, if they're so religious, why don't they obey the rules of the government? I've heard Jesus told His disciples to pay taxes, so why won't they obey the emperor's rules and sign the allegiance?"

"They can't . . . *we* can't, because—"

Athenius interrupted. "Christians are cowards. I went to the coliseum once, thinking to see some courage in action. But at the first hint of the animals, they all backed down. Swore allegiance to the emperor, every one of them." He spat in disgust.

"Some do," said Polarian, as he wondered how he would fare before the lions. "But hundreds haven't."

"And what about families?" Athenius went on. "You tell me you won't go to a party because of your wife, but Christianity has *split* families. And those

Jewish books say that's what's *supposed* to happen! How can you accept that Jewish nonsense? You're a Roman, by Jupiter! Is that what you want Rome to become? A lot of hotheaded fanatics who are ready to walk away from their parents, wives and children just to follow the ideas of some dead Jew?"

Athenius was not even pretending to listen anymore. But Polarian persisted. "Athenius, more often than not, it is the families who reject Christians. My parents disowned me for following Christ." Polarian looked up at the ceiling and breathed in deeply. He would never forget the last time he saw his father's face, so full of anger and hatred.

In a flurry of anger, Athenius continued, "They claim Jesus is both a god and a man. If he's not a true god, at least He has to be a sort of superhuman. And these Christians trick you. They're not honest. They tell you they have only one God; and then when you take up with them, they tell you the secret: God is really three gods! What's more, I've heard they're cannibals. They drink blood and eat human flesh. Polarian, you were always a great student. Can't you see through this nonsense?"

Polarian stood. "There's a lot I could say, Athenius, and I'd love to say it. But I won't, unless you want to listen." He lifted his linen wrap from a hook on the wall and threw the wrap over his shoulders. "I'm glad I've met you here today. I will pray that the true God will reveal Himself to you and that you will know His love. If you ever want to know more about Jesus Christ, you can come visit Rhoda and me any evening. I'm living at the Upper Market hill, along the Way of Hera. Take the first little road to the right behind the lyceum. I do hope you come. Bring your wife, if she wants to come. By the way, I have the best goat cheese in all of Rome. Good night."

As he walked away, Athenius shook his head. "Deluded . . ." he muttered. But he remembered Polarian's address.

INTELLECTUAL ATTACKS

In the previous chapter I mentioned two *external* pressures on the Early Church and two *internal* pressures. We discussed one of the external pressures, persecution. Now we change our focus to another external pressure, intellectual attacks.

The Early Church had no sooner lost its original leaders then it faced vigorous intellectual attacks. But God raised up defenders of the faith, a group of prolific writers who became known as apologists. "Apology" comes from the Greek word *apologia,* which means to "make a defense." Although all Christians ought to be able to give a defense, or answer, to those who ask or challenge the faith, we sometimes use the term "apologists" to refer to a group of Christian writers (primarily Greek) who wrote important defenses of the faith in the early centuries of the Church. Sometimes they wrote to the emperors. Generally their goal was to influence public opinion regarding Jesus and to open minds so that people would consider becoming Christians.

Unfortunately, most of their writings are little read today because the questions they were dealing with were specific to their times. But their names are important to us, for once again, these are people who made it possible for us to enjoy the faith today. The apologists include men with names mostly unknown to us: Justin Martyr and his disciple Tatian, Aristides, Athenagoras, Tertullian, Theophilus of Antioch, Origen, and Milito, who was the bishop of Sardis. Let's take a moment in our journey through Church history to get acquainted with a few of them.

JUSTIN MARTYR

The most visible of all the apologists was Justin Martyr (ca. 100-ca. 165). People did not have last names back then, so you can guess how Justin got his. Justin was put to death under the Roman official Rusticus. Justin was one of the most competent defenders of the Christian faith that the Church has ever known. Born in Shechem, where Jesus had spoken to the woman at Jacob's well, Justin was raised as a pagan and saturated with pagan philosophy. He was drawn to the faith through his interest in philosophy and theology. While living in Ephesus, Justin was converted when he read the Old Testament prophets and reflected about Christ's fulfillment of the prophecies. As he put it:

> Straightway a flame was kindled in my soul, and a love of the prophets and of those men who are friends of Christ. Theirs is the oldest and truest explanation of the beginning and end of things and of those matters which the philosophers ought to know, because they were filled with the Holy Spirit. They glorified the

Creator, the God and Father of all things, and proclaimed His Son, the Christ. I found this philosophy alone to be safe and profitable.[1]

As Justin's faith grew, he put his philosophical skills to work in defense of the gospel. His most famous work, *Apology,* was addressed to the Emperor Antoninus Pius, while his *Second Apology* was addressed to the Roman senate shortly after the ascension of another emperor, Marcus Aurelius, in 161. Justin attempted to persuade the emperor of the validity of Christian thinking. He also battled against a movement called Gnosticism. We will take a look at this unusual belief system in a later chapter.

Justin and the other apologists, though certainly learned scholars, were not pure intellectuals—dry, dusty or dispassionately professorial. They were energetic and profound, with a burning passion for the truth. They were so struck with the power and awe of the Christian faith that they were compelled to defend it so that future generations would have the truth.

As a young man, Justin searched energetically for truth in a variety of philosophical schools. One day while meditating alone by the seashore, perhaps at Ephesus, he met an old man who exposed the weaknesses of his confident thinking. The stranger then pointed him to the Jewish prophets who bore witness to Christ. Justin had already been impressed by the remarkable moral consistency of Christians in the face of death. These themes were to occur later in his writings. Justin responded wholeheartedly by becoming a Christian. He took his new faith into the philosophical schools. He believed he now possessed in Christ a more perfect philosophy, revealed fully by the God who had been known only in part through the wisdom of the ancient world.[2]

Throughout his life, he wrote so that others would embrace Christ as the truth. The longest of Justin's three surviving works is entitled *Dialogue with Trypho.* Trypho was presumably an educated Jewish man who objected to Christianity. Justin patiently explains why the message of Christ in the New Testament supersedes the Old Testament.

John Foxe records Justin's death with unusual brevity: "Justin and six of his companions were apprehended. Being commanded to deny their faith and sacrifice to the pagan idols, they refused to do either; they were, therefore, condemned to be scourged and beheaded."[3]

A DIFFICULT TASK

It is impossible to overemphasize the importance of Justin Martyr's contribution to the defense of Christianity, which at the time was a young, little-
known religion. Although Christians understood that their faith was not
new (since it was the true outworking of the Jewish faith), most people were
not sure what a Christian was. For the average Roman citizen, a Christian
was a member of a small group of unusual people who believed that a man
from Nazareth had come back from the dead. Not much would have challenged that understanding, since there were few means of exposing people
to the Christian faith. The New Testament did not exist in one volume as we
know it today. At the time, it was a series of scattered letters, some of which
were never included in the New Testament. There were no Christians books,
radio or TV stations, or Christian colleges.

The task of the apologists was formidable. They had to argue the
defense of the gospel philosophically while respecting its supernatural content, such as Jesus' miracles and His resurrection. Often, they could not
preach openly about the topic because of persecution. They turned to semi-
private instruction. Justin Martyr, for example, held classes in a rented room
over the public baths. In safer times, some apologists such as Clement of
Alexandria and Origen, founded special schools of instruction to explain
the basics of the Christian faith.

The apologists swam against the stream of popular culture. When
pagan emperors accused Christians of being atheists because they did not
believe in the Greek gods, the apologists had to explain why the God that
Christians believed in was, in fact, the true God. When common rumor
reported that Christians were incestuous, the apologists had to prove that
the titles "brother" and "sister" did not mean that Christians were biologi-
cal brothers and sisters but that such terms indicated the rich fellowship in
the family of believers. When reports spread that Christians were cannibals, the apologists demonstrated that references to "eating Christ's body"
and "drinking his blood" at the Lord's Supper, were figurative of Christ's
death on the cross and did not indicate that Christians ate human flesh or
drank blood.

By the second and third centuries, relations between Christians and
Jews had become increasingly hostile. If Jesus were the Messiah, why did the
Jews not accept Him? The apologists presented a defense for this perceived

failure of Christianity. They argued that the fault was not in the Messiah but in the nation of Israel, which was filled with apostate people who refused to believe.

They sometimes found themselves in the awkward position of defending the Christian faith against those who called themselves Christians. A plague of heresies contaminated the Early Church, spreading from within. Many called themselves Christians but proposed another gospel. One of these heretics was Marcion, who claimed the God of the Old Testament was not the Creator of the universe but a fickle and evil lesser god. Marcion rejected all of the Old Testament and much of what became the New Testament because they didn't agree with his theology.

Justin Martyr, again making a sturdy defense of the faith, asserted that Marcion was impacted by the devil himself. This was the only explanation for why Marcion would so blaspheme God as to deny that He was the Creator of the universe.

Though the apologists are little read by people today, they helped guard the faith for us. Their defense was scholarly, almost always courteous and extremely forceful. Their defense encouraged believers to hold steady, and it must have eased the persecution by swaying the opinion of pagan political leaders.

ARISTIDES

Aristides lived in Athens, Greece in the year 140. He wrote to the Roman emperor Antoninus Pius with great conviction, to argue that the ancient cult religions were totally unable to meet the cry of the human heart. He systematically laid out the contents of the gospel to show that Jesus alone could meet human aspirations. Eusebius, the first Church historian, states that Aristides was "a man of faith and devoted to our religion."[4] In one of his works, Aristides provides a description of God and then examines various religions to see which one truly measures up to the appropriate understanding of God. Christianity alone, he argues, provides a belief system which does justice to a proper understanding of the nature of God.

Imagine explaining the basics of Christianity to people who have no grasp of it whatsoever. You cannot offer them a book or a tape, and their thinking is thoroughly pagan. How would you explain the basics of the faith? Here is Aristides' profound yet succinct statement:

> As for the Christians, they trace their origins to the Lord Jesus Christ. He is confessed to be the Son of the most high God, who came down from heaven by the Holy Spirit and was born of a virgin and took flesh, in a daughter of man there lived the Son of God. . . . This Jesus . . . was pierced by the Jews, and He died and was buried; and they say that after three days He rose and ascended into heaven. . . . They believe God to be the creator and maker of all things.[5]

Though this explanation may seem elementary to you, remember the audience. Aristides is forthright in his description of the Christian faith. These clear, careful statements maintained the basics of the Christian faith through the tumultuous early centuries. It was simple statements such as these that God used to maintain pure doctrinal truth so that the Church could remain alive and well.

TERTULLIAN

The most exuberant apologist was Tertullian (160-ca. 220), who wrote voluminously on an extremely wide array of topics. He has been called a "fiery fanatic" who "penned sizzling theological treatises."[6] Although referred to as the "last of the Greek apologists," he is also known as the father of Latin theology since he was the first Christian writer to produce literature in Latin.[7] He is also referred to as the "phrase-maker of the Western church," because he was the first to use the word "Trinity" and he developed the formula ("one substance, three persons") to describe it.[8]

Quintus Septimus Tertullian lived most of his life in Carthage, the capital of the Roman province in Africa, where his father was a government official. Tertullian traveled extensively (Rome, Greece and the Middle East) and received an excellent education. He studied law and the classics, wrote easily in Latin or Greek and was thoroughly familiar with philosophy, literature, history, physiology, logic and psychology.[9] He could have lived a life of ease, but in 197 he converted to Christianity, after hearing of those who died for the faith. From that moment on, Tertullian turned his vigorous, bright personality and his thorough training to the defense of the gospel.

Tertullian's writings (197-212) discuss three major issues: (1) Christianity's attitude toward the Roman's state in society, (2) the defense of Christian beliefs against heresy and (3) the moral behavior of believers.

A DISCIPLINED, VIGOROUS MAN

Aggressively outspoken, Tertullian chose to use his witty and vigorous style to call Christians away from their lethargy and moral laxity to a rigorous and ascetic Christian faith. Tertullian applied his Christianity with great single-mindedness. He was deeply disturbed by the apathy of many believers in Carthage, a city with a population of three-quarters of a million people. One portion of his writing challenges Christians not only to live rigorous and disciplined lives but also never to flee from persecution. Tertullian was drawn to the Christian faith in part because of the courage of the martyrs, and it was he who first said that "the blood of the martyrs is the seed of the church," meaning that those who died for their faith brought others to faith (which was the truth for Tertullian).

Tertullian was also concerned that pagan philosophies could corrupt the basics of Christianity. Another of his well-known phrases was "What has Athens to do with Jerusalem?" Tertullian could see nothing in the Greek philosophers that could mix with the gospel of Jesus Christ. No Greek philosopher in Athens had anything to offer, according to Tertullian.

HIS WRITINGS

While Tertullian's name is largely unknown to contemporary believers, his writings helped preserve the gospel for us. So prolific are his writings that one could spend years becoming thoroughly familiar with them. His masterpiece was the *Apology*, in which Tertullian aggressively argued that Christianity should be tolerated and not persecuted. In his writing *To the Heathen*, which was written the year he was converted and the same year as the *Apology*, he wrote that believers should not be punished for their convictions but should be judged on the basis of their morally upright actions. His longest work consisted of five books entitled *Against Marcion*, in which he defended the use of the Old Testament by the Christian Church. To us this might seem strange, but as we have seen, the issue was

a controversial one at the time. Non-Jewish Christians thought the Old
Testament was a purely Jewish document, with no significance for
Christians. Tertullian, in his usual aggressive style, argued that the Old
Testament had great validity for Christians. If you have not yet discovered
the wonders of the left side of your Bible, you might enjoy reading some
of Tertullian's arguments defending the importance of the Old
Testament.

In *Against Marcion*, Tertullian argues in support of the Oneness of
God the Creator and Jesus the Savior. We may wonder why he makes a big
deal about such an obvious truth. But that truth is obvious to us partly
because Tertullian so valiantly defended it and explained it so forcefully.
It is in his work entitled *Against Praxeas* that Tertullian develops the doctrine of the Trinity and first uses the term "Trinity" that is so common in
our vernacular today. His work helped sustain that truth through the ages
to us. Like our understanding of many great doctrines, our understanding
of the Trinity was bought at great price. The energy, study and suffering
of the apologists shaped our history so that we now use their formula-
tions quite casually. We say "Three in One and One in Three" without realizing the struggle involved in reaching such a formulation.

One of Tertullian's works is *Testimony of the Soul*, the first Christian
writing on the topic of psychology. In *To Scapula*, Tertullian reasons with
the political leaders in Africa. Christians don't fear death, he argues, so
their suffering is not the reason to avoid killing them. No, the Roman
leaders should abstain because they will bring upon their own heads the
guilt of murder. In *The Prescription of Heretics*, Tertullian accuses heretics of
violating the "church's property rights" by quoting the Bible. He wrote
extensive commentaries on the Gospel of Luke, Paul's writings and even
the Lord's Prayer. *De spectaculis* would not be received too enthusiastically
today, since in it Tertullian argues that Christians should not attend public sports events. An equally unpopular work for our culture would be his
De cultu feminarum in which Tertullian vigorously condemned current
feminine fashions as immodest. In *De exhortatione castitatis* he claims that
to be truly monogamous, one cannot marry again should the first partner
die. Tertullian specifically requested his own wife not to remarry if he died
first! If she insisted on remarrying, he asked her at least to marry a
Christian.

Most of Tertullian's work does not touch on areas quite so mundane. Far more typical would be *Ad martyres*, written to imprisoned Christians to encourage them to hold steady and to help them understand that their deaths would only be a means by which they would escape the prison of this world.[10]

Though Tertullian wrote about a great variety of things, he did not shotgun problems by shooting in any and every direction. One might say that he "rifled" his writing, aiming at very specific targets. Tertullian struck blows wherever the faith was threatened. In his defense of the Christian faith, he always drew people to the truth of Christ Jesus. This core theme can be seen in the following example, in which he attempts to convey who Jesus really is:

> When a ray is projected from the sun it is a portion of the whole sun; but the sun will be in the ray because it is a ray of the sun; the substance is not separated but extended. So from Spirit comes Spirit, and God from God, as light is candled from light for. . . . this ray of God . . . glided down into a virgin, in her womb was fashioned as flesh, is born as man mixed with God. The flesh was built up by the Spirit, was nourished, grew up, spoke, taught, worked, and was Christ.[11]

Using the sun as an analogy, Tertullian provides a picturesque glimpse of God's taking upon Himself human flesh in the person of Jesus. While this may seem mundane to us, it was this type of vigorous defense that was used by God to preserve the truth we so casually enjoy today. Even though Tertullian took a brief detour into a heresy called Montanism, he was quick to correct his ways, for God's supernatural hand was upon him as a preserver of truth.

ORIGEN

"Pious, popular and persuasive"[12] is how William Barker begins his description of Origen (ca. 185-ca. 254), one of the most profound teachers of third-century Christianity. The oldest of seven, Origen was born in Alexandria, Egypt. By the age of 18, he had become a teacher. The depth of his knowledge, both in spiritual and in secular topics, along with his winsome ways made him an immensely popular teacher. His intellectual acumen was exceeded only by his extreme piety and love for God. As a result of misunderstanding the application of Matthew 19:12 ("some are eunuchs for the sake of the Kingdom of God"), he castrated himself, an act that he later regretted. He was overly zealous about martyrdom, which naturally concerned his mother!

When Origen's jealous bishop banned him from his hometown, he remained in Caesarea, teaching and writing. His great work was *De principiis*, which became the most highly regarded theological treatise of its time. Another comprehensive and exhaustive work was his *Hexapla*, which consisted of the Bible arranged in six columns, comparing the Scriptures in different languages and versions.

This brilliant thinker, popular preacher and prolific author was seized, along with hundreds of other believers, during Emperor Decius's Decade of Horror (250-261). Although he was not killed, he was so savagely tortured that he died shortly thereafter. Jerome referred to Origen as the "second teacher of the church," second only to the apostle Paul.[13]

OUR INDEBTEDNESS

In the rush of contemporary life, few have the time or interest to think about people who lived in the second and third centuries. We have enough trouble remembering basic details about George Washington or Abraham Lincoln. How can we give more than passing attention to people from another culture, who lived so far away and so long ago? Yet these are the ancestors of our faith, on whose shoulders we stand, and we owe it to ourselves and to them to pause long enough to realize who they were and what they did. The recurring theme of this book is that had they not been faithful, you and I might *not* have the gospel. They brilliantly defended that which we often take for granted. And as our American culture becomes increasingly paganlike, new apologists are needed who will study the skills and understanding of the early apologists. As the Church is able to defend its faith, it becomes stronger. And that is important because a weakened Church will never be able to portray and teach a Christ who saves civilization.

To further assist you in understanding the key individuals and events of chapter 2, study questions, charts, diagrams, time lines and links to biographical websites are available on the Internet at www.jimgarlow.com. Please follow the site links to *How God Saved Civilization*, chapter 2 study helps.

TROUBLES BRING NEEDED CHANGES

HERESIES, SCHISMS AND DEVELOPMENTS

Dates covered: A.D. 150-590
Key persons: Irenaeus, Marcion Motanus, Constantine,
Augustine, Ambrose, Jerome, Gregory I

Mercel woke to gray clouds on the spring morning of their third anniversary. Lotius was snuggled fast asleep under the down cover. Today was not their wedding anniversary. They had been married for five years. No, three years ago today they had waded into the Arc River to be baptized in the name of the Father, the Son and the Holy Spirit.

Lotius turned over and mumbled.

"Good morning, Lotius," said Mercel, kissing him gently on the forehead. She loved him so much more since they had both begun to obey and love Christ.

But Lotius rolled over and went back to sleep. Mercel felt a stab of loneliness. Was Lotius changing? His original joy was gone. He spent less time with her and more time with a group of strange friends. He was consumed with knowing special things . . . secret words and coded sayings. When she voiced her fears, he would laugh and tousle her hair as if she were a little girl.

"Trust me!" he would say. "I'm learning enough for both of us."

"Why learn secrets?" she would ask. "Isn't it enough to know Christ?"

"But I am learning *more* about Christ, dear Mercel," he would answer. "There is a deeper way, a better way than the one we first knew."

Mercel rose quietly and brought the fire back to life. She brought in fresh water from the stone pot in the garden and started the water boiling. Lotius loved to drink an herbal infusion for breakfast. She prepared a platter with goat cheese, figs and the recently harvested grapes, and quietly carried it to him.

"Wake up, sleepyhead!" she teased, and kissed him gently on the cheek. Why had he been so distant recently? It was as if he had forgotten she was his wife. He had changed so much over the last months, and Mercel didn't like what she saw.

Lotius finally sat up in bed and ate his breakfast without a word of thanks.

"It's our anniversary today. Remember our baptism three years ago?" said Mercel quietly. "I'm feeling so glad that Jesus died for us."

"Mercel," said Lotius, still chewing on his bread, "I've changed my mind about that. You see, the true Christ did not really die. It was an illusion. Physical things are evil. True spirituality has nothing to do with a physical resurrection. I've come to understand who I really am. As the apostle Thomas said, 'There is light within a man of light.'" At these words, Mercel could take no more.

"Lotius, what has happened to you? Are you even a Christian any-more?"

Lotius threw aside the remains of his breakfast and jumped to his feet. "I can see they're right! They warned me about women. Until you understand true wisdom, you are a weight around my neck. What can I do with you?" Without another word, he dressed quickly and left the house.

"Dear Jesus," sobbed Mercel, as she sank to her knees beside her bed. "Please send someone to help me. I know he's wrong, but I am powerless to show him!"

Over the next several months, Lotius spent many hours in spiritual exercises while Mercel did more and more of the chores on the farm. Patiently she listened to him as he tried to explain it to her. The physical world was unimportant, evil. Jesus could not have died in the flesh. Women and men were really the same, and marriage wasn't that important. If you wanted to be truly spiritual, you had to be like a woman and a man all at once. The best way to know God deeper was to know yourself. The explanations went on and on.

Mercel could only pray. She tried to show Lotius that the Bible didn't teach such things, but he would put his own meaning into the Bible's words.

One day, two years later, Lotius's older brother, Monin, was visiting from Lyon. He came with a book in his bag. "Look!" he exclaimed, "I was able to borrow a copy of Irenaeus's work, *Against Heresies*. It was hard to get it. I've read it over, Lotius, and I think what we've been learning from the Gnostics is wrong. The book is very convincing."

"Only because you're my brother," said Lotius, "I'll hear you out."

For a week, Mercel could hear Lotius and Monin arguing in the garden. She didn't mind doing *all* the work now. She prayed hard as she made the evening soup and kneaded the bread. Finally God had sent someone Lotius would listen to. Maybe this man Irenaeus could convince her stubborn husband to believe the true gospel of Christ. When he left for home, Monin gave Lotius his precious book.

Mercel sensed the battle in her husband. She kept quiet and prayed, loving him as much as he would allow her. But God is faithful. After eight months, Lotius begrudgingly admitted that he may have gone too far in some things.

Mercel was happy. But Lotius never regained the exuberance that had once characterized his Christian faith. He never studied the Gnostic way again, and he continued following Christ; but he seemed to carry a spiritual scar. Mercel longed for the old days, before the detour called Gnosticism.

INTERNAL ATTACKS

Having survived persecution, the Early Church successfully fought off intellectual attacks, thanks to God's gift of the apologists. Both persecution and doctrinal opposition were *external* attacks. The young Church was not prepared for what happened next: The attack suddenly became *internal*, a cancer that threatened from within. The first internal attack was heresy, a divergence from orthodox, biblical views. Because the church was so young, it had not officially formulated many of its beliefs. Some heretics seemed unaware that they were departing from orthodoxy. Their beliefs forced the Church to gather for councils and conferences to determine what was truly biblical. Often heretics were denounced many years after having espoused a particular belief system.

ARIANISM, PELAGIANISM, NESTORIANISM
AND OTHER HARD WORDS

One heresy that seriously threatened to take the Church off course was promulgated by Arius (ca. 250-336). Arianism taught that there was a time when Jesus did not exist and that although Christ had some divinity, He was not equal with God the Father. The first worldwide council, the Council of Nicea, decisively rejected Arianism in 325. As a result, you and I understand the humanity and divinity of Christ.

Another dangerous heresy was the teaching of Pelagius (late fourth century, early fifth century). Pelagius had an overly optimistic view of human nature. He taught that apart from God's grace, people can take the first steps to God; they needed only reason and determination to be able to choose between right and wrong, good and evil. Pelagius denied original sin, the doctrine that there is something terribly wrong at the core of humanity, that we are born spiritually dead and unable to bring ourselves any degree of spiritual life. Pelagius underestimated the seriousness of sin and human slavery to sin. Ultimately, according to Pelagianism, we don't really need

God's grace of Christ's death on the cross because we can practically save ourselves by our good works and asceticism. The great churchman Saint Augustine (354-430), bishop of Hippo in North Africa, vigorously attacked and eventually won the day against Pelagius's human-centered doctrine. Pelagianism was condemned at several Church councils from 412-418.

Nestorius (died ca. 451), bishop of Constantinople, one of the most important churches in the Roman Empire, stirred up a controversy which led to his being deposed as bishop. Nestorius objected to the growing devotional movement which elevated the virgin Mary's title to *theotokos,* or "God-bearer." According to Nestorian teaching, Mary was the mother of Jesus the man but not the mother of God the Son. Furthermore, Jesus had two distinct natures, human and divine, and He switched from one to the other depending on whether He was doing normal human things or performing miracles.

Whether Nestorius was trying to preserve orthodox Christian belief or to blaze a new heretical path, Nestorianism contradicted what the Bible, the orthodox churches and the Church councils had said about Christ. The term "God-bearer" meant that Jesus of Nazareth was *fully* God and that His humanity and divinity were united in one person. Nestorianism was formally condemned at the Councils of Ephesus in 431 and Chalcedon in 451. Nestorian churches, centered in Persia, broke away from Catholic churches. Despite many efforts to find a way to agree, the breach was never mended.

Another group which denied the biblically orthodox teaching that Christ was 100 percent God and 100 percent man were the Monophysites (after the Greek *mono* meaning "one" and *phusis* meaning "nature"). The Monophysites said Christ had only one nature, and that nature was divine. In making this claim they rejected the belief that Christ had a genuine human nature. The Council of Chalcedon condemned Monophysitism in 451.

And there were more—the Ebionites, the Docetists, the Modalists, the Novatians, the Manicheans, the Donatists, the Pneumatichoi—most of whom distorted the biblical teaching and the emerging consensus in the Church about the nature of Christ and the Trinity (the "Trinity" is a theological shorthand for the biblical teaching that God exists as God the Father, God the Son and God the Holy Spirit).

However, one heretical teaching shook the Church more than any other. It was both subtle and powerful and still exists today—Gnosticism.[1]

GNOSTICISM

Not a single thought pattern or a distinct movement, Gnosticism was a group of movements, largely disconnected. Its very shapelessness made it a difficult enemy. Its influence in the Early Church nearly corrupted the gospel we know and love. The word "Gnosticism" comes from the Greek word *gnosis* which means "knowledge." Gnostics believed that to advance spiritually, one had to gain special, secret knowledge; and as one learned more, one progressed from one level (aeon or emanation) to the next. If one climbed this "ladder of secret knowledge," one could escape the evil, material world and move toward the good and the spiritual. This thinking is sometimes called radical dualism, because spirit is set against physical matter. What can be touched and seen is evil; what one cannot see or touch is intrinsically good.

VIEW OF CHRIST

The implications of Gnosticism were enormous for Christianity. Gnostics believed that the true Jesus was not human, for if He had a body, then how could He be spiritually good? Gnosticism attacked the heart of the gospel. If Jesus didn't have a real body, He could not have suffered and died on the cross and could not, therefore, have been physically raised from the dead. Nor would His physical body have ascended into heaven. The apostle Paul said, "If Christ has not been raised, your faith is futile; you are still in your sins" (1 Cor. 15:17). Gnostic doctrines denied the very foundations of the Christian faith. Gnosticism was the single greatest threat to Christianity throughout the second century. Gnosticism's "evangelists" were Simon Magus, Saturninus who taught at Antioch in the early 100s, Marcion who died in about 160 and Valentinus. Among those who combated these doctrines was John the Apostle. The book of 1 John is written partly to combat early Gnostic tendencies. Much of John's phrasing refutes the false teaching of Gnosticism ("This is how you can recognize the Spirit of God: Every spirit that acknowledges that Jesus Christ has come in the flesh is from God" [1 John 4:2; see also 1 John 1:1-4]).

Many years later, another Christian would take up the battle against a much stronger Gnosticism.

IRENAEUS

Irenaeus (ca. 125-200) studied under Polycarp, who himself had been a disciple of the apostle John. We know little about him, except that he was faithful to the gospel when he served as bishop of Lyon in Gaul (present-day France). The name Irenaeus means "peaceful," and that word describes him well. Yet Irenaeus was ready to defend the faith fearlessly against falsehood and especially against Gnosticism, which he studied thoroughly and whose seductive errors he quickly identified. His *Against Heresies* demonstrated how unbiblical Gnostic teaching was. Irenaeus showed that a loving God created a good world and a perfectly innocent couple, Adam and Eve. The couple's fall into sin spelled the need for Christ, the new Adam. Christ was born of a woman and received a glorified but physical body at the resurrection.

Irenaeus further attacked Gnosticism for its elitist snobbery. The over-inflated sense of self-worth that came from Gnosticism's "secret knowledge" caused their followers to become "puffed up with conceit and self-importance."[2] So expansive was his influence and so brilliant was Irenaeus's writing that he has been called "the founder of Christian theology."[3]

SCHISM

Heresy was not the only internal attack upon the Early Church. The second was schism. Schism is a nice way of saying *church split*. Church splits are not a uniquely modern occurrence. Even under Paul's ministry, Christians identified with one or another faction instead of keeping their unity in the truth of the gospel. In the Early Church, the first major Church split occurred under the influence of a man named Marcion.

MARCION

According to tradition, Marcion (died ca. 160) was a ship owner who began to develop his own unique theological views. In Sinope, Pontus (a province within Asia Minor), he locked horns with the bishop, who (according to some) was his own father. As a result of this theological altercation, he was excommunicated. He arrived in Rome in about 130, where he promptly wore out his welcome and was again excommunicated in about 144.

What was so controversial about Marcion's beliefs that he was twice excommunicated? It was his view of Scriptures. He thought the God of the Old Testament to be imperfect, so he cut the Old Testament books from the Bible. Even the New Testament needed editing, according to Marcion. He did not accept Matthew, Mark, Acts or Hebrews; and he admitted only a portion of Luke's Gospel and 10 of Paul's letters into his private canon. He believed that Paul was the only apostle not guilty of corrupting the original gospel message of Christ. He further believed that Jesus was not born of a woman but simply appeared as a full adult man in a synagogue in Capernaum in A.D. 29. He is sometimes accused of being a Gnostic because he believed that Jesus did not have a human body. Jesus' crucifixion and resurrection were "appearances."

In practical areas, he was an ascetic, believing in a highly disciplined treatment of his body. He rejected marriage, saying it was not acceptable to Christians. The Marcionites, as they were called, set up their own congregations with their own traditions and pastors. Their ideas spread through Italy, Arabia, Armenia and Egypt, and their influence continued into the fourth century.

Some good, however, did come out of Marcionism. Marcion's treatment of the Bible forced Church leaders to resolve the fundamental question as to what books were truly canonical (God-inspired). Marcion set off a reaction which resulted in recognition of our Bible. So even in the midst of schism, God was working to bring about His good and perfect will by compiling the most miraculous source of spiritual food, heavenly manna, sufficient for all needs—the written, trustworthy Word of God.

MONTANUS

In 156, another controversial movement arose that divided the Early Church. Montanus began to prophesy that the Age of the Paraclete (after the Greek word referring to the Holy Spirit) had come upon the Church and that Christ's millennial kingdom and the heavenly Jerusalem would soon descend. A rigorously ethical life was therefore necessary. Montanus condemned what he saw as laxity of spiritual discipline in the Catholic church, calling church members "psychics" (soulish people) as opposed to the

Montanists who were "pneumatics" (spirit filled). Montanist asceticism disallowed second marriages, required a return to the earlier fasting practice of twice a week (Wednesday and Friday) and insisted that true Christians should never flee from persecution.

To many, Montanism seemed like a return to the spiritual fervor and increased expectation of the imminent return of Christ as seen in the Early Church. In addition, Montanism was a prophetic movement with Montanus as the lead prophet joined by two prophetesses, Maximilla and Priscilla (later a third prophetess, Quintilla, joined them). The movement spread rapidly from Phrygia to Europe, Africa and other parts of Asia Minor (present-day Turkey). Montanism gained widespread credibility when Tertullian, the brilliant defender of Christianity, joined the movement near the end of his life in about 207.

Montanus's writings have not survived, so historians can learn about Montanism only from biased anti-Montanist writers. Nevertheless, the large number of orthodox writers who were against Montanism indicates a significant distrust of the movement. One problem was the unrealistic demands of Montanist asceticism and its harsh system of penances for violations. Another problem, the one at the heart of the dispute, was Montanism's rejection of the legitimacy and authority of established bishops in favor of the Montanists' own spirit-filled prophets.

A third problem related to the limits of revelation: the idea of a fixed set of canonical Scriptures was gaining force in the Church. Did the new revelations from the Montanist prophets fit in to that understanding of revelation? The orthodox Church decided they did not, and Montanism was formally condemned in several local synods just before 200 and later by Pope Zephyrinus.

RESULTS OF MONTANISM

Montanism came with the same blustery promise as the charismatic movement of the 1970s in America. It challenged the moral laxity of orthodox Christians and insisted that rigorous, holy and disciplined living was good and right. But Montanism was plagued with weaknesses. In its rigor, it became judgmental and its zeal was unfocused. As with other divergent movements, it did more good for the Church in the opposition it stimulated than it accomplished by spreading its peculiar doctrines and rules. Just as the Marcion controversy forced the Early Church to consider what should be *in* the New Testament, the Montanist movement forced it to decide what should *not* be included in the New Testament. The Church recognized the importance of the closed canon; that is to say, a dependence on the authority of the written Word, by which all declarations made by contemporaries would be judged.

THE BIBLE

It is very impressive, indeed, to look back over time and through history and see how God's hand built the canon we have today—the Bible. Consider:

- A.D. 30—if a child were asked to get the Bible, he would have asked, "What is a Bible?" If asked to get the sacred writings, he would have run for a copy of the 39 books of the Old Testament (had he known where to find one!).
- A.D. 200—a child would recognize the Muratorian canon (the four gospels, the 13 letters of Paul, the book of Acts, two letters of John, Jude and Revelation, along with the Wisdom of Solomon and the Revelation of Peter).
- A.D 250—a child would not have had in his Bible, James, 2 Peter, 2 and 3 John, Jude or Revelation, but he would have been familiar with *The Shepherd of Hermas*, the *Letter of Barnabas*, *The Teaching of the Twelve*, *The Apostles*, *The Gospel of the Hebrews*, *The Acts of Peter* and *The Didache*.

How did the Church rule out of all these candidates? Can we be sure they got the right collection? Why did the Church fathers include some books and not others? The Eastern church, centered in Constantinople (Byzantium), had arrived at a consensus by 367. That year, Athanasius wrote an Easter letter that listed the 27 books we have in our New Testament. Excluded were *I Clement* and the *Letter of Barnabas*. Athanasius encouraged new believers to read *The Didache* ("teaching") and *The Shepherd of Hermas*, but these were not to be read as inspired canonical books. The Western church, centered around Rome, approved the same 27 books in the New Testament at the Council of Hippo in 393 and at Carthage in 397.

CONFIRMATION VERSUS AFFIRMATION

These councils did not *confirm* what was to be included in the New Testament. They merely *affirmed* what the Holy Spirit had already confirmed. The attendees at these Church conferences merely acknowledged what was already known to be true: the 27 books of the New Testament were uniquely inspired by God, with a particular ring of authenticity. David F. Wright states it this way:

> Although churchmen in a literal sense created the canon (the Bible), they were only recognizing the books that had stamped their own authority on the churches. The criteria for accepting a book as canonical (authentic) were sometimes complex. Above all, it had to be written or sponsored by an apostle, and also be recognizably orthodox in content, and publicly used by a prominent church or majority of churches. . . . But the eventual shape of the New Testament shows that the Early Church wanted to submit fully to the teachings of the apostles. It had been created by their preaching and now grounded itself upon their writings.[4]

Certain books, such as the Acts of Paul, were considered forgeries and were not included in the canon. Other books were disputed for a time: Hebrews (due to its unknown authorship) and James, for example. There was discussion about the differences and overlap between John and the other Gospels, but all four were finally included. Revelation was particularly disputed, since it was so difficult to interpret and because the heretical Montanists loved it so much.

AMAZING PROCESS

To some, deciding on the canon may seem arbitrary. However, it is truly amazing that given the Church's record of disagreeing about nearly everything, opinion about the canon was so unified. The 27 books of the New Testament were accepted throughout the Christian Church, even though the process took over 250 years and involved hundreds of churches, thousands of believers and many headstrong church leaders! Some might be disappointed that the Bible didn't miraculously drop out of heaven, complete with its 66 books, leather-bound and in King James English. But it is apparent that

God's hand was always at work in and throughout this spectacular process and the story is an exciting and thrilling one.

Another amazing development that helped tie the message of the New Testament into a succinct, memorizable saying was the Rule of Faith (Latin: *regula fidei*). The Rule of Faith, which eventually developed into the Apostles' Creed,[5] was explicitly Trinitarian and included affirmations about God the Father, God the Son and God the Holy Spirit. It appeared nearly spontaneously very early in the second century in many far-flung churches in the Roman Empire. This Rule of Faith was an effective tool for the Church to declare the truth of the Bible and to weed out heresies.

CHURCH STRUCTURE

The Bible provided the sure foundation on which Church councils could solidify doctrinal beliefs and church government. During this period (150-450), churches began to use buildings (relatively rare before 250). The New Testament offers some principles for the development of Church structure; and later portions of the New Testament speak of offices such as bishop, presbyter and deacon. Several Church councils took place involving Peter, Paul, Apollos and other Church leaders, which began to establish Church practices as they related to earlier Jewish customs (see Acts 15). But the New Testament Church appears to have been structured loosely and had not yet dealt with questions that would arise as the gospel made its way through the Gentile world where different cultural questions were involved.

LEADERSHIP

It appears that leadership in the Early Church was by appointment, often with prophetic prayers and the laying on of hands by a group of elders. But an extremely significant idea which drastically broke down the firm distinction in the Old Testament between the Levitical priests and the people (and by extension to our time, between clergy and laity) was the New Testament principle that the Levitical priesthood was completed and eclipsed by Christ and that the entire Body of Christ is a priesthood: all believers were now called to be a kingdom of priests and to have been given a ministry of reconciliation.[6]

The earliest distinction in Christian ministry was made between itinerant and local ministries. Itinerant preachers were traveling missionaries, wandering prophets like the apostle Paul; others stayed in one place to establish local churches. Though Paul traveled extensively, he placed men like Timothy in charge of the churches he founded. The local ministers were often referred to as presbyters, or elders, which comes from a Jewish term meaning "respected old men." Spiritual maturity, however, was valued above age. Eventually the term *episcopos*, which means "overseer, or bishop," came to be used interchangeably with presbyter. By the time of Ignatius (only a decade after the last book in the New Testament, the Revelation of John, was written), the terms "bishop," "presbyter" and "deacon" were used in specifically defined ways.

ONE-MAN RULE

The second observable development in the structure of the Church was the development of the monoepiscopate: One (*mono*) person was an overseer (*episcopos*) of a designated geographical area. The Church soon developed the custom of placing one person in charge of a given congregation or even a collection of congregations. From the first day of the Church's existence on the Day of Pentecost, when Peter emerged as an obvious leader, one-man rule had been logical and effective. A one-man episcopate developed in Alexandria; and even in Jerusalem, James, brother of Jesus, became the leader of a group of elders ruling the church.

There is plenty of scriptural evidence for the plurality of elders, a system advocated by many churches today and throughout history. However, even in the Bible, there is a special place of honor for the principle, or teaching, elder. God has always tended to raise up one individual to be the leader among the elders. This emphasis gradually led to monoepiscopates. To explain the emergence of strong one-man rule, Bruce Burke and James Wiggins describe how early Christians met in private homes. The largest home would obviously be the most usable; and since the house owner would be the normal host, he would have the honor of leading the worship service.

A second reason for the rise of one-man rule was the need for stability. Itinerate, or traveling, pastors could not meet the needs of the people in the same way that a local, stable pastor could, so individuals emerged in roles of leadership.[7]

The one-man rule policy could have been justified on pragmatic, or practical, grounds, but some felt the need to buttress this form of government with a theological argument known as Apostolic Succession. This teaching appeared in the writings of Clement I as early as A.D. 96 (just when John was probably completing the book of Revelation). Apostolic Succession advocated an orderly and continuous succession of authority from the apostles down through the centuries. The apostles laid hands on, or ordained, their successors, who consequently laid hands on, or ordained, their successors and so forth.

The problem with this teaching on succession is that it cannot be verified historically. Who laid hands on whom? The theory is fascinating but unsupported by the evidence. However, what *can* be proven and defended historically is the apostolic teaching that has been handed down from generation to generation. Identifying a historical line of succession is less important than testing teaching based on the Scriptures. The Church today should be faithful to the spiritual apostolic succession. But no one can rightfully claim that he can prove who ordained whom in a tight succession, extending century after century.

ONE NEW TESTAMENT MODEL?

God slowly developed certain structures to help sustain the Church. Some groups claim that their structure is truly New Testament, thus implying that other people's are not. However, we see variety even within the New Testament. In the early New Testament the model of structure was quite loose and was based upon gifts (charisma). In the later years of the New Testament, the Church was more highly structured, with offices such as bishop, elder and presbyter.

VARIETY TODAY

A variety of church models is available today, each with its own strengths and weaknesses. Some church governments are clearly episcopal, with a highly centralized, structured organization. The Roman Catholic church, with the Pope and a strong hierarchy of authority, is a good example. Other groups, such as independent Baptists, are totally congregational, with no official or legal ties to any other Baptist church, though loose unions of such churches often enjoy fraternal relationships. A third form of government, halfway between episcopal and congregational, is the presbyterian form of government. Presbyterians have a group of elders in each congregation who meet together with elders from other congregations on regional and national levels to decide church policy issues. Presbyterians have some components of centralized control (episcopal) and other components that allow for local church autonomy (congregational). Some might argue that the presbyterian form of government includes the best of both worlds, while its critics would say that it includes the worst. Though the Church will probably always argue about structure, the point is that God has used many different structures to accomplish His plan. We Christians (His kids) ought to try being as gracious as He is about this issue!

SUSTAINING THE GOSPEL

There are basically two opposing views about Church structure. One argues that structure doesn't work. When people organize, difficulty, conflict and infighting arise. The more optimistic view holds that the Church would not exist today were it not for Church government. In fact, the structures have worked so well that after 2,000 years we still have the purity, the beauty, the power and the majesty of the gospel of Jesus Christ. In order to get to us, the gospel *needed* a structure. The gospel needed a cradle, the Church; and the Church required structure. Somehow, after all these years, in spite of a variety of Church structures, the gospel has survived; and we have it today.

CHURCH BUILDINGS

In the very first days of the Church, believers met outside in the Temple courts and inside in people's homes. There was spontaneous giving to one another, and people even sacrificially gave up their property and inheritances to keep the movement going. As the early Jesus movement rapidly grew, the Church continued the pattern, and members even went from house to house to preach the gospel. Even a significant number of synagogue leaders put their trust in Christ. It was these "house churches" that provided the base and basis of the earliest Church (archeological digs yield Church buildings very rarely before 250).

Equally controversial was the issue of church buildings. The original believers on the Day of Pentecost gathered near the Jerusalem Temple as the apostles had instructed them. As time passed, they began to meet in homes, a practice apparently followed for over 200 years. In about 250, the first Christian Church building was erected. (Little did these early Christians know how much this decision would cost the later followers of Christ!) The Church chose to erect buildings partly because of explosive growth and partly because believers in communities and cities desired to meet together. Christians may have patterned their places of worship after the Jewish synagogues with which they were familiar.

Before their exile to Babylon (in the Old Testament), the Jews had worshiped in the Temple in Jerusalem to which they made an occasional pilgrimage. During the 70-year exile, the Jews observed that the pagan Babylonians had local places for worship. Therefore, upon their return from Babylon, they not only reconstructed the Temple in Jerusalem but also provided synagogues in their local communities.

BELIEFS

Early in their history, Christians developed creeds, brief statements of their beliefs. The word *credo* means "I believe." Although it appears that the earliest Christians greeted each other with the simple affirmation "Jesus is Lord," they later wrote more complicated creeds in response to the aberrations of heretical movements. The fourth, fifth and sixth centuries produced a great number of creeds in response to theological controversies about the Trinity. We may wonder why there was so much infighting about such creedal documents. How important is it to be able to explain everything? The creeds were very important, however, because Christians had no books or bookstores, no Christian radio or TV, no cassettes or videos, and no printed Bible. The printing press would be invented hundreds of years later, so the only copies of Old Testament Scriptures were hand-written—a laborious process. Such copies could only be owned by the rich or by church leaders, whose responsibility it was to read them in public for the sake of the Church. We get the impression that Paul's letters were handled this way. He had only a few copies made and then circulated them by trusted messengers to be read to the churches. We must remember, too, that many people were illiterate.

Creeds were a succinct way for Christians to recite the essence of their faith. No doubt they would teach them to their children and use them as a means of "giving an answer for the hope that was in them" (1 Pet. 3:15). Tertullian said it this way: "Only where the true Christian teaching [creed] and faith are evident will the true Scriptures, the true interpretation, and all the true Christian traditions be found."[8] The creed we know best is the Apostles' Creed (which was not written by the apostles of Christ). This creed, which is very similar to the phrases of the second century Rule of Faith, developed to its final form by the eighth century. Of the earlier creeds, the best known are the Nicene Creed, formulated at the Council of Nicea in 325, and the Chalcedonian Definition, from the council of Chalcedon in 451. These seemingly obscure Church councils and creeds formulated the basics that almost all Christians believe today. This was the primary period of the formation of Christian beliefs as we now understand them. And as a result of the labors of those who attended the Early Church councils, we have an understanding of Christian truth today.

WHO IS JESUS?

These Church councils were crucial in the life of the Church, because they were attempting to answer *the* question: Is Jesus really God? Arius, an influential and persuasive preacher in Alexandria stated that only the God the Father was God Almighty. Jesus, being a son, was different and inferior in authority, power and substance. Such a radical statement touched off a theological firestorm. Arius had quite a following, and Emperor Constantine was unhappy that a theological eruption was occurring in the Church. He called Arius and other theologians to work out their differences at the Council of Nicene in 325. Athanasius (ca. 293-373), bishop of Alexandria, where Arius was a pastor, had vigorously withstood the Arian position and embraced the position of the Nicene Council. Arius and his followers were so powerful that they banished Athanasius from Alexandria on five separate occasions! Arius claimed that Christ was not quite God and not quite man but something in between. Athanasius insisted that Jesus was both God and man at the same time. The dispute was bitter and vitriolic. The emperor was annoyed at having to be drawn into the fray. In the end, Arius lost; and the Nicene Creed was reaffirmed in the famous council at Constantinople in 381. As a result of the struggles of Athanasius, we are able to affirm today that Jesus is both God and man at the same time.

THEOLOGICAL DISPUTE

How can the Church experience such bitter disputes over the doctrine of Christ? Doesn't its attitude nullify the power of the gospel? Shouldn't we be embarrassed that followers of Christ were so hostile to one another over theological issues? Yes, we *are* embarrassed. We *are* disappointed. At the same time, I am thankful that Athanasius was willing to suffer the anguish of banishment and the exhaustion and tension involved in a long Church dispute in order to stand for the truth that I now value so highly. If I didn't realize that Jesus is fully God and fully man, my whole life would change. If Jesus had not been God, He could not have asked for my complete allegiance. If He had not been human, He could never have understood my struggle with sin, nor could He have truly stood in my place. I thank God for those who came together in great councils to debate, think through, argue about and articulate biblical truth. I thank God that people gathered in Arles in 314, in Nicea in 325, in Constantinople in 381, in Ephesus in 431 and in Chalcedon in 451.

I am glad that some of my Christian ancestors were willing to invest their lives to establish Christian beliefs. Do I wish they could have arrived at their conclusions without arguing? Of course. But dispute is part of the process. Perhaps God is not nearly as bothered as we are about a good frank discussion. He planned the Christian life to be worked out in the context of history, people living in space and time—people like you and me.

Consequently, where two or three are gathered, there in the midst shall be a theological dispute! Was it the Church's finest moment? Well, no and yes. No, because it was a dispute. Yes, because they arrived at a strong statement of biblical faith. Not only *in spite of* dispute but also, in some sense, *due to* dispute, the Church was made stronger.

CONSTANTINE

One of the greatest changes in church history happened in 313. In 284, Diocletian became emperor and divided his empire in two, East and West, and appointed Galerius as Caesar in the East. Galerius was furiously anti-Christian; by 298 he was removing all believers from civil positions and the army. By 303, a great persecution had begun. Bibles were taken, churches were burned, and worship services were prohibited. The persecution became even more intense in 305. But Galerius was unsuccessful in crushing the Christian movement, though he had killed Christians by the thousands. Finally on April 30, 311, six days before his death, Galerius issued the *Edict of Toleration*, which allowed Christians freedom of worship.

Meanwhile, a soldier named Constantius, who had risen to the rank of Caesar, died in 306, leaving his son, Constantine, as the new leader. His would-be adherents gathered around him and formed an army to battle one of his opponents, Maxentius, at the Milvian Bridge outside Rome. According to tradition, Constantine had a vision of a flaming cross with the accompanying words "In this sign conquer!" According to some, he became a Christian and put the insignia of the cross on his soldiers' shields. Later, according to tradition, Christ appeared to Constantine with a symbol of a cross with the Greek letters *chi* and *rho*, which are the first two letters of the Greek word for Christ, *Christos*. Having put these on the soldiers' shields, Constantine went confidently into battle—and won. When he became emperor in 313, he issued the *Edict of Milan*, which granted complete religious freedom within the entire Roman empire. Not only did Constantine put an end to persecution, but he also sponsored Church councils in order to resolve theological disputes, prohibited pagan sacrifice and provided financial aid to Christian causes. He built *basilicas* (church buildings); and through the influence of his mother, Helena, located and preserved many of the sacred sights associated with the life of Christ in the Holy Land.

VICTORY OR DEFEAT?

When we see that Christianity was encouraged in the Roman Empire by such a powerful leader as Constantine, we may be tempted to think, *The Church was doing fine*. But we need to look more closely, because what appeared to be the Church's greatest victory proved to be its worst stumbling block. Just when the Church seemed to have developed from a persecuted sect into the official religion of the Roman Empire, a huge stumbling block was introduced—now, thousands flocked to the faith not by conviction but by convenience. What looked like a huge step forward had been a tragic step backward. Once Christianity became the religion of the state, everyone in the Roman Empire by definition was a Christian.

Constantine forcefully baptized thousands, and thousands more came into the Church to avoid the wrath of the state. Overnight the whole dynamic of what it meant to be a Christian in the evil Roman Empire changed: pagans became nominal Christians or Christian in name only; underneath they continued their pagan beliefs and morals. The Church undoubtedly tried to teach the faith to the masses, and some of the masses of pagans undoubtedly came to genuine faith in Christ. But the stumbling block of nominal Christianity has been a continual and severe problem in Western Christianity since the time of Constantine.

AUGUSTINE THE THEOLOGIAN

On November 15, 354, Monica gave birth to a son in the small town of Tagaste, in Roman Africa. A devout Christian, Monica prayed for her son every day. But for many years, those prayers seemed to go unanswered, for Augustine chose to follow his pagan father's lifestyle rather than to seek to please Christ, as his mother had tried to teach him to do. Sensuous and pleasure loving, Augustine took a mistress, who bore him a son, and dabbled in various philosophical systems. When we read Augustine's later writings, we learn what he thought of his own licentious lifestyle—his work is full of discussions about the sinfulness of human nature.

CONVERSION

While in Milan, Augustine heard Bishop Ambrose preach. He was stirred so deeply that he began to feel dissatisfied with his womanizing. His mother was hopeful he would live a more respectable life and was encouraged when Augustine agreed to separate from his mistress, but he later took another. Then on a summer day in 386, he thought he heard the voice of a child from a nearby garden telling him to "pick it up and read it." To him, this voice was a call from God, an exhortation comparable to Romans 13:13,14, calling him to leave his wicked ways. On Easter of 387 he was baptized by Ambrose and started home to share the good news with his faithful mother; but when he arrived, Monica had already died. Back in Africa in 391, Augustine moved to the coastal city of Hippo, where he lived for the rest of his life as pastor, preacher and administrator. Full of passion, power, intelligence and piety, Augustine became one of the most colorful and influential figures in the major Church councils, many of which occurred in North Africa.

DEBATER AND WRITER

Augustine, by his courageous, passionate and intelligent writing, influenced not only his contemporaries but also Christians for centuries to come, Not one to hold back, he waded unintimidated into every theological controversy of his day—where he debated with vigor! He attacked the Manichaeans, the Donatists, and the Pelagians (who drew from him the works for which he is best known today). Augustine wrote 15 long treatises to confront those who were claiming that man could be saved by his own efforts. In his argumentation, Augustine was not ashamed to include references to his long years of debauchery. His early, careless lifestyle was an important part of his theological understanding. No writer before him had written so profoundly about the depth of human depravity. In fact, it would be nearly 1,150 years before anybody would again write as convincingly on this topic. That individual, who would borrow from Augustine, was John Calvin (1509-1564).

INTERPRETING THE END OF THE ROMAN EMPIRE

Augustine lived at a time when the great Roman Empire was beginning to unravel. He wrote about the crisis for 15 years, and his thoughts were published under the title *The City of God*. In 10 books he defended basic Christian doctrine and launched an attack against paganism. Twelve more books outlined a philosophy of history and spoke of the long-term conflict between the City of God (the Church), and the City of the World. The two cities, predicted Augustine, would continue doing battle until they were finally separated into heaven and hell. The City of the World, as demonstrated by the empire, would someday fall. And fall it did. As the invasion of the empire pressed southward, Augustine's city, Hippo, with some other cities, held out against siege. But Augustine himself lay dying on August 28, 430, as the Vandals were breaking into the city of Hippo.

The powerful influence of the North African church had now ended. The Church would face outside control and persecution that would leave it devastated, following the loss of tens of thousands of martyred Christians. In his famous book *The City of God*, Augustine argues that the true Church presses ever forward. Cultures and nations rise and fall, come to glory and fade, but the Church remains. In a time when our own American culture has used up all its Christian reserves and stands at the edge of moral bankruptcy, it is comforting to know that the authentic City of God will continue.

America may or may not continue as we know it, but the gospel will!
Augustine died as his city and nation were collapsing, but the gospel he proclaimed has remained strong to this day. Augustine, the greatest and most
influential theologian in the Western church, knew that the City of God—
God's kingdom—would survive long after the Roman Empire had crumbled.

AMBROSE THE ORATOR

Ambrose was an influential fourth-century Church leader. So popular was
he as the governor of Milan that he was elected bishop. He was baptized,
and he released all his wealth to the Church. He began to study theology
and quickly demonstrated his exceptional leadership by managing the
administrative affairs of the Milanese church. But he is perhaps best known
as an eloquent and influential preacher, arguing persuasively against
Arianism.

PASTORAL ABILITY

Since Milan served as home to the Roman emperors in the West, Ambrose
became advisor to the royal family. His preaching career at his metropolitan
church affected three different emperors. Due to his connection with the
emperor, Ambrose found himself and his congregation caught in a political
war. During a season of attacks, Ambrose kept his church congregation
gathered in the cathedral and occupied their minds by introducing the
singing of hymns that he himself had composed. So skillful were his preaching and teaching that he won young Augustine to the Christian faith in 386.
His preaching style was more like that of a lawyer than an orator. His influence in worship styles was so significant that some liturgical practices today
are still known as the "Ambrosian rite." His hymns were written in a popular style that made them very easy for the common people to sing. In addition to his exceptional pastoral skills, he was a brilliant thinker who gave
leadership in various Church councils.

Perhaps his finest moment came when he publicly demanded that
Emperor Theodosius repent for ordering the killing of 390 people in
Thessalonica. Bowing to the conviction of the Spirit and the influence of
Ambrose, Theodosius repented. Ambrose died on April 4, 397, a few
moments after a bishop served him his last Communion. So influential was

Ambrose that if one were to sculpt a "Mount Rushmore of the Early Western Church," its four faces would be Augustine, Jerome, Gregory and Ambrose.

JEROME THE BIBLE TRANSLATOR

If Augustine was the brilliant theologian and Ambrose the brilliant orator, Jerome (340-420) was the Bible translator. In 405, Jerome completed his translation of the Old Testament from Hebrew into Latin, the *Vulgate*, one of the most significant events in Church history.

A DIFFICULT PERSONALITY

Jerome was regarded as an "unrestrained controversialist"[9] with a "crusty disposition."[10] Another scholar puts it this way: "In the charitable mind of the Church, his service to Christian scholarship and zeal for aesthetic life has been allowed to outweigh the ambiguities of his character."[11] Simply stated, Jerome was not a pleasant man to be around!

HIS MAJOR GIFT TO HUMANITY

Jerome was born in Stridon in Dalmatia and completed a classical education in Rome. Because of his intense intellectual skills, he eventually secured the position of secretary to Pope Damasus. He garnered a substantial audience of wealthy people, particularly upper-class women intrigued by his scholarly brilliance. In 386, two years after Damasus died, Jerome went to Bethlehem to head up a monastery. His move to the Holy Land was due partly to his bitterness at not being chosen bishop of Rome and partly to a desire for seclusion in order to complete his translation of the Bible. Jerome began working on his translation in 382 and insisted on working only with the original Hebrew and Greek texts. Twenty-three years later, in 405, he had translated the entire Bible. Although his translation included the Apocrypha (books Catholics, not Protestants, accepted as inspired), in his opinion the Apocryphal books were Church books not canonical books. Martin Luther and his fellow reformers would heed Jerome's advice many years later and remove those books from the Protestant Bible. Though his personality was a challenge (to put it mildly), he became, by virtue of his amazing translation task, one of the greatest men of this period of Church history. From him would come the academic discipline of Bible translation, and all who call themselves Christians today are indebted to Jerome. A charming personality is not a prerequisite to Bible translation!

GREGORY I

Gregory I (540-604) was not nearly so cantankerous as Jerome. In fact, so spectacular was this leader that he is known as Gregory the Great. A leader with exceptional organization and administrative skills, Gregory gave the pope and the city of Rome much of their power and influence. In the political vacuum left by the collapse of the Roman Empire, Gregory created structures that allowed the pope to exercise great power.

ONE MAN'S INFLUENCE

In 590, Gregory himself was elected pope, a position which he hesitatingly accepted. The city of Rome was in a disastrous situation, devastated by floods, plagues and famines, and crammed with the poor and homeless. Gregory was an amazing administrator, for he was able to set up a massive welfare program for the city's poor, while accumulating great wealth for the church in Rome. Gregory also sponsored many missionary campaigns, including one to the English. To England, he sent another Augustine (not to be confused with the one already mentioned), one who was known as the Apostle of the English. Gregory's influence impacts all English-speaking people, since the gospel was established in England through Gregory's initiative. From England, of course, the gospel spread to America many years later. You may know the Christian message today due to the missionary activity of Gregory.

ROMAN SUPREMACY

So politically popular and wealthy was the Roman church under Gregory's leadership that he could press the issue of the supremacy, or preeminence, of Rome. In one sense Gregory is the first authentically *Roman* Catholic pope. Many popes existed before him, but Gregory's influence was profound. He stood, popular and powerful, at the threshold of the Middle Ages, having shaped the future by the power and influence he gave to Rome.

AN INFLUENTIAL ORIGINATOR

Under Gregory the Great, the mass was organized in the form familiar to us today. Gregory also emphasized the doctrine of purgatory and encouraged believers to gather and worship relics (pieces of clothing or bones from ancient saints). Some regard him as the originator of the Gregorian chant, which opened the door for musical worship. His most influential written work was a book on pastoring, which remained well known through the Middle Ages. In spite of the fact that some of his doctrinal positions remain questionable, Gregory had a remarkable commitment to pastoring and led a significant Catholic church while the secular Roman Empire was crumbling around him.

THE FALL OF THE ROMAN EMPIRE

This brings us to the close of a chapter filled with developments in the Church as it faced a crumbling culture. Many thinkers have tried to explain the collapse of the Roman Empire. Ultimately, however, we can only say that in the plan of God, one of the most powerful kingdoms on earth crumbled forever. On August 24, 410, Alaric attacked Rome and held it under siege for three days. Although the impact was not felt by the empire immediately, the symbolism was staggering. This was the first time in 800 years that Rome had been controlled by a foreign power. Even Jerome, many miles away in Bethlehem, proclaimed, "The city which has taken the whole world, is itself taken!"[12] Almost overnight the empire was invaded by barbarians with unusual names: Visigoths, Ostrogoths, Vandals, Lombards, Franks and Saxons. Under the weakened rule of Honorius (395-423), the Roman Empire began to disband. City after city began to fall as the Goths entered Spain and the Vandals pressed further south. The massive, unconquerable Roman Empire would exist no more.

THE MUSLIM FAITH

Though we do not have time to do justice to it, we must mention the rise of the Muslim faith. One hundred fifty years after Rome fell, Mohammed (570-632) allegedly received his first vision in 610 and proclaimed himself to be a prophet of God. By 622, he had founded a Muslim community; and within eight years, he had launched his first military campaign at Mecca. By Mohammed's death in 632, Islam had spread through much of Arabia, Palestine and Syria. Eight years after that, Islamic forces invaded Egypt and North Africa, effectively eradicating the one million Christian believers! A few years later, very few Christians remained in that region.

ALIVE AND WELL?

It is difficult to close a chapter and say that the Church was alive and well. How can one can talk about the martyrdom of one million people and then glibly state, "The Church is alive and well"? Well, you can't say it *glibly,* but you can say it *soberly.* The Church being alive and well does not depend, nor has it ever depended, on people's escaping persecution and death. Sometimes it seems that the Church can only really be alive and well when it is at the point of death! God works mysteriously and has taught us in His Word that one can only gain his or her life by losing it. Christ promised that His followers would share His suffering. And so, in spite of the staggering losses of the Christian Church and in spite of the gains of Islam, we proclaim in faith that the true Church of Jesus Christ was alive, and it was well! It was the Roman Empire that fell, not the true Christian Empire. The City of God survived. Had Christianity fallen, this chapter would be the last in this book. But you have many exciting adventures to read; and as I write, the Church is 2,000 years old and still counting.

To further assist you in understanding the key individuals and events of chapter 3,
study questions, charts, diagrams, time lines and links to biographical websites are available
on the Internet at www.jimgarlow.com. Please follow the site links to
How God Saved Civilization, chapter 3 study helps.

THE GRAND DETOUR

THE EARLY MIDDLE AGES

Dates covered: A.D. 590-1300
Key persons: Boniface, Bede, Charlemagne

Lintrin pointed his finger at his brother and shouted defiantly, "You may be two years older than me, Ansolt, but that doesn't make you right!"

The young man Ansolt folded his arms in frustration and squinted. "Lintrin, we agree that whoever has been smashing our cherished statues at Saint Matthew's Cathedral is clearly doing something that is wrong before God and man. But please don't tell me the statues have special powers and now those powers are lost to us."

"You do not believe, but many have believed . . . even over hundreds of years many have believed."

"Believe what? That stone and marble people and faces have special powers?"

Lintrin pleaded, "Remember when Father was sick."

"What of it?"

"Well, I prayed to the statue of Saint Luke because I heard the priest say that Luke had been a doctor."

Ansolt rolled his eyes and sighed, "So?"

"So, Father recovered in a week. In one week! Everyone thought he was going to die, but he lived!"

Ansolt placed his hands on his brother's shoulders and pleaded, "Lintrin, remember what Mother taught us. It's God who heals. Not a statue."

"If they're only statues, why are you so sad and angry?"

"Because the statues do have a purpose and value. When I see the statue of Luke, I am moved at how God used a physician to care for the weak, the frail, the lost. When I see the statue of Peter, I am stirred to worship God for loving that fisherman who had many weaknesses like my own. Lintrin, the statues mean a great deal to me, too, because the statues inspire me to live honorably before God."

"But I prayed to that statue and Father was healed," defended Lintrin. "The statues are more than reminders and inspirations. The statues have powers to heal."

"You wait and see," protested Ansolt. "Many people want to destroy the statues because of your view. They call your praying to an image of Luke, idolatry."

"It isn't idolatry," protested Lintrin.

"But the statues aren't magical either."

The two brothers did not have to wait long for another act of vandalism. Four days later, in the middle of the night, a group of men rode into town in the early morning hours, broke into the cathedral and pushed over 14 beautiful statues which included portrayals of Abraham, Joseph, Moses, David, Matthew, Luke, Mary and other biblical figures.

When Ansolt and Lintrin arrived at the cathedral, the large wooden door at the main entrance barely hung by one hinge. Broken stone was all over the floor. Marble arms, heads and torsos were everywhere. Lintrin cried, as did many others. They felt they had been robbed of saints to pray to, saints that actually heard them.

Though Ansolt felt differently about the statues, he too felt a keen loss. Ansolt barely spoke, "We'll never be able to replace them."

Lintrin, with tears flowing, mumbled his anguish. "Now, who will I pray to if Father gets sick again? Who?"

Ansolt winced and thought, *Lintrin, will you ever understand?*

DARK AGES OR GOLDEN AGE?

Some historians identify A.D. 590 as the beginning of the Middle Ages while other scholars refer to it as the Dark Ages due to the tragic events that occurred. The period lasted for nearly a thousand years, but the first 500 years of this period saw the steady rise of Church influence in every corner of Europe.

How should we view the Middle Ages? The answer will depend on which scholar you read. Those who refer to these years as the Dark Ages imply that there is little to learn from this period. Most Protestants look in vain for signs of true spirituality during these years. Some Catholics, in contrast, see it as the Golden Age, because the Church made a brilliant attempt to establish a truly Christian society. Neither view does justice to this historical period. Martin E. Marty observed that "the Dark Ages were neither so dark, nor so aged, as were told; The Golden Age was neither so untarnished nor so long."[1]

The temptation is to wade through the Middle Ages as a "painful thousand years," in order to get to the Reformation and Martin Luther. Protestants unashamedly jump from the first few centuries of Christianity all the way to Reformation exploits. But if we do that, we miss the amazing conquests that occurred in this period.

[The Middle Ages] gave birth to all the great universities of the world from Oxford and Cambridge to Leipzig to Mainz; it oversaw the establishment of all the great hospitals of the world from St. Bartholomew's and Bedlam in London, to St. Bernard's and Voixanne in Switzerland; it brought forth the world's most celebrated artists from Michelangelo, Buonarroti and Albrecht Duhrer to Leonardo da Vinci and Jan van Eyck; it gave the splendor of gothic architecture—unmatched and unmatchable to this day—from Notre Dame and Chartres to Winchester and Cologne; it thrust out into howling wilderness and storm-tossed seas the most accomplished explorers from Amerigo Vespucci and Marco Polo to Vasco da Gama and John Cabot; it produced some of the greatest minds and the most fascinating lives mankind has yet known—were the list not so sterling it might begin to be tedious. Copernicus, Dante, Giotto, Becket, Guttenburg, Chaucer, Charlemagne, Wycliffe, Magellan, Botticelli, Donatello, Petrarach and Aquinas.

But of all the greatest innovations that medievalism wrought, the greatest of all was spiritual. Medieval culture—both east and west—was first and foremost Christian culture. Its life was shaped almost entirely by Christian concerns. Virtually all its achievements were submitted to the cause of the gospel. From great cathedrals and gracious chivalry to bitter crusades and beautiful cloisters, every manifestation of its presence was somehow tied to its utter and complete obeisance to Christ's kingdom and as a pursuit of beauty, truth, and goodness.

Of course, the medieval church had its share of dangerous and scandalous behavior.[2]

In the pages ahead, we will attempt to record the glowing advances made by the Church in the Middle Ages, while acknowledging the catastrophic failures of the Church's imperfect leadership. We will stand amazed, yet again, to watch God protect His Church in spite of the glaring deficiencies of its most visible and articulate representatives. As Kenneth Scott Latourette says in his fascinating book, *The Thousand Years of Uncertainty*, it is difficult to write about this period using a strictly chronological approach. Although we will follow a time sequence, sometimes concepts and larger movements will force us to move out of a strict chronological sequence.[3]

THE BARBARIAN INVASION

At the close of the last chapter, we discussed the rise of Islam, which continues to expand to this day and remains the single greatest threat to the expansion of Christianity (the chapter "What a Time to Be Alive" will touch on this expansion). In 600, however, the Church was only partially concerned with the newfound religion, Islam. Their more imminent struggle was against the barbarians. The barbarians remain

> mysterious to us, since they have no recorded history. But from time to time, for causes that may be equally mysterious to us, these peoples began to spill outwards over the edge of their own proper territory toward other and perhaps more fortunate lands; one race or tribe presses another, and the ripples spread onwards until they reach the utmost oceans, and then they can spread no more. When this happens, written history becomes aware of the movements, and begins to concern itself with the barbarians.[4]

The Roman Empire was unable to defend itself against these rapidly expanding barbarian groups. Some, such as the Huns, simply passed through, leaving a pathway of destruction. Others, such as the Goths, had a more highly developed civilization than some of the more primitive groups. A few of the invading barbarian groups had become Christian before they invaded, but they tended to embrace Arian theology (that Jesus was not coeternal with the Father), instead of the Catholic understanding of the Christian faith. In the 500-year span from 500 to 1000, the Western branch of the Church wrestled with the barbarian influence and attempted somehow to convert the barbarians.[5]

MISSIONARY ACTIVITY

In the previous chapter, we told of Gregory I, the skilled administrator who was elected pope in the year 590. One of his greatest contributions to Christianity was an unquenchable zeal for converting barbarians to the gospel of Jesus Christ. One of the well-known missionaries sent out by Gregory I was

Augustine of Canterbury (who died around 604), not to be confused with Augustine (354-430), the famous bishop from Hippo. The later Augustine arrived in Kent, England, in 597 and was soon successful in converting to Christianity King Ethelbert, whose wife was already a Christian. The Christian example of both the king and the queen opened the way for many of their followers to embrace the Christian faith. Augustine's rigidity, however, caused him to try to remake Canterbury into a "little Rome," thus alienating many English people. However, in spite of his inflexibility, he was successful in laying the foundations of the Christian faith in England.

Augustine's arrival in Kent in 597 corresponded with the death of one of the greatest of the Middle Age missionaries. Columba (521-597), who was born in Ireland, became an amazingly energetic missionary to Scotland. He arrived on the island of Iona in 563 and established a monastery there that became his headquarters. The monks he sent out from Iona played a crucial role in the evangelization of both Scotland and England. Columba "was fresh and full of zest, which led to his being called the 'saint of the young.'"[6] A biblically-based environmentalist, Columba seemed ahead of his time. He believed that Christ had redeemed *all* of creation and argued that to reject the beauty of the earth was to reject the kingship of Jesus Christ, the Lord of all of life. His great passion and tireless occupation was copying the Scriptures.

BONIFACE

Over 100 years later, another great missionary, Boniface (680-754), left his native England to become the "apostle of Germany." A brilliant scholar and preacher, Boniface began his initial missionary endeavors in Germany in 716, but was driven home to England by the eruption of war. By 719, he was once again ministering in Germany, organizing the country into respective sections to make it more manageable. By 754, he had accomplished so much, and had gained a position of such authority, that he could have taken a satisfied retirement. Instead, however, he took one more evangelistic trip to Frisia, where he and his helpers were martyred.

THE VENERABLE BEDE

Much of what we know about the expansion of Christianity at this time is due to the skilled writing of Bede (ca. 673-738), who entered a monastery when he was seven years of age. He became a deacon at age 19 and a priest at age 30. In 731, he completed the *Ecclesiastical History of the English People*. He is also known for lending his scholarly authority to the agreements that were worked out at an important meeting in the Synod of Whitby in 664. This special meeting determined that Roman traditions would prevail over Celtic customs in the Church.

MUSLIM INVADERS

Conflicts between Celtic and Roman traditions paled to insignificance in the face of invading Islamic armies. The next three men—a grandfather, father and son—dealt with war, and they shape our understanding of the eighth century. The grandfather was Charles Martel (ca. 688-741). When his father, Pepin II, died in 714, Charles's stepmother imprisoned him, claiming that she had authority over the government. After escaping prison and winning a decisive battle in 717, he succeeded in overthrowing his half-brothers and their mother, to become the mayor of Austrasia. By 719, he was the ruler of the Frankish realm. But he is best known for his 732 victory over the invading Muslims at the famous Battle of Tours, which stopped the Islamic advance in Europe for the next century.

Charles Martel's son, Pepin III (ca. 714-768), became the sole inheritor of the Frankish kingdom, functioning as mayor of the palace from 741 to 751 and finally becoming king of the Franks from 751 to 768. Pepin played a specific role in Church history because he was a formidable defender of the pope of Rome. On two separate occasions he led expeditions into Italy, defeating the pope's enemies in 754 and 756 and giving their territories to the pope. This land gift is referred to as the Donation of Pepin. Pepin drew up a Deed of Donation and placed this document, together with some symbolic keys, on the tomb of Saint Peter. The significant donation of land, which was later confirmed by Pepin's son, Charlemagne, marks the beginning of the political authority of the pope in Rome.

CHARLEMAGNE, FOUNDER OF EUROPE

Charles Martel had political influence, but he had only marginally helped the Church. His son, Pepin III, proved to be a great help to the Church. But

Pepin's contribution is minor when compared to the consolidating influence of his son, Charlemagne (Charles the Great, 742-814). Little is known of his early life, but by 771 Charles had become the sole ruler of the Franks. When the Lombards threatened the pope, he appealed to Charlemagne for help. Charlemagne drove the Lombards back and became their king. He next turned his attention to conquering the Saxons, against whom he waged a series of battles from 772 to 804. The Saxons eventually converted to Christianity and were included in the Frankish Empire. When Charlemagne attempted to fight against Spain, however, he was defeated.

In 800, when Pope Leo III called on him for assistance, Charlemagne responded and helped banish the pope's enemies. Christmas Day A.D. 800 is a date you may remember from your study of history. In Rome on this day, Charlemagne was formally crowned emperor by a grateful Leo III. The significance of this coronation is much debated, and many see it as an attempt to renew the old Roman Empire, at least in the West. The fact that Charlemagne allowed himself to be crowned by the pope symbolized a blossoming relationship between the Church and the state. This was the embryonic form of the *Holy* Roman Empire. Charlemagne took a vivid interest in Church policies. He continued as a protector of the papacy and its properties. He financially assisted reformers and missionaries, and was personally involved in discussions of orthodoxy and heresy. He even assisted in establishing synods (conferences) to reform the morals and elevate the education of the clergy. Deeply committed to education, Charlemagne encouraged monasteries to teach reading and writing.

THE CAROLINGIAN RENAISSANCE

The changes effected by Charlemagne were known as Carolingian, and became the core of a reform movement that would last for the next 200 years. The Carolingian Renaissance brought a fresh intellectual vigor to the age, complete with a revival of classic learning and a renewed emphasis on education, manuscript copying and libraries. Alcuin of York (735-804) was the greatest and most influential figure in the renewal of learning in the Frankish Empire. He and other scholars brought profoundly significant educational advances to Charlemagne's palace school at Aachen.

Regretfully, Charlemagne's personal life was not characterized by high morals. His home was plagued by jealousies among his many wives, concubines and children. His daughters were not women of virtue. His eldest son attempted a rebellion in 792, and the sons whom he trained to follow him had all died before he did. His empire was left to his only surviving legitimate son, Louis, who became emperor when Charlemagne died in 814. Louis and others who succeeded him were not marked by Charlemagne's unusual ability, and within a century the empire had disintegrated. The system that had been built on deep personal loyalty to Charlemagne and on his overwhelming military strength, was unmatched by any of the leaders who followed him.

ICONS AND IMAGES

So far, we have spoken of several battles: Christianity versus Islam, Celtic Christianity versus Roman Christianity, Charles Martel versus the Muslims, and strong rulers versus barbarians. But another war was also raging: the Icon Controversy. This spiritual debate took place throughout the eighth and ninth centuries and concerned the role of images, pictures and statues. Was it right to have an icon, an image or a statue? Those who felt such images were wrong as aids to worship in the Church were called Iconoclasts, which means "image breakers." To worship or even to venerate such images was so offensive to some that they would smash images.

The first major controversy over images stirred from 726 until the Second Council of Nicea in 787. Emperor Leo condemned the use of icons in 727, but Pope Gregory supported them in 731. By 754, three hundred Byzantine bishops had endorsed image breaking. But by 769, the famous Council of Lateran condemned the decision of the 300 bishops! The matter was finally put to rest at the Second Council of Nicea, which condemned Iconoclasm and declared the use of sacred images in worship to be an acceptable practice of the Church. But that did not totally settle the matter. A second Icon Controversy broke out from 813 through 843.

Why would people fight over this seemingly minor issue? Iconoclasts supported their action by citing the second commandment, which prohibits worshiping any graven image. They felt that icon worship, or even the use of such physical images in worship, was pagan idolatry. Icon advocates, on the other hand, insisted that such images were a useful visual aid in instructing the faithful.

Eventually the controversy began to pit East against West and revealed the political stress that was beginning to show between the emperor and the pope. Some historians see Emperor Leo's iconoclastic desire to destroy the images as an attempt to reduce the power of the Church in the East. Others see it as a device by which the emperors were trying to remove public education from the hands of the clergy.[7] Whatever explanation we choose to accept, in this issue of images we see the Church exercising its argumentative talent, a trait that has been particularly fine-tuned through the centuries! However, lest I appear too glib, we must remember that maintaining scriptural principles is the only way to keep the Church from self-destructing, so we must accept the difficult process of confrontation that a desire to remain true to the Bible often produces.

GENUINE OR NOMINAL CHRISTIANS?

With the destruction of the Roman Empire in the 500s, the pope became more influential. The result was a liaison between the pope and the political rulers. This close working relationship between Church and state often resulted in people's being coerced into becoming Christians. One of the most unfortunate portions of Church history is the period in which ecclesiastical leaders, aided by civil authorities, coerced by the use of the sword untold tens of thousands to "convert" to Christianity. Rather than trying to rationalize it to contemporary critics, present-day believers do better if they simply repent for what was done in the name of Christ. The pope "stepped into the ruins of the fallen Empire in the West and proceeded to build the medieval Church upon Rome's bygone glory. . . . It took centuries, but the popes, aided by Christian princes, slowly pacified and baptized a continent and called it Christendom, Christian Europe. Baptized masses, however, meant baptized pagans."[8] How does a Church full of "baptized pagans" affect those who are really sincere about God? Genuine Christians withdraw. And that is exactly what many true Christians did. They were called monastics.

MONASTICISM

Monasticism comes from a Greek word which means "the act of dwelling alone." Monastics were those who took so literally the scriptural admonitions not to love the world (see 1 John 2:15-17) that they drew away from it entirely. The goal of the monastics was to become holy by isolating themselves from the cares and sins of a pagan world. Some evidence of monasticism is seen very early in the history of the Church, developing as early as the fourth century. The father of monasticism is Antony of Egypt, who died in 356. By the Middle Ages, monasticism had begun to flourish. Godly people were not sure how to respond to the wickedness and worldliness of nominal Christians. They could not turn to the Roman Catholic church as a haven of holiness, for it too was tainted by debauchery. Those who followed a monastic life took vows of poverty, obedience, service, celibacy and, in some cases, silence (never to speak again!). In many cases the monastics or monks were "cenobite"; that is, they lived in communities. They worked and prayed together. Others were "mendicant"; that is, they had a traveling ministry, helping the poor and doing good deeds. Frances and Dominic are examples of mendicants.

Some monastics were influential in leading reform movements and revivals that called for holy, righteous living. One such revival movement was the Cluniac Reform, which started in Cluny, France, in 909. This reform movement touched many, who repented of sinful ways and began walking in righteousness. However, a century later those in Cluny were themselves in need of revival. The Cistercians (1098) reacted against the laxity that eventually affected the Cluniac orders, and called again for holiness and a closer walk with Christ.

Monasticism separated many Christians from society and kept them living in isolation, according to a particular set of rules. Such communities can be both criticized and praised. In one sense they were quite obviously too isolationist. To keep men in monasteries and women in convents not only created an artificial existence for these Christians, but it also kept them from fulfilling the mandate given at creation to bear children. These talented and godly men and women not only deprived the world of their gifts in many cases, but they also deprived the world of some very capable offspring! Imagine what strong, loving families they could have had, had they lived as married couples.

On a more positive note, however, we must admire the courage and strength these Christians exhibited in forsaking marriage for the sake of living holy lives. These people did influence their society. The monasteries became centers of learning, as well as posts for agricultural experimentation. Many of the advances in science, particularly agricultural science, occurred in the monasteries.

EAST-WEST TENSIONS

During the Middle Ages an enormous tension began to mount between the Christian East and the Christian West. Greek had become the primary language of the regions to the east of Rome, with Constantinople serving as the capital. The regions west of Rome preferred Latin and looked to Rome as their primary city. Struggles between the East and West lasted for centuries. As early as 680, Eastern and Western Churches disagreed with regard to the celibacy (nonmarriage) of the clergy. The Eastern church allowed priests to marry; the Western Church preferred that they remain single. The Icon Controversy in the 700s created further tensions and suspicions between Eastern and Western Christians. In 857, another deep split occurred, an omen of things to come. This controversy was the Photian Schism and involved three issues:

1. Who's in charge?
2. How should we understand the Trinity?
3. Can a lay person become the patriarch (spiritual leader) of Constantinople (the most influential city in the East)?

In 858, Emperor Michael removed the then-ruling patriarch and put a layman, Photius, in his place. That appointment touched off a firestorm of controversy that rivals any contemporary political intrigue, and even many Hollywood melodramas. This intense conflict involved the reinstatement of the deposed patriarch and an excommunication! Along with the political aspect of the Photius crisis came an intense battle over the phrasing in one of the Church creeds regarding the relationship between God the Father and God the Son. Photius, who was reinstated as patriarch in 877, aggressively disagreed with the placement of three words ("and the Son") in the Nicene Creed. In an effort to solve the controversy, the pope agreed to drop the offensive language from the Creed, but only if the Eastern Church agreed that Rome, not Constantinople, had complete authority and jurisdiction over the Church! Needless to say, such a demand was highly offensive to the East and was an indicator of what would later develop into a full-blown split.

THE YEAR 1054—THE BOILING POINT

If the Photian Schism seems an embarrassing display of politics and pettiness, you will be even more surprised by the events that occurred during a worship service in the Church of Holy Wisdom in Constantinople. Patriarch Michael Cerularius refused to accept Leo IX (from Rome) as having authority over Constantinople. To demonstrate his displeasure, Cerularius closed any Eastern church whose leader was loyal to the western, Roman pope. Hoping to solve the problem, Leo IX sent Humbert (who died in 1061) as his representative. Michael Cerularius was in no frame of mind to accept instructions from Pope Leo's ambassador. When Cerularius (from the East) refused to accept Roman authority (from the West), Humbert, in a public act with profound consequences, announced that he was *excommunicating the entire Eastern Church*! Now that was one very interesting church service! East and West disagreed over other matters as well, such as rules for fasting, unleavened bread, clergy celibacy, lay involvement in the Church, and the relationship of Church and state. Once again believers demonstrated their inability to get along.

The growing tension between the two halves of the Church boiled over during the Fourth Crusade in 1204, ending any hope for reconciliation between the East and the West. On July 5, 1203, the crusading armies arrived in Constantinople, the capital city of the East. Until this time, the Crusades had seen only Muslims as their enemy. However, these out-of-towners were so poorly received in Constantinople that they decided to retaliate against fellow Christians. On Good Friday, 1204, the Western-sponsored Crusade army raped and slaughtered Christians in the name of Christ! The Roman Catholic church and the Eastern Orthodox church separated completely from that point on.[9]

THE HOLY ROMAN EMPIRE

By now, you are probably asking yourself what happened to the basic truths of Jesus, grace and faith. Are they lost? Why are we not hearing about preachers who declared the gospel and about hearts hungry to respond to it? Unfortunately, Church leadership was inextricably intertwined with politics in the Middle Ages. The pope's heavy political involvement was sometimes caused by an absence of cohesive secular governmental structures, and at other times it was driven by sheer greed for power and control. The Church's prime mission, to preach the gospel and to seek the lost, was overshadowed by the complexities of political controversies.

In 962, Pope John XII crowned Otto I, "The Great" (936-972), as Roman emperor. This created the Holy Roman Empire which "represented medieval man's belief of the unity of Christendom and his admiration for the past glories of Rome."[10] Although the empire of German King Otto I was smaller in landmass than the lands that had made up Charlemagne's empire 150 years before, this union of Germany and Northern Italy, which was called the Holy Roman Empire (it wasn't holy, it wasn't Roman, and it wasn't an empire), continued for the next 900 years, until 1806. During the tenth and eleventh centuries, the Holy Roman Empire was the most influential state in Europe. But the cozy relationship between pope and emperor ended quickly. Otto the Great removed popes when he wanted to and nominated his own candidates in their place! He insisted that all papal elections be submitted to him for approval.

POPE VERSUS EMPEROR

As might be expected, most popes refused to bow to the emperor's demands. The most intense controversy broke out during the reign of Henry IV (1056-1106). Pope Gregory VII, eager to assert his independence from the emperor, issued a special bulletin in 1176 which declared that the pope had the right to depose any secular rulers, even the emperor! He then tried to curtail Henry's influence by asserting that Henry could no longer appoint (invest) bishops or spiritual leaders. This Investiture Controversy was the focal point of a power struggle from 1075 to 1122 and was typical of the intensity of conflict between secular and spiritual authorities that would go on for many years. Pope Gregory warned Henry not to invest bishops any longer. Henry, emperor of the Holy Roman Empire, repudiated Pope Gregory's claim. The pope responded by excommunicating the emperor and calling for his removal! Pope Gregory, a careful tactician, gathered rebellious German nobles into his camp and brought the emperor to his knees.

By 1077, the emperor saw his authority eroding rapidly in Germany. Humiliated, the emperor came to the castle of Canossa, where the Pope was temporarily living. Pope Gregory, however, seized the moment of humiliation and ignored the emperor for three days. During that time the emperor stood before the castle gates in humble clothing, pleading for the pope's forgiveness, which the pope finally granted.

But the story does not end there. Henry was later able to defeat the rebellious German nobles who had aligned themselves with the pope. He turned the tables on the pope and managed to drive Pope Gregory from Rome!

How was this problem to be resolved? A compromise was finally reached in 1122, in what is called the Concordat of Worms (a city). The compromise that ended the Investiture Controversy stated that Church elections would be free from the emperor's control but that he would have a representative present. Bishops who were elected would swear political allegiance to the emperor, but their *spiritual* authority would come only from fellow churchmen. Although the Holy Roman Empire continued until Napoleon dissolved it in 1806, it ceased to have a powerful political influence after the year 1250. Its continued existence was "a testament to the aspirations and ideals of medieval men for a united Christian commonwealth in which the temporal and spiritual authority work together for the benefit of Christendom."[11] The attempt was noble, but most would question whether this was the best way to live out the gospel. From our perspective in history, the experiment seems largely to have failed.

THE CRUSADES

The Crusades, which took place from 1095 to 1291, are undoubtedly one of the most bizarre detours the Church ever took, removing the Church far from its fundamental goals. The Crusades consisted of eight military expeditions established for the purpose of recapturing the Holy Land from the Turks. Pope Urban II was able to inspire far more zeal than he was common sense as he encouraged people to leave their European homeland and travel en masse to conquer Palestine. Some of the Crusades were aborted and never made it to Israel. Others successfully established the Latin Kingdom of Jerusalem. But the Crusade members were not the chivalrous nobles they were meant to be. They were often unruly, wicked men who stole, pillaged and raped their way from one city to another. They cared not whether the village was Christian or Muslim. They were equal-opportunity villains who destroyed anyone and anything in their way. Now 900 years later and on the exact days, repentant Christians traveled the same route, asking forgiveness for what had been done in the name of Christ!

The most peculiar of all the Crusades was the Children's Crusade in the year 1212, in which unsuspecting parents placed their children on ships that they believed would be guided to the Holy Land, where Muslims would naturally surrender to an army of children! The wicked shipowners had other intentions. Hundreds of children were sold into slavery!

If the health of the Church was determined by the Crusades, one would have to declare it sick to death.[12] But again, God's mercy didn't end. Although the Church, at times, appears almost out of view, the Church was preserved—with all its purity and with the power of the gospel. Because of this resiliency, we have the gospel 900 years later.

To further assist you in understanding the key individuals and events of chapter 4, study questions, charts, diagrams, time lines and links to biographical websites are available on the Internet at www.jimgarlow.com. Please follow the site links to *How God Saved Civilization*, chapter 4 study helps.

GROWING
CONFLICTS

THE LATE MIDDLE AGES

Dates covered: A.D. 1000-1517
Key persons: Anselm, Peter Abelard, Thomas Aquinas, Innocent III,
Francis of Assisi, Joan of Arc, Erasmus, Savonarola

Odette watched Maman throw the first handful of dirt into the open hole that held her father's casket. There wasn't money for a carved and polished stone house, like the other graves had, or even a fancy stone marker. *Papa deserved better,* she thought. *Why was money so important?* She thought of her father's weak smile and strong words to her just before he died—only Thursday, yet it seemed years ago. "Take care of Maman," he had told her. "She's not so strong now." Odette lowered her head and kicked at the dirt in the cemetery. Tears refused to come.

Père Gerard held her mother's elbow as they walked back to the house. Odette shuddered when she saw him touch Maman. Odette did not like the priest. Odette held baby Gaëlle in her arms while Anne-Marie sucked her thumb and clung to Odette's skirt. Together they followed Maman and Père Gerard into the small, cold stone hut in which Odette had lived ever since she had been born, nine years ago. Papa had tended sheep for a rich stocking merchant who lived in nearby Arles, in southern France. Only a few weeks ago, Papa had been healthy. But then that no-good farmworker had slipped while shearing and had cut Papa's arm with the shears. The sore had grown worse and worse, until . . . now Papa was in heaven.

She stamped her foot as she walked. Papa *was* in heaven. She didn't agree with Maman, and she didn't agree with Père Gerard, who told her that Papa was not with Jesus but in a place called purgatory.

They sat in the chairs Papa had carved for them. Maman served the precious goat cheese to Père Gerard. Maman had made the cheese herself along with some anise cakes that she usually baked only when celebrating Christ's birth into the world. Anne-Marie and Odette watched quietly.

"My dear Madame Buvois," said the priest, drinking one more glass of Maman's sweet cider. "You and Etienne have been faithful members of my parish ever since I came here five years ago. I am so happy I can be here now to help you in your distress."

"Thank you, Père," replied Madame Buvois.

"There is one more thing you can do for Etienne, now."

Again, Odette knew she wouldn't agree. How could anyone help Papa now that he was dead?

"You know that Etienne is now in purgatory."

"Yes, Père."

"You may be able to help him get to heaven faster."

"Of course, Père; but you see that we live simply, and now I do not know how I can provide for my children, especially since they are all girls. I have no fine young man to take over the shepherding. Odette is a wonderful help, but I don't know how we will manage." Odette gritted her teeth. She knew what Père Gerard was going to say next.

"I certainly understand your concern," he said softly. "But I don't need to tell you that the things of heaven must take precedence over the things of earth. Have you nothing at all with which to buy an indulgence?"

Odette was nearly screaming inside. *Don't tell him!* she thought, and then she found herself praying. *Dear God, don't let her tell him about the coins!*

But her mother said, "I have only two gold coins that Etienne's grandmother left him."

"But that's wonderful!" exclaimed the priest, taking another anise cake. "That will reduce his time in purgatory by about a thousand years!"

"Yes," said Madame Buvois. "I love him very much. I must help him."

Tears welled up in Odette's eyes. She rubbed at them angrily and pushed Anne-Marie away from her.

The priest continued, "The Lord will honor your great sacrifice."

Odette's mother drew two gold coins from their secret hiding place beside the hearth. She caught her mother's eye and shook her head as hard as she could no! But Maman gave them to the priest and placed the sealed document he gave her in return back in the hole, covering it with the brick.

The priest rose to leave but then turned and spoke to Madame Buvois again.

"Chère Madame," he said, with a slight bow of the head, "I want you to realize that God may test you yet again."

"What do you mean, Père?" asked Maman, her eyes wide with fear.

"Well, your health is not perfect, and the girls need protection from sickness and accident. Remember that Etienne refused to buy relics from me last year. And the Lord has visited him now. Had he protected you as he should, he would have been alive today."

Odette felt her fists ball up hard. She wanted to punch the priest's face. *Oh God,* she prayed silently, *how can I hate Your servant so much, when I love You even more?*

"Etienne did not believe in relics," Maman answered quietly.

"I know, dear woman. And look where he is now. I believe it is your Christian duty to protect yourself and your girls."

"But, Père," replied Maman, "I have nothing left!"

Father Etienne moved back to the chair where he had been sitting and placed his hand on the smooth, carved wood. "These are beautiful chairs. And the table, too, is elegantly carved. They would fetch a fine price at the Saturday market. I'm sure the price would be enough to cover this!" Odette watched him pull from the deep pocket of his black robe a velvet bag, tied with gold strings. Carefully he pulled from the bag a piece of bone about three inches long.

"This came to me from a very reliable source in Rome," he explained in a soft, reverent voice. "It is a piece of bone from the leg of the apostle Peter himself!"

Odette could stand it no more. She was no longer worried about appearances or about the baby being asleep or about what the villagers would think. She flew upon the priest, pounding her fists on his black robe, the tears flowing down her cheeks.

"I hate you!" she screamed. "You're not from God. Leave my Maman alone. I will protect Maman. God will protect Maman. Get out! Get out!" Odette wept and pounded her fists against the man.

Nothing changed. Maman had decided. She was convinced she had to sell her table and chairs in order to pay for the precious portion of Peter's bone. Maman honestly believed that because she now possessed the bone, her family would be safe.

SCHOLASTICISM: THE AMAZING HUNGER FOR LEARNING

During the twelfth and thirteenth centuries, an inexplicable quest for learning burned its way through Europe, and many universities were created. *Uni* means "one," and *versity* refers to diversity. A university was the gathering of great diversity in one place. This quest for learning was labeled Scholasticism, a complex term with multiple definitions. The University of

Paris had its origin in what were called cathedral schools. As the name implies, these schools started in the large churches called cathedrals. A cathedra was the seat or chair of the bishop, where he lived and presided. Thus, cathedrals were influential churches serving a jurisdiction of smaller churches. The University of Naples was founded by a political leader, Fredrick II in 1224. Some universities were founded by towns. Oxford University and the University of Bologna were among the earliest to be founded. In time, the universities at Paris and Oxford had residence halls, or dormitories, a totally new concept. Generally, only about half the students received degrees. Many came to listen to some well-known teacher for a while. By the end of the Middle Ages, there were 80 universities. Before there were such centers, talented professors would wander from town to town, tutoring students privately.

ANSELM OF CANTERBURY

Anselm (1033-1109), born in Italy, became known as the founder of Scholasticism. Anselm's father wanted him to follow a political career and was displeased when his son chose to become a monk. Anselm's teaching abilities caused the school located at his monastery to become a prominent center of learning. Due to his frequent visits to England, he became popular among the clergy there. When the archbishopric of Canterbury became vacant in 1089, the English wanted Anselm as their leader. However, William II (also known as Rufus), had come to the throne in 1087 and was very happy not to have to deal with anyone in that position, which he left open for four years. Finally, the king needed someone to hear his confession, since he was seriously ill. As Anselm came to hear the king's confession, William II thrust a pastoral staff into Anselm's hands, insisting that he become archbishop. Anselm protested, saying "You have yoked an old sheep with an untamed bull to the plough of the Church, which ought to be drawn by two strong oxen."[1] Anselm, who initially refused, finally accepted after negotiating for the return of lands taken by William II from the cathedral of Canterbury. While William II agreed to this and other promises, he promptly broke them after Anselm accepted the position; and he even went so far as to block Anselm from making necessary trips to Rome. Since this was at the time of the Investiture Controversy, it was six long years before a compromise was reached. However, Anselm did not waste much time fighting with kings. He was a scholar. Scholasticism, in part, refers to the attempt to use logic in order to understand faith. He believed that one could demonstrate the existence of God through reason, not merely by Scripture. Anselm became well known for his Ontological Argument for the existence of God. He believed that the mere fact of the existence of the *idea* of God necessarily implied the existence of God. One should not assume that he sacrificed faith at the altar of reason. Quite the contrary. He believed that faith must precede reason. He stated, "I don't seek to understand in order that I may believe, but I believe in order to understand."[2] In other words, Anselm, though a profound scholar, placed the highest emphasis on faith. He is regarded as the greatest scholar between Augustine, in the fourth century, and Thomas Aquinas, who came 200 years after Anselm.

PETER ABELARD

Another great philosopher who contributed significantly to the use of reason in the Christian faith was Peter Abelard (1079-1142), a French philosopher and theologian. Born in Brittany, Abelard studied under Anselm at several different locations and went on to become a profoundly influential and popular teacher himself, attracting large numbers and becoming one of the great influencers of the minds of the twelfth century. Among his students was Peter Lombard, author of *Sentences*. In attendance at his lectures were 2 future popes, 20 future cardinals and 50 future bishops.[3]

Abelard's life was filled with pathos. While in Paris, he lived in the house of Fulbert, the canon of Notre Dame. Abelard fell in love with Fulbert's niece, Heloise, who gave birth to a son. Abelard offered to marry her. She declined, thinking that her marriage to Abelard would destroy his career in the Church. She entered a convent. Fulbert was incensed and ordered Abelard castrated. Abelard then moved to the monastery at Saint Denis. He and Heloise continued a lifelong correspondence of spectacular love letters that proved them to be among the world's most faithful lovers.

Abelard's tragic and frustrated romance was only one of his problems. By 1121 he was condemned as a heretic and was forced to seek refuge. Abelard was criticized for giving reason too high a place in the study of theology. His disclaimers are passionate: "I do not want to be a philosopher if it means resisting St. Paul; I do not wish to be Aristotle if it must separate me from Christ." His personal motto revealed his Christian convictions: "I understand so that I might believe."[4] But his arguments didn't satisfy his critics.

THOMAS AQUINAS

No one influenced the theology of the Middle Ages more than one overweight Italian. Thomas Aquinas's (1225-1274) large physique earned him the denigrating nickname of "Dumb Ox." But his theological brilliance and passion for Christ later earned him another nickname, "Angelic Doctor." Educated at the universities of Naples, Paris and Cologne, Aquinas became a Dominican preacher and scholar, and taught in Paris and Rome. He attempted to merge the philosophy of Aristotle with biblical theology. His system of thinking is known as Thomism. He became the single most influential Roman Catholic scholar until the 1960s. Protestants, as a rule, condemn his mix of the Bible and Greek philosophy, complaining that he compromised many Bible doctrines. Aquinas believed that theology was the queen of all sciences and that philosophy should be the servant of theology. Philosophy, he believed, *establishes* what theology *assumes*. Theology, for example, assumes the existence of God. However, it is the job of philosophy to establish it.

Aquinas put great emphasis upon the capacity of human reason. In fact, he felt that the image of God in every person *was* human reason. Sin, he said, diverts the will but not the intellect. His masterpiece, entitled *Summa Theologica*, was written between 1265 and 1273. It was a systematic summary of all the theological, philosophical and ethical issues that were debated in medieval universities. In additional to his commentaries on several Old and New Testament books, he wrote commentaries on the principal works of Aristotle and on Peter Lombard's *Sentences*. (Lombard [ca. 1100-ca. 1160] compiled the most widely used theology textbook in the Middle Ages and was known as "Master of the Sentences." His *Four Books of Sentences*, written between 1150 and 1152, were the culmination of an effort to systematize all theological writings from the previous 50 years.)

Aquinas's attempt to merge faith (theology) with reason (philosophy) was used by the Roman Catholic church to justify their teachings on transubstantiation, which states that in the celebration of Communion the wine and the bread turn into the actual, literal blood and body of Jesus. Only by rather complex reasoning was Aquinas able to give philosophic foundation to this unique teaching. Aquinas was the theological Mount Everest of this 1000-year period.

MYSTICS AND PRE-REFORMERS

You may be assuming that the Middle Ages was merely about wars with Muslims, wars between East and West, wars over creeds, wars between popes and emperors and wars in the universities; but there was more. Between the 1100s and the 1500s, two groups still hungered for intimacy with God and longed to see revival in His Church. These were the Mystics and the Pre-Reformers.

Mystics hungered for and experienced unusual intimacy with God. In contrast to Aquinas, they were nonrationalistic and extremely emotive. They felt their faith, which did not mean they were incapable of sound reasoning. I only mention them here so that the reader does not assume that the Middle Ages was devoid of Christians who articulated a profound passion for Christ. The Mystics, who provide a brighter light than many in the midst of the Dark Ages, are so important to our story of the Church's survival that the next chapter will be entirely devoted to them.

The chapter after the one on the Mystics will explain the movement known as the Pre-Reformation. Faithful Christians, such as Peter Waldo, John Wycliffe and John Huss, helped prepare the terrain for Martin Luther's Reformation in 1517. You can look forward to reading their stories in the next chapters.

CONFLICTS BETWEEN POPES AND COUNCILS

One of the most embarrassing conflicts to occur during the Middle Ages was the theological and ecclesiastical tug-of-war between popes and

Church councils. In 1309, Clement V moved the papacy from Rome to Avignon, France. For the next 68 years (1309-1390), the papacy remained in Avignon, in what is referred to as the Babylonian captivity of Church history. This relocation set off a vitriolic struggle within the Roman Catholic church.

The conflict was not merely between Rome, Italy and Avignon, France. It was between two men—both claiming to be pope at the same time! In 1377, Catherine of Siena (we'll discuss her in a later chapter) persuaded Pope Gregory XI to move the papacy from Avignon back to Rome. But Gregory died the next year (1378), and the cardinals in Rome elected Urban VI as the new pope, who was to reside in Rome. Some of the cardinals regretted electing him and gathered to elect Clement VII (?-1394), who went to reside in—you guessed it—Avignon. This period, known as the Great Schism, created a most unwieldy situation: two men claiming to be pope at the same time! France, Spain and Scotland followed Clement, the French pope in Avignon. England, Germany and Northern Italy regarded Urban of Rome as the true pope. This embarrassing standoff continued, even though other popes succeeded Clement (in France) and Urban (in Rome). Finally, a great solution was proposed: have a Church council and resolve the schism once and for all!

The Council of Pisa (Italy) in 1409 had high hopes of dealing with this controversy. By this time, 1409, Gregory XII was the pope in Rome and Benedict XIII was the pope in Avignon, France. The solution seemed obvious. Elect a new pope, and have Gregory and Benedict both step down. The cardinals at the Council of Pisa elected Alexander V. But neither Gregory nor Benedict would step down. So now there were *three* men all claiming to be the *one* true pope! The three remained for another five years, until the Council of Constance (1414-1418)! This council was a long affair (as many Church councils proved to be). Located on the German/Swiss border, the town's population swelled by tens of thousands and prostitution and debauchery skyrocketed while Church leaders tried desperately to resolve the problem. Finally, the decision was made to elect a new pope, Martin V, and to depose the other three popes (one of them, John XXIII, fled from the council in 1415). Sadly, though the problem of having too many popes at the same time was resolved, the papacy was left badly tarnished and much criticism of the ecclesiastical office was generated.

Joachim of Floris (ca. 1132-1202), a fiery Italian Cistercian abbot and author, began to attack the very idea of the papacy. Those who followed him—such as Wycliffe and Luther—unhesitatingly called the papacy the Antichrist. However, the papacy maintained a strong political grip, even if it had lost spiritual authority. So strong, in fact, was the papacy, that it won out over the councils. After this the Church was led by a pope (one man) much more than by a council (a committee).

CONFLICTS BETWEEN CHURCH AND STATE

But even as the Church wrestled with internal problems, the feuds between Church and state intensified. This friction was best dramatized in the life of Thomas Becket (ca. 1118-1170) and his friend King Henry II who ruled England from 1154 to 1189.

Becket loved luxury and entertainment, which made him more than a chancellor to the pleasure-loving king. Becket was a close friend. Consequently, in 1162, when the Archbishop of Canterbury died, Henry seized the moment to appoint his friend as the new archbishop. Henry was counting on Becket to strengthen the ties between Church and state. However, Henry was in for a surprise.

When Becket became the archbishop, he changed. Becket became a highly disciplined, sober individual who championed the rights of the people and defended the position of the Church. However, Becket's change in lifestyle strained relations between him and the king. The conflict between the two former friends grew more intense when, in 1164, Becket objected to the king's Constitutions of Clarendon. Finally Henry exiled Becket to France. Six years later, in 1170, assuming that all was calm, Becket returned to Canterbury, England.

In a casual conversation with four of his knights, King Henry expressed his annoyance with Becket and stated a wish that he would no longer have to deal with him. The knights took it literally, went back to Canterbury and murdered Becket at the altar of the Canterbury Cathedral in 1170. The assassination shocked the English people and created enormous anger toward the king. So forceful was the outrage over Becket's death that the king withdrew his attempts to control the clergy and did penance for defying ecclesiastical authority. In the words of T. O. Kay, "The bishop achieved more as a martyr than as an archbishop."[5]

THE POPE VERSUS CIVIL RULERS

Some issues just won't go away. Leadership was as much an issue in the 1300s as it had been earlier. No one stirred up the authority issue more in the fourteenth century than Marsilius of Padua (ca. 1275-ca. 1342). In June 1324, he completed his revolutionary political document entitled *Defensor pacis*, in which he stated that the Church must come under duly and validly appointed rulers. He observed that people by themselves were given to strife and that the purpose of the state was to establish order. The state needed to have the power of coercive law. No part of the community could validly resist law or its duly appointed rulers. The Church, as a part of society, should submit to that law and those rulers. Marsilius was far ahead of his time, embracing the thinking of the Renaissance. Predictably, he was seen as an archheretic by the pope.

HERETICS AND THE INQUISITION

Heresy was given a new definition in the Middle Ages. In earlier centuries, heresy referred to incorrect beliefs or theology. However, in the earlier years of the history of Christian faith, one didn't necessarily know what truth was until a particular teaching was advanced. At that point the Early Church leaders would meet and judge whether it was heretical or orthodox. Thus they established what was acceptable, or what we would today call orthodoxy. For example, when certain teachings arose declaring that Jesus was simply man and not God, Church leaders came together to establish what we understand regarding the dual nature of Christ; that is, He is man and God at the same time.

With the passing of years, however, heresy took on a new definition. Anyone who did not accept the *organizational* structures of the all-powerful Roman Catholic hierarchy and bureaucracy was named a heretic. People who disagreed in the slightest ways with the Church were tried and tortured. This systematic torturing of people was referred to as the Inquisition, which took place during the twelfth, thirteenth and fourteenth centuries. Prior to the Inquisition, the Church had been in the habit of excommunicating heretics; but with the advent of the Inquisition, more dramatic measures followed: confiscation of property, torture and/or death or execution.

The prime instigator in crushing out the opposition during the Middle Ages was Pope Innocent III. He followed a guilty-until-proven-innocent approach to heretics and applied torture freely to crush the heretics. Though we have trouble understanding such actions, we must remember that variation of belief was considered a threat to "the social, ecclesiastical, and doctrinal order of Christendom. Church and state were two aspects of a single society and political and social unity, were the results of ecclesiastical unity. To destroy heresy was thus to preserve the integrity of the faith and also the security of society. To the Christian monarch, the heretic was a rebel; to the Christian Church, the heretic was murdering his own soul."[6]

The leaders of the Roman Catholic church unleashed their disapproval on three kinds of groups:

- anti-institutional groups—people who organized in a way contrary to the established structures of the Roman church;
- ascetic groups—highly disciplined, pious communities who advocated strong accountability in the Christian life;
- enthusiasts—passionate, zealous, excited Christians (Peter Waldo and the Waldensians, for example, were condemned as heretics).

INNOCENT III

Innocent III was unanimously elected Pope in 1198. At only 37 years of age, he brilliantly reorganized Roman Catholic bureaucracy. "Convinced that he truly was the 'Vicar of Christ, appointed to convey the divine law to all mankind, he set out to make his authority uppermost in the feudal and ecclesiastical relationships that he reformed.'"[7] He contended that he had the right to choose rulers, including the emperor, "justifying this action not as a temporal ruler but as a 'spiritual judge' over all men."[8] Innocent III never forgot his ordination sermon, based on Jeremiah 1:10, which states, "See, today I appoint you over nations and kingdoms to uproot and tear down, to destroy and overthrow, to build and to plant." With this in mind, he wrote to King John a couple of years later: "The King of kings . . . so established the kingship and the priesthood in the Church, that the kingship should be priestly, and the priesthood royal . . . setting one over all, whom he appointed his vicar on earth."[9] To paraphrase Innocent, "I'm in charge here."

Innocent III epitomizes medieval Christianity at the peak of its political authority. He is, without question, the most eminent of the medieval popes. Ironically, very few persons today have ever heard of Innocent III, whereas one of the poorest (by choice) and humble persons of the same period is extremely well known today—Francis of Assisi.

FRANCIS OF ASSISI

In contrast to Innocent's unquestioned power is Francis's unquestioned powerlessness. Francis was born to a wealthy cloth merchant in Assisi, which is now northern Italy. By the age of 20 he went on a military adventure which ended with his serving one year as a prisoner of war, due to a border dispute. In 1204 this experience, combined with a severe illness, caused Francis to reevaluate his life. He became disillusioned with his extravagant ways and his materialism, and began a process of inward prayer and meditation. In 1205, he made a pilgrimage to Rome and decided to change places with a beggar outside of Saint Peter's Basilica for one day. This proved to be an eye-opening experience to him. In addition, he chose to embrace a leper, which was considered unacceptable, and even kiss his sores, which was totally repugnant to most people! After returning home, he heard a voice speak to him from a painting of Christ, telling him to repair the church. After using his father's funds to repair the church, his angry father denounced him, declaring Francis to be insane. By 1209, the words of Matthew 10:7-10 had become his guideline, as he embraced a beggar's life. He preached poverty, repentance, brotherly love and peace. The funds he received were used to repair churches. He began to attract followers, who would eventually be called Franciscans. A 16-year-old woman named Clare left her wealthy family to follow Francis, and soon had followers of her own, who would be called the Poor Clares.

Francis left Italy and traveled through France and Spain to convert Muslims. At one point, he traveled to the Holy Land to persuade the Crusaders not to attack the Muslims, but the Crusaders paid him no attention. They attacked, and were promptly defeated by the Muslims. Francis went instead to the Muslim camp and began preaching to the sultan, who received Francis with hospitality.

As the number of followers increased, Francis realized that he needed formal approval to organize. He secured permission from, of all people, Innocent III, who was not totally pleased with some of Francis's extreme ways. The Fourth Lateran Council of 1215 sought to curb some of the "excessive enthusiasm" of the Franciscans. But formal approval was granted, and for a moment the world's most powerful pope came into the life of the "world's favorite Christian saint."[10]

But this gentle lover of God's creation lacked administrative skill, so Cardinal Ugolino (later Pope Gregory IX) directed more and more of the policies of the Franciscans. When the leadership of the Franciscans was handed to Elias of Cortona in 1223; the order began to place a strong emphasis on education. Francis was offended, sensing a betrayal of the simplicity of the gospel and a temptation to pride in learning and to a love for material possessions (books). Even more troubling to Francis was the friars' new involvement in politics.

With the Franciscan order wrested from his control, Francis abdicated his leadership in 1223, and by 1224, had moved to a life of solitude on Mount La Verna. While in prayer there, he allegedly received the *stigmata*, bleeding wounds in his body at the places where Jesus had been wounded on the cross. It is said that Francis performed many miracles. He was, according to William P. Barker, "the brightest personality in the dreary late medieval period of history."[11] Again, the irony is that Francis humbled himself and God exalted him; Innocent exalted himself, but few would know his name today.

COUNCILS AND TRANSUBSTANTIATION

Fourteen councils or synods were held at the Lateran Palace in Rome between the seventh and eighteenth centuries. Only five of these stand out as significant to us today:

- 1123, the First Lateran Council ended the Investiture Controversy;
- 1139, the Second Lateran Council condemned clerical marriage and asked secular powers to assist in detecting heresy (a euphemism for asking political leaders to kill anyone who disagreed with Church policy);
- 1179, the Third Lateran Council laid out extensive regulations for the clergy—including a condemnation of those who kept concubines!— and began an attack on the Waldensians (those who followed Peter Waldo), the Albigensians and the Cathari (two heretical sect groups in the eleventh through the thirteenth centuries);

- 1215, the Fourth Lateran Council affirmed the doctrine of transubstantiation;
- 1545-1563, the Council of Trent reaffirmed the doctrine of transubstantiation in spite of criticisms by Protestant reformers.

A STUDY IN CONTRASTS

Nothing better illustrates the contrasting faces of the Church than two men who lived at the same time in the Middle Ages. Innocent III (1160-1216) was the most powerful Pope, a "high-water mark" in papal authority and influence. His real name was Lotario dei Conti di Segni (now you see why they renamed him when he became the pope!). At the opposite end of the spectrum was Francis of Assisi (1182-1226), the "gentle lover of everyone and everything in God's creation."[12] Saint Francis, in contrast to Innocent III, gave away everything he had and refused to associate himself with any role of authority or power. These two men intersected ironically when the most powerful pope, Innocent III, was asked to approve the formation of the Franciscans, a collection of persons who followed Francis due to his *lack* of possessions and power.

BUBONIC PLAGUE

Life in the Middle Ages was hard—very hard. The single event that best epitomized the pain of the Dark Ages was the dreaded disease that swept Europe, beginning in 1347: the Black Death. Timothy Paul Jones writes in this graphic way:

> In October, 1347, an unwelcome passenger scurried aboard a cargo ship. It was a rat with a disease-laden flea fixed on its hide. The ship's sailors brought home something more costly than their cargo. Dark spots swelled between their legs and beneath their arms. The blots oozed black blood and putrid pus.[13]

For four years the Black Death ruled Europe and Asia Minor. In Constantinople it killed 88 percent of the population. In Paris alone, 800 people died daily. Corpses rotted on the streets, unburied and unblessed.

"And no bells tolled," one man wrote, and "nobody wept, no matter what his loss, because almost everyone expected death."[14] The cause of the disease was not known at that time. Instead of blaming it on its actual cause, a flea, the dying hordes blamed it on the fact that the pope was living in exile, or on the Jews, whose communities they promptly burned. Others blamed it on their own personal immorality. Between 1347 and 1350 the Bubonic Plague took the lives of somewhere between 24 million and 40 million Europeans. Life in the Middle Ages was very hard!

JOAN OF ARC

If life was hard for men in the Middle Ages, it was considerably harder for women. But when they do emerge, they form some of the "highest mountain peaks" of Church history. Such was the case for Joan of Arc (1412-1431), a young French peasant girl originally known as Jeanne la Pucelle. As if disease, sickness and hardship were not enough in the Middle Ages, war was rampant.

Joan of Arc was born during the troubled period known as the Hundred Years War. By 13, she had begun to see visions and hear the voices of the archangel Michael, Saint Catherine and Saint Margaret encouraging her to save France. One of her visions confirmed the legitimacy of the rule of King Charles VII, whose disputed claim was dividing the country. In 1429, Joan convinced a skeptical Charles to put her in charge of 10,000 troops to relieve the interminable siege of Orléans. Dressed in men's clothing, she became an instant heroine when the battle was successful. Consequently, she asked to stand with Charles VII as he was crowned and anointed at Rheims.

With the taste of victory so sweet, Joan led a contingent to recapture Paris, but she lacked sufficient troops. She was captured on May 23, 1430, and sold to the English, who had Church officials put her on trial for witchcraft. She was held in prison until the trial, which continued from February to May of 1431. While questioned in the trial, she answered the interrogators with boldness, candor and unusual perception, in spite of the fact of the probable consequences. Under great pressure, she renounced the voices but later retracted that denial. As she was burned at the stake in 1431, she uttered the words, "Jesus, Jesus."[15]

Her death, however, spurred the French to greater resistance; and they finally drove the English out of their country in 1453. In 1456, the Church decided to reopen the trial and reconsider the charges made against her (a little late for Joan!). In the final Church trial, her initial sentence was considered unjust by Pope Callistus III.

RENAISSANCE AND REFORMATION

Movements are difficult to label, and it is even more difficult to explain their beginnings. Such is the case with the Renaissance. The Renaissance refers to a movement in Europe during the fourteenth, fifteenth and sixteenth centuries. The word "Renaissance" comes from a French word meaning "rebirth." The term is understood to have begun in fourteenth-century Italy through the writings of several great writers, artists, thinkers and political leaders:

Francesco Petrarch (1304-1374)	Giovanni Boccaccio (1313-1375)
Lorenzo Valla (1407-1457)	Marsileo Ficino (1433-1499)
Giovanni Pico della Mirandola (1463-1494)	Niccolò Machiavelli (1469-1527)
Leonardo da Vinci (1452-1519)	Michelangelo (1475-1564)
Raphael (1483-1520)	

The Renaissance was an attempt to merge ancient Greek wisdom with traditional Christian faith. In southern Europe (primarily Italy) the Renaissance was essentially secular, even mildly antireligious. Although many Renaissance leaders were Christians, they separated religion from their studies.

Northern Europe, however, had a different form of rebirth, regarded as more traditionally Christian. The Renaissance accomplishments in northern Europe were tied to traditional Christian faith. For example, the northern Renaissance leaders passionately studied the writings of the Early Church fathers in an attempt to make the Bible more understandable. These leaders were generally referred to as Christian Humanists and came from various nations, such as England, France and Germany. Although their names may be unknown to most of us, their impact on our lives has been significant:

John Colet (ca. 1467-1519)	Thomas More (1478-1535)
Faber Stapulensis (died 1536)	Rudolph Agricola (died 1485)
Johannes Reuchlin (1455-1522)	Desiderius Erasmus (ca. 1466-1536)

The best known of all the Christian Humanists, and the one who will be mentioned in later chapters in conjunction with the Reformation, was Erasmus.

You may be reeling from a list of names you will never remember, partly because you cannot pronounce them. But these Christians who lived 500 years ago have had an impact on your life. An entirely new method of schooling, training, equipping and developing our minds came from the passions of these men. For example, the Bible was translated into the language of the common people, in part through the scholarship of Erasmus. (Luther used Erasmus's copy of the Greek text of the Bible when he compiled a German Bible.) Contrary to what one might think at first glance, these are not a group of dead men from long ago. Their influence is alive today in the things we do and the ways we think.

If you are a Protestant, the Renaissance in northern Europe has had an immeasurable impact in your life. The Renaissance was intertwined with the Protestant Reformation in such a way that the political, economic and religious factors all converged. The Renaissance paved the way for the Reformation. Although the Renaissance and Protestant Reformation were not identical movements in northern Europe, they shared a common goal: the renewal of Christians and a strong emphasis upon training and educating laypeople.[16]

The significant differences between the southern European Renaissance and its northern counterpart are instructive for us today. Southern Europe's emphasis was humanistic, while northern Europe's movement was labeled Christian humanism. Christian humanism teaches that God created the human mind with the purpose of knowing Him and understanding His ways. Northern Europe perceived academic study to be God-centered. Southern Europe experienced a human-centered, or anthropocentric (*anthropo* means "man"; *centric* means "centered"), understanding of truth.

We see this same division today. Secular humanists believe in the potential of the human mind without any other authority. They conclude that truth is relative. A Christian humanist believes in the full potential of the development of the human mind yet is committed to developing it under the authority of God's Word and the ways of Christ. Both groups believe in the development of the mind, but one group sees humankind as the source of truth while the other sees God's Word as the ultimate source of authentic truth.

THE GUTENBERG PRESS

As the Middle Ages began to draw to a close, the explosion of new ideas and the challenges for reform were greatly aided by a tremendous technological advance—the printing press. This invention made books readily available for scholars and laypeople.

Johannes Gutenberg (ca. 1400-ca. 1468) invented the principle of moveable type in approximately 1450, in either the city of Mainz or Strasbourg. His first printed book was a Latin Bible, often referred to as the Gutenberg Bible. The invention of the Gutenberg press had profound significance a few years later with the spread of Martin Luther's teaching on the Reformation. This innovation during the late Middle Ages is as significant as the invention of the computer was in the last half of the twentieth century.[17]

INTERNAL REFORMATION

We have discussed the tragic debauchery, greed and avarice of some of the leaders of the Roman Catholic church. Equally forceful, however, were the attempts to bring internal correction to the Church by godly and devoted followers of Christ. There were many bright lights throughout the Dark Ages. Most of those names come under the category of internal reformers.

"Internal" refers to the fact that these were pro-institutional men and women. They worked from the inside. They never left the Roman Catholic church. They lived in it and loved it. They always believed it could be changed. Girolamo Savonarola (1452-1498) was the Billy Graham of his era. He was an awesome gospel preacher in Italy. So profound were his sermons that the city of Florence was heavily impacted by his clarion call to a godly walk. But, as has happened so many times in Church history, authorities attempted to silence him. They branded Savonarola a heretic and tried to get him to recant. After torture failed, he was found guilty and condemned to death. He was hanged, his body was then burned, and the ashes were scattered in the River Arno.

Another internal reformer of the Church in the tumultuous Middle Ages was Francisco Ximenes (1436-1517). Ximenes was one of the most outstanding figures of Spanish history, whose devotion to truth created an explosive spiritual and intellectual awakening throughout all of Spain. He is regarded as "an ardent reformer and a zealous missionary. He reformed the monastic houses . . . routing out heresy. . . . His greatest concern was for the conversion of the non-Christian peoples of Spain."[18]

A brilliant scholar who started a university and advanced the study of the Bible, Ximenes, with his colleagues, was a pioneer in preparing the way for the Bible to be translated from its original languages of Hebrew and Greek into the language of the common people. He stands tall as one of the greatest of the internal reformers, operating within the Roman Catholic church.

DISTORTIONS REGARDING FORGIVENESS

In spite of the fact that there was much call for internal reformation, the Church of the Middle Ages was sluggish and bogged down in many non-biblical perceptions. No one concept more demonstrates this than the term "forgiveness." When you and I consider forgiveness today, we think in terms of that which is supplied by Jesus by His death on the cross. That was not true of the common person living in the Middle Ages. There was no understanding of mercy, grace or forgiveness. To those living in the Middle Ages, forgiveness could only be obtained by overt acts—permission-giving acts—events provided for by the Roman church. One act was baptism. Another method of obtaining forgiveness was the saving of relics (bones of saints or certain objects associated with saints). Another was the act of penance. Penance referred to some assigned action that would allegedly accrue God's favor. One example of penance was Pope Urban II's declaration that anyone going on the First Crusade would receive forgiveness of sins. Another pope declared that pilgrimages to the Holy Land or to the city of Rome would provide forgiveness of sins.

Another way to obtain forgiveness was through the purchase of indulgences. An indulgence was a document one could purchase which would grant remission from punishment. This practice led to abuse. Unscrupulous Church leaders, aware of the fund-raising capacity of such a technique, used it to fleece the unsuspecting peasants. Knowledgeable people were offended and angered over this horrific practice. The reformer, Martin Luther, was one of those.

Luther's disdain for the sale of indulgences eventually helped overthrow this system. You might wonder why people would tolerate such abuse. It is important to remember that the Church was all powerful. Priests, clergy, popes and cardinals were to be believed. If you attempted to challenge them, you could suffer excommunication, which condemned you to suffer eternal torment in hell (since there was no salvation outside the Church). At least these horrible abuses stirred an enormous hunger for biblical truth. They created such a massive vacuum that when the truth finally emerged, it exploded across much of Europe.

What is critical to understand is how God's grace and love worked in various people and nations in spite of the flagrant abuses and distortions within the Church. What the Middle Ages teaches us is to distinguish between the *organizational* church and the *true* Church. The *organizational* church demonstrated much wickedness, but the *true* Church of Jesus Christ is always alive. If one could see the underside of Church history, one would find thousands of untold, unknown, unnamed saints of God who faithfully persevered the gospel miraculously and inexplicably for you and me.

Though much of the Middle Ages proved to be a grand detour, the gospel was preserved. And we enjoy it today because of the faithfulness of thousands of unnamed followers of Christ who passed the truth of the gospel from one generation to the next—in spite of the 1,000-year detour.

To further assist you in understanding the key individuals and events of chapter 5,
study questions, charts, diagrams, time lines and links to biographical websites are available
on the Internet at www.jimgarlow.com. Please follow the site links to
How God Saved Civilization, chapter 5 study helps.

INTIMACY WITH GOD

THE MYSTICS

Dates covered: A.D. 1100-1600
Key persons: Bernard of Clairvaux, Bonaventure, Johannes Eckhart,
John Tauler, Catherine of Siena, John Ruysbroeck, Thomas à Kempis,
John of the Cross, Teresa of Avila

Artis lay awake beside his wife. The three children slept in the other corner of the room. *Why?* His mind was tormented with never-ending questions, but nobody else seemed worried.

Even his wife had gotten tired of listening to him. "You're one simple peasant," she sighed. "Why do you think you should be able to know and talk to God?" She would shrug and turn back to her churning.

Artis lay looking through his cottage window at the faraway stars. He felt as alone as those tiny stars looked in a black sky, trying to bring light but flickering as if about to go out.

Life was a struggle. Why was it so hard for him and his family and for the other peasants in his village? Those lying in the castle just at the other edge of the forest wore silk and satin fineries on Sunday. And even in the monasteries, plenty of wealth was evident.

Brother Thomas and the nuns were extremely kind, especially to his children at the monastery school. Yet the village priest was indifferent to Artis's questions about how to know God. Why was this pretentious man any better able to know God than the honest villagers who stopped to talk to Artis every day? Why was the priest given the privilege of knowing God, when he didn't care at all if Artis knew anything? Why could the pope hear from God, but no one else? Couldn't God speak for Himself? Did He want to? Did He hide from Artis and his family on purpose?

Artis loved his job as village cobbler. Everyone visited his shop eventually! As he repaired their shoes, they would tell him of their troubles: sick children, bad crops, a death from childbirth; and sometimes of their joys: a newly wed son, a healthy baby, a gift received from a wealthy relative. *In some ways, my shop is a happier place than the church,* thought Artis, with an immediate twinge of guilt.

He spread the thin blanket over his wife, who shivered in her sleep and snuggled in closer to him for warmth. Artis smiled and tucked his arm under her head. If God had made love between a man and a woman to be close, good and warm, wouldn't He want to be warm and close with His children, too?

"God," Artis whispered. "I'm only a cobbler. And I'm sorry that I don't like Your priest. Can You be as angry as he says You are? Please, I want to know You. Show me Yourself, if I'm allowed."

Artis woke slowly the next morning. The rooster's crowing met with the jarring thoughts and doubts of last night. Another hard day of work and with no assurance that God cared about him. As he pulled his rough cloak over his bare shoulders and splashed water from the basin on his face, he tried not to think about all the whys. He made no mention of them at breakfast. The brown bread and goat's milk warmed him in preparation for the new day.

As he arrived in the village, he sensed something was wrong. His first client was the baker and Artis got the whole story quickly. In the next village the night before, a man named Cross had explained some very unusual things about God.

Artis felt a thrill run through him. Did God want to communicate with him after all?

"Let's go over tonight," offered the baker. "I can see you want to know more!"

His wife stayed with the children, and Artis accompanied his friend to the next village that night. They pushed into the small crowd to hear what a plain-looking monk called John of the Cross was saying. Artis was shocked, but an intense joy pierced through his doubts. John of the Cross said that God wanted to talk with them. He wanted to be with them. He would even speak to them, if they would listen.

I've been listening for years! Artis thought. *He's never said a word to me.* As if John had read Artis's mind, John continued: "The reason you don't think God talks to you is because you don't know how to listen. I will stay in your village for three more days. I will teach you how to listen to God, how to talk with Him and to know how much He loves you."

Artis had never heard such words before. With hardly a thought for the shoes piling up on his workbench, he listened to John of the Cross the entire day.

God, You must want me to know You. I prayed to You only last night, and You brought John to the next village. Thank You. I love You. Artis could hardly sleep again. He was about to know the God of the universe! A wonderful new life would open before him. Cautiously, he began to follow John's instructions. Every night, he talked to God himself, without asking the priest to do it for him. He couldn't help but believe that God was really listening.

A REFRESHING BREEZE

Would the Church find its way again, after its tragic detour into greed, corruption, moral decay, debauchery and the excessive use of power? God's promises are sure. His Holy Spirit began to move, and a refreshing breeze stirred gently in His Church. Some Christians who reacted to the abuse in the Church by seeking a deeper spirituality were known as the Mystics. They were not without personal faults and even lacked the theological clarity that would come during the Reformation. In fact, some Mystics held rather embarrassing theological positions. So why refer to this movement as a "refreshing breeze"?

For all their confusion, the Mystics had a heart to know God. They longed for communion with God. They hoped to discover a mystical union with God and to lead others to the same discovery. They saw what others did not see; they felt what others could not feel; they grew to know and embrace what others seemingly did not know. And their personal devotion and commitment to Christ are convicting. Their love for others and their examples of practical service are motivating.

DEFINITION

Mysticism is the belief that a person can establish direct union with God by cultivating the spirit, or the soul, and by developing a sense of inwardness. In order to cultivate the spirit, the Mystics exercised strong personal discipline, both in their devotional and in their physical lives. Only such discipline could lead them to a powerful union with God.

The dangers of such an emphasis on experience and on self-discipline as a means of union with God are evident. When taken to extremes, such practices deny the historic nature of the Christian faith. Some Christians would argue that it is impossible to be a Christian and a mystic at the same time, because the Christian faith is based not on *our* attempts to draw near to God, but on *His* work in reaching down to save us. Our faith is not in our experience but in Christ, who died and rose from the dead. Other Christians criticize Mysticism because it bypasses the *objectivity* of God's revealed Word—the Bible—and substitutes in its place *subjectivity*—the emotions.

WHY MYSTICISM IS NEEDED

Although Mysticism has its dangers, I believe that within certain parameters, it is a good and healthy component of true Christianity. If by mysticism we mean receiving esoteric visions that run counter to Scripture, then it is distinctly anti-Christian. But if by Mysticism we mean a sense of God's presence in the Christian's life, and a dependency on His guidance to make decisions in conformity with the written Word (the Bible), then such mysticism is merely the living out of a vibrant Christian life.

SIFTING HISTORY

Some of the Mystics that we are about to study crossed acceptable theological boundaries, making us wonder if they knew the same God the Bible reveals. However, students of history learn to sift the past—absorbing the good, while identifying and rejecting the bad. As Christians, we must even sift biblical stories in this way. God never hid the sin and faults of those He chose to reveal His name and to accomplish His purposes. Moses, David, Peter and Paul were all flawed. And in the history of the Church, we see flawed heroes. They were all flawed. We are all flawed as well! But when we study Church history, we learn from the failures of those who have gone before us. Can some of the Mystics be considered failures? Of course. Did they overemphasize emotion and experience? Absolutely. Yet their deeply devotional, Spirit-guided lives can teach us much.

KNOWING GOD

Let us define biblical mysticism as a union with God that does not deny the authority of the written Word of God (the Bible). In one sense, every believer ought to be a *mystic* (small *m*), even if he is not a *Mystic* (capital *M*). Every believer has a true human-divine encounter, which can be described as knowing God. No one can be a Christian without this personal knowledge of God (John 17:3: "Now this is eternal life: that they may know you, the only true God, and Jesus Christ, whom you have sent.") All believers want to know Him better and to grow in their knowledge of Him.

The Mystics of the Middle Ages seemed to pursue such a relationship with ease. They really knew their God. They enjoyed incredible fellowship with Him. They talked to Him, and they heard from Him. They experienced God. And in this sense, we envy them.

A LOOSE COLLECTION OF INDIVIDUALS

Mysticism was not an organized movement. It was a phenomenon experienced by a collection of individuals largely unrelated to each other, across a 500-year span. Some of them knew each other and clearly influenced and taught each other. But many of them had never heard of each other (especially those who were several hundred years and many miles apart). In the pages that follow, we will examine nine individuals. We will start in the High Middle Ages (1100-1300; "high" refers to the middle portion of the Middle Ages), examine several Mystics in the closing portion of the Middle Ages (1300-1500) and look into the lives of two Mystics who lived during the counter-Reformation period (late 1500s). These Mystics are

High Middle Ages

Bernard of Clairvaux (1096-1153)   Bonaventure (1221-1274)

Johannes Eckhart (1260-1327)

Late Middle Ages

John Tauler (1300-1361)   John Ruysbroeck (1293-1381)

Catherine of Siena (1347-1380)   Thomas à Kempis (1380-1470)

Counter-Reformation Period

John of the Cross (1542-1591)   Teresa of Avila (1515-1582)

Unfortunately, space in this book does not permit us to go into depth concerning other notable Mystics such as

- Hugo of Saint Victor (1096-1141), who merged intense academic research with a carefully cultivated inner spiritual life;
- Henry Suso (1300-1366), who offered practical, easy-to-read treatises on how to live a Christlike life;
- Gerhard Groote (1340-1384), who contended that all instruction, including the Bible itself, should be put in a common language for all;
- Jacob Bohme (1575-1624), a Protestant who lived after the Reformation and who held very strongly to a direct connection with the divine presence of God—his views became heretical.

BERNARD OF CLAIRVAUX

Bernard (1090-1153) was one of the most influential spiritual leaders of the Middle Ages. He founded the famous Cistercian Abbey at Clairvaux, France, in 1115. So magnetic was his spiritual life and so keen his administrative skills that the new order spread rapidly. Before he died, his order had already spread to 68 houses (centers where his followers lived and ministered). The Cistercians paid a price for their popularity, however, since they came into conflict with the Cluniacs (the reform movement that started in Cluny). So highly regarded was Bernard's devotion that both Martin Luther and John Calvin referred to him 400 years later in the most complimentary ways.

Bernard concluded that he could not trust philosophy to make Christian truth understandable. True understanding came by walking in humility and by communing with a loving God. Anyone who wishes to understand Bernard of Clairvaux's Mysticism can read some of his writings. From 1112 to 1153, Bernard wrote 500 letters dealing with life; over 100 sermons (86 on the Song of Solomon), a book entitled *Grace and Free Will*, in which he demonstrates that salvation comes only from God; a book entitled *On the Degrees of Humility*, which outlines how to walk in humility; and another entitled *Why and How God Is to Be Loved*.

Although he was the most influential and powerful preacher of his age and participated in the great Church events of his time, Bernard turned down offers that would have advanced him in the hierarchy. Bernard remained a lowly abbot until his death on August 20, 1153. Bernard demonstrated both an exceptional grasp of the Bible and a profound command of language, unparalleled among any who lived in his time frame. We can still experience his particular blend of biblical knowledge, deep piety and writing skills when we sing his hymns: "Oh Sacred Head, Now Wounded" and "Jesus, the Very Thought of Thee," written 850 years ago.

BONAVENTURE

Bonaventure (1221-1274) was a profound thinker who became the leader of the Franciscan Order in 1257. His strong administrative skills were exceeded only by his qualities of meditation. His academic treatises, written early in his life, were spectacular: *Commentary on the Sentences* and *The Journey of the Mind to God*. Trained at the University of Paris at the same time as the famous Thomas Aquinas, Bonaventure became convinced that only through prayer and meditation could one reach true union with God. This union would then bring insight into divine knowledge. He agreed with

Saint Francis that the entire purpose of doctrinal teaching was to further the soul's progress toward God, and he shared Augustine's conviction that the purpose of life was to "know God and the soul." To Bonaventure, "all other knowledge, including philosophy, was pertinent only to the degree that it assisted . . . the mind to God."[1] Any attempt to acquire knowledge for itself would lead only to error, for faith must always be the foundation upon which knowledge is founded. Wrote Burke and Wiggins, "The union of the human soul with God was the foundation of Bonaventure's intellectual commitment. He was a first-rate theological proponent of Christian Mysticism. . . . He epitomized the ideal of 'faith seeking understanding'. . . . Theology as lived experience was his vision."[2] Bonaventure was the architect of a structure of Christian truth in which faith was the foundation upon which the Church built a superstructure of doctrine, received through the intellect. Without a personal, vital faith as its foundation, the Christian's carefully constructed doctrinal superstructure comes crashing down around him.

JOHANNES ECKHART

Johannes Eckhart (1260-1327) is rarely known by his first name. He is generally referred to as Meister (Master) Eckhart, a title that implies his academic and intellectual capacities. Trained at the University of Paris, he became one of the most outstanding preachers of his time. Sometime after the year 1307, he came under the influence of a movement known as the Brethren of the Free Spirit, who emphasized pious living and a mystical understanding of truth. His mysticism got him into deep trouble. In 1326 he was accused of heresy in 28 propositions that he had written. In the Inquisition at Cologne, he offered to recant anything he had said or written in which he would be shown to be in error. Consequently, he was never formally excommunicated. However, he died soon after the hearing, and two years later Pope John XXII formally condemned his beliefs on 17 of the 28 points.

For what particular beliefs was he condemned? Eckhart stated that a person can be absorbed into God's being, so as to be, in effect, lost in God. Such language, so heretical to Church leaders, captured the hearts of many disciples both in Eckhart's time and even in our own. John Tauler, Henry

Suso and (indirectly) Jan van Ruysbroeck were his students; and even some of the reformers, including Martin Luther, were profoundly impacted by Meister Eckhart's teaching. His influence continued into the twentieth century (for example, in the life of Rufus Jones [1863-1948], who was the spokesman for the Society of Friends and the founder of the America Friends Service Committee).

If Bernard was the preacher/organizer and Bonaventure was the architect of learning built on piety, then Eckhart was the master of long-term mystical influence. Although the pope condemned many of his beliefs, his students continued to study Eckhart's ways and to flourish in their walk with God. A true follower of Christ will produce other followers, called disciples. One of the reasons that the Church is alive and well is that throughout its history, Christians have been willing to invest their lives in those who would come after them. They knew they were not on earth merely to absorb truth but to convey to the next generation what God had done for them. The Christian Church is a "relay of truth," one generation passing the baton to the next. Eckhart is a spectacular model of that.

JOHN TAULER

John Tauler (1300-1361) brought to his mystical emphasis an insistence that personal union with God results in loving service or works. Tauler did not hide from the world in the luxury of isolated contemplation. He was an activist, and he expected Mysticism to drive others to action. His selflessness was reflected already in 1314 when, as a boy of about 14, he left his father's wealth and entered the Dominican Order under his beloved teacher, Meister Eckhart. Tauler belonged to Eckhart's loosely knit fellowship, known as the Friends of God. He may have been drawn to mysticism because of the tragic turbulence and theological controversies in Germany and France in the war among Emperor Louis IV of Bavaria, Fredrick of Austria and Pope John XXII. In addition, Tauler witnessed a series of catastrophes: the Basil, Switzerland, earthquake of 1356, the horrific Black Death Plague (1347-1350), and a pope who went into exile. In an age of declining morals, Tauler's call to repentance produced great fruit, though it also brought him persecution.

Tauler and his friends minimized the distinction between clergy and laity, insisting that all God's people are equally worthy. He never forgot the downtrodden, either. Ignoring a pope's command during the bubonic plague of 1348 and 1349, he ministered with skill to the ill and forgotten. So convicting and practical was this fourteenth-century Dominican Mystic that Martin Luther read and reread him, 150 years later. His practical and simple sermons were "a bugle-call for a vital relationship with God and a blunt rejection of salvation-by-ceremonies, leading some to label him a Protestant before Protestantism."[3] Tauler's great contribution, not merely as a Mystic but as a Christian, was his capacity to focus on the fundamental basics of the Christian life: loving God and loving one another.

JOHN RUYSBROECK

Raised by a pious uncle, John Ruysbroeck (1293-1381) was ordained in 1317 and lived an austere life with two fellow Mystics for over 26 years. The simplicity of their lifestyle began to attract others, and John became a "director of souls." Through his writings, he influenced Gerhard Groote, the Brethren of the Common Life, and Tauler. He wrote the classics *The Adornment of the Spiritual Marriage* and *The Spiritual Espousal*, which were an explanation of the text "Behold, the bridegroom cometh"(Matt. 25:6, *KJV*). In typical mystical style, he refused to accept credit for his writings, claiming that the concept came directly from the Holy Spirit.

Ruysbroeck was accused of pantheism (not an unusual accusation to be directed at Mystics) but attempted to refute that accusation by writing against Bloemardinne, a popular female author, who embraced pantheism. (Pantheism is the belief that God is in all things and all things are God. This is not to be confused with the Christian belief that God is omnipresent.) Ruysbroeck "stressed humility, charity, flight from the world, meditation on the life and passion of Christ, and the abandonment to the divine will."[4] That's not a bad legacy to leave behind!

Ruysbroeck is included in this list of nine Mystics because of his writing on the relationship between the Bride and the Bridegroom. Mystics frequently saw their union with God in profoundly intense metaphors. He captures the essence of this chapter title—"Intimacy with God." One could not possibly read his writings without wondering, *Is it possible for me to have a deeper relationship with my God?* It is the mark of a true saint of God, to cause people to hunger for a deeper knowledge of Him.

CATHERINE OF SIENA

Catherine of Siena (1347-1380) was born in Siena, Italy, as the youngest of several children. Even in childhood, her mystical gifts began to emerge. But her mysticism had a strongly practical emphasis. By age 16, she was taking care of the ill and the dying—a practice she continued throughout her life. In 1370, she received a vision known as a mystical death, which included such things as hell, purgatory and heaven.

Catherine wielded tremendous political clout. Her influence was so great that she was, more than anyone else, responsible for the return of the papacy from Avignon, France, to Rome in 1376. She wrote aggressively to princes and political leaders urging them to stop all wars. And she was equally active in denouncing clergy for greed and immorality. She labored tirelessly to repair the deep schisms in the Roman Catholic church, working at the request of Pope Urban II. Catherine was exceptional at understanding spiritual applications to political life. She left behind over 400 letters, 26 prayers and a writing known simply as the *Dialogue.*

Catherine was not an isolationist, as some Mystics were. She was an activist, applying her intimate conversations with God to the very heart of society. She was afraid of no one but challenged all to a radical obedience of God, whether they were king, priest or pope. If this is what a Mystic does, then Lord, give us more Mystics.

THOMAS À KEMPIS

Thomas à Kempis (1380-1470) is the author of the world's most popular book outside the Bible, *The Imitation of Christ.* Born in Kempen, Germany, he attended the Deventer school, founded by Gerhard Groote. When he arrived there, he was referred to as Thomas of Kempen, as opposed to his family name of Thomas Hammerken. Ordained in 1413, Thomas spent most of his life earning a living by copying manuscripts (this was before the printing press) in a poor, little-known monastery at Zwolle. Biographers indicate that Thomas's personal life was profoundly uneventful, mentioning only that he was unhappy during the period of time in which he had to serve as the business manager of the monastery. His writing, *The Imitation of Christ*, has been translated into more languages than any other book except the Bible.

How odd that the author of the world's second best-selling book remains a mystery to us. Almost nothing is known about him! What a paradox. But this would not be a paradox to a Mystic. To Thomas, the imitation of Christ was the surrender of self. While it seems strange to publicity-hungry Americans that so little would be known about the world's most successful author, this fact would please the modest, quiet Thomas, for he was much more consumed with imitating Christ than with fame. Such humility is the mark of a truly good Mystic.

JOHN OF THE CROSS

Although born to a noble father, John (1542-1591) was raised in near poverty by his widowed mother. In 1563, he took the name John of Saint Matthew and became a Carmelite priest. But his life was changed when he met Teresa of Avila, with whom he agreed to work to found the newly approved order of the Discalced (barefoot) Carmelites. Reflecting his newfound vigor for Christ, he changed his name to John of the Cross. Little did he know what lay ahead. His attempts to reform the Carmelites met with tremendous resistance, which resulted in persecution and a nine-month imprisonment at Toledo in 1578. In the deprivation of this period, he wrote *The Spiritual Canticle*. After escaping prison, he served in several monasteries and preached at the college in Baeza.

But the reform efforts of John of the Cross continued to stir such animosity that his critics successfully persuaded the Pope to excommunicate him. Apparently, however, John never learned of this before he died in 1591. His passion for God, and the brokenness caused by his imprisonment are reflected in such works as *The Ascent of Mt. Carmel*, *The Dark Night of the Soul*, and *The Living Flame of Love*. In his writings, John contended that it is only in the "nights" of life that the soul is led to rely entirely on God's divine grace and mercy. When John died, after a long illness, the controversy about his reform still raged around him. Not until 135 years after he died was this great Christian leader recognized. Though criticized, imprisoned and excommunicated during his life, he was canonized in 1726.

One reason I have included John in this list of Mystics is to show that many of the so-called Christian greats were not considered great while they were alive. Our most revered Christian heroes were sometimes only tolerated and were frequently severely persecuted during their lifetime. It was only after their deaths that the truth emerged, and their greatness was understood. John of the Cross, who was not particularly appreciated while he lived, is now considered to be one of Christ's most passionate followers.

TERESA OF AVILA

Teresa (1515-1582) was a Spanish Mystic, born in Avila. One of 11 children, she was her father's favorite. At age 20, this vivaciously happy woman entered the Carmelite Convent. In spite of her paralyzing ill health, Teresa was known for her brightness and exuberance. She delighted in entertaining friends at her lovely apartment and thoroughly enjoyed her contacts with aristocratic women around her town. With the passage of time, she felt increasingly guilty about taking advantage of such privileges, and in 1555 underwent a second conversion. At age 40, she began to experience visions of Christ, union with Him, and the "prayer of quiet."[5] Four years later she felt her heart pierced by a fire-tipped sword held by an angel. She was never the same. At about this same time, she met some of the Discalced (barefoot) Franciscans and decided to start a similar simple, austere branch of Carmelites. Offended by the apathy and lethargy of the clergy, she confronted the established Church, calling it to passion for Christ. She gave herself tirelessly to converting unbelievers and attempted to heal the growing division between Catholics and Protestants. A skilled administrator, Teresa founded 16 religious houses, two of which were for men. At this time she was joined by John of the Cross, who was to become her lifelong colleague and whom she called both her "son and her father."[6] Traveling across Spain in unbearable heat and cold, on springless carts, she encouraged the occupants of the more than 30 religious houses, which had joined her reform movement.

Instead of accolades and encouragement, Teresa received accusations, jealousy and suspicion. Such accusations were not empty threats at the time, for Teresa lived during the time of the Spanish Inquisition. An accusation could quickly become a death sentence. Overcoming her constant ill health, she refused the temptation of a contemplative life and pressed ahead. Her encounter with God had called her to energetic service, which she gave zealously until she died on October 4, 1582.

Teresa's writings can be almost embarrassing because of the erotic overtones she uses to describe her love for God. However, she demonstrated a profound understanding of human psychology, displayed wonderful common sense and, in spite of her poor health, maintained a phenomenal sense of humor that has made her popular to this day. After her first autobiography entitled *Life*, she wrote a second autobiography entitled *The Book of Foundations*. In the tradition of the Mystics, she wrote *The Way of Perfection* in 1556 and *The Interior Castle* in 1577. In these writings her descriptions of union with God as spiritual marriage would probably make some readers wince.

It is easy to see why we include her on this list of nine influential Mystics. Her literary and ministry output alone would qualify her, since she eclipsed almost all of her contemporaries. However, we include her also because her highly personal language of union with God is typical of the Mystics. In fact, their descriptions about their relationship with God are *so* personal that we find them embarrassing. Why did these Christians write this way? The answer is simple. The strict rationalism of Teresa's day completely overlooked the deep cry of the human heart to truly know God. If we understand the context in which Teresa lived, we have a little more sympathy for the emphasis she placed on personal passion and devotion.

SCRIPTURE TESTS MYSTICAL VALIDITY

These nine Mystics reveal tremendous spiritual commitment. Moreover, the Mystics we haven't mentioned in great detail, such as Hugo of St. Victor, Henry Suso and Gerhard Groote, also evidenced the same passionate quest to serve God. However, this chapter ends with a warning.

Some Mystics went so far in their emphasis on inner experience that they deny the objectivity (Scripture) of Christ's work. Jacob Bohme (1575-1624) was one of these. His descriptions of the inner self violate foundational scriptural principles. Bohme was more than a Mystic; he was a

Theosophist. Theosophy is *not* Christian; it is an older version of New Age beliefs, more in keeping with Buddhism than with the Bible.

Theosophy is not fundamentally God-centered but man-centered. It teaches that man's spirit is so highly developed that it can exercise control over the forces of the universe, producing the miraculous. It is not evident to what extent Bohme believed the definition of Theosophy I have just described, but his beliefs paved the way for *anti*biblical thinking. Bohme is listed as a grave reminder that without the "tracks" of the Scripture, the "locomotive" can be derailed. Zeal (that's the coal coming from the coal car into the locomotive) is not a substitute for truth (the railroad tracks themselves). One may have dreams and visions, but these must be submitted to the scrutiny of the Scriptures. Otherwise, they have no biblical or Christian validity.

DEEP FAITH IN THE MIDST OF SPIRITUAL APATHY

Why spend an entire chapter on the Mystics? First of all, they were responding to the stark, empty, lifeless rationalism of the scholastics of the Middle Ages. People longed for a deep, personal and emotive faith. But that wasn't the only problem. During this period, three people claimed to be pope at the same time, each attempting to excommunicate the others. The authority of the Church had been undermined by such scandals. Burke and Wiggins state it this way:

> Outbreaks of religious enthusiasm began to be experienced in diverse places. The church, which now desperately sought to maintain its authority by authoritarian means, was crippled in its efforts by the scandal of the Great Schism. The thunderbolts of papal interdict and excommunication darted back and forth between Rome and Avignon (France) with no apparent ill effects for either. Europeans realized that the efficacy (effectiveness) of such actions was less than for centuries had been thought. The "Ark of Salvation" (meaning the church) had surely come upon rough seas that threatened to sink her, or at least required drastic measures to keep her afloat.[7]

The Church of Jesus Christ was in serious trouble. The wickedness of the Middle Ages had taken its toll. To discover the faint pulse of the Church we must look not at the authority structures of the time but at individuals on the underside of the Church—individuals who were attempting to faithfully maintain the gospel as they walked with God. The Mystics were not popes or cardinals or in high positions of authority. They were educated men and women with outstanding leadership and administrative skills. But the secret of their ongoing influence is not in their personalities or skills. Their influence was their passion for Christ. Although they were unhappy with the state of their Church, they stayed in it with the hope of reforming it from within.

THE ROMAN CATHOLIC HERITAGE OF ALL PROTESTANTS

I have talked openly of the corruption of the Roman Catholic church. One might be tempted to think that since I am a Protestant, I write with an anti-Roman bias. Such is not the case. Protestants can only trace their heritage to approximately 1517. As they go back farther, they realize that they, too, have a Roman Catholic heritage. As a contemporary Protestant, I am extremely indebted to the Roman Catholic church throughout the Middle Ages. I can't condone the immorality and greed. But the Roman Catholic church was wide and deep and broad enough to include people who had a deep abiding personal faith. Through them the gospel was sustained through the nearly 1,000 years known as the Dark Ages. To trace my spiritual heritage, I would have to search back to the apostles through this 1,000-year period. And I might find it leading back through one of the Mystics, nearly all of whom were Roman Catholic. It led through the Pre-Reformers, all of whom were Roman Catholic. The gospel was sustained through the efforts of some of the counterreformers, all of whom were Roman Catholic. It is important for all Protestants to appreciate what was sustained through the Middle Ages by the Roman Catholic church. Although in the Middle Ages one cannot affirm that the organized, visible church always acted nobly and righteously, nonetheless, God's hand was working through His true Church—godly people who acted in wisdom, honor, kindness and mercy.

To further assist you in understanding the key individuals and events of chapter 6, study questions, charts, diagrams, time lines and links to biographical websites are available on the Internet at www.jimgarlow.com. Please follow the site links to *How God Saved Civilization*, chapter 6 study helps.

DYING FOR
A CHANGE

THE PRE-REFORMERS

Dates covered: A.D. 1200-1500
Key persons: Peter Waldo, John Wycliffe, John Huss

Felice watched Leemus come in from his Wednesday-night encounter with his friends. He was whistling a delightful tune she'd never heard. How rewarding it was to see her son becoming a strong, loving young man. Felice depended on him since his father had died. But one thing puzzled her. Why was he only happy on Wednesday nights? Who were these friends who were able to turn a somber and stolid young man into the picture of joy? There was only one explanation. It had to be a woman. But why hadn't Leemus introduced her? Why would he hide such happiness?

Felice waited several months for Leemus to share his secret with her. Finally she could stand it no longer. "Son, you are the joy of my heart and a true help to a lonely widow . . ."

Leemus did not wait for her to finish; he threw his arms around his mother and whirled her off her feet. "You're the best mother in the world!" he exclaimed as he planted a kiss firmly on her forehead.

Felice set her hair straight and sat down at the small wooden table in her warm kitchen. "Who is she? You can't hide her forever."

Leemus pulled up the other chair and sat down with a thump. He laughed heartily.

"Now what are you talking about, Mother?"

"She must not be a French girl."

Leemus touched his mother's flushed face. "Mama, what's the matter?"

"Well, you come home on Wednesdays so happy. You must have found a girl. All the rest of the week you seem quite glum, especially at Sunday Mass—when you come, that is."

Leemus sighed and pushed his broad hand through the mass of curly brown hair that had always been such a challenge to keep tidy. "Mother, I don't want to hurt or disappoint you. I don't know how to say this in a way you'll understand. There *are* a few lovely young Christian ladies I know. Unfortunately, none of them seems interested in me!"

"Then why do you come in every Wednesday as if you're in love?"

"I suppose I am in love, in a way." Leemus sat up straight and pulled his chair a bit closer to the table. He took his mother's hand in his.

"Mama, I'm going to tell you some things you may not understand at first. But hear me out."

Felice looked lovingly into the sincere eyes of this boy who had never given her a sad moment. How could she not trust him?

"I don't enjoy Mass," began Leemus, "because I no longer believe what the priest says." Felice gasped and put her free hand to her mouth. But Leemus pressed on. "On Wednesday nights, I attend a meeting with a group of men here in Lyon. It's a small group, but it's getting bigger every week. We meet with Peter Waldo. We're called the Poor Men of Lyon."

Felice gasped, "Waldo." She had heard of this dangerous teacher. "Father Justin has warned us against Waldo, Leemus!"

"I know, Mother, but listen to me." Felice lowered her head, and Leemus continued. "He's teaching us the Bible; He reads it to us. Mother, you'd be amazed to hear what the Bible really says!"

"But we have the Church," whispered Felice.

"Yes, Mother. I thank you for teaching me to love the Church. I do love God's people. But some of the authorities in the Church we know are not teaching us what God really says. Peter Waldo and we Poor Men of Lyon do more for God's people than the rich bishops!"

"No, no, no! How can you be talking like this! I never raised you to leave the truth!" Felice began to cry quietly.

Leemus could hardly bear it. He stood and walked around the table to her side. Placing his hands gently on her shoulders, he leaned down and kissed her hair. "Mother, I love you so. But I love Christ more and I must follow Him, not the Church if the Church is unfaithful to His gospel. Even Peter and John said they had to obey God rather than men." Felice wiped her eyes with her handkerchief and Leemus continued, "Mother, have you ever seen a Bible?"

"Once."

"Mother, I've held one! Peter Waldo reads it aloud! The truth I have discovered is beyond description, so much richer and fuller than what the priests have told us. And I'm able to show others what's in it. Mama, you can't imagine the joy of sharing God's Word with God's people!"

"I'm a simple woman, Leemus. I can't even read. How can I go looking for truth somewhere else? The Church has truth for me. The priest is knowledgeable. He can read the Bible and explain it to me. I don't need some group of rebels to explain another truth to me."

"Mother, I understand how you feel. It was frightening for me at first, too. Until I began to hear for myself the Word of God. Oh, Mother. You can't believe the wonderful things that are in the Bible. Did you know, for example, that Jesus' death completely covers our sins? We aren't accepted by God because of the money we give or what we do for the priest. Jesus' sacrifice on the cross has taken our guilt away if we place our faith in Him!"

"Oh, Leemus, I do have faith in our Savior! You know that."

"Yes, Mother, I know you do. I'm so sorry to hurt you. But it's partly because of people like you that I get so angry with the Church. You have a believing heart and your church has never taught you the comforting words of Christ. Mama, look at me." Leemus drew his mother gently to her feet.

"Mama, I may not be safe much longer. There are many who hate us. I want you to know that I love you more than you could imagine. I pray that you will discover the depth of Christ's love for you; I pray for you every day, Mama. Don't be afraid." He took Felice in his arms and held her tightly.

The next Wednesday, on his way to a Bible study, Leemus was assaulted by several drunken, angry townsmen who knew that this Poor Man of Lyon was fair game. The authorities never bothered to bring them to justice. As Leemus lay bleeding in the street, drifting in and out of consciousness, his mother's name was on his lips. "May she know Your Word, dear Savior." Before the night was out, Leemus had joined those Waldensians who had given their lives for the gospel.

THREE MEN WHO LAID THE FOUNDATION

Much of the Church's leadership in the Middle Ages was so corrupt that it is offensive to mention the specific sins that were characteristic of its clergy. But God was not done with His Church! In fact, He is never done with His Church! He is always working, sometimes on the underside of history, to bring forth His will, to reestablish His Church as truly alive and well.

In 1140, God brought on the scene the first of three spiritual giants who would lay down their lives for the cause of truth in this historical period. Inspired by their example, Martin Luther would step out to call the Church from its lethargy, decadence and theological corruption.

PETER WALDO:
TRUTH OVER WEALTH

Peter Waldo (1150-1218) had an easy life. Born in 1150 in Lyon, France, to a wealthy merchant, Peter would himself become a successful businessman and a moneylender. But in 1175 or 1176, Peter Waldo (occasionally spelled Valdes) experienced a life-changing conversion as radical as that of the apostle Paul. He became so consumed with a passion for the Scripture, that he hired two priests to translate major segments of Scripture into French for the people of Lyon. When Waldo read the admonition to give all to the poor, he did precisely that. He handed over his house to his wife, and gave the rest to the poor. He settled his daughters into a convent and began traveling to preach what he had discovered in the Bible. His enthusiasm and consistency of life quickly attracted followers. Soon the Waldensians, as they were called, were matching up in pairs and imitating their leader. They traveled extensively, preaching and teaching. Because they were not well educated in many cases, they became known as the Poor Men of Lyon. They had no training in how to preach, so they simply memorized long portions of Scripture and quoted it everywhere they went. Their barefooted, uneducated approach invited disdain, contempt and amused scoffing which, within a decade, would become organized persecution.

At one point they enjoyed moderate success. Pope Alexander III gave them tentative approval to exist as an organization. However, they could not preach without the express permission of the local church authorities in each region. The Waldensians paid little attention to this. They went where they wanted and preached when they wanted. This disregard of protocol began to anger Church leaders. In addition to their preach-anywhere policy, their lifestyle of poverty was an open condemnation to the wealth and luxury of the established Church. This was intolerable to many clergy. The Waldensians exposed the worldliness of the clergy and labeled the Catholic church the "whore of Babylon."[1]

As would Martin Luther some 300 years later, Waldensians appealed to the Word of God as their only authority and, therefore, did away with such beliefs as purgatory and the veneration (worship) of the saints. By 1182, only seven short years after Peter Waldo's conversion, the Archbishop of Lyon threw them out of his city. Two years later, they were officially branded heretics at the Council of Verona (1184). For the next 35 years, Waldo and his itinerant preachers were forced underground. They were chased into the French Alps, where they were hunted like animals.

The persecution, however, did not stop the growth of the Waldensians. By the end of the 1200s, they had infiltrated most of Europe. Though numerous, they were persecuted with intensity. Far from the mild approval the Waldensians had received from Pope Alexander III (who became Pope in 1159), the hatred of Pope Innocent III (who became Pope in 1198) was vitriolic. He even declared a crusade against them in the year 1209. Along with others, the Waldensians were the victims of the widespread theological trials known as the Inquisition. In spite of this they could not, they would not, be silenced. The most outstanding hallmark of the Waldensian movement was their determined missionary preaching of the New Testament, which they always did in the language and dialect native to the area in which they found themselves.

Peter Waldo's conviction and his pure respect for the Word of God, as well as the courage of the hundreds and thousands who followed him, resulted in the first crack in the foundation of the aberrant Church during the Middle Ages.

JOHN WYCLIFFE: ENGLAND'S BRILLIANT MIND

The second giant to lay down his life as a predecessor to the Protestant Reformation was John Wycliffe (ca. 1329-1384), considered the most influential person in England in his time.

John Wycliffe was born sometime between 1325 and 1329, in Hipswell in the Yorkshire area of England. He attended Oxford University in the 1340s and earned three degrees, completing his doctorate in theology in 1372. His first teaching position was in 1361 at Balliol College, at Oxford University, but he met with little fame in his early teaching years. It was a decade and a half later that Wycliffe caught the attention of Oxford, England, and even the pope in Rome. In approximately 1376 he had begun to deliver lectures against the debauchery and wickedness of clergy. He specifically attacked the churches for owning massive amounts of land. He challenged clergy who were unworthy to become true men of God and shepherds to the people.

These criticisms met with the hearty approval of the peasants, who were weary of sending enormous sums of money to support Rome's luxurious lifestyle, and were even more enthusiastically received by emerging civil leaders who began to object to the massive accumulation of wealth on the part of the Church. John Wycliffe's popularity was heightened because of an embarrassing event in Roman Catholic history; known as the Great Schism, this was a period from 1378 to 1417 during which not one, not two, but three men claimed to be pope at the same time.

But God's agenda for purifying His Church went far beyond mere political infighting. God raised up John Wycliffe to discover the more serious deformities of the Church's theological corruption. By 1378 Wycliffe was systematically denouncing the doctrinal framework of the Church, demonstrating how antiscriptural it was. His work did not go unnoticed. As early as 1377 the ecclesiastical authorities were so infuriated that they drew up arrest orders against Wycliffe. Though threats of arrest and assassination swirled around him, Wycliffe remained unmoved. God had supernaturally placed John Gaunt, an influential member of the English nobility, as a political umbrella over Wycliffe. Gaunt did for Wycliffe what Frederick the Great would do 200 years later for Martin Luther; that is, provide political protection from the powerful and inflexible bureaucracy of the Roman Catholic church.

OPPOSITION

In spite of Wycliffe's broad popular appeal, strong opposition mounted against him in Oxford by 1380, the year that he was officially condemned. Even influential political leaders were unable to withstand the strong-arm tactics of the Church authorities to crush Wycliffe and, above all, to silence him.

Wycliffe was stripped of his teaching position at the university and banished to Lutterworth, a small and nondescript preaching assignment. But his influence could not be stopped. With time on his hands, Wycliffe did in that small town what he may never have done had he stayed at the university, and the project he finished did more to accomplish his goals than any amount of political fighting would have. From 1382 to 1384 he accomplished the greatest passion of his life, to produce the Bible in the language of the common man. Wycliffe was no hack translator. He insisted on working with the original languages, rather than translating from the Latin. His English version was a masterpiece, which set the standard for English prose.

Meanwhile, Wycliffe's theological attacks on the Church did not stop. He exposed the pope as a mere mortal. Christ alone, he contended, was the head of the Church. Wycliffe branded the pope as the Antichrist. By 1381 he specifically attacked Rome's unusual interpretation of the Lord's Supper (transubstantiation). This was ultimately an attack upon the abuses of the clergy. He wanted the monks and friars to take care of the people. He chastised them for having no concern for the poor. Wycliffe felt a village priest should be more of a shepherd than a hireling. He felt that the truth of God's Word should be available to all and should be communicated in a language all could understand. When he was asked the question, "How must the Word of God be preached?" Wycliffe answered, "Appropriately, simply, directly, and from a devout, sincere heart."[2]

LOLLARDS

Wycliffe's beliefs were disseminated through a band of men known as the Lollards (the name Lollard is believed to mean "stutterer," or "stammerer"; in other words, an inarticulate speaker). These preachers fanned out over the countryside to preach the basics of the gospel message and to read the Bible to the people. While a few of them may have been scholars, most were poor and undereducated. Thus, they became known as the Poor Preachers. Often barefoot and poverty-stricken, they walked the countryside to bring the Bible message to the peasants. These Poor Preachers, or Lollards, were profoundly influential in disseminating the Christian gospel. It is amazing that we do not know the name of a single one of them. But had they not been faithful, *you* might not have received the gospel. This group of men, destitute and on many occasions persecuted, walked to virtually every village and hamlet in England to carry the very simple message of Jesus.

As Wycliffe's influence increased, his health diminished. Ostracized and broken, he died in 1384. One would think that his death would be adequate to meet the anger that the pope and the religious hierarchy had for him, but his death and burial were not good enough. Forty-four years later, Pope Martin V insisted that Wycliffe's body be exhumed, burned and his ashes scattered in the river. That was the pope's way of expressing his desire to forever squelch Wycliffe's influence. But just as his ashes were carried by that river to multiple points, so his message went all over the world. And the fact is, the enemy has never been able to defeat the truth for long.

JOHN HUSS: MARTIN LUTHER'S "JOHN THE BAPTIST"

John Huss (Jan Hus) was born between 1369 and 1374. Although the date of his birth is uncertain, his death was documented in every detail. Huss was born in Husinetz in Southern Bohemia. A highly gifted student, he was forced nonetheless to work at a menial job to provide a living. He finally received his bachelor's degree from the University of Prague in 1393 and his master's degree in 1396. From his widowed mother it is said that he inherited his strong moral character, his deep piety and his intense love of learning.

In 1401, Huss was ordained a Roman Catholic priest and the following year he was made rector of the university. That year was also significant because one of his acquaintances returned from England with documents that would change his life and significantly alter Church history. Jerome of Prague (remember many people did not have last names at this time) had been at Oxford University studying under the famous Dr. John Wycliffe. Although Huss was a fiercely independent thinker, he was profoundly influenced by John Wycliffe's writings and translated the *Trialogus* of Wycliffe into the Czech language. Since Huss accepted many of Wycliffe's presuppositions, he was headed for trouble.

John Huss's character and studious temperament won him acclaim by both his archbishop and his king. Archbishop Zbynek appointed him as a preacher to the entire synod, a position of great honor. Knowledge of Huss's preaching skill had spread far and wide. In 1402 he was appointed director of Bethlehem Chapel, an auditorium that filled twice daily to hear the fiery preacher declare the power of the gospel. Bethlehem Chapel had become well known for what is called "vernacular preaching"; that is, preaching in a way that people understood.

Huss's popularity caught the attention not only of the archbishop but of the king as well. King Wenceslaus IV (Wenzel) was recognized as a staunch defender of the national Bohemian church, as opposed to a distinctly Roman church. Patriotism in Bohemia was on the rise. Huss's understandable, folksy preaching further fueled the fires of nationalism.

As mentioned above, the Roman church had been embarrassed by the fact that two individuals both claimed to be pope at the same time—one in Rome and one in Avignon, France. This split resulted in factions and divisions in the Church. Finally a plan was proposed to depose both of them. Huss agreed with this plan, as did many others. Unfortunately, his archbishop did not share his view. In the meantime, both popes were becoming increasingly angered over Huss's teaching of Wycliffe's ideas. By 1409 word came from Rome to silence John Huss. When that attempt failed, the pope excommunicated Huss and his followers in 1411. This simply made Huss far more determined. He increased his attack on indulgences and openly exposed the pope's attempts to raise money to finance his private causes. So vehement were Huss's criticisms that they began to alienate the king, who had once been his strong supporter. By 1412, Huss and his followers were forced out of the city of Prague. He then devoted himself to writing *On the Church (De ecclesia)*.

CONSTANCE

A resolution to Huss's problems seemed possible when he was encouraged by Emperor Sigismund to appear before the Council of Constance in 1414 for the purpose of explaining his views. The emperor assured him that he would be protected and gave him a pass for safe conduct. He arrived in Constance on November 3, 1414, but was never given the opportunity to explain his theological views as he had been promised. To Huss's shock, his arrival in Constance was met with only brief questioning, followed by imprisonment for eight difficult months.

On July 6, 1415, after refusing to recant the truth of his teaching, he was burned at the stake. A moving and compelling 72-page account of his death was written by Poggius Bracciolini, the papal legate who delivered the summons which informed John Huss that he was to appear before the Council of Constance. Although Bracciolini was an employee of the pope and obviously in opposition to Huss's teaching, his writings indicate that he was profoundly moved by the demeanor and, finally, the death of John Huss. Few books have greater melodrama than Poggius Bracciolini's account, entitled *Hus the Heretic*. It recounts the traumas, trial and sentence of John Huss as a blasphemer. When his guilty sentence was pronounced, a riot broke out that extended from the room into the community. Chairs were broken and pieces were thrown around the room. The mob dispersed and became increasingly hostile. The corpse of the prince bishop of Cleve, who had died during the council, was trampled beyond recognition, as the mob vented its anger against the Church hierarchy for voting to burn John Huss at the stake. John Huss could have easily escaped at that point. The enemies panicked, convinced that Huss had slipped away during the riot. They tried to seal off the gates of the city to cut him off. When the tumult had stopped, they discovered that he had gone back to his cell and was on his knees praying for courage for his death which would come the next day. That night, alone in his cell, he wrote to his friends back in Bohemia:

Dear Beloved, the few minutes of life which are left to me I shall . . . use to bid you goodbye. . . . Fifteen months ago I left you to defend what I have taught you, before the assembled fathers of this council at Constance. . . . I have failed in my endeavor, because I was not permitted to speak freely. . . .

Because I did not care to sacrifice my conscience . . . they threatened me with prison, hunger and thirst, which threats they very soon carried out, because I was not permitted to return to my shelter, but was led to a prison cell, far from the center of town upon a high wall. . . . After that I was questioned again and told that a recanting would bring me freedom. But I could not recant without feeling guilty, and the promised riches could not change my conviction. . . . I was cast into a damp hole in the tower . . . for eighty days. After that I was asked again whether I had re-considered. . . . Then I was cast into a still more dismal prison, where the waves of the lake splashed through the air hole of my cell . . . and wetted the straw of my bed so that it became foul and rotted under my body. I had to relieve my bowels into a hole at my feet and often weeks passed before the high waters washed the excrements away, so that a terrible odor remained which nearly killed me. Fever ravished my bones, a biting rash covered my skin and stinging blisters grew upon my tongue, aggravated by the salty food I received, making swallowing a pain. My teeth loosened and dropped out into the foul straw, my strength left me and the light of my eyes waned. The nails of my fingers grew inward, because I could no longer bite them off and my beard was full of vermin which tortured me continually, bored under my skin and multiplied in the festering sores of my body. My garments rotted and failed to cover my nakedness during (the six months) of such imprisonment. Then I was hauled up again and asked to recant . . . and I . . . recanted what I had taught you . . . and thus earned for myself a better cell. But when I laid down to sleep, the fear of my soul, and remorse gripped me, because I had been illoyal to God and my conscience. . . . With the first light of day I informed my enemies that I rued my recanting and . . . I was let down again into my hole in which I had to suffer until a few weeks ago. An escape had been arranged for me, with the help of some who loved me, but my conscience forbade me to avail myself of their help. . . . I have grown so sick and weak in body that the end of my days does not frighten me any longer. The only thing which hurts me is that I cannot see you once more in this world and that I must cease to preach the honor of God and the gospel of His Son.

My writings . . . were burnt, although not a word of them had been understood. . . . Their wrath went so far that they destroyed a well in Constance, because I had (quenched) my thirst there. . . . I write all this for you my beloved, so that you may know that God has stood by me powerfully in all my tribulations and has strengthened me, so that I might manfully die tomorrow, and I hope that my work will be sealed with the roasting of my flesh. . . . Don't avenge my death. . . . Remain peaceful. . . .

I would cry much for you, but a servant of God, whose honor shall be mine, must desert, for Him, and for the sake of Christ, his wife, child, brother, sister, home, possessions and all that is dear to him. And so I shall dry my tears and bow under the hand of the Lord. Amen.

Written at Constance, during my last night, on the 5th day of July 1415, on which day I was just 42 years old—John Huss[3]

Huss quietly lay down to sleep after he had prayed and then handed the letter to his friend, Count Chlum. It was rumored that he had been offered an escape but he refused to accept it because "his conscience spoke against it."[4]

Reportedly, the door of his cell had actually been left open and some of his friends forcibly carried him as far as the street, but he refused to go further because he believed that God's hand would rescue him with honor; or perhaps because he feared that his escape would somehow cause harm to the cause he served. On the day that he died he rose early and sang several songs, after which "he fell upon his knees, prayed loudly and sobbingly to God, thanked Him for the days of his life, for the joys and trials, from childhood until today."[5]

Bracciolini (who had brought the original summons to John Huss to appear before the Council of Constance, where Huss was imprisoned and condemned) records a moving exchange between Huss and himself. Bracciolini requested Huss not to bear him any malice, whereupon Huss asserted that he would never have malice toward anyone, including Bracciolini. Huss was then led to a public area where a large crowd had gathered. Once again they demanded that he recant, at which time he responded, "manfully and with the high courage of the apostle: . . . I stand here under the eye of God, and I can never do what you ask me, were I not to blaspheme Him and prostitute my conscience."[6]

The attempt to get Huss to recant during the meeting in the church turned chaotic. As his accusers tore at his clothing and ripped it to pieces, his defenders became more irate. Finally Huss's enemies pressed Huss's defenders too far. When they grabbed his head and began to cut his hair, a fight broke out. One Bohemian knight named von Meneszsch, who had hidden in his boot a long dagger, drew it out and plunged it into the ribs of a man who was shearing Huss's hair. The man was killed instantly. Immediately the enemies of John Huss turned upon von Meneszsch with knives and attempted to kill him. Miraculously, he defended himself against several individuals and escaped through a small door. Bracciolini records the conclusion of the event with these words: "Huss, however, cried and clasped his hand above his shorn head and prayed God for a blissful end."[7]

Huss's torture grew worse. As he stood before his enemies, they ridiculed him by attempting to throw pieces of earth into his face. Huss responded to this and the horrible curses that were yelled at him, by folding his hands and praying, "Oh Lord, Jesus Christ, into Thine hands I deliver my soul, which Thou hast redeemed with Thy blood. Father in heaven, do not hold against them the sins which my enemies commit against me. . . . Enlighten their deceived hearts, so that the truth of the holy gospel may open their eyes and its praise be spread everywhere, for ever and ever, amen."[8]

At this point in the events, Huss's writings, along with several of Wycliffe's thrown in for effect, were burned in a fire in front of him. The events of Huss's death spread over a major portion of the day, during which people were provided free drinks. The mob, increasingly inebriated, became more ruthless. At approximately five in the afternoon Huss's tormentors forced him to lead a procession through the streets of Constance.

> [Bracciolini indicates that] there were only a few streets in Constance through which the procession did not wind its way and its duration was longer than two hours. Many cried, many made fun, and many prayed for Huss. In the meantime, it is reported that Huss sang the Psalm 31: "In Thee, O Lord, I put my trust. Bow down Thine ear to me."[9]

As they arrived at the place where Huss would be burned, his accusers demanded one final time that he recant. He replied: "Today you will roast a lean goose, but a hundred years from now you will hear a swan song, whom you will leave unroasted and no track or net will catch him for you."[10] This proved to be a prophecy. The name Huss in Bohemian actually means "goose." And the "swan" is interpreted by many to refer to Martin Luther, who 100 years later would *not* be burned at the stake for saying many of the same things for which Huss contended.

At this point "the hangmen seized moistened ropes, tied the victim's hands and feet backward to the stake, squeezed oil-drenched wool between his limbs and the stake and emptied so much oil over his head that it dripped from his beard." The fire was then lit in six or more places, but it did not burn well, due to the fact that the wind was not blowing. John Huss had to wait for over half an hour until the smoke started rising around him. An elderly man, believed by Bracciolini to be almost 80 years of age, ran with more fire and placed it around Huss, saying jeeringly that this was so "you might depart to hell sooner." By now, smoke was bellowing and the flames licked higher on the body of John Huss. Three times the crowd heard him call out, "Jesus Christ, Thou Son of the living God, have mercy upon me." After the third time, the smoke cleared for a moment and the crowd could see that his head had sunk to his chest. Bracciolini states that "he had died before a flame had touched him." Two hours later, his cremated body was thrown into the Rhine River. Bracciolini concludes his letter to his friend Nikolai with these striking words: "I wanted to acquaint you with this story of a heretic, my dear Nikolai, so you might know how much fortitude of faith Huss had shown before his enemies and how blissful, in his faith, this pious man's end had been. Verily, I say unto you, *he was too just good for this world!*" The letter was simply signed, "Poggius, Written on the day of Calixtus, in October 1415."[11]

After such a startling account of a most gruesome death, every reader must be asking the question, Why? Why was this man executed? What had he done to deserve so much anger, hostility and brutality? What was his great crime? His sin? The answer is simply that he believed the Bible to be God's Word. He believed it to be the final authority. He believed that people should not be able to *purchase* forgiveness for their sins with money (indulgences). He believed in the simplicity and the holiness of the Early Church. He believed that not only the bread, but the cup as well should be served to people in the Communion service. He believed that clergy should stop abusing the laity and stop taking advantage of them economically and emotionally. He believed that the true Church of Jesus Christ was not an organizational structure but was comprised of people who really knew their God.

Such were the crimes that bought him an agonizing death. And because he died, because he stood firm, the truth marched on. Truth, as it always does, won out on that hot July day in 1415, and it is still winning today. Because of the faith, the fortitude, the confidence and the resilience of people like John Huss, we can say with integrity—truly, the Church is alive, and it is well! And a healthy Church saves (preserves) civilization.

To further assist you in understanding the key individuals and events of chapter 7, study questions, charts, diagrams, time lines and links to biographical websites are available on the Internet at www.jimgarlow.com. Please follow the site links to *How God Saved Civilization*, chapter 7 study helps.

THE SPIRITUAL EXPLOSION

MARTIN LUTHER AND THE REFORMATION

Dates covered: A.D. 1483-1546
Key person: Martin Luther

Olga stared lovingly into the unfocused eyes of her 10-day-old grand-daughter. In an hour, Gertrude would be baptized. How fortunate they were to have such a fine pastor. With gratitude she whispered, "You won't have to live what I lived, little Gertrude. You've been born into a new world." She lifted the baby's soft head up against her cheek.

Memories of her father's small farm across the Elbe river near Wittenberg filled her mind. Father would walk with her to the Castle Church on Sunday to listen to fiery young Martin Luther. She remembered the day Luther had reached out to touch her curls as he walked by. "Love God with all your heart, little one." With a boisterous laugh, Luther then climbed the winding stairway into the pulpit. As he preached, his zeal was contagious and filled her heart with warmth. Luther challenged her to think differently about her faith. So many things had changed because of Luther.

Olga smiled. How proud she had been of her father. He was an unedu-cated farmer who didn't even know how to read, but her father had under-stood the issues perfectly and could make the theological issues of the day easy to understand.

"What difference does it make, Father," she had asked him, "if Jesus' body is really in the bread and the wine at Communion?"

Her father would patiently and passionately explain to her Luther's thinking: If you admitted to Jesus' being sacrificed again each time Communion came, then His death was not once and for all, as the Bible taught. If His death wasn't once for all, then He didn't really have to die. "It makes light of Jesus' sacrifice and puts the power of salvation into the hands of men instead of God!"

By the time Olga had turned 18 and had married, the theological war that had been brewing between the professors of Wittenberg and the lead-ers of the Roman Catholic church had put the whole town in tumult. Her father had even been afraid for Luther's life one night. But now, on a sunny morning in April 1547, she was sitting with Gertrude on her knee, and by God's grace Luther had not been killed. Instead, he had brought about a complete change. Gone were all the silly superstitions she had feared as a girl. Gone was the belief that her soul was at the mercy of the Church lead-ers. Gone was their fear of the village priest. Most people could read now. Her brothers all could, and she had taught herself to read, using the book of Ephesians, translated by Luther in the tower of Wartburg.

"You won't have to give away your hard-earned money to get me out of purgatory, Gertrude!" Olga understood now that there was no purgatory. She could remember, before Luther's teaching, going without her dark bread, coffee and sausages for breakfast when the priests would come by asking for coins. Her parents didn't dare seem hard-hearted toward their ancestors, but Olga knew that even back then her father hadn't put much stock in the indulgences he was forced to buy. "God's not stupid enough to need papers to remind Him who needs punishing. And He's not so poor He needs money," he used to say. "Those greedy priests just want money for their fancy cathedrals."

Gertrude whimpered, so Olga rocked her, humming a tune Martin Luther had made up himself. "You might not understand the church service, today, little Gertrude," she whispered to her granddaughter. "But as soon as you can understand German, you'll know what's going on in church. You won't need to learn Latin! You can read God's Word in German and understand the preacher." Olga had learned so much about the Bible, now that preaching was a regular part of the service. And she felt so welcomed by God. She could take both the elements of Communion. She loved the congregational singing. And the fact that priests could now marry gave them much more sympathy with the ordinary folk.

If there was anything Olga regretted, it was only that her husband's family had refused to come to Gertrude's baptism today. The reforms that Olga delighted in had not come without a price. Her in-laws had not spoken to her since the early 1520s—over a quarter century of hardened silence. To them, Lutherans were heretics and traitors. Gertrude began to cry. "Shh," said Olga, patting her back and rocking her. "Nothing to cry about. Maybe you wish Dr. Martin himself could baptize you, ja? But he did much for you. And now he is happy in heaven. Not purgatory!" Olga laughed and looked at the clock. "Time for church, now, little one. Maybe we can even go through that very door where it all began on October 31, 1517."

CONVERSION BY LIGHTNING BOLT

It is impossible to overestimate the impact of one individual—Martin Luther, the highest "mountain peak" in all Church history. Luther was born to a simple peasant miner in 1483 in Saxony, Germany. His parents were simple and poor, but in spite of their poverty, they insisted that Martin receive a good education. He attended schools in Magdeburg and Eisenach and finally enrolled at the University of Erfurt in 1501. Luther's father wanted him to become an attorney, so Martin began the study of law. However, this study came to an abrupt end on July 2, 1505, when Luther was knocked to the ground by a bolt of lightning during a severe thunderstorm. Lying on the ground, paralyzed with fear, he cried out, "Saint Anne, help me and I will become a monk!" Though he said he later regretted those words, his conscience was strong; and two weeks later he had changed academic direction, left law school and entered the Augustinian monastery at Erfurt, Germany.

His father was most unhappy and objected strenuously. But Luther was extremely stubborn when it came to principles, and he took his monastery vows in September of 1506, receiving ordination on April 4, 1507. Though his father attended Luther's first Mass, he took the occasion to scold his son for disobeying his wishes. Luther's sensitivity caused him to take this rebuke very hard. Luther went into the monastery, in part, because of his deep feelings of sinfulness and an overwhelming sense of guilt. An outstanding student, he had no joy in his religious faith. The agony of his guilt, however, was the very tool God would use to produce such great faith in Luther. The passion of that transformation would in turn change the course of the world.

In 1508, Luther was teaching in a brand-new little university, Wittenberg University. While working there, he had the occasion to fulfill a dream, for he was asked to travel to the Holy City, Rome, with a fellow monk. How he had always longed to see Rome! There, surely, he would find true piety, true righteousness. However, when he arrived in Rome, Luther was stunned. The Italian priests were far from pious. Crassly commercial, they flaunted their wealth and seemed to approve the state of spiritual lethargy into which the Church had fallen. Luther's spiritual sensitivity could not bear such abuse. He returned to Wittenberg, deeply disappointed and troubled.

By 1511, Luther had earned his doctorate at Wittenberg, and began teaching Genesis and Psalms. But he found in the Scriptures only an angry judge, an unapproachable God. Luther was plagued by his guilt and unfulfilled in his spiritual quest. His confessor, a priest named Staupitz, directed him to the crucifixion account. From 1513-1514, Luther began to discover that the term "God's righteousness" meant that God had made man to be righteous. This truth exploded in Luther's heart and affected his entire perception of Christian reality. His preaching and teaching were radically altered. By 1515, he was lecturing from Romans on his theology of the Cross. Luther began to teach that salvation was not earned but that man's justification was a gift from God. Grace was God's profound gift to humanity.

THE SCRIPTURES

Finally, Luther's long spiritual crisis was coming to an end. But with his peace, he gained some convictions that flew in the face of everything the Church of his time was teaching. And the source of all his "new" ideas was the Word of God. Luther began to realize the value of the Scriptures as he taught that by knowing God's Word, one can discover that one is justified by faith and that grace is available to all. Luther's discoveries not only healed his own soul, but they also began to capture the hearts of his fellow faculty at Wittenberg University. They, too, began to embrace this radical new teaching that Jesus' completed work on the Cross was sufficient for sinful man.

Did he have any idea how much his thinking would change the lives of ordinary Christians? It is not likely. October 31, 1517, the eve of All Saints' Day, Martin strode down the narrow street toward the church. He was on his way to the door of the Castle Church, which functioned as a local newspaper/bulletin board/chatroom. Taking a small mallet and some short nails from his robe, he lifted a paper to the church door, tacked it on and turned for home. Little did he know that within three weeks his 95 statements of protest, known as the Ninety-five Theses, would be spread all over Germany.

THE NINETY-FIVE THESES

The theses were protests against the abuses of the Catholic church. They protested transubstantiation, the doctrine of purgatory (added to Catholic beliefs in the early 600s by Gregory I), prayers for the dead, the sale of indulgences, and other abuses.

As Luther's ideas spread, more and more people began to understand the freedom of his message. Soon, Luther's popularity and audacity attracted the attention of the Vatican. The pope and the Catholic church leaders began to target him, asking him to defend his theses in public. Luther's tenacity and conviction under this challenge became well known. In April 1518, they summoned him to a great debate with the purpose of shaking him from his theories of grace. When that failed, another trial was scheduled for October 1518. Luther again refused to recant. Finally, in July 1519, the Church brought in its theological heavyweight, Johann Eck, a famous university professor from Leipzig, Germany. At one highly dramatic moment, Eck forced from Luther an admission that he had been influenced by the thinking of John Huss, who had been burned at the stake as a heretic 100 years earlier. By admitting this connection, Luther was placing himself in the same camp as a heretic. And everyone knew what happened to heretics!

Luther's pen was even mightier than his debating skills and probably got him into more trouble. In 1520, he wrote four provocative works that shook the foundation of the papacy:

- *Treatise on Good Works*
- *To the Christian Nobility of the German Nation*
- *The Babylonian Captivity of the Church*
- *On Christian Freedom*

Hostility between Luther and Rome intensified. The pope ordered Luther's books burned and had Luther excommunicated. Luther's audacious response was to excommunicate the pope!

LUTHER STANDS FAST

In 1521, Luther went to yet another debate, the Diet of Worms. No, this was not a German weight-loss scheme. A "diet" was a debate or a meeting, and this particular one occurred in the town of Worms (pronounced Vorms). Once there Luther was not asked to debate theology, as he had expected, but to recant. Luther replied that he had come to discuss. "Do you recant?" came the insistent demand. Luther requested 24 hours to reflect, knowing what would happen if he refused. The next day, he appeared before a hushed audience.

"Did you write these books?" asked the interrogator.

"These, and many not here," replied Martin.

"Will you recant?"
Luther responded,

> Here is it, plain and unvarnished. Unless I am convicted of error by the testimony of Scripture, or by manifest reasoning, I stand convicted by the Scriptures to which I have appealed, and my conscience is taken captive by God's Word, I cannot and will not recant anything. For to act against our conscience is neither safe for us, nor open to us. On this I take my stand. I can do no other. God help me. Amen.[1]

The Edict of Worms was a death warrant for Luther, designed to silence him for good, although he supposedly enjoyed political protection from Frederick of Saxony. As he left the famous Diet, his coach was abducted and he was held hostage for eight months in Wartburg Castle. However, it was not his enemies but his friends who whisked him off the road that night, in order to protect his life.

THE BLESSINGS OF FORCED SECLUSION

But God's hand was mighty even in those circumstances, for those eight months were some of the most profitable ever spent on behalf of the Church. Luther translated the New Testament into the common German language of the day, using Erasmus's newly compiled Greek text of the New Testament. Luther's forced study break while kept prisoner by his friends, for his own protection, may not have been to his liking; but it was to the tremendous benefit of the Church.

We are so used to having Bibles and reading them, that we cannot imagine a church that would withhold God's Word. But the Church of that time did not want its people reading the Bible. How could uneducated, illiterate peasants properly interpret and understand the Bible? This was the domain of the Church rulers and priests. Of course, it wasn't difficult to keep people from reading it because most people could not read anyway. Even if they could, where could they get any books? Books were expensive and rare. But Luther was dedicated to making the Word of God available to everyone. After all, had not the Word been the source of his real understanding of God's love? Luther's Reformation resulted in the mass-produced Bible, available to common people in their own language.

LUTHER AND WORSHIP

Bible reading was only one of Luther's radical ideas. Another was his view of public worship. Until Luther, the Mass had been said in Latin, did not include a sermon and consisted of much repetition. The congregation did not participate in worship as it does in our churches. Luther, a passionate man who loved music, incorporated congregational singing into the Church.

Just to the right of the door on which Luther nailed his critique of the Church's practices, stands a fortresslike stone cylinder, a tower attached to the Castle Church. A stairway winds its way to the top of this tower, on which is inscribed in the stone the words *Ein feste burg* ("a mighty fortress"). Luther's best-known hymn was inspired by those words: "A Mighty Fortress Is Our God." That song represents the vigor and vitality with which Luther viewed not only congregational singing but also the entire worship service.

TRADITIONS UNDER ATTACK

Luther threw the Church into turmoil by tearing down many of its powerful traditions. He argued that the virgin Mary was not necessary as a mediator between God and man. He did away with the doctrine of purgatory, appealing, as always, to the Scriptures for the authority to do so. He preached consubstantiation (Communion wine and bread represent the *real presence* of Christ) instead of transubstantiation (Communion wine and bread *become* the body of Christ). This emphasis on the simple power of Christ's sacrifice helped the people to understand that they could not see such things as holy water, shrines, wonder-working images, rosaries and candles as some kind of magical talisman to make God do what you wanted Him to do. A great sense of freedom came with the Reformation. Finally free of superstition, papal taxes, the sale of indulgences and immorality among the priests, God's people worshiped Him with joy and enthusiasm.

LUTHER THE MATCHMAKER

One of the most radical elements in Luther's reforms came in 1521, when Luther declared that the priests were free to marry. But where would they find wives? Luther didn't think twice—he opened the convents! Reentering life from monasteries and convents, these Christians must have been puzzled by their sudden need to make choices. They needed companions, but what would all the single men from the monasteries and the single women from the convents do? Where would they find marriage partners? Luther didn't leave them puzzled for long. He lined up the nuns and matched them with priests.

According to the story, one lady was unhappy at the sight of her assigned partner. This assertive woman took one look at the elderly man who fell to her, and said, "I will not marry that old goat." When Luther inquired whom she *would* marry, she answered, "You!" And marry Luther she did. Katherine von Bora proved to be a spectacular wife, mother and "first lady of the Reformation." Not only did she bear six children (Luther loved each of his children and mourned deeply when two of them died at an early age) but she was also an outstanding friend, confidant, lover, hostess and counselor.

LUTHER THE MENTOR

Luther also gave attention to his students. Luther's home was flooded with young scholar-theologians who wanted to learn from the greatest name in all of Europe. Katherine bore up under Luther's popularity with the greatest of skill, opening her home continually. Lack of funds caused the Luther family to take in boarders to help make ends meet. In addition, they took in four children from a relative, bringing the household to over 20 people! Visitors poured into the home on a continual basis. Some of these wrote of laughter and theological debate around the Luthers' heavy wooden table, which one can still see today in that Wittenberg apartment. Luther's young, exuberant scholars filled a whole book with notes from those evenings (these notes have been published under the name *Table Talk*). On one occasion, Katy (as Dr. Luther called her) was feeling ill and went to the bedroom. When her absence was unnoticed, she came back into the living area where a lively theological debate was going on. She announced her pains and ailments to the group—in Latin, the official language for theological debate. Thereafter she was included in the theological sparring. Luther's home life provided a stunning model for Protestant parsonages.

By the time Luther died on February 18, 1546, at the age of 64, he had shaken the world. More books have been written about Martin Luther than about any other figure in all of Church history, with the exception of Jesus Christ. Luther had a strong personality and plenty of vitality. He had a tender conscience and an unusual passion for God. These qualities do, in part, explain his influence. His own personal charisma, devotion and energy turned a major segment of the population away from superstition and tradition, to a renewed and joyous celebration of God's love for them and His grace.

LUTHER'S SOLAS

Luther had four great passions for all believers that can explain the great changes he initiated.

- *Sola scriptura*, "by Scripture alone." God used His own Word to unstop the dam behind which His power and that of His Church had been constrained. Every statue of Martin Luther in Germany today shows him clutching the Bible close to his heart. "It is by the Word of God and the Word of God alone," he would often say. In this Word, he did not find prayers for the dead, intercessors other than Christ, or a works-based righteousness.
- *Sola Christus,* "by Christ alone." When Luther read the Bible, he discovered that people had direct access to God through Christ, and this became the second of the Reformer's mottoes. Luther's radical commitment to the sufficiency of Christ and His work led him to denounce any mediator but Christ. Neither Mary nor dead saints nor priests should be allowed to take over the role that Christ alone was given. Luther believed that people had direct access to God through Christ.
- *Sola gratia*, "by grace alone." Christ comes to us by the grace of God. It is He who initiates, who comes to seek and to save the lost. He works in us to draw us to Him. He initiates relationships with us.
- *Sola fide*, "through faith alone." Our response to God's grace is one of faith. Man can never save himself. Salvation is through Christ and Christ alone, through His profound grace and through radical confidence (faith) in Him.

Luther's death in 1546 did not see the end of his influence. *Sola scriptura, sola Christus, sola gratia* and *sola fide* became the hallmark of virtually every Protestant group that followed Luther. Once again, God's hand of grace and mercy was moving through difficult events and times on behalf of the Church and all humanity. Luther's theology purified and corrected the Church which put her (the Church) in place to bless the rest of culture—to be God's instrument in saving civilization.

To further assist you in understanding the key individuals and events of chapter 8, study questions, charts, diagrams, time lines and links to biographical websites are available on the Internet at www.jimgarlow.com. Please follow the site links to *How God Saved Civilization*, chapter 8 study helps.

THE CHAIN REACTION

THE EXPANDING REFORMATION

Dates covered: A.D. 1518-1572
Key persons: Ulrich Zwingli, Conrad Grebel, Felix Manz,
Menno Simons, John Calvin, John Knox, Ignatius of Loyola

Ulrich Zwingli has been killed on the battlefield," Grandma announced as she came through the door with the eggs. Sixteen-year-old Gretchen looked up from her books. Grandma sighed, "He was so young, only 47."

"It serves him right," muttered Gretchen.

"Gretchen!" exclaimed Grandma. "How can you say such a thing about the man who sat you on his knee, who was your pastor, who ate at your table and taught you the beautiful truths of our Savior?"

"How can I ever forgive Zwingli for what he allowed to happen to Father?"

Grandma had no answer. She stood behind Gretchen, stroking her long, blond hair. "We must let our heavenly Father judge all men."

Gretchen's mind went back five years to the hushed, nighttime conversations. She had been 11 and would listen at her bedroom door to the troubled voices of Father and his closest friends. Zwingli was their hero and Gretchen often heard his name when they discussed the biblical way to understand Communion. Gretchen loved theology and listened carefully. She was surprised to learn that Pastor Zwingli and Martin Luther couldn't even agree on Communion.

Father was sad, troubled and preoccupied with his thoughts. Sometimes he didn't feel like taking Gretchen for their evening walk along the Limmat River. As tensions increased in town between Zwingli's ideas and brother Martin's ideas, in public her father refused to tell Gretchen stories about the fascinating brother Martin. Then one day the cloud lifted from her father's face.

"The town council has adopted brother Martin's beliefs," he told her happily, as they watched the ducks swimming lazily in and out of the water plants growing by the shore. Father and his friends spoke more openly after that.

Gretchen delightedly replied, "Maybe we'll have some peace then." Gretchen had always hated fights, harsh words or conflict of any kind. There were moments when her brothers were playing soldier and fighting that she would throw herself between them and shout, "Stop. Stop. Don't kill each other!" She would think, *I wish I'd been born at another time. No one seems able to get by without anger and violence.*

But the peace in town didn't last long. Tensions began building again and Gretchen was sent off to her room at night. From her position at the door, she learned that her father and his friends no longer agreed with Pastor Zwingli! Gretchen lay on her bed and cried that night, begging the Lord for peace among His people.

One Saturday, shortly before her 12th birthday, Gretchen's father called her into his study. His voice cracked, "We're not going to church tomorrow morning."

Gretchen sat down quietly at his feet, near the fire. She could tell something was terribly wrong.

"Why, Father? Heidi's new baby sister is being baptized, and I promised her I would go home with her to celebrate."

"I've tried to keep these problems from you, Gretchen. I know you hate conflict, but I feel more strongly than you might think that baptizing babies is wrong. It leads the Church into apathy. People think they are God's children just because water was placed on their heads when they were babies. Being a Christian means more than a few drops of water. It is dying to self with Christ. Baptism is a symbol of that dying and of our hope in Christ's resurrection. New life is marked by true faith and baptism is a symbol of that faith. I'm coming to believe, Gretchen, that we should baptize not only new adult believers, but that we should rebaptize those who have only been baptized as infants."

"Will you rebaptize me? The Limmat River is warm right now, Father."

"Zwingli's government will not allow it," her father responded.

"What would Pastor Zwingli and the city council do if you baptized me again?"

But her father stood abruptly. "I'm sorry, my sweet dove. I wish I could make things the way you dream of them. Tonight we are moving out of our house. We will be living in a large cave some way out of town."

Gretchen could hardly believe her ears. She clung to her father's rough shirt, tears rising in her eyes.

That night, she discovered how cold and damp a cave can be at night. There wasn't enough room to bring much from home, for the cave was crowded with a dozen families. Heidi's family was not there and Gretchen missed her friend. Father refused to hide all the time. He took turns on watch at night, but during the day, he insisted on preaching in the villages surrounding the city.

One night they were huddled together in the warmest, driest section of the cave when Gretchen heard shouts from the guards. A far-off sound of whinnying horses came through the night air. Then from the woods nearby came the sound of clashing swords. As they had practiced many times, everyone moved to the prearranged spots and the children remained absolutely silent. Eventually, the night became quiet again. But one of the young men returned, badly wounded.

"They have taken nine of us!" he whispered, with a sob of pain and grief. "They will drown them. Oh, we shall never see them again!"

Mother refused to be held back. She would go to Pastor Zwingli and the city council. Surely they would not harm her beloved husband, so faithful to Christ and to His gospel! Those left in the cave begged her not to go, but she was determined. She kissed Gretchen and the boys and told them to wait for her. But she never returned. Father and the others never returned either.

Two months later, a woman at the fish market told her how her husband had seen Gretchen's father one morning in the woods near the river. Her father, hands bound, along with other men, was being thrown into the Limmat by soldiers who mocked, "So you want to rebaptize! We'll see to it that you are!"

Gretchen's mind was jolted back to events at hand. She said in a flat, dull voice, "Zwingli is dead. You are just, Lord. Please bring peace to Your Church."

From the kitchen, Grandma, through her tears, whispered, "Amen, Lord Jesus."

THE SPREADING REFORMS

The door had been opened and the gospel had been released. The Bible was in the hands of common people. Things would never be the same again. Martin Luther had ushered into Europe not merely a fresh theology, but a new worldview. Try as they might, the officials of the Roman Catholic church were unable to "get the horse back in the barn." What had happened in Wittenberg began to spread across Europe like a wildfire.

ULRICH ZWINGLI

Ulrich Zwingli (1484-1531) made a theological journey parallel to Luther's in many ways. Born in 1484 in Wildhaus, Switzerland, Zwingli received his bachelor's degree in 1504 and his master of arts degree in 1506. He was the priest of Glarus for 10 years, then moved to Einsiedeln. There, his preaching began to change, as his understanding of the gospel altered. Zwingli became far more evangelical, and courageously denounced certain common practices, such as the use of mercenary soldiers. He had witnessed 6,000 of them die in a war for which they had been hired.

In 1518, only a few months after Martin Luther had placed the Ninety-five Theses on the door in Wittenberg, Zwingli became pastor of the Grossmünster in Zurich, Switzerland. His preaching revealed the widening chasm that existed at the time between Rome's practice and the gospel. Although thoroughly influenced by events at Wittenberg and by Martin Luther's explosive teaching, the pastor wanted to avoid a clash with Rome, if at all possible. However, he chose a peculiar method of keeping the peace. Zwingli secretly married, which was against the Church's practice, and then unsuccessfully sought permission for priests to marry. Many nuns and priests followed his example. His influence in Zurich caused upheaval in the Church, not only regarding the issue of clergy marriage but also in other realms. Images and statues were removed from the spectacular cathedral in the heart of Zurich. The Mass was replaced by a simple worship service with singing and teaching that people could understand.

DISAGREEMENT OVER THE LORD'S SUPPER

Although Zwingli followed the pattern of Luther in many issues, he vehemently disagreed with him on the interpretation of Communion. While Roman Catholics believed in *trans*ubstantiation and Luther believed in *con*substantiation (Christ was somehow profoundly, *literally* present in the Communion), Zwingli believed in the *spiritual* presence of Christ. He was convinced that Jesus was uniquely but *spiritually* present when the Lord's Supper was celebrated. (The Anabaptists, who will be mentioned later, held a fourth position—that the Communion service was a memorial, or reminder, to what Christ had done on the cross.)

One would think that the Reformers, having fought so valiantly for the truth and having agreed on so much, would have been able to work through their differences on this issue or at least agree to disagree and remain in fellowship with one another. However, we must not forget that the very reason these men had made such an impact was partly due to their ability to analyze an issue, hold convictions about it and not budge from those convictions, no matter what the cost to their own lives, families, congregations or country. These were men of intense conviction, living in an era that demanded uniformity, so they were not afraid to clash once again. In 1529, a political leader named Philip of Hesse brought Luther and Zwingli together in what is referred to as the Marburg Colloquy. But Luther and Zwingli, sitting across the table from each other as arranged by Philip with the hope that it would cause them to reconcile, only antagonized each other further. The Reformers left that meeting more divided than ever. Of the 15 propositions of Reformation, they could agree on 14. Only one remained—the one describing Communion. This issue would splinter the Reformation movement and leave it tragically disunited.

BIRTH OF THE ANABAPTISTS

Zwingli's leadership in Zurich did not go unchallenged. Some residents of the town felt he was still too committed to Roman ways. Conrad Grebel (ca.1498-1526) and Felix Manz (1490-1527) were Zurich residents who attempted to persuade Ulrich Zwingli and his colleague, Leo Jud, to become more radically biblical in the reform movement in Zurich. By September of 1524, Zwingli was totally alienated from his former colleagues Manz and Grebel.

BAPTISM

Although Grebel and Manz disagreed with Zwingli in several areas, the most difficult practical problem was the believer's baptism. Zwingli's colleagues felt that only people who were old enough to understand the gospel should be baptized. Zwingli himself, however, continued to follow the Roman Catholic method of infant baptism. The Zurich city council, fearful of divisiveness in the city over this issue, sided with Zwingli. It was a heated exchange.

Zwingli was highly agitated, and those who opposed him (once his brightest disciples and students) claimed that he was abandoning views he once held. By January of 1525 the breach between Zwingli and his former followers was opened even wider when Grebel decided to perform a baptism (or *re*baptism) by immersion for the first time. The Anabaptist leaders (as they would later be known) believed that the Greek word *baptizein* meant "to immerse," and decided to baptize people by plunging them into the freezing, January river water of the Limmat River that ran through Zurich.

The name Anabaptist means to "rebaptize." Luther and Zwingli agreed with the Roman Catholic church that children could be baptized as infants. But Anabaptists believed that a person could not choose Christ until they were of age, and that baptism was to be reserved for those who had confessed Christ in faith. The issue of baptism became explosively divisive. The Lutherans and Zwinglians began to torture the Anabaptists and to punish them by drowning. They would taunt their victims by shouting, "Do you want to be rebaptized? We'll rebaptize you!" And they would drown them.

GREBEL DIES; MANZ KILLED

The believer's baptism movement began to grow rapidly, with hundreds responding. By October of 1525, Grebel was going from house to house, witnessing to one or two people at a time or to any small group who would listen. He called people to repentance and emphasized the baptism of believers. One of their large meetings was to occur on the 8th of October. But Grebel, Manz and others were arrested while they were preparing to meet in the woods. Grebel's physical constitution had already been worn down by a previous time in prison and months of fugitive existence. The second arrest was too much for him. He died and thus became the first martyr of the Anabaptist movement.

On January 5, 1527, Manz was sentenced to death for embracing the idea that only believers should be baptized and that the state should have no influence in Church issues. He was led from the Wellenberg prison, still bound, past the fish market to a boat. As he walked, he was still witnessing to those who stood along the streets and the banks of the Limmat River. He continued to praise God that even though he was a sinner, he would have the privilege of dying for the truth. He once again openly declared that believer's baptism was the only true baptism according to the Bible. His mother's voice could be heard above the sounds of the crowd. What did she say? Did she encourage him to recant, to give up his faith so that his life could be spared? Oh no! Instead, she encouraged him to remain true to Christ in this tremendous time of testing. Finally, he was placed in a small boat just below the council hall building (which still stands) in Zurich. Slowly the boat began to move downstream where it collided with a small anchored fishing hut. His arms and his legs were bound so he was unable to swim to save his life. He was heard to cry out with a loud voice, "Into Thy hands, oh Lord, I commend my spirit." He disappeared under the waters of the Limmat River, where only two years before he had baptized his first converts. Bernard Wyss recorded that Manz's execution took place on January 5, 1527, at three o'clock on a Saturday afternoon. He was the second martyr in the Anabaptist movement,[1] but he was far from the last.

THE RADICAL REFORMATION

The Anabaptists are frequently referred to as Radical Reformationists. The term "radical" refers to returning to the very "root" (*radix*) of the Christian faith. The Anabaptists liked being called radicals, because they desired to return to biblical roots. They were a simple people with a simple faith, but they did think about what they were proposing. They introduced the phrase "discipleship of Christ" as a description of what to mature in Christ means. Anabaptist thinker Hans Denck spoke of the "indwelling Word" which affects moral renewal in the human spirit. In the Anabaptists' earnest search for morality and integrity, they relied unabashedly on the power of the Holy Spirit. They were courageous and slow to compromise with the contaminated world in which they lived.

How were they treated for this simple faith? They were martyred by the thousands—and not at the hands of the normal enemies of the Cross. They were martyred by fellow Reformers—by followers of Martin Luther and of Ulrich Zwingli. They were considered a threat for "having gone too far." But their resiliency and the beauty of their spirit in the face of severe persecution shows us once again that the true Church of Jesus Christ will not be coerced. Ironically, the term "true Church of Jesus Christ" has an Anabaptist ring to it. They firmly believed that the organizational church structures (councils, the priesthood, church regulations) should not be confused with those who were part of the true Church.

It is painful to admit that such theological intolerance existed. From our century, however, we must attempt to understand the world in which they lived. Theological uniformity within a given political region was perceived to be an absolute necessity. All who lived within a particular country or province *had* to be of the exact same theological persuasion. This was a part of the political and social fabric of the time. No variation was allowed.

Thus, religious dissidents were seen as a threat to the political system, and justice was necessarily quickly executed for the sake of the public peace.

The second major issue that affected the way the Anabaptists were treated, and which separated them from the other Reformers, was the relationship between the Church and political powers. Believing that the state should not have intervention in spiritual matters, the Anabaptists were the first to advocate a separation between Church and state. (Their lineage can be traced to the New World, where the Baptist colony of Rhode Island did not require an officially endorsed religion.)

THE MANY BRANCHES OF THE ANABAPTIST MOVEMENT

Rather than being a uniform group, the Anabaptists included a variety of approaches to the Christian faith. For example, some were pacifists. Their descendants, the Mennonites, do not participate in war to this day; they list themselves as conscientious objectors. Unfortunately, some of the splinter groups within the Anabaptist movement became increasingly bizarre, practicing polygamy and claiming to receive strange revelations. However, this was not typical of most Anabaptists who were moral, decent Christians with an intense love for God, which drew persecution.

FOUR CATEGORIES

The origin of the Anabaptist movement is generally traced to January 21, 1525, when the city council of Zurich ordered the leaders of this movement to stop stirring up theological controversy. To the Anabaptist purists, this order was another political attempt to coerce them. A few nights later, they baptized one another and were thus named Anabaptists, or rebaptizers. With the passage of time the disconnected collection of people called Anabaptists were divided into four main categories:

1. *Mainline Anabaptists:* These included the Swiss Brethren, the Mennonites and the Hutterites, all of whom were spiritual descendants of Jacob Hutter.
2. *Spiritualists:* Andreas Carlstadt (1480-1541), Thomas Muntzer

(1489-1525), Kaspar Schwenkfeld (1489-1561) and Sebastian Franck (1491-1542) were prominent leaders. The Spiritualists were more subjective than other Reformers. One of the major tenets of the Reformation was *sola scriptura,* which meant "by Scripture alone." Spiritualists were much more comfortable with the unique nudging of the Holy Spirit on the heart of the believer in contemporary life. They believed that God could speak truth to the heart of the spiritually sensitive. While there is a measure of truth in such a statement, their followers were unfortunately quite vulnerable to abuses of biblical interpretation.

3. *Rationalists:* The most popular group in this category was known as the Socinians, who were named after Laelius Socinus (or sometimes Sozzini, 1525-1562) and his nephew, Faustus Socinus (1539-1604). They interpreted everything in light of reason and their strict rationalism led them to reject such basic things as the deity of Christ.

4. *Revolutionaries:* A key example of these are some of the followers of Thomas Muntzer (1489-1525). The Munsterites, as they came to be called, attempted to usher in the kingdom of God by the sword. The Muntzer Revolt occurred in Westphalia, when a group of Munsterites seized the large church and took control of the town council by force from early 1534 until June of 1535. This was their way of bringing in the kingdom of God. They felt that it was justifiable to kill "pagans" (those who disagreed with them) when necessary.[2]

MENNONITES—MOST INFLUENTIAL

It is extremely important, however, to point out that the second, third and fourth groups (Spiritualists, Rationalists and Revolutionaries) all waned in influence with the passage of time. The term "Anabaptist" tended to be associated with the Mennonites and Brethren. The best-known leader of the Anabaptist movement was Menno Simons (1496-1559). Simons had become a Roman Catholic priest in 1524, but by 1527 he had serious doubts about the traditional view of the Communion, the Mass, and infant baptism. He hungered for deeper moral seriousness. He began to study the

Scripture and from 1535 preached a message of repentance. In 1537 he was reordained—a symbolic act which meant that he was breaking with his Roman ties. He traveled widely as a preacher, gathering together people who embraced his idea of a "new creature," that one should take seriously Paul's teaching of dying to the old Adam (see Rom. 5:12-21) and rising up in newness of life in Christ (see 2 Cor. 5:17).

JOHN CALVIN
THE THEOLOGIAN

Although Martin Luther is the best-known Reformation leader, John Calvin is regarded as the greatest systematic theologian and disciplinarian of all the Reformers. He was born July 10, 1509, in Noyan, France, approximately 50 miles north of Paris, the fourth son of Gerard Cauvin (later spelled Calvin). Martin Luther nailed his theses to the door of Wittenberg only two years before Calvin's birth. Unlike this older brother of the Reformation, Calvin was a quiet young man. However, he had the same determination and strength of will. Calvin, a gifted and conscientious student, began attending the University of Paris by age 14. Calvin's academic brilliance was already obvious. Little is known, however, about his religious attitudes before his 25th birthday. In 1533 young John experienced a "sudden conversion." In the introduction to his commentary on the Psalms he wrote the following regarding his conversion experience: "Since I was more stubbornly addicted to the superstitions of the papacy and to be easily drawn out of so deep a ruin, God subdued my heart—too stubborn for my age—to docility by sudden conversion."[3]

On October 31, 1533, the 16th anniversary of Martin Luther's nailing of the Ninety-five Theses on the Wittenberg door, Calvin's friend, Nicholas Cop, preached a sermon as the newly installed rector of the University of Paris. Its Lutheran content raised such a ruckus that both Nicholas Cop and John Calvin were forced to flee Paris University.

THE INSTITUTES

In 1536, at age 27, John Calvin released the first of what would be many editions of his famous *Institutes of the Christian Religion*, usually simply referred to as the *Institutes*. These amazing volumes were a spectacular accomplishment for a person of Calvin's age, and as they were revised through the years, they became his legacy to the Christian Church. Even after five centuries, the *Institutes* remain very much the "Mount Everest" of systematic theology. They serve as defining volumes for a major branch of the Christian Church.

Calvin was courageous and dedicated, with a heart for the Church and a broad knowledge of the Scriptures. But Calvin's brilliance was in his ability to sytematize and to organize that knowledge. He applied his orderly intelligence to all he did. In his flood of writings, he presents a carefully structured exposition of the truth. No one had ever so thoroughly arranged the Scriptures of the Bible into a systematic outline. His *Institutes* are regarded as a classic to this day.

GENEVA AND STRASBOURG

In writing his *Institutes*, Calvin immediately became an influential and full-blown Reformer. Guillaume Farel persuaded John Calvin to come to Geneva to help reform the city and bring it into alignment with biblical ways. This attempt to establish the city of God on earth was an abysmal failure and resulted in both Farel and Calvin's making a hasty retreat from the city in 1537. Many people chafed under Calvin's heavy hand.

From Geneva, he went to Strasbourg, France, where he continued writing, thinking and pastoring. In 1539, he wrote his commentary on Romans, which would be the first of many commentaries. Meanwhile, back in Geneva the tumult was continuing. So unrestful was the city that city fathers encouraged Calvin to return in hopes that he would help restore peace. After 10 long months he finally agreed, convinced that God's hand was upon this call to the city.

He arrived in Geneva in September of 1541 and remained there until his death of tuberculosis on May 27, 1564. Calvin's return to Geneva was anything but peaceful, however. It was filled with controversy—political, ecclesiastical and theological. He carried on an aggressive campaign for moral reform of the citizenry. By 1548 his opponents had won control of the city council and made life even more challenging for him. A strange turn of events would cause him to regain control of the city in 1555.

Michael Servetus had denied the doctrine of the Trinity. In an era which disallowed any kind of theological pluralism, Calvin condemned him as a heretic and a blasphemer. Apparently with Calvin's tacit approval, Servetus, the gadfly medical genius (he was the first to discover the pulmonary circulation of the blood) and amateur theologian, was burned at the stake. To historians, this event would be the black cloud hanging over Calvin. He should not be remembered exclusively for this one tragic incident, however. His daily life was filled with service. He performed weddings and baptisms, and he preached every day in Saint Pierre Church, where he spoke often of his vision that Geneva should become a visible city of God. He established the Geneva Academy which trained hundreds of young pastors.

It was said among the French Protestant Huguenots (countrymen of the French-born Calvin) that a degree from his school was the equivalent of a death certificate. Most of the young Frenchmen who studied at the Geneva Academy and returned to France as pastors would be arrested and condemned to sit chained to the benches of the king's galleys to row until they died, which usually took only a year or two. But new students kept arriving.

DOCTRINE

Calvin's beliefs are frequently characterized by the acronym T.U.L.I.P. These five doctrinal points do not describe everything Calvin taught, but they were the points on which his system differed from the Roman Catholic doctrines of his day.

- *T for Total Depravity*—Adam's fall into sin is so great that no human could ever have any capacity to respond to that which is good.
- *U for Unconditional Election*—God chooses people *un*conditionally; that is, God's choice is not based upon anything one might do or any response one might make.
- *L for Limited Atonement*—Christ's death on the cross is only for a few select persons. Christ's death was effective for only a few, and in this sense was not for all people.
- *I for Irresistible Grace*—If one had been selected to receive salvation, he couldn't possibly resist it.

- *P for Perseverance*—Once one is truly saved, it is impossible to fall from that condition. This is also known as eternal security.

EVALUATION

In the 1500s, Calvinism, as it came to be called, spread rapidly through Scotland, Poland and Holland and eventually to America. Presbyterian denominations and Reformed denominations point to John Calvin as their founding father. Depending upon the theological tradition in which you were raised, John Calvin is either your hero or a villain. I was raised in a distinctly Wesleyan tradition, so Calvinism was not a particularly positive term. However, we need to acknowledge the profound influence of this godly man. He was a brilliant theologian of the Reformation who also longed to see God's justice established on earth, bringing morality and peace to an entire city. While we view these events through the eyes of our twentieth-century pluralism, we are forced to admire Calvin's remarkable attempt to live out the Bible in community and city life. Finally, we must appreciate Calvin because he grasped the depth of human depravity in a way few did. Perhaps only Augustine (in the fourth century) and Jonathan Edwards (in the eighteenth century) shared Calvin's sensitivity to the depth of sin in the human heart.

HIS THOUGHTS

Though Calvin was tormented by much controversy and severe criticism, his motives become evident in his writings during his final illness before his death in 1564:

> I have lived amidst extraordinary struggles here; I have been saluted in mockery at night, before my door, by 50 or 60 shots from arquebuses. Think how that would terrify a poor timid scholar such as I am. . . . then, later, I was hunted out of this town and went to Strasbourg. . . . I was recalled, but I had no less trouble than before in trying to do my official duty . . . whilst I am nothing, yet I know that I have prevented many disturbances that would otherwise have occurred in Geneva. . . . God has given me the power to write. . . . I have written nothing in hatred . . . but always I have faithfully attempted what I believe to be for the glory of God.[4]

OTHER REFORMERS

When the Spirit of God is doing something new in history, He generally moves upon more than one individual, although there is often a point man. When God is up to something, He tends to release the same truth on numerous people at the same time. Such was the case in the Reformation. [5] Before examining Martin Luther, we looked at Peter Waldo, John Wycliffe and John Huss. Martin Luther became the pivotal, or turning, point because the soil was so well prepared by the Pre-Reformers so that the seed could take root. Yet Martin Luther was not the only one experiencing this explosive truth from God. We've mentioned Ulrich Zwingli and John Calvin, along with the Anabaptists. A host of other lesser-known yet influential leaders also helped invigorate the Church:

- Martin Bucer (or Butzer, 1491-1551), a peace-loving German who attempted to establish alliances and agreements whenever possible. He had a profound influence on Calvin and wanted very much to establish harmony among Lutherans, Zwinglians and other reformers. Under invitation by the English archbishop, Thomas Cranmer, he went to Cambridge and revised the English *Book of Common Prayer*.
- Berthold Haller (1492-1536), a reformer in the city of Bern, Switzerland. He had been a fellow student with Phillip Melanchthon from Wittenberg, where Luther had launched the Reformation. Haller, like Bucer, liked peace. He disliked controversy and yet spent his last years in disputation with the Anabaptists.
- Guillaume Farel (1489-1556), a fiery, explosive French Reformer who in 1530 was successful in persuading the city fathers of Neuchatel, Switzerland, to follow Reformation teaching. He was equally influential in convincing the town fathers of Geneva to do the same two years later. "More evangelistic preacher than original thinker, Farel was a memorable pulpit personality whose sermons made an impact on all hearers, including the cool, cerebral Calvin."[6] It is a memorable side note in history that Calvin became very upset with Farel because he chose to remarry at age 70, taking a younger wife!

- Pierre Viret (1511-1571), a Reformer extremely active in the French cantons in Geneva, Lausanne and many other cities. He was a close associate to both Farel and Calvin.
- John Oecolampadius (1482-1531), who started his ministry as a cathedral preacher in Basel, Switzerland, in 1515 as a Lutheran but changed back to Roman Catholicism and thereafter entered the monastery. In 1522 he changed his mind again and became a pastor in Basel and later a professor at the university. Oecolampadius is credited as the one who brought Reformation changes to the city of Basel. So respected was he that he was invited to participate in the famous Marburg Colloquy, put together by a political leader, Phillip of Hesse, in an attempt to help the Reformers gain uniformity. Oecolampadius suffered from poor health and died only seven weeks after hearing of the death of Ulrich Zwingli, his good friend.
- Theodore Beza, a right-hand man to John Calvin in Geneva.
- Phillip Melanchthon, a right-hand man to Martin Luther, whose work at Wittenberg he continued after Luther passed away.

We will have to wait for heaven to have time for all the stories of those whose names are lost in the woodwork of history and yet who were used by God to bring back fundamental and basic biblical truths to His Church. They were part of His plan—a mighty plan, an awesome plan to reestablish God's dreams for His people, His Church. Through their devotion and endurance, you and I have the advantage of the biblical tenets of the Reformation—something we might not have, had it not been for such Reformers.

THE BRITISH ISLES: JOHN KNOX

Leaving the continent of Europe, we go now to the British Isles. In Scotland, a Reformation hero stood as tall and mighty as John Calvin in Geneva. His name is John Knox (1513-1572). Little is known of his early life, except that he was reared in Haddington and attended the University of Saint Andrews. He embraced Reformation views because of the influence of a very close friend, George Wishart. Archbishop Beaton arrested Wishart because of his positions and then refused to allow John Knox to intercede on his behalf. The day George Wishart was burned at the stake at Saint Andrews, John Knox was catapulted into the Reformation movement. Scotland was looking for a leader. The populace was prepared for a revolution, since there was a great deal of intellectual fomentation, as well as anger, about the many abuses by the clergy. The Scottish people wanted a simple, pure faith. Knox became a natural leader.

However, his journey to leadership took him along a difficult and painful route. For 19 long months he served as a slave after he was captured at Saint Andrews. Upon his release, he became a royal chaplain. But life would not become any easier for him. In 1553, he was forced into hiding when the Catholic advocate, Queen Mary, ascended to the throne of England. John Knox took refuge in Geneva, where he became a disciple of John Calvin in both his theology and his form of Church government. In 1555 he returned to Scotland, pastored a congregation and married Marjorie Bowes.

CONTROVERSY

By 1556 he was condemned for heresy in Scotland for his Reformation views and forced to return to Geneva once again. It was in 1558 that he wrote his epic *The First Blast of the Trumpet Against the Monstrous Regiment of Women,* in which he advocated a rebellion against any ungodly rulers, but he specifically condemned female monarchy. This offended not only Queen Mary ("Bloody Mary") but also Queen Elizabeth, who followed her half-sister Mary to the throne. Finally, in 1559, he had the privilege of returning to his homeland for good. It would not be a serene setting, however. Upon preaching a fiery sermon against idolatry, a rebellion ensued. By 1560, the same year that his wife died, the parliament adopted the "Scot's Confession," which Knox had helped to write. It was thought that this confession of faith would bring the long-sought peace. Much to the contrary! The period from 1561 to 1567 was one of intense struggle among the newly empowered Protestants, the old Catholic regime and many nobles who supported the Reformation only because it gave them the opportunity to wrest Church lands from the Catholic church. Eventually, Protestantism became the faith of Scotland.

FEARLESS AND HUMBLE

Finally, after much struggle, the Scottish church that Knox had dreamed of had come to fruition, following the pattern of John Calvin's Geneva. Knox himself had stood courageously and consistently against political leaders who had tried to crush his theological views. As one writer noted, "His fearless and successful opposition to regent and queen marked him as a true patriot. But the man himself was the key to his great achievements—tireless, sincere, simple, practical . . . not without humor and tenderness."[7]

Knox's modest and unassuming personality is faithfully reflected in his grave marker—a paving stone, engraved only with small initials, that lies in the road on High Street in Edinburgh. This modest grave does not keep us from recognizing that Knox was one of the most influential men in the entire Scottish nation. Thanks to his willingness to endure the most turbulent of times with dedication, the Scots, too, can thank God that the Church is alive and well.

THE COUNCIL OF TRENT

The Roman Catholic church tried hard to stop the Reformation. Some of its efforts were noble endeavors to clean up and purify the Church from within, through well-placed, spiritually sensitive Roman Catholic leaders who loved their Church and their God. These leaders also loved God's people. They sincerely wanted the Roman Catholic church to reflect the nature of the Church as God originally envisioned it. Thus, the Catholic Counter-Reformation developed, taking its name from the fact that it attempted to counter the Protestant Reformation. Tragically, however, some leaders of the Counter-Reformation were spurred simply by the desire to control land, power and wealth; and they used the Counter-Reformation as an attempt to preserve the status quo—the privileged position of the Roman Catholic church.

The Council of Trent (1545) had the stated noble goal of restoring the Church to God's original design. Pope Leo X had been a pleasure-seeking pope; but his successor, Pope Paul III, was reform-minded. He wanted to see authentic change, for the Roman church was in desperate need of reform. A commissioned report indicated that the clergy were worldly, that offices were corrupted by bribery, that immorality was high, that indulgences were mere excuses for greed and that prostitution was rampant in Rome. To deal with these problems, the council met sporadically from 1545 to 1563. One positive outcome was the abolishment of the sale of indulgences, a practice against which the Protestants had been preaching for years. However, the council could do nothing to heal the deep breach between Catholics and Protestants.

The council reaffirmed its theological positions. They maintained seven sacraments, whereas the Protestants had kept only two: baptism and Communion. They reiterated belief in transubstantiation. They insisted that Mass should be said in Latin. Most offensive to Protestants was the fact that Bibles were not allowed in the hands of common people, under the guise that laity might inadequately interpret Scripture. Consequently, the Council of Trent accomplished only minor modifications within the Church and deepened the split between Catholics and Protestants.

IGNATIUS OF LOYOLA AND THE RISE OF THE JESUITS

Approximately five years before the Council of Trent convened, an organization was founded which produced amazing spiritual results. Ignatius of Loyola (1491-1556) received approval from Pope Paul III on September 27, 1540, to found a new order known as the Jesuits. The Jesuits would become one of the greatest reforming and missionary forces of the Catholic church. On August 15, 1534, Ignatius and six of his friends gathered in Paris and vowed to live lives of poverty and chastity. By 1539, it was obvious that this was a permanent community, so they wanted the blessing of the pope, which they received in 1540.

Ignatius was a deeply spiritual man, hungry to please God. His dedication came, as it has for many of God's children, through a tragedy. While fighting as a knight in the spring of 1521, he was struck by a cannonball that fractured his left leg. During his long period of recuperation he read about the life of Christ and the lives of the saints. This was to forever alter his life. His spiritual journey is reflected in the devotional manual he wrote, *Spiritual Exercises*. So convicting and influential was his writing that to this day his works are studied. You can even sign up to study his book in courses entitled "Ignatian Spirituality" in Protestant evangelical graduate schools.[8]

During his recuperation from his wound, he made the decision to be in a life of combat for Christ. The Jesuits, or Society of Jesus, as they were sometimes called, were expected to demonstrate militaristic obedience. The *Constitutions* which Ignatius wrote from 1547 to 1550 called for the Jesuits to be "ready to live in any part of the world where there is hope of God's greater glory and the good of souls."[9]

CRITICIZED FROM BOTH SIDES

Conservatives within the Roman Catholic church criticized Ignatius because they felt he was too Protestant. On the other hand, Protestant Reformers were critical of him because the Society of Jesus clearly was an effort to hold people within the Roman Catholic church. Regardless of his critics on both sides of the Catholic/Protestant divide, Ignatius accomplished an amazing missionary work. The Jesuits were committed to education and founded universities wherever they went. By the time Ignatius died in 1556, his followers numbered over a thousand and were working in over 100 locations, including India, China, Japan, Abyssinia and South America. Ignatius's dedication drew people of the caliber of Frances Xavier, who successfully expanded the mission work of the Society of Jesus even more.

Ignatius was frequently ill. In 1551, he implored his colleagues to accept his resignation. Because they refused, he stayed on as director until his death on July 31, 1556. The Jesuit Order continued to be powerful after his death. Members of the order were disciplined, hardworking, committed and willing to sacrifice. They suffered the pain of rejection and were expelled from numerous countries. They also experienced martyrdom in Europe and later across various mission fields in the nineteenth century. In time, they became the largest teaching order in the United States, with high schools and colleges established across America.

SAINT BARTHOLOMEW'S DAY MASSACRE

We have seen the expansion of the Reformation and how God's truth exploded across major parts of Europe. We have also explored the way in which God was purifying the Roman Catholic church from the inside. Yet at the same time, the Church was violently divided. The massive conflict between Roman Catholics and Protestants was not only religious but also political. Europe was torn apart by it. For example, Phillip II of Spain (1556-1598) united the Catholics and led an attempt to abolish the spread of Protestantism. The Dutch dreaded his invasion of their towns. Dutch Protestants finally won independence from Spain in 1581. The English seized the opportunity to break Spain's hold, and defeated the Spanish Armada in 1588. Catholic/Protestant conflicts became so intense that a series of four wars (Bohemian, Danish, Swedish and French) would cover three decades and be known as the Thirty Years' War from 1618 to 1648.

One of the most tragic events during this period was the slaughter of 30,000 French Protestants, beginning on the Feast of Saint Bartholomew, August 23, 1572, in Paris, and continuing for the next six weeks all over France. The events leading up to this horrific slaughter have the intrigue of a contemporary soap opera. But tragically, they were not simply a television show or a movie. This was reality. French Protestants were killed by the thousands.

The tragedy began at a festive celebration of the marriage of Henry of Navarre, a well-known Protestant leader, to Marguerite of Valois. Marguerite was the sister of King Charles IX and the daughter of Catherine de Médicis, a forceful Catholic leader. The wedding was supposed to bring together the Protestant and Catholic leaders who had been at war with each other for over a decade. But Catherine was planning more than her daughter's wedding. She was plotting the assassination of a well-known Huguenot (French Protestant) leader named Gaspard de Coligny. Coligny was a strong Protestant leader and a war hero who had become close to King Charles IX, only a teenager at the time. The plot to kill Coligny was planned for August 22, 1572, but it failed when the would-be assassins only succeeded in wounding the elderly statesman. Allegedly, Charles, the young king (knowing how his fellow Protestants resented this political marriage), remarked, "If you are going to kill Coligny, why don't you kill all the Huguenots in France so that there will be no one left to hate me?"[10] And that is precisely what Catherine tried to do.

THE PLAN CARRIED OUT

At 4:00 A.M. on August 24, 1572, on Saint Bartholomew's Day, the massacre began. Mobs roamed the streets of Paris, murdering Huguenots by the thousands. The Protestants were a well-educated and prosperous element of French society, and vocal about their beliefs. Not only was it easy to know who they were, but apparently some of the more obscure homes had been labeled with a secret mark on the door, so the mobs would know where to go. In a matter of hours a full-scale class struggle was on—the lower class against these middle-class business owners. Bodies were piled up and thrown into the river Seine. Don't forget that John Calvin was originally Jean Cauvin, a Frenchman. Calvinism had started in France in 1555 and had grown rapidly to include over 2,000 churches and some 400,000 adherents. Some estimates maintain that as many as 100,000 of them were killed in less than 50 days, although more conservative estimates place the number between 30,000 and 40,000.

HUGUENOTS' EXIT

The intrigue didn't stop there, and the plot thickens. In 1589, Henry of Navarre, the Protestant groom at the infamous wedding, became king. As king, Henry IV of France vacillated and converted to Catholicism! However, he intended to bridge the gap with his former Protestant friends by publishing in 1598 the Edict of Nantes, a document which provided civil and religious rights to the French Protestants. The guaranteed rights were overlooked, however, and another war broke out which continued until 1628.

During this period, Huguenots were sometimes left in relative peace if local authorities were favorable to them. However, at other times and in certain areas they were persistently tortured, abused, and practically exterminated. A group of courageous Protestant women were imprisoned in the Tour de Constance, where several of them remained for over 30 years. Pastors and leaders were taken to row on the galleys, where they perished after a year or two. Others were tortured to death. Children were taken from their parents, and Protestants were not allowed to worship freely or hold jobs. Thousands of Protestants experienced forced "conversions" to Catholicism. Some 400,000 escaped the country, taking refuge in England, Germany and America while Louis XIV revoked the Edict of Nantes, thus allowing Protestants no protection whatsoever.

Nonetheless, the conflicts and persecutions surrounding the Huguenots do not diminish the providential grace of God. The Lord is able to bring good out of the most painful Church circumstances and failures.

The hunger for spiritual reform was expanding at an incredible pace even as Protestants fled France, and that reform would benefit all believers in Christ. Even the most troublesome times could not stop God's great creation—the true Church—which He designed as a gift to civilization.

To further assist you in understanding the key individuals and events of chapter 9, study questions, charts, diagrams, time lines and links to biographical websites are available on the Internet at www.jimgarlow.com. Please follow the site links to *How God Saved Civilization*, chapter 9 study helps.

It'll Never Happen in Britain

THE ENGLISH REFORMATION

Dates covered: A.D. 1526-1559
Key persons: William Tyndale, Henry VIII, Thomas Cranmer

Bedtime came early when winter arrived in Chesterton, England. The three older Smithton children never wanted to go to bed, but they loved nightly prayers with their father, John. Mother was putting baby Susannah to bed. When they had washed up with the cold water in the basin, the oldest child carried an oil lamp in from the kitchen and set it on the small table near Father's cozy chair. John Smithton reached for the priceless Bible his father had passed on to him. He picked up the Bible carefully, lovingly. He waited until his three oldest children had settled on the sheepskin at his feet, near the crackling fire.

"Why do we read the Bible every night, Father? What about another book for a change?" asked nine-year-old Matthew.

"Pardon me?" asked his father, coming back from his thoughts.

Matthew questioned, "Does reading the Bible and praying really help?"

"Three days ago," said seven-year-old Ann, "I prayed that I wouldn't have to gather eggs from the chickens anymore, but you asked me to do it again! My prayer didn't work."

"Well," said John, trying to control the smile that tugged at the corners of his mouth and knowing that he would ask her to collect the eggs again tomorrow.

"Of course prayer works," answered 11-year-old Thomas, in a very grown-up voice.

"I don't know if I can remember ever getting anything I prayed for," argued Matthew.

There was a noticeable pause as John Smithton pondered his answer. The children knew him to be wise, but he was also careful in his speech. They sat still, waiting while the oil lamps flickered, casting eerie shadows on the whitewashed stone walls.

John knew prayer worked. But how to explain its mystery to these questioning children?

"Let me give you an example of an answer to prayer in our family. It was a very special answer. See this Bible in my hand?"

How could they not know that Bible, since they saw it every night and all day on Sundays?

"Yes," said the children in unison.

"Well, your grandmother and grandfather prayed for a long time that our family would someday own a Bible. This Bible cost your grandfather three month's wages, and it's still expensive to buy one. But I want to tell you not only about your grandparents' prayers but also about another man's prayer—the one who brought the Bible to England."

"Did he bring that one to Grandma?" asked Ann.

"Was that the only one he brought?" piped in Matthew.

"Well," replied John, "what I mean is that one man prayed that the king would let us and other Christians in England have a Bible of our own, to read as we do, around the fire, around the table and whenever we want."

"But, Father," objected Thomas, who had heard many stories of the Church, "they killed him."

"Well yes, as a matter of fact, they did kill him," said John, realizing that the children were, once again, not likely to be in bed by the time his wife had said they should be.

"Why did they kill him?" asked Matthew. "Tell us the story, Father, please!"

"This man longed for every English family to have a Bible so that we could all love it and read it and know God better. So he worked very hard to translate the Bible."

"What's 'translate?'" asked Ann.

"You translate for baby Susannah," explained her father gently. "You know her baby language and you tell us what she means." Ann nodded. "Well," the Bible was written down in a language we don't speak here in England. So somebody who understood that language had to write it again in ours, so we can understand it. But of course, it's a big book and he wanted to be very careful, because it is God's Word. He wanted everything just right."

"But why did they kill him?" asked Matthew, eager to get on to the exciting part.

"They killed him because the king did not want us to have a Bible. Right before he died, he prayed to God and this is what he said, 'Oh Lord, will you open the king's eyes?'"

"Was the king asleep, Father?" asked Ann.

"You might say that, Ann. You know when you're supposed to be doing your studies and Mother says to you, 'Wake up, Anne'—what does she mean?"

"Not to look out the window but to learn my numbers."

"Yes, dear. And that's what this man wanted. He wanted the king to stop paying attention to the wrong things and to pay attention to God's things. He was asking God to change the king's heart—change the king's mind—so he would be willing to let everybody in England have a Bible."

"Did everybody get a Bible the next day?" asked Matthew.

"Not the next day," said John, "but it wasn't long."

"I suppose he was asking for what God wanted all along," said Thomas, thoughtfully, "not like our prayers for a new suit of clothes or fancy sweets from town."

That night the Smithton family read from a Bible that had been translated by William Tyndale, a man who had been executed but whose prayer just before his death had been that God would open the eyes of the king. And God did! When God's Word came to England, England entered the Reformation.

ENGLISH REFORMATION

The English Reformation is a story of the faithfulness of William Tyndale. In Europe the Reformation had grown out of Luther's protest. In England, the Reformation grew out of two dissimilar events: The first was Tyndale's insistence on translating the Bible into English, and the other was the self-centered desire of a king who wanted a divorce. Those two events dislodged a nation from its Catholic allegiance and catapulted it into the Protestant camp.

WILLIAM TYNDALE

As the Reformation spread across Europe, Henry VIII staunchly disallowed any Reformation teaching in England. So impressed was the pope with Henry's faithfulness to the Catholic church, that he assigned to him the title "Defender of the Faith." But God—through William Tyndale—had different plans for England. Born in 1494 in Gloucestershire, Tyndale completed a bachelor's degree at age 18 and a master's degree at age 21. After lecturing at Oxford for a year, he went to Cambridge, where he began to study Greek and became a promising linguist. Although charged with heresy and acquitted in 1522, he became increasingly focused on a life calling: the translation of the Greek New Testament into English. Luther had done it for the Germans. Someone had to do it for the British. But he couldn't live in England while translating, or he might be arrested. So Tyndale fled to the continent and worked in hiding.

FIRST AND SECOND VERSIONS OF THE ENGLISH BIBLE

Tyndale saw his dream come true in February 1526, when 6,000 copies of his English New Testament were completed on the continent on Peter Schoeffer's press. How discouraged and perplexed he would have been, had Tyndale known that Bishop Cuthbert Tunstall would buy up all 6,000 copies that very year, only to burn them at a church. What irony that a bishop of the Church would burn copies of the Bible at the foot of a cross named after the apostle Paul, a man who had written more than half the letters of the New Testament.

William Tyndale knew about Bishop Tunstall's plan and actually cooperated with it! Why? Because Bishop Tunstall had advised Augustine Packiengton, his accomplice, to buy all of the copies of the Bible no matter how much they cost. Packiengton went to Tyndale to make an offer. When Tyndale found out who was buying them and how much he was ready to pay, he accepted the offer, even though he knew they would be burned. Tyndale was a clever businessman and publicist, as well as a man who knew "that in all things God works for the good of those who love him, who have been called according to his purpose" (Rom. 8:28). Tyndale figured that he would receive enough money to retranslate the Bible and do a much better job on the second version than he had on the first. When he realized what was happening, he exclaimed,

> "I shall get money [from him] for these books, to bring myself out of debt, and the whole world shall cry out upon the burning of God's Word. And the over plus of the money, that shall remain to me, shall make me more studious to correct the . . . New Testament, and so nearly to imprint the same one again; and I trust the second will be much better . . . than . . . the first." And so forward went the bargain: The Bishop had the books, Packiengton had the thanks, and Tyndale had the money.[1]

TRANSLATION WORK CONTINUES

Although turbulence in Europe and fear of being caught caused Tyndale to stay on the run from city to city, by January of 1530 he had accomplished another major portion of his goal, having translated the first five books of the Old Testament. His revised edition of the New Testament was released in 1534. So spectacular were Tyndale's translation skills that his work is still consulted and is reflected in every English version of the Bible to this day—particularly in the King James Version. It is claimed that 90 percent of the King James Version reflects Tyndale's original translation skills.[2] In 1535, Tyndale again revised his New Testament and continued to translate the Old Testament from Joshua through 2 Chronicles.

BETRAYAL AND ARREST

On May 21, 1535, Tyndale was arrested and imprisoned, betrayed by a young Englishman named Henry Phillips. Tyndale's letters and journals during a 16-month imprisonment reflect his emotional and physical pain. During this period, he was tried and condemned by university professors of theology. Writing to the authorities, Tyndale stated:

> I suffer greatly from cold in the head and am afflicted. . . . (I request) a warmer coat also, for this which I have is very thin; a piece of cloth too to patch my leggings. My overcoat is worn out; my shirts are also worn out. . . . A woolen shirt, if he will be good enough to send it. I have also leggings of thicker cloth to put on above . . . and I ask to be allowed to have a lamp in the evening; it is indeed wearisome sitting alone in the dark. But most of all I beg . . . (to) permit me to have the Hebrew Bible, Hebrew grammar, and Hebrew dictionary that I may pass the time in that study.[3]

PRAYER IN DEATH ANSWERED

It is doubtful he was granted his request. Instead, here is what is recorded in John Foxe's *Book of Martyrs* regarding Tyndale's final moments: "He was there tied to the stake, and then strangled by the hangman, and afterward consumed with fire in the town of Vilvorden, A.D. 1536; crying thus at the stake with fervent zeal and a loud voice, 'Lord! Open the King of England's eyes.'"[4] And to this final cry from Tyndale, John Foxe, author of the greatest book ever written on martyrdom, added, "Tyndale's prayer was answered."[5] In 1538 (only two years later) the king issued a royal injunction making the Bible available in every parish church in England. England was about to be thoroughly reformed.

HENRY VIII

The story of England's reformation switches from the death of a Bible translator to the unchecked demands of a self-centered king—Henry VIII, who was king from 1509 to 1547. No one would have imagined in the early portion of the 1500s that a divorce would be the pivotal factor in bringing the Reformation to England! After all, King Henry VIII had vigorously attacked Martin Luther's teachings in 1521. Henry's change in ecclesiastical preferences was not stimulated by theology, however. His troubles stemmed from the fact that he had no male child to whom he could pass on his title; he had one surviving daughter named Mary. To remedy this problem he decided to rid himself of his first wife, Catherine of Aragon, but this was no easy task. Originally Catherine had been Henry's sister-in-law, but when her husband had died (Henry's brother), she became Henry's wife under a special provision of the law. But to annul the marriage, Henry needed permission from the pope; but the pope was hesitant to grant an annulment which might offend the emperor, who was a relative of Catherine's.

When Cardinal Wolsey failed to negotiate the pope's permission for the divorce, Henry VIII impatiently dismissed him and put another man in his place. Unfortunately, the replacement, Sir Thomas More (1478-1535), was even more opposed to the divorce than was Wolsey! The king then dismissed the second negotiator from the case. But the king was not to be discouraged in his effort to get a new wife. After a complex theological polling of favorable university professors, the king amassed support for his divorce.

Finally, on June 1, 1533, Henry's marriage to Catherine was declared invalid and his marriage to Anne Boleyn was declared valid. But there were still problems to deal with. What about the pope? He had not approved this! Thanks to the genius of a brilliant lawyer, Thomas Cromwell, a piece of legislation was produced in 1533, entitled the Act of Restraint and Appeals, in which Henry, as king, was referred to as one "who owed no submission to any other human ruler."[6] This legally creative thinking manifested itself again the next year with the 1534 Act of Supremacy, which declared that "the king is rightfully the supreme head of the Church of England." Thus, Henry's marital problems were solved, for as head of the Church, he was free to decide whatever he wanted about religious matters.

Henry had never particularly wanted to rule a church. He had only wanted a divorce. Now that he was the head of a church, what should it look like? If it was no longer tied to Rome, should it be a Catholic or a Protestant church? All Henry had wanted was a divorce. But now he found himself the head of an entire church! What was he to do with a church?

THE TWO THOMASES

To answer that question he turned to the same two people who helped get him out of his previous marriage and into his present one: Thomas Cranmer, who was placed as archbishop of Canterbury on March 30, 1533, and Thomas Cromwell. They had to work carefully, however. While Cranmer, Cromwell and their accomplice, Bishop Latimer, were clearly Lutheran in their views, many of the older bishops were still thoroughly Roman. Working carefully to offend as few as possible and to establish unity in this brand-new church organization, leaders in the newly formed Church of England agreed to the Ten Articles which were published in 1536. The articles, while containing some Roman Catholic views, were distinctively Lutheran about some points. The doctrine of transubstantiation (regarding the Communion) was no longer advocated, and the number of sacraments was dropped from seven to three. In 1536 and 1538 the Injunctions were released for the purpose of defining the articles in an even more Lutheran way. Included in the Injunction of 1538 was a call for Bibles, which had been William Tyndale's final prayer. The king insisted that there be one Bible set up in a convenient place in every parish. Priests were warned not to dissuade people from reading the Bible. In fact, they were to encourage it. William Tyndale's prayer was answered—only two years after his death!

PROTESTANT OR CATHOLIC?

As time went on, Henry VIII became even more Protestant, or so he insisted. On the surface, he appeared to be acting in a politically expedient fashion. He decided to dissolve the monasteries, not because he was so thoroughly

Protestant, but rather because they contained great wealth, which he confiscated. In 1539, Henry insisted on passing the Six Articles Act, which moved the Church in a slightly more Roman Catholic direction and prescribed a penalty if one denied transubstantiation or disagreed with celibacy for priests. This latter issue was a problem for Archbishop Cranmer, who had married the niece of Andreas Osiander, a well-known Lutheran Reformer and university professor. It was said that Archbishop Cranmer had to keep his wife in hiding after these articles were passed until he could get her back to Germany for safekeeping.

CRANMER'S NARROW ESCAPE

Meanwhile, Thomas Cromwell, Henry VIII's trusted attorney, had come under suspicion by some of the king's advisors. They persuaded Henry that Cromwell was out to manipulate him. Cromwell arranged for Henry VIII to have yet another wife, Anne of Cleves, whom he married on January 6, 1540. When the marriage proved to be a disaster, Henry VIII was extremely irritated with his attorney, who paid dearly for his lack of matchmaking skills. Cromwell was immediately impeached and condemned; he was executed on January 28, 1540.

Miraculously, Thomas Cranmer managed to stay alive despite Henry VIII's infamous outbursts of rage that "never spared a man in his wrath or a woman in his lust."[7] Henry VIII died on January 28, 1547, and young Edward VI, Henry's son by his third wife, Jane Seymour, became king.

VIA MEDIA

The Church of England was by now mostly Protestant, or at least followed a via media—somewhere in the middle! In 1549, *The Book of Common Prayer* was issued, which established the liturgical and worship life of the Church, followed to this day. The Anglican church beliefs were decidedly Protestant by the time they were compiled in what came to be known as the Forty-two Articles, and finally in 1553 in the Thirty-nine Articles, which exist in Anglicanism (the Church of England) to this day.

BLOODY MARY

All the effort to formulate the Thirty-nine Articles, a statement of beliefs in theology, seemed vain when one month later Edward VI died and Mary

Tudor, the daughter of Henry VIII and Catherine of Aragon, became queen at the age of 37. It is not by accident that she quickly earned the name Bloody Mary. Proud of her Spanish ancestry and determined to solidify her tie with the Roman church, she married her cousin, Phillip II of Spain. Mary was forceful and the parliament compliant. It voted on November 27, 1554, to take England back into the Roman Catholic church. With this act, Parliament had the authority to burn all Protestants at the stake. Mary had hundreds martyred during her reign, from 1553 to 1558. Protestantism, which had been exploding in England, passed through a most tragic season. Those who could leave the island left quickly. Those who didn't get away quickly enough were executed.

LATIMER AND RIDLEY

A massive mopping up operation began. John Rogers, a special friend of William Tyndale, who had helped compile the Bible, was the first to be killed. Two well-known and popular bishops, Nicholas Ridley and Hugh Latimer, were held as prisoners in Oxford for 18 months until their fateful day on October 16, 1555. As the fire was lit, Hugh Latimer looked at his frightened colleague and said, "Be of good comfort, Master Ridley, we shall this day light such a candle by God's grace in England as, I trust, shall never be put out."[8] Looking out of the tower in which he was held, Cranmer witnessed the execution of his two friends, knowing full well what was in store for him.

CRANMER'S RECANTATION

Thomas Cranmer did not have to wait long. He was next to be tried. The charges against him included adultery, due to the fact that he was married (remember new rules had been enforced regarding celibacy of priests). Papers were drawn up which would allow him to recant what he believed. To his shame, he signed the papers! The archbishop had compromised his faith, but he would have one more chance to redeem himself.

On March 21, 1556, after three long years in prison, the old man who was once the archbishop of a nation was led through the streets of Oxford to Saint Mary's Church. He was forced to listen to a sermon which explained why it was necessary for him to die. The old archbishop wept openly throughout the sermon. Finally, he was allowed to speak. Everyone expected him to affirm his recantations, for after all, he had signed them. But instead, Thomas Cranmer, in his final moments, demonstrated the courage which had made him such a great leader for so many years. He recanted the recantations that he had signed! And he even went further. He said that when it was time to throw him into the fire, he would thrust his right hand into the fire first, "for as much as my hand offended, writing contrary to my heart, my hand shall first be punished for it; for when I come to the fire it shall be first burned."[9] His accusers were stunned. They grabbed him, threw him near the flame and, as he had promised, he extended his hand while stating, "this unworthy right hand," and finally crying out, "Lord, Jesus, receive my spirit!" He continued to cry out until he died.[10]

THE AMAZING LADY JANE GREY

When Queen Mary burned an archbishop, the nation was horrified. Public opinion had turned against her, but she wasn't done yet. In a horrible act of cowardly vindictiveness, she executed 16-year-old Lady Jane Grey. Estep properly states that, "made of sterner stuff than some of the most illustrious martyrs, she deserves to be widely recognized. The story of Lady Jane's martyrdom reveals not only the brilliant defense of a young girl under the most difficult of circumstances but also the deep convictions that the new faith was capable of nurturing in so young a heart."[11]

Only four days before Jane was beheaded, Master Feckenham, a well-trained Roman Catholic, was sent to this 16-year-old for the purpose of theologically outsmarting her and coercing her to recant. The transcript of the exchange between the adult theologian and the teenage girl about to be killed is astounding. He attacked her faith, but she answered with the profundity of Scripture. At one point she was asked how many sacraments there were. She stated there were two. He then corrected her, claiming there were seven, whereupon she simply inquired, "By what Scripture find you that?" When he challenged her regarding transubstantiation, she countered by arguing that Jesus could not have meant that bread was literally His body, any more than He had meant literally His statements, "I am the vine" or "I am the door." Surely Master Feckenham did not believe that Jesus was a plant or a piece of wood?

This teenager, held in the tower of London, then went on to challenge the theologian, "How many Christs are there?" She went on to argue, "If Christ

hung on the cross, then how could one also be partaking of His body? Either
He hung on the cross and that body is real, or the body one takes in communion is real. There couldn't be two unless there were two Christs." One can only
imagine that the theologian who was sent to extract the recantation must have
been inwardly shaking his head. Certainly he could never have expected this. In
one more attempt, Feckenham challenged her: "You ground your faith upon
such authors . . . and not upon the Church to whom you ought to give credit."
Lady Jane Grey answered, "No, I ground my faith upon God's Word, and not
upon the church. For if the church be a good church, the faith of the church
must be tried by God's Word, and not God's Word by the church."[12]

Observes Estep: "When one considers Jane's age and the situation in
which she found herself, her testimony is all the more amazing. It indicates
how deeply the cardinal principles of the Reformation had taken hold of an
obviously brilliant and articulate young girl."[13] But Estep notes that while
Mary knew how to burn martyrs, she was a failure at everything else. In the
brief five years of her rule, there are 273 known martyrs, 60 of whom were
women. Thankfully, as she came to the end of her bitter reign, there was no
offspring to continue the terror. She died, much to the relief of Englishmen,
on November 17, 1558; and for reasons that are obvious, she is known to
this day as Bloody Mary.

ELIZABETH

As Mary's death was announced, church bells rang and celebrations erupted. Elizabeth had become Queen at age 25. Protestant refugees flocked by
the thousands from Frankfurt, Germany, Zurich and Geneva, Switzerland.
The pope, infuriated that Elizabeth was clearly Protestant, excommunicated her in 1570 (even though she wasn't even a member of his church!). This
is not to imply that Elizabeth had an easy reign. Roman Catholic clergy
within the country plotted to reestablish Catholicism; and there were several serious attempts to overthrow the new queen, but none succeeded.

Armed with an astute sense that surpassed her years, Elizabeth was
uniquely aware of the challenges she faced for governing the nation. With
Roman Catholics on one end and Calvinists, Puritans and Anabaptists on
the other, she tried to find a middle way. During her reign, the Thirty-nine
Articles were revised and firmly established, and *The Book of Common Prayer*

became the official form of worship. The Act of Uniformity, which required all laypeople to attend the Church of England (Anglican church, or as it is known in this country, the Episcopal church), passed on April 28, 1559, only one day earlier than the Act of Supremacy, which gave her complete authority over the Church. The Elizabethan Settlement, as it is called, was here to stay and England was firmly Protestant.

FINDING GOD'S HAND

We finish this chapter with a sense of ecclesiastical exhaustion. To the uninitiated, the story of the Church sounds more political than spiritual—an organization totally mired in political chicanery rather than a group of people hungry for God. The Church, which God placed on Earth as His vehicle to preserve civilization from self-destruction, seemed to need to save itself.

The explanation goes beyond the separation I have tried to show between the organizational, visibly structured church (such as a denomination) and the true Church (those who are truly saved). What is important to see in this story is the faithfulness of God's hand to execute His goodwill in history. Why God chooses to work at what seems to us an excruciatingly slow pace, we cannot say. Someone once said, "Although God is never late, He misses all the good opportunities to be early!" However, we must remember that God is exercising great patience with us, allowing us the opportunity to turn to Him before He comes in final judgment. God shows infinite patience with the world. In spite of avarice, greed, debauchery and conniving, God is somewhere, somehow at work, even in the messiest centuries. It may look as if He has forgotten His people or is powerless to act. However, the same God who created this world knows how to rule it. Often when He seems most absent, He is most present.

SEEING THROUGH THE EYES OF ETERNITY

When Tyndale was to be burned at the stake, history looked bleak for God's people. But within two years, God would change the king's heart! As Queen Mary was viciously stamping out the life of a spectacular young believer, she was undoing herself! The day Lady Jane Grey was executed, Mary appeared to be winning. But two short years later, she was dead herself, a despised woman. The world stands in awe of Lady Jane to this day! Now I ask you—was God's hand present? Yes. Were the results what we wanted? No, not at that time. Had I told you Tyndale and Lady Jane were snatched from the executioner in a Christian version of Robin Hood, you might have been more reassured. But in the midst of persecution and sorrow, God was moving. These two martyrs became heroes, and their deaths exposed the true villains of history. God vindicated their deaths by allowing His Church to move forward and prosper. The Church, though battered and bruised, was still functioning as the preserver of truth, civilization's only hope.

To further assist you in understanding the key individuals and events of chapter 10, study questions, charts, diagrams, time lines and links to biographical websites are available on the Internet at www.jimgarlow.com. Please follow the site links to *How God Saved Civilization*, chapter 10 study helps.

A Fire
in England

John Wesley and
the Methodists

Dates covered: A.D. 1703-1791
Key persons: Susannah Wesley, John Wesley, Charles Wesley

Eighty years old and still preaching! Forrest shook his head in amazement at the announcement of John Wesley's 80th birthday. At least the old preacher had listened to reason and stopped traveling by horseback. Forrest was happy to see the positive reports of his hero's ministry. Twenty years ago, Wesley had received boos and jeers. Forrest rested his head against the high-backed chair where he always read his Bible in the morning sun. He allowed his mind to caress the memories. He could see himself, an unkempt, foulmouthed miner's boy, 10 years old, who could drink nearly as much as his father, Thomas. The year was 1740; the place, Bristol, England. They would awake in the dark and be on the road by 5 A.M. Often Forrest would have to shake his father awake, having dragged him home from the tavern the night before. If all else failed, he would break the ice off the water bucket, and throw a dipperful onto his father's face. That cold morning in November started the same as many others had before, only an hour later, but it would change Forrest's life. Once again Forrest had wakened his father; once again he had received a blow across his shoulders, this time for having let the coal fire go out; once again he had stood between his mother's fear and his father's rage, managing to soften the blows that she, too, received.

As Forrest and his father walked listlessly to a new day's work, they joined the other miners along the road. Curses and foul talk mixed in the air with the morning mist and the stench of workers unwashed from their carousing the night before. Ahead of them, a murmur had arisen in the crowd. Forrest lifted his head. A little amusement was always welcome, for it would buy him a few minutes of free time. But as they approached the shouts, he realized it was only a field preacher. *How annoying those men are,* he thought. *It is easy for them to hand out rules. They don't have to work in the mines*! Forrest looked at the short man who spoke so boldly to all these strong miners. It took some courage, he had to admit. His dad stopped to stare and to curse. They listened a little longer. Thomas spat on the ground. Then Forrest watched his father bend down and pick up a fair-sized stone. With amazing precision for a man who seemed constantly drunk, Forrest's father hurled the stone straight at the preacher. The preacher's shoulder was struck by the stone and he stumbled and turned to peer through the mist. Forrest's father advanced belligerently.

Oh, no! Forrest thought. It was one thing to make fun of the man, another thing to injure him. His dad might end up in prison and then what would become of the family? Forrest pushed ahead of his father, trying once again to keep him from striking out. But the preacher had not backed away. He had jumped off the box on which he had been standing and was coming straight toward them. Gently, the preacher reached out and drew the young boy to the side. He looked straight into Forrest's face. Forrest had cringed and closed his eyes, expecting the worst. But instead of an explosive rain of blows, Forrest heard the strong voice of the preacher. Forrest watched his father's reaction to the preacher's calm words. "For you Christ has died. For your sins, He was crucified."

What Forrest saw next, he could not believe. His father, a physically powerful man, could easily have beaten the preacher to a pulp; but instead, his father's eyes filled with tears. He slumped and fell weeping to his knees before the preacher. "God, forgive me!" he begged. "Forgive me, forgive me, a poor sinner."

Forrest followed his father to meetings held by the preacher every morning from that day on. It had taken some getting used to, seeing his dad sober, learning to read, insisting that he treat his mother and sisters as a gentleman should. The change was so spectacular that even the preacher, Mr. Wesley himself, was amazed. But best of all was the change in his mother.

Forrest remembered the first morning he had heard a soft, lilting tune coming from the barn. He had put his head round Bessie, the cow, to find his mother rocking slowly on the milking stool, her tears mixing with the milk. "Jesus, the name that charms our fears, that bids our sorrows cease," sang his mother quietly. "'Tis music in the sinner's ear; 'tis life and health, and peace." Forrest had stood beside her and quietly joined in. He knew the song, too, for it was Mr. Wesley's brother who had written it. "He breaks the power of canceled sin, He sets the prisoner free; His blood can make the foulest clean; His blood availed for me."

Forrest's thoughts raced to the present. Thomas, his father, had died in 1761, at the age of 49. But Thomas had become a lay preacher himself long before that. *Dad would want me to write John Wesley a note of congratulations and tell him how he taught me to be a true man of God, a good husband and a loving father,* thought Forrest. *But most of all I must thank Mr. Wesley for showing me Jesus.* He reached for the drawer in his writing desk and pulled out a sheet of his finest stationery. He would do it immediately.

JOHN WESLEY

Finally, all eight children were asleep and Susannah dropped onto her own bed, exhausted. But in the night a piercing scream woke her. Smelling the acrid odor of smoke, she jumped out of bed. "Samuel!" she called, shaking her husband awake. "The children!" Samuel and Susannah dashed from room to room in the English country home, gathering up the children and herding them out into the cool evening air at some distance from the burning structure, where they stood watching the flames destroy their house. Susannah clutched her children and wondered, *Was this the hand of God or of the parishioner who had been so angry with Samuel's preaching and decisions in the church?*

As the flames crackled, Susannah stood shivering next to the neighbors and parishioners. They had given up fighting the fire. *So many happy and sad memories,* thought Susannah. Of the 19 children born to her, 11 had died in infancy, but she thanked God for the eight she now had. She glanced down at them, crowded around her in the shadows of the old oak tree. She tried to account for them. What did a house matter? She gazed back at the flaming structure. Suddenly, she stepped forward and screamed, "John!" She ran toward the house, calling her five-year-old's name. "John! John!" Samuel ran after her and grabbed her from behind, restraining her, holding her close. Immediately the men from the church and the community ran forward again. One man climbed on the shoulders of a friend and others helped a third to stand on his shoulders. Gradually a human ladder formed, the men leaning where they could against the wall. It seemed agonizingly slow to Susannah, but they broke through the window glass and pulled a frightened John Wesley from his bedroom window into the night air. Down he was passed from one to the next until finally one man ran back and placed him in his mother's arms. Susannah Wesley held John close. "Truly," she said with Zechariah 3:2 in mind, "you are a brand plucked from the burning."

Susannah's statement would later be understood by Wesley to be an announcement of destiny. And destiny it was. The boy who was pulled from the fire as a "brand plucked from the burning" would have unimaginable impact on Christianity. It was not apparent that day in 1709, nor was it obvious even during the first 35 years of his life. But by 1738 a series of events would occur through which God would make Wesley into one of the single most influential leaders in all of Christian history.

CHILDHOOD AND EARLY EDUCATION

John Wesley was born in 1703. He was the 15th child born to Samuel and Susannah Wesley (only eight children survived infancy). The Wesley home, in contrast to what one might think, was highly orderly and managed methodically. Susannah was a genius at organizing her home and making certain her children were equally organized in their personal spiritual development, their theology and their academic pursuits.

The fire in the above true story was not an accidental fire. A member of the church where Samuel Wesley was the rector, became so upset with the pastor that he decided to torch the parsonage! Perhaps the kind of resistance that Samuel Wesley endured would help his son, John, to endure the volumes of criticism he would later receive. As was common for the young Wesley men, John went off to Charter House School in London in 1714 and finally to Christ Church College at Oxford University in 1720.

PREPARATION FOR MINISTRY

Although Wesley completed his bachelor of arts degree in 1724, it was not until four years later that his thinking began to solidify into ideas, strategies and ministry goals that would affect an entire nation. Many of the books Wesley read shaped his thinking.

At age 23, Wesley was reading Jeremy Taylor's *Rules and Exercise of Holy Living and Dying*. Two words from the title give us hints of themes in Wesley's future ministry. One is the phrase "holy living." Years later, people all over the world would know John Wesley as one of the primary forces that had restored an emphasis upon holiness to Christianity. Also intriguing in Jeremy Taylor's book title is the term "dying." It would be said many years later that Methodists "knew how to die well," meaning that they experienced great peace when it was time to go from this life to the next.

In 1725, John Wesley was ordained to the ministry by Bishop Potter. The following year he began to read the *Imitation of Christ* by Thomas à

Kempis, another book that shaped his thinking. But we see in the very fact that he chose to read it, the longing in his heart for righteous living and a disciplined walk with Christ. In that same year, 1726, he was elected a fellow, which is essentially a teaching assistant at Lincoln College, part of Oxford University. This was no small honor, and Wesley understood it to be a position of significance, one he would relish for years to come.

In 1726-27, Wesley was influenced by another writer, one William Law, who wrote *Christian Perfection and a Serious Call*. The phrase "Christian perfection" would surface in Wesley's preaching and teaching in the years ahead. His name would forever be linked to the phrase "Christian perfection," but it was an emphasis that gained for him many critics.

Finally, in 1727, he received his master of arts degree and, as was common in his day, he always listed "M.A." after his name from that time on. In 1728, he was officially ordained as a priest in the Anglican church, the Church of England.

EARLY MINISTRY

John Wesley's father, Samuel, looked forward to his son's graduating and becoming a priest. He had dreams of young John serving with him in his church. In 1729, Samuel's dream came true when John came to serve with him in the small community of Epworth. However, after his Oxford years, John found Epworth to be an understimulating environment. He had thrived on his years at Oxford and couldn't wait to return.

Upon returning to the campus, he was drawn to a group of like-minded students—serious students, not the party animals that populated Oxford at the time. John's friends were known as the Holy Club. Their desire was simple: to practice primitive Christianity. "Primitive" in this case meant New Testament Christianity. They wanted to return to the simplicity and purity of living out the Christian faith as people had lived it in the New Testament.

By 1730, the members of The Holy Club had begun systematically to visit prisons, attend to the poor and take care of the sick. The orderly manner in which they lived their lives caused them to be nicknamed "Methodists." To be a Methodist was not a compliment. Methodist meant that one was very methodical, and methodical they were with so many hours a week of involvement in ministry.

So serious was Wesley about biblical study that he called himself *homo unius libri,* meaning "the man of one book." It certainly didn't mean that he read only the Bible; Wesley read widely. But his commitment to biblical authority had emerged in full force by this time. His early ministry period ended on April 20, 1735, the same year that his father died.

THE ATTEMPT TO BE A MISSIONARY

In September of 1735, Wesley was approved to become a missionary to the New World, to the Georgia Colony. He was sent by the evangelistic wing of the Anglican church, known as the Society for the Propagation of the Gospel. On October 21, 1735, he set sail on the ship called *Simmonds,* to what would be a very disappointing season of his life. One with the personality and academic credentials of John Wesley was poorly fitted for the rough, and in his opinion, barbarous world, in the Georgia Colony. He went with the intention of being a missionary to the Indians. What sent him home three years later was not the Indians, but his inability to adapt to the white people of Savannah, Georgia.

One of the prime examples of his inability to adapt was revealed in a courtship issue. Historians have speculated that John thought all women were like his mother, who had been a highly organized administrator, a brilliant theologian and an articulate defender of her political positions. John mistakenly assumed that what a woman needed was a cerebral and theological point of connection.

During the course of Wesley's life he courted several women. While living in the Georgia Colony he was drawn to one named Sophia Hopkey. John and Sophia enjoyed many wonderful moments together, and a marriage seemed natural. But Wesley consistently had great difficulty courting women. He could discuss theology with them. He enjoyed their company. But he did not seem to know how to meet the emotional needs of a woman. Whatever the reasons for his failure, one woman after another courted John and married someone else. The story of his later marriage is one of disaster.

Sophia Hopkey, like those who would follow, grew weary of waiting on Wesley for a proposal. She began to court someone else whose engagement proposal she accepted. Wesley was crushed. In typical Wesley rigidity he kept the letter of the law and refused to serve Communion to Sophia and others. This infuriated the roughshod residents of the Georgia Colony. His authoritarianism was not appreciated in a colony that prided itself in its rugged individualism. The result was that John Wesley literally ran for his life.

On February 1, 1738, he landed back in England, much to the shock of his sending agency, the Society of the Propagation of the Gospel, which refused him permission to return. John resigned his pastorate in Savannah and moved on to the next phase of his life, which was the one that caused him to be included in this chapter. If John Wesley had died before 1738, he would not have rated any notice at all from historians. Instead, countless books have been written about him and those he has influenced.

CONVERSION AND EXPANDED MINISTRY

On May 24, 1738, Wesley attended a small Bible study on Aldersgate Street in London in the shadow of Saint Paul's Cathedral. Someone stood and read from the preface of Martin Luther's commentary on the book of Romans. Much has been made of Wesley's response to what was read. Some of it may be legendary. But it was most assuredly pivotal.

> About a quarter before nine, while he was describing the change which God works in the heart through faith in Christ, I felt my heart strangely warmed. I felt I did trust in Christ, Christ alone for salvation; and an assurance was given me that He had taken *my* sins, even *mine*, and saved *me* from the law of sin and death.[1]

The key phrase from this important quote is "I felt my heart strangely warmed." That became the hallmark phrase of the "people called Methodists."[2]

Wesley's life was significantly changed from that moment on. He would repeatedly look back to it as the time when his faith became vital. So significant was that moment to the many who would later follow Wesley that the "warmed heart" would be a hallmark of not only Methodists but also many others who would be influenced by the movement. To have a warmed heart meant that one truly did experience God. It meant that faith was not merely cerebral. Being a Christian was not merely a process of embracing theological dogma or truth. One could actually know God, feel

Him and sense His presence. Wesley, perhaps for the first time, *felt* his faith. The necessity of such a heart confirmation of one's faith would become a significant characteristic of the people called Methodists.

But Wesley's conversion was not the only significant thing that occurred in that pivotal year, 1738. On November 30, George Whitefield arrived back from a preaching mission in Georgia. Whereas Wesley's Georgia experience had been disastrous, Whitefield told spectacular accounts of people's responding to the gospel. An aggressive preacher and evangelist, Whitefield challenged Wesley to leave the safe sanctuaries of the Church of England and preach outdoors.

Outdoor preaching was not a new phenomenon. Many had tried it already, some with positive and some with negative responses. Outdoor preaching had proved to be an effective method of delivering the gospel to those who would not be likely to enter a church, but it was also an effective method for receiving injuries from stones, hurled by those who wished preachers would *stay* in the churches. Of all preachers, John Wesley was not the kind to preach outdoors. He thrived on the liturgy and even expressed his appreciation of the attire worn by the Anglican priests.

But Whitefield's influence upon Wesley was significant. On April 2, 1739, Wesley embarked on an event that would forever change his life—outdoor preaching. The response of the coal miners walking to work at 5:00 A.M. in Bristol, England, was far more than Wesley could have anticipated.

The response to Wesley's preaching was dramatic. Within a short period of time he was worrying not so much about preaching outside, as about what to do with all the people who were responding to the gospel. He quickly saw that young believers needed spiritual cultivation. So he borrowed from his German friends, the Moravians, the idea of organizing people into small accountability groups. These were simply called the United Societies. At the time, Wesley never envisioned that the numbers of his converts would be so large and so exuberant that they would insist on separating from the Church of England that he loved so much. However, as is often the case in revival, the old wineskins simply could not contain the new wine. The United Societies would one day become the foundation for the Methodist church, a movement totally separate from the Church of England; but that separation was still 50 years away.

THE REVIVAL EXPLODES AND MATURES

By 1744, the revival was no longer a new event, but it continued to attract large numbers of people. With success came persecution. Wesley was maligned for almost every position he took. So many articles and pamphlets were printed against him that an annotated bibliography of the material fills an entire book. But criticism didn't dampen the spirit of what became known as the Wesleyan revival. Across England people continued to come to Christ. But that only posed additional problems for Wesley.

How do you take care of so many baby Christians? How do you encourage them to keep growing? How do you keep them from going back to their previous ways? And how do you find and train enough leaders to care for all the new believers? How do you encourage and help those leaders? Perhaps no figure in Church history was better equipped to solve the organizational challenges of a massive new movement than John Wesley. He had clearly inherited the organizational genius of his mother, Susannah.

Wesley began to strategize about how to conserve the tremendous fruit of this massive move of God. He began to train and equip laypersons for ministry on a scale unprecedented in all Church history.

THE ANNUAL CONFERENCE

In 1744, he organized his first annual conference, which proved to have many long-term results. He did it for the purpose of directing, equipping and encouraging all the lay preachers who were traveling under his ministry. The annual conference would be a predominant mark of Methodism and all of the denominations that find their roots in this awakening. Later, most denominations would borrow from Wesley's annual meeting. Why was it important? This was Wesley's time to bring together the key lay pastors who had traveled the assigned regions (circuits) of England. A lay preacher traveled a circuit of 5 or 10 locations where he was assigned to minister. As more and more people came to Christ, the circuits had to be subdivided, because one person could not keep up with the demand.

LAY PREACHERS

Who were the lay preachers attending these conferences? Where did they come from? How did Wesley decide to use them? We need to understand the context of the Wesleyan Revival. We view the Wesleyan Revival positively

from our perspective. But in the early years of the revival, Wesley was severely criticized. First of all, he was an enthusiast. He preached with vigor. He
believed that one could feel one's religion. Such outward emotion was considered very unsophisticated by most Anglican priests. In fact, of all the
Anglican pastors at the time, only about 40 were sympathetic to the great
evangelical awakening. Most of them were unwilling to help cultivate the
lives of new believers. What was Wesley to do?

He tried desperately to keep up. He traveled tirelessly from one part of
the nation to another, preaching several times a day. On one particular occasion he arrived late back in London to preach to a group of people, including his mother, Susannah, who had gathered. In his absence, a layman by
the name of Thomas Maxfield stood and preached. When he was finished,
he dismissed them and sent them home. Wesley arrived a few moments
later. He stopped by his mother's house to find out what had happened. He
was furious when he learned that a layman had had the audacity to stand
and preach. He was determined to correct Thomas Maxfield for his unpar-
donable action, until his mother said to him, "Rebuke him if you will John,
but he is as called to preach as you are."

John Wesley never rebuked Thomas Maxfield. Instead, he began to train
lay preachers to spread out across England to proclaim the gospel and to
organize into small Bible study groups those who responded to the gospel.
In the years that followed, Wesley trained 653 lay preachers, 57 percent of
whom stayed with his ministry till their deaths. This does not include another category of lay ministers called the local preachers who did not travel, but
who had spiritual responsibility over a small geographical area.

JOHN WESLEY'S RIGHT-HAND MAN

The rapid growth of the Wesley Revival caused Wesley to need several generals for his vast army. His key right-hand man was his brother, Charles,
who was close to him both emotionally and spiritually. They had shared
experiences at Oxford University and spiritual experiences as a part of the
Holy Club in that university town. In 1749, John Wesley officiated at the
wedding of his brother, Charles, to Sarah Gwynne, which proved to be a
happy and successful marriage.

Charles's spiritual insights and musical genius profoundly influenced
the evangelical awakening in Britain. Charles was younger than John, a bit

more somber than the exuberant John, and was converted just three days before his older brother. A faithful companion to John for over 20 years of travel, Charles had to leave John and their missionary work in Georgia in 1736, due to sickness. The same was to occur in 1756 when Charles, once again, could not physically withstand the rigors of traveling with John.

However, Charles's frailer constitution did not prevent him from having a solid, influential ministry. And he wrote over 6,500 hymns; some of the better-known are

- "Hark, the Herald Angels Sing!"
- "Christ the Lord Is Risen Today"
- "O, For a Thousand Tongues to Sing"
- "Jesus, Lover of My Soul"
- "Love Divine, All Loves Excelling"

MARRIAGE

In 1749, the same year that John performed the wedding ceremony for Charles and Sarah, he developed a meaningful relationship with a woman named Grace Murray. Frankly, she could have been and should have been the "Mother of Methodism." But once again, John, whose relationships with women often suffered, lacked the ability to relate appropriately in courtship. Instead, in 1751 he married a Mrs. Vazeille. Why he married this rather strange and neurotic woman is a mystery. He had had numerous opportunities to marry outstanding women. It is believed that his marriage with Mrs. Vazeille may never have been physically consummated. Wesley and his wife were formally separated in 1755, but due to his constant travel schedule, it seems unlikely that he ever spent much time with her. In 1781, he simply notes in his diary that she died.

This minor-key strain in John Wesley's life offers a simple but intriguing footnote of history: all great saints of God still have feet of clay, or areas in which their lives fall far short of God's desires. All the greats of Church history have some point of observable weakness. Yet as God looks down from heaven, He sees beyond those flaws and instead causes the strengths of His saints to flourish and to work His will. Certainly, this truth is demonstrated in Wesley.

HIS WRITING

In 1766, Wesley wrote *A Plain Account of Christian Perfection*. The title reveals one of the major thrusts of early Methodism: one should be able to experience pure motives, pure love. One's love of God and love of neighbor should be evidenced in very practical ways. One's *methods* may be tainted by the fall of Adam, but one's *motives* could be so pure as to be referred to as Christian perfection. Wesley was severely criticized for this position. No one can live perfectly, his critics exclaimed. And they were right. But Wesley was defining "perfection" differently. He was not using the Latin word *perfectus,* which means "unimprovable." Wesley, influenced by the Desert Fathers (Early Church monastic leaders), was using "perfection" from the Greek understanding of *telios.* According to this view, perfection was a moving target, a being all one can be at a given moment with full awareness that one can yet improve. The Latin understanding of perfection was static, a "having arrived." The Greek understanding, which Wesley embraced, was a journey, a growth experience, with new levels to be gained. Wesley's critics rarely understood these important distinctions. And contemporary critics of Wesleyanism still fail to grasp this important fact. Tragically, even some who call themselves Wesleyans do not comprehend the significance of the difference between the Latin *perfectus* and the Greek *telios.* The generations that would follow him would further refine and define the Wesley experience of sanctification, or living above sin. One of Wesley's great contributions to Christianity is precisely at this point. He challenged people to become all they could be for God. The result was untold numbers of people who desired to live with exceptional Christian maturity.

His view of Christian perfection was the source of only one of many controversies. By 1770, he was locking horns more intensely over Calvinism, opposing all of John Calvin's five theological points. Wesley embraced:

1. *Prevenient Grace*—God puts a safety net under humanity known as prevenient grace. Grace means God's special favor—His love for us. *Pre* means "before"; *vene* means "to come." So prevenient grace is God's special grace that comes before we even knew Him, before our conversion.

2. *Conditional Election*—God's choosing us is conditional, based upon our responding to Him.

3. *Unlimited Atonement*—Christ died for all and atonement is unlimited.

4. *Grace Can Be Resisted*—The grace of God can be, and tragically many times is, resisted.

5. *Loss of Salvation*—Instead of eternal security, people can and tragically do fall from their saved condition.

These beliefs are frequently labeled as Arminian, named after Dutch theologian Jacobus Arminius (1560-1609). Frequently, Wesley's views are referred to as Wesleyan/Arminian.

To be called an Arminian in Wesley's time was despicable. But Wesley did with that title what he had done with Methodism. He made it respectable. When the members of the Holy Club were nicknamed "Methodists" back at Oxford University, the term was meant to be pejorative. But Wesley kept the name Methodist and made it respectable. In fact he usually referred to those who followed him as the people called Methodists. He did the same thing with the accusation of Arminianism. He simply accepted it and made it reputable; he launched the magazine in 1778 known as *The Arminian Magazine*.

By 1778, the movement had matured both in its self-understanding and in its respectability in London. The persecution of Wesley had come to an end. Oddly enough, this fact concerned Wesley. He thought he must be doing something wrong to be receiving so much acclaim! That year marked a special, joyous time for him. He opened the beautiful City Road Chapel in London, which still stands as one of the hubs of the explosive Methodist movement. Across the street from the City Road Chapel is a cemetery where Susanna Wesley, John's mother, is buried. Also buried there are Isaac Watts, the famous hymnist, and John Bunyan, author of the popular book *Pilgrim's Progress*. Directly behind City Road Chapel is the burial place of John Wesley (he died March 2, 1791) and some of the key leaders of Methodism.

HOW GOD USED WESLEY

What are the great contributions of John Wesley to Christianity? What did God do through him? What was the Church's state of health during John Wesley's time, the phenomenal 1700s? One of the most surprising things we notice about Wesley was his flurry of activity. Few people have ever accomplished what he did. One writer suggested that "no Christian evangelist since St. Paul, Luther and Calvin could look back on more concrete results of his ministry."[3]

Another writer observed that with the exception of some people in political, scientific and military spheres, John Wesley received more biographical attention than any other Englishman during his century.[4] Methodist scholar Albert Outler noted that Wesley's phenomenal accomplishments emerged from obscurity and failure. He observed that

> if John Wesley had died at any time before his 36th birthday (17 June, 1739—a full 12 months *after* Aldersgate), his name would not rate a footnote in the history books. Considering situations in the spring of 1739. . . . he had failed as a teacher and had earned a reputation for being a little crack brained.[5] "He had been a leader of a religious society at Oxford, another sect society in Georgia, still a third in London—with no visible or lasting effects. . . . he published . . . a theological manifesto that had stirred no ripples. . . . he had . . . no power base. . . . (he had) next to nothing to show for 36 full years of high-minded diligence."[6] It is truly amazing that only 10 years later John Wesley was the "head of the most effective mass movement in eighteenth-century England."[7]

ENERGY AND EFFICIENCY

Wesley rose at 4:00 A.M. daily and was extremely efficient during his 18-hour days. He rode a quarter of a million miles, and probably knew England better than any other person of this century.[8] The list of cities and villages that Wesley visited is so extensive that it would be easier to count the places that he did not visit than the ones he did.[9] It is remarkable that John Wesley continued traveling by horseback until he was 70, covering 4,000 to 5,000 miles a year and as many as 80 miles a day.[10] It is believed that Wesley spent more time in the saddle than any other man who has ever lived, Bonaparte and Caesar not excepted.[11] To Wesley, the saddle became a library chair. In March of 1770, Wesley wrote:

> Nearly 30 years ago, I was thinking, How is it that no horse ever stumbles while I am reading? History, Poetry, and Philosophy I commonly

read on horse back, having other employment at other times. No account can possibly be given but this: Because then I throw the reins on his back. I then set myself to observe, and I aver that, in riding above a hundred thousand miles I scarce ever remember any horse (except two, that would fall head over heels anyway) to fall, or make a considerable stumble, while I rode with a slack rein.[12]

Only in his latest years did he leave his horse and ride in a carriage.

AUDIENCE

It is believed that John Wesley preached in excess of 40,000 times. Most days he preached as many as five times. The number of persons to whom Wesley preached is equally amazing. On September 21, 1773, he preached to an estimated 32,000 people in a large outdoor natural amphitheater known as Gwennap Pit. Although it is possible that the size of the crowd was overestimated, the numbers remain, by any standard, a staggeringly large crowd to preach to without the modern benefits of a public-address system.

Wesley wrote 233 books. In Wesley's era, ideas belonged more to the world than to individuals; and it was acceptable to borrow heavily (what today would be called plagiarism), so some of his books would more appropriately called revisions of works by other authors. However, it is still an amazing accomplishment. He was so faithful in journaling that one can trace almost exactly what he did each day of his life—the cities where he preached, his sermon topics and even the conversations he had with his friends.

LAY MINISTRY

But Wesley's life was much more than a burst of activity. He accomplished something profound. One of his most amazing innovations was his use of laity for ministry.

From our perspective, we do not realize how radical and unique this was. Church historians have noted that what Wesley did was revolutionary. It was unthinkable for laity to be involved in any significant ministry, and Wesley himself might never have used lay preachers, except for the enormous number of converts and the unwillingness of the clergy to help train them. But the Methodist movement grew under the leadership of its lay preachers until the membership at the time of Wesley's death was over 120,000.[13] Another writer has suggested that if you included the adherents of Methodism, the number following Wesley would have approached a million.[14] With such a large movement and so few Anglican clergy being supportive, Wesley desperately needed and managed to train an enormous army of lay workers. He trained over 600 traveling lay preachers. In addition, there were many local preachers. Local preachers did not travel but simply had oversight in their respective village or hamlet. In 1850, only 60 years after Wesley's death, there were over 20,000 local preachers. In addition to these two categories of lay influence, there was a third, that of the class leaders. There was roughly one class leader for every 10 Methodists. Some writers believe there were as many as 25,000 persons functioning in this particular ministry.[15] In addition to the lay preachers, local preachers and class leaders there were trustees, stewards, exhorters and other ministry positions. Wesley's high view of the role of laity was unprecedented in all of Church history.[16]

One of Wesley's most outstanding gifts was the ability to replicate himself. Of all the lay preachers he trained, none of them compared to Francis Asbury (1745-1816), who was sent by Wesley in 1771, at age 26, from Bristol, England, to Philadelphia. Although Methodism's arrival in the New World predated Asbury's arrival by several years, Asbury is the primary reason for Methodism's explosive growth in the newly formed nation. His statistics are nearly as impressive as Wesley's own. He traveled constantly by horseback over the course of four and a half decades. He covered an astounding 300,000 miles! He preached 16,000 sermons. He actually had no home. Consequently, he instructed those in Britain to address letters simply: "Francis Asbury, in America"! And, given his notoriety, the letters addressed this way probably found him. Asbury's quick ability to understand the New World, something Wesley never did, made him the perfect match for America. American Methodism's first bishop is responsible for the rapid expansion of the gospel in the colonies and later in the new nation.

EVANGELISM

Another area in which Wesley had a profound impact on Christianity was his view of evangelism. Christ's universal atonement, the fact that Christ died for all, was a jolting and profoundly liberating thought to Christians so deeply impacted by Calvinism. It validated people who otherwise would cower in fear, believing themselves not a part of the elect. Maybe Christ might have died for them! This thought gave value to people who previously had felt worthless.

ORGANIZATION

A fourth major way in which God used John Wesley was through his success in maintaining and preserving converts. Writers on this topic frequently contrast John Wesley with George Whitefield, another great evangelist. Whitefield preached to crowds as large as Wesley's, yet few people thought of themselves as followers of Whitefield after he died. What was the difference? Very simply, it was Wesley's organizational genius. Whitefield did not have a vast army of laypeople. He didn't have class leaders watching over the spiritual care of 10 other individuals. These unique organizational features of Methodism enabled it to sustain, nourish and maintain a massive movement.

HOLINESS

A fifth way in which God profoundly shaped the Church through Wesley was through his call to holiness. He did not believe that one should just barely sneak inside the gates of Christianity while continuing in sin. Sinning Christianity was not a part of Wesley's understanding of biblical truth. He called on believers to live in Christian perfection, to mature and to grow. In fact, if they didn't, they were sometimes reprimanded. In the class meetings, which were held weekly, the class leader would stand and ask the question, "How is it with your soul?" Every person was to be ruthlessly honest and explain how he or she was doing in spiritual growth. This kind of honesty and accountability, fueled by the expectation that one could have pure motives, caused holiness to be the heart cry of many of the followers of John Wesley.

A WORKINGMAN'S RELIGION

A sixth profound way that God shaped the Church through John Wesley was the validation of the lower socioeconomic classes. Although many wealthy people followed Wesley, most of his converts were poor. Wesley's presentation of the gospel to them gave them a sense of hope and value. The fact that they could function in roles of responsibility (such as class leaders, local preachers or lay pastors) gave them opportunities to develop in ways that the contemporary culture did not. Evidence shows that the people trained to be class leaders and local preachers became so confident in their organizational skills to mobilize other people that later generations of them became leaders of labor unions, organized on a local basis. Wesley's powerful, emotive presentation of the gospel grabbed the hearts of the lower classes and resulted in a complete transformation of the nation.

Closely associated with this confidence was social reform. Wesley said that there was no holiness that is not social holiness, meaning simply that holiness pervades an entire culture. Through the influence of the massive Wesleyan movement, the conditions of a nation were altered. Child labor laws were instituted which brought an end to the abuse of children. Most significant was Wesley's influence through a member of parliament by the name of William Wilburforce, who almost single-handedly brought an end to slavery in the entire British Empire. Methodism's emphasis on holiness saved marriages and reunited families. The result was the transformation of a nation.

Anyone who looks at England in the 1700s and sees the work of John Wesley, this tireless, passionate saint of God, would agree that the Church of Jesus Christ was truly alive and well. And a healthy Church was and still is God's great plan for preserving anything of value within civilization. The Church—God's people—"salted" into the nature of everyday life is God's one and only plan for saving civilization.

To further assist you in understanding the key individuals and events of chapter 11, study questions, charts, diagrams, time lines and links to biographical websites are available on the Internet at www.jimgarlow.com. Please follow the site links to *How God Saved Civilization*, chapter 11 study helps.

FIRE IN THE
NEW WORLD

THE FIRST
GREAT AWAKENING

Dates covered: A.D. 1667-1833
Key persons: Roger Williams, Francis Makemie, Solomon Stoddard,
Jonathan Edwards, George Whitefield, Junipero Serra

Winford hacked at the next dry cornstalk. The stalks made good bed-
ding for the cows through the cold winter. Over the last few years at
the farm, the palms of his hands had toughened so that even the rough
stalks could not pierce his calloused skin. He straightened up, proudly sur-
veyed his 23 acres, and watched with delight as the rolling hills and wooded
areas softened as a shower of sunlight broke past the forest line.

As the light poured down upon him, he began to think about his family. Life was hard in New England in the 1740s. Over the last nine years, his
wife, Ruth, had given birth to six wonderful children, but two infants had
died from sickness through the cold, harsh winters. Ruth's devotion to raising four small children didn't provide her the time to help Winford in milking the cows or hitching the horses. He missed her help in the outside
chores, but he loved Ruth's care for the children and was eager to celebrate
their ninth wedding anniversary tomorrow. Yet he kept wondering how the
children would grow up.

Winford stacked the stalks on his wagon. He knew rugged farm life
was not the problem. Children needed to work hard, to honor their parents
and to help their neighbors. No, Winfred was worried that his children
would never learn about God. The duties of the farm left them little time
for church. One day rolled into another without a break. Each season
seemed as difficult as the last. Right now, preparation for the cold
Massachusetts winter was an endless task. But in the spring he had had
just as much work, clearing the land of trees, one by one, and of the endless rocks. So far he had cleared over 12 acres from which he had harvested
two crops of corn.

Winford knew that he and Ruth could teach the children some things
about God, but their training was limited—neither of them was a scholar or
Bible teacher. It was Winford's mother who had taught him about the Bible;
he could only remember a few things now—some stories and a few commandments. He thought about his childhood and the times his family went
to the local Congregational church up to the time he was 12 when they
moved too far away to attend. Now, as a father, he felt very responsible for
how his children would grow in the Lord, but the nearest church was two
miles away as the crow flies and more than four when taking the family
wagon over the bridge. *How important is it for my children to know about God?*
he thought. *Why did he and Ruth not care more about spiritual things?*

Winford's thoughts were interrupted by a cry. He looked around the fields but saw no one. As he bent over to cut loose another stalk, he heard another scream. When he looked up this time, he saw Mary Bensette running along the fence line that separated his farm from the Bensette farm. She was waving her arms and hollering something to her husband, John, who was plowing some 50 yards away. Concerned, Winford dropped the large corn knife and ran toward the fence. Finally, John heard his wife's call as well and ran toward her. The three of them arrived at a common point at almost the same moment. "What is it, Mary?" John and Winford asked at the same time.

"Whitefield," she gasped, totally out of breath.

"Where?" said John.

"At First Congregational . . . right now!"

"What are you two talking about?" exclaimed Winford, wondering at this coded message.

"It's Whitefield," explained John, as if this one word were enough.

"Who . . . or what is Whitefield?" Winford asked, with an edge of impatience.

"George Whitefield!" John said. "The great preacher from England, in our town! Whenever George Whitefield comes, things happen. It's amazing. We heard him several years ago when he spoke in Northampton. We never saw anything like it before. If you've never heard him, you must go now and hear him for yourself."

Winford looked at Mary. Her face was happier than Winford had ever seen it. "I'm busy this afternoon," said Winford, "maybe I'll go another time."

"Now!" demanded Mary. "You must go now."

"But Ruth . . . and the kids . . ."

"I will watch the children and you will take Ruth." Winford had never seen Mary so dogmatic. There was no arguing.

Less than an hour later, Winford and Ruth were sitting in the large field behind the schoolhouse. Though Winford felt skeptical at first, he couldn't help smiling. Just an hour ago, he had been wondering whether he should try to get back to church, and here he was, listening to a preacher! And not just any preacher. As Mr. Whitefield began to preach, several began to cry out . . . frightened at the thought of facing God without the forgiveness of sins.

One person to the left of Winford fell facedown on the ground. Winford and Ruth felt a twinge of discomfort as they watched the two demonstrative listeners. But their attention was quickly drawn back to the preacher from England. As Whitefield's booming voice echoed across the hills, easily heard by the hundreds who had gathered to hear him, Winford put his arm around his wife's shoulders. Ruth looked up at him. They didn't need to say anything. Both of them knew that they had been putting their own daily concerns above their faith in God. Were Christ to return today, He would not find them ready to meet God. But they wanted to be. Winford pulled his wife tight against his side and lowered his head. Hers, too, bowed in repentance. Their little homestead would never be the same again; Christ had moved in.

THE NEW WORLD

Our interest in Europe lessens now, as we see something of great significance happening in the New World: what we refer to as America. The seventeenth century was an intensely active and vigorous time in the founding of religious groups in the New World. Wrote Earl Cairns:

> Nearly every one of the Protestant churches of the Reformation came to be represented in America between 1607 and 1732. Distance from Europe, the early rise of voluntarism and consequent control of the Church, recurrent revivals, the influence of the frontier, and the relative religious radicalism of the "groups" who came to America has made American Christianity amazingly creative in its activities.[1]

Many motives have been suggested in trying to explain why people would leave their safe homeland in England in order to come to a dangerous and unknown New World. Some argue for the profit motive. Others contend that overcrowded living conditions were bad enough to force people abroad. The New World offered limitless expanses of land. But when we examine the writings of those who came, we see that religious freedom was the driving force that caused most people to risk the transoceanic voyage to eke out an existence in the New World.

JAMESTOWN

The cost of a trip to the New World was so high that people had to join together in joint-stock companies, a forerunner of the modern corporation, in order to finance the trip. The Virginia Company sent settlers to Jamestown (in what is now called Virginia) in 1607. Robert Hunt, a chaplain, helped establish the Anglican church there and was the first to serve Communion to the colonists as they sat on logs, shaded by the sail that had been removed from their boat.

Two events which influenced the destiny of the future nation occurred in 1612 and 1619, respectively:

- colonists learned that they could grow tobacco;
- colonists began to purchase slaves from Dutch traders for the purpose of working the tobacco plantations.

The colonists could not have imagined that 242 years later the consequences of their business maneuver would lead their new nation into civil war, with tragic results. As the years passed, more and more Puritan Anglicans migrated from England. In 1624, the Virginia Company was dissolved, for Virginia was now a royal colony with a governor appointed by the king. The Church of England (the Anglican church) was the official, established church of the colony.

PURITANS AND SEPARATISTS

The Puritans got their name from the fact that they wanted to purify the Church of England. Many felt they could best accomplish the purifying process by staying within the Church. Some, however, argued for separation from the Church of England and became known as Separatists. At that time, separating from the Church was not the same as it is today. Today one can go from one church to another with very little recrimination, because there are many acceptable denominations. However, in England at the time, there was only one legally recognized Church, funded by the government, and every individual was automatically a member, unless you opted out of membership.

Separatists were harassed, threatened and sometimes imprisoned. Ruffians would just happen to disrupt their worship services. Weary of such treatment, Robert Browne led some Separatists to Holland, where they would be free to worship as they wished. However, these Englishmen realized with regret that their children would soon be absorbed into the Dutch culture, and the English were unhappy about this notion. Leaving Leyden, Holland, the Separatists decided to go to the New World where they could establish a pure Church. In August of 1620, 102 English Separatists left England for the New World, sailing from Plymouth harbor. Their destination: Virginia. However, a storm blew them northward and they landed in Massachusetts. So unprepared were they to face the first brutal winter, that half of them died within a few months. But they were a hardy, courageous and well-organized people. Before they had left the Mayflower, 41 of the men on board signed the Mayflower Compact, a legal document to govern them. The compact stated that the purpose of the new colony was to bring glory to God and to advance the Christian cause. Consequently, the Church was the center of not only their spiritual life but their social life as well.

NEW WORLD SETTLEMENTS

Though the first few years nearly destroyed them, large numbers of Puritans eventually began crossing the ocean. After 1628, the towns of Salem and Boston were organized. Their church government was a Congregational system, in which each congregation had complete autonomy and the right to self-government. Because they all shared the same Calvinistic theology, they had a nearly total uniformity of faith. In 1631, the Massachusetts General Court made church membership mandatory. Truly, it was a New Israel, as they liked to refer to it. Boston was perceived to be the "city set on a hill." Its reputation soon drew over 20,000 more Puritans from England. Expansions of Puritans continued westward across the fertile Connecticut River valley. The Cambridge Synod of 1646 outlined the unity of theology and church government. The representatives who gathered there agreed on the Westminster Confession as their doctrinal statement and on the Cambridge Platform as their form of church government. Each church was independent of other churches, but all were bound together by a common church covenant. Agreeing with the covenant was the requirement for joining the church. Everything looked good. Their dreams were fulfilled!

But the Puritans had forgotten Old Testament history. A generation devoted to God was often followed by a generation who "did that which was

right in [their] own eyes" (Judg. 21:25, *KJV*). The Puritans had failed to antic-
ipate that within a few years a generation would arise that would not be committed to the covenant principles. All the original adult citizens were in the
New World because they loved the principles of God's covenant. But their
children and grandchildren had not chosen this structure, and would not all
desire to follow it. This painful problem would create a massive dilemma.

ROGER WILLIAMS

Puritan churches with Calvinist theology and Congregational government
were not the only ones developing in the New World. Roger Williams,
another Anglican-trained Cambridge graduate who embraced the views of
Separatism, had ideas of his own. Although initially he seemed to fit right
in, differences quickly emerged. Williams opposed the idea of a state church
and argued that one particular denominational group should not be funded as the official state church. In addition, he felt that political leaders
(most of whom were pastors) should have no power to choose for another
man how he was to worship. Williams also felt that the Native Americans
should be allowed to maintain their own land. Eventually his views became
so objectionable that he was driven out of Plymouth. He wandered southward, where friendly Native Americans helped him through the bitter winter. In 1636, he founded Providence (in what is now Rhode Island) on land
that he purchased from the Native Americans.

OTHER OUTCASTS

Roger Williams was not the only one forced to leave Plymouth. Ann
Hutchinson, about to give birth to a child, was forced out in the bitter winter and had to walk all the way from her Massachusetts community to
Providence. Along with Roger Williams, she helped found in 1639 what is
believed to be the first Baptist church in America. Members of this new
church were rebaptized, perhaps by immersion, the mode of baptism that
would become characteristic of all Baptist churches. (There is a debate
about whether the first Baptist church was in Newport or Providence. But
in either case, the Baptist movement was started in Rhode Island under the
Roger Williams's charter.) This expression of the Christian faith would
spread so rapidly across America that it would become the largest

Protestant denomination. Williams passionately advocated the separation of Church and state, and freedom of conscience in worship.

ESTABLISHMENT

However, in Williams's day, 9 of the 13 colonies had an established church. The Anglican church made enormous gains in the New World. It displaced a strong Catholic hold in Maryland, becoming Maryland's established church in 1702, and a Dutch Reformed hold in New York in 1693. It took over South Carolina in 1706, Georgia in 1758 and North Carolina in 1765. All of these colonies remained Anglican until after the American Revolution. The credit for this rapid Anglican expansion goes in part to the Society for the Propagation of the Gospel in Foreign Parts, which was founded in 1701 and which sent more than 300 missionaries to the colonies, among whom were the two Wesley brothers. Only a few islands of Catholic influence remained.

A PATCHWORK OF GROUPS

Roger Williams, with his Baptist views, was not the only one to clash with Puritans over the issue of the separation of Church and state. Quakers (the Society of Friends), founded by George Fox, made their way to the New World and quickly clashed with the New England Puritans. New Jersey was divided into East and West after 1674, and West Jersey became a Quaker settlement. The Quaker movement is most closely associated with the name William Penn, a wealthy man with massive landholdings (now known as Pennsylvania). Penn chose to open his colony to virtually anyone. The result was that an enormous variety of Christian faiths quickly assembled, giving the state a most spectacular and unusual patchwork of unique groups. Quakers were joined by Mennonites, Moravians and Lutherans (who had begun their American adventure in the Dutch colony of New Amsterdam). Pennsylvania and the middle colonies became known for an intriguing religious diversity, while the southern colonies preferred Anglicanism and the northern colonies Congregationalism.

FRANCIS MAKEMIE

In 1683, an Irishman who became known as the father of American Presbyterianism arrived in the colonies. Educated in Scotland, Francis

Makemie (1658-1708) was commissioned to serve as a Presbyterian missionary to America. He founded the First Presbyterian Church in America at Snow Hill, Maryland, in 1684. He was an aggressive evangelist, covering New York, Maryland, Virginia and North Carolina. By 1706, he had brought Presbyterians together from several backgrounds (Irish, Scottish, Welsh and English) and unified their beliefs around the Westminster Confession. Events in the Old World would soon bring a large influx to the New World.

By 1715, due to economic discrimination against Presbyterians in Ireland, a staggering 100,000 Presbyterians had come to America. So rapid was the growth of Presbyterians that they soon joined the Anglicans, the Baptists and the Congregationalists as one of the largest churches in the colonies. Notes Cairns:

> The various churches created by the Reformation were transplanted in America during the first one hundred and fifty years of the history of the colonies. Except for a while in Maryland and the Middle colonies, an established Church held sway until the American Revolution. After the Revolution, the separation of Church and state made the churches of America dependent upon voluntary support for money to finance their ventures and upon evangelism to win the unchurched and the children of the members of the church into the fellowship of the church.[2]

EDUCATION AND CHURCH GROWTH

Nothing is so impressive about the growth of Protestant Christianity in the New World as its deep commitment to Christian education. It is remarkable to think that Harvard College was founded in 1636, only 16 short years after the colonists arrived—a remarkable feat, considering the fact that almost all of their energy went into surviving. Named for John Harvard, a man who willed his library and half of his estate to the new college, Harvard was started for the purpose of making the gospel known. William and Mary College was founded in Williamsburg, Virginia, in 1693, with the hope that it would produce good ministers. Yale College was founded in 1701 to give youths religious education. Colleges and churches flourished. Edwin Scott Gaustad has done a thorough analysis of the growth of churches in the New World. From 1660 to 1740, the growth was spectacular:

- Anglicans went from 41 congregations to 246;
- Baptists, from 4 to 96;
- Congregationalists, from 75 to an amazing 423;
- Dutch Reformed, from 13 to 129;
- Lutherans, from 4 to 95;
- Presbyterians, from 5 to 160;
- Roman Catholics, who recorded modest gains, from 12 to 27.[3]

"JEREMIADS" AND "DECLENSION"

With this massive growth and the addition of colleges to train the youth in Christian ways, one would naturally assume that the Church was really alive and well. But such was not the case. Puritans arriving in the New World naïvely assumed that everyone else coming to the New World was here for the same purpose. Puritans, you will remember, wanted freedom of worship, or at least they wanted to worship in their particular way and expected everyone else to want to do the same. As more people arrived, and as a second generation came on the scene, not everyone was interested in the covenant.

So distressing was this apostasy to the pastors that they began preaching in "Jeremiads," sermons calling apostate people back to their faith. Another term used to describe the loss of spiritual fervor is "declension," which means a decline in interest in spiritual things. The original colonists were not prepared to deal with the lack of spiritual fervency in their offspring.

SOLOMON STODDARD

Deeply concerned about this decline in spirituality was one of the most brilliant and influential Congregational pastors in Western Massachusetts for half a century. Solomon Stoddard (1643-1729), pastor in Northampton,

Massachusetts, from 1672 until his death in 1729, would become the grand-father of Jonathan Edwards, whom we will discuss later. In a noble attempt to entice unbelievers into the faith, he embraced an extremely controversial method known as the Halfway Covenant. This agreement allowed non-members to have their children baptized and to receive Communion even if they were not certain of their salvation. Stoddard believed that the Lord's Supper could become a "converting ordinance."[4] The Halfway Covenant was a desperate attempt to try to remedy the difficulty of having a substan-tial percentage of the population not participate in worship services. It should not be assumed that Solomon Stoddard wanted to compromise the faith. He advocated more effective preaching and had seen firsthand the fruit of courageous proclamation of the gospel.

In his nearly 60 years of ministry he had witnessed five outbreaks of spiritual zeal, which he nicknamed "harvests." However, the practice of the Halfway Covenant was so identified with his name that it came to be known as Stoddardism. His influential grandson, Jonathan Edwards, would later roundly criticize this practice instituted by his grandfather.

By 1730, in spite of the rapid increase in the numbers of churches and colleges founded for the purpose of perpetuating the faith, young Jonathan Edwards would cry out for the kind of harvest that his grandfather had observed five times. Solomon Stoddard died in 1729 and Jonathan Edwards became the pastor in Northampton, Massachusetts. A little over a decade later he would have the privilege of seeing the revival he longed for.

FIRST GREAT AWAKENING

In the 1730s, something began to stir among the colonists. Among the first to sense it were a Reformed pastor and two Presbyterian pastors. Theodore Frelinghuysen (1691-1747), born in Prussia, stirred his Dutch Reformed congregation in Raritan, New Jersey, with his profound and motivating preaching. Two Presbyterian pastors, a father-son team by the name of William Tennent (1673-1746) and Gilbert Tennent (1703-1764), worked in Pennsylvania. William, concerned with the lack of well-trained pastors, began to train young students in his home in Neshaminy, Pennsylvania, in 1736. His building for training was jeeringly called the Log College, but in spite of modest facilities, it produced many dedicated pastors who had effective ministries on the frontier. His critics "branded his graduates 'half educated enthusiasts.' But Tennent may have had the last laugh. Two of them eventually became president of Princeton University!"[5] As it became apparent that a revival was under way, William was joined by his son, Gilbert, in the training at the Log College. When it was decided later to establish a formal institution for training Presbyterian pastors, Log College was moved and renamed the College of New Jersey. Today you know it by a different name: Princeton University.

NEW LIGHT AND OLD LIGHT

The revival did not come without conflict, however. Many Presbyterians spoke derisively of the revival, feeling it was all zeal with no truth. Gilbert Tennent became a great defender not only of revival but also the revivalist who would stir the fires—George Whitefield from England. Presbyterians, unable to work through their differences over the revival, split into two camps: the New Light (which accepted the revival) and the Old Light (which could not accept it). Although Gilbert argued tirelessly for the revival, he worked diligently to try to bring the two splinter groups back together. He went on to serve as a trustee of what is now called Princeton University and was one of the prime fund-raisers for the building of Princeton University's famous Nassau Hall.

If Theodore Frelinghuysen was the first to recognize the revival, and William and Gilbert Tennent were the early trainers of the revival, Jonathan Edwards (1703-1758) was the theologian and the most visible representative of the explosive movement.

JONATHAN EDWARDS

Jonathan Edwards graduated from Yale in 1720 at age 17 and went on to become assistant pastor under his grandfather, Solomon Stoddard, in 1727. His brilliance has caused him to be regarded as a "theologian, revivalist, philosopher, psychologist and aesthetician."[6] Although he was nearsighted, which caused him to bend over the pulpit to read his sermons from full manuscripts, his preaching had a profound impact on people. His 1741 sermon entitled "Sinners in the Hands of an Angry God" is still highly regarded to this day. In supporting the revival, he was accused of being an advocate of experimental religion, meaning that he placed too much emphasis on the exuberance of preaching, a call for decision, and the emotional response of people, which was labeled "enthusiasm." Bear in mind, enthusiasm was not a positive term as it is today. The word "enthusiast" was a derisive, demeaning term, referring to people who were not sufficiently rational.

DEFENDING THE REVIVAL

Although Edwards himself could hardly be called an enthusiast in terms of uncontrolled emotionalism, he was a profoundly sensitive man with deep humility to match his extraordinary intellect. He was loathe to condemn the moving of God's Spirit, and continued to defend the revivals, in spite of the fact there were some excesses. He felt revivals were irrefutably the work of God's supernaturally moving on the human heart. Rationalistic theologians, who were in vogue in the day, scoffed at Edwards's defense of religious enthusiasm and traditional Calvinism. Although Edwards acknowledged that some of the weeping, shouting and other bizarre physical manifestations might be excessive at times, he considered them appropriate responses for those contemplating the reality of damnation—eternity without God. He felt it was appropriate to preach the terror of that reality, which thus aroused people's emotions, or affections as they called them in Edwards's day.

Most of Edwards's preaching and writing was concerned with defending the revival and battling Arminianism. So influential was he in his persuasive skills that he brought evangelist George Whitefield (1714-1770) to embrace Calvinism, which later caused Whitefield to break fellowship with John Wesley in England. In defending the revival, Edwards wrote

- *A Faithful Narrative of the Surprising Work of God* (1737)
- *The Distinguishing Marks of a Work of the Spirit of God* (1737)
- *Some Thoughts Concerning the Present Revival of Religion in New England* (1742)
- *A Treatise Concerning Religious Affections* (1746)

His writings defending Calvinism were so profound that he is regarded by some as America's greatest philosophical theologian. These writings included

- *Treatise on the Freedom of the Will* (1754)
- *The Great Christian Doctrine of Original Sin Defended* (1758)

HEARTBREAKS AND THE FINAL YEARS

After defending the revival and seeing the full impact of it in his city and his church, Edwards was run out of his own pulpit in 1750. His forced resignation was caused by his refusal to serve Communion to those who were not living consistent Christian lives. It is indeed an irony that "for the next several years, America's mightiest speculative thinker humbly served as a missionary to the Massachusetts Indians while serving a tiny parish at Stockbridge."[7] The heartbreak of being released from his pulpit was preceded in 1747 by another desperate disappointment. His daughter had been engaged to David Brainard (1718-1747), one of the most heroic and celebrated missionaries to the Indians. But before the wedding date, Brainard contracted tuberculosis and died in Jonathan Edwards's home at the age of 29. Shortly thereafter, his own beloved daughter died as well.

In 1758, Jonathan Edwards was invited to serve as president of Princeton, which was a redeeming moment. However, he died a few months later from a smallpox inoculation. Jonathan Edwards was without a doubt the giant of one of America's most significant spiritual events, the First Great Awakening.

GEORGE WHITEFIELD

By the time George Whitefield arrived from England in 1740 for his first of seven trips to America, the revival was already well under way. Edwards had noted that "in the spring and summer (of 1735), the town seemed to be full of the presence of God; it never was so full of love, nor of joy."[8] Although Edwards had reported 300 new converts by 1736, it was Whitefield's revivalist preaching that tied the entire movement together from north to south. Evangelists in those days did not have microphones. Whitefield didn't need one; in Bristol, England, it was claimed that he preached to 20,000 people at one time. Even Benjamin Franklin, who was not a Christian but a Deist and who was skeptical of the claims that Whitefield could be heard by so many people, paced out the anticipated area that would be occupied by the crowd and calculated how many persons might be standing per square yard. A quarter of a mile from the speaker's stand, Franklin climbed a tree and perched himself, not expecting to be able to hear the speaker. But when Whitefield started preaching, the force of his voice was so great it nearly knocked Franklin out of the tree! Franklin further noted that Whitefield was so persuasive in raising money for his orphanage that Franklin purposely left his purse (as it was then called) at home so he would not be moved by Whitefield's appeal. However, according to Franklin, he was so moved by Whitefield's request for funds that he ran home, got his purse and gave everything he had! Now that's one of the signs of a revival! The genius of George Whitefield was his capacity to tie the entire revival together. In his seven trips to the colonies, he visited every one of the 13 colonies, from Maine to Georgia. When one adds Whitefield's preaching endeavors in England, Ireland, Scotland and Wales to those in America, the number of meetings is over 18,000! Whitefield averaged 10 sermons a week until he died of asthma in Newbury Port, Massachusetts, at age 56.

SOUTHERN COLONIES

While Edwards dominated the revival in New England, and Gilbert and William Tennent, along with Theodore Frelinghuysen, were the prominent leaders in the middle colonies, the southern colonies produced its own visible leaders: Samuel Davies, a Log College graduate and later president of Princeton, initiated the first phase of the revival. Under the guidance of a Baptist preacher named Shubal Sterns and his brother-in-law, Daniel Marshall, the revival spread like wildfire through Virginia and North Carolina. Debereuz Jarrat, an evangelical Anglican who preached with the fervency of a Methodist, also was an influential leader in the southern colonies.

THE IMPACT OF AWAKENING

It would be a mistake, however, to portray the Great Awakening by simply discussing famous preachers and theologians. The Awakening ultimately was not about churches or pulpits or books. It was about changed lives. Earl Cairns estimates that from 30,000 to 40,000 people were converted, out of New England's population of only 300,000.[9] Some estimate that as many as

50,000 people were converted between 1740 and 1742.[10] Over 150 new churches were added, while other churches were once again filled to capacity. In addition to the spiritual vigor in the New England area, thousands more flocked to the churches in the middle and southern colonies.

As if that were not enough, over 50 new colleges were founded. Some of them were

- Princeton University (in 1746), whose presidents were all evangelical until the turn of the twentieth century
- Columbia University (in 1754), originally called King's College
- Brown University (in 1764), founded by Baptists and originally called Rhode Island College
- Rutgers University (in 1766), originally called Queen's College
- Dartmouth University (in 1770)

In fact, "with the exception of the University of Pennsylvania, every collegiate institution founded in the colonies prior to the Revolutionary War was established by some branch of the Christian Church."[11]

CAUSES AND EFFECTS

What caused the Great Awakening? What could touch 150 towns in New England alone (not including the middle and southern colonies)?[12] How can we summarize such a movement of God's Spirit? The first and profound contribution of the Great Awakening was the emphasis on knowing God in a personal way. Religion, to many, had become a cerebral exercise, a mental assent to doctrines. Whenever the Christian faith is reduced to mere dogma, its power and appeal are gone. The Great Awakening, supernaturally inspired by the Spirit of God Himself, drew people into an authentic, personal experience with God, which is the central cry of every human heart.

Revivals are often divisive, and the First Great Awakening was no exception. The Awakening clearly created theological splits between the liberals led by such persons as Charles Chauncy and Jonathan Mayhew. The real test of any authentic spiritual awakening is not theological controversies but its ability to transform culture. Lefferts A. Loetscher, along with colleagues Sheldon Smith and Robert Handy, noted that the social effects of the Great Awakening cannot be ignored. The Awakening elevated the common man. By giving him a self-authenticating religious experience, it made him able to experience God, independent of professional ministers and church synods. Lay activity and lay authority in the Church increased.[13]

DISESTABLISHMENT

Ironically, the Awakening hastened the separation of Church and state. It emphasized the individual Christian "in his inner religious experience rather than church or theocracy."[14] This comment means that the Awakening caused churches and Christian people to realize they were not dependent upon the government to sustain their Church. This era began the end of Established Churches. Disestablishment meant that churches would exist upon the voluntary contributions of those who attended them, not on government funding. This seemed a new and radical idea. In fact, it had not been experienced on a wide scale in Church history for over a thousand years. Most contemporary Americans probably assume that the way their churches operate, sustained on the tithes and offerings of their members, is normal. But such a structure is an American invention. For a millennium, churches and governments had been so intertwined that the churches were receiving tax support. Once the disestablishment movement started, it gathered momentum quickly, affecting Maryland and New York during the American Revolution. In 1786, the Anglican church lost its privileged position in Virginia. In New Hampshire disestablishment occurred in 1817, followed by Connecticut the next year. In Massachusetts the Congregationalist church was separated from the state in 1833. The bold new American experiment was under way, and it had been partially spawned by the revival fires of the First Great Awakening.

CHURCH GROWTH

The fact that disestablishment (no support from the state) didn't devastate American Christianity is proof, in part, of the vigor, reality and authenticity of the Great Awakening. What disestablishment produced was a massive surge of American Christianity. The growth of Christianity from 1660 to 1740 was followed by new growth from 1740 to 1780:

Anglicans almost doubled, growing from 246 to 406; Baptists more than quadrupled, going from 96 churches to 457 churches; the Reformed Movement increased from 129 churches to 328; Lutherans grew from 95 to 240; Presbyterians tripled from 160 to 495 churches; and Congregationalists, which were leading the pack in 1740 with 423 churches, nearly doubled to 749.[15]

Certainly, spiritual authenticity and vigor cannot be measured in numbers alone. However, numbers are important indicators, and here we notice that the Christian faith was keeping pace with the rapidly expanding American colonies. Solomon Stoddard's dream of another harvest had come, and this harvest had truly been a "hundredfold return."

ROMAN CATHOLICS

Within a 150-year span, virtually every Protestant denomination was transferred to America. But Roman Catholics arrived on American soil a full century before the Mayflower set sail. It is believed that priests accompanied Spanish colonizers into Florida in approximately 1521. In 1526, Mass was offered by two Dominicans who were part of a 600-man exploration team. One year later, however, 400 were dead. This did not deter massive Roman Catholic missionary endeavors, which continued to flourish in the New World. Explorer Coronado came to the New World in search of gold, not to bring Christianity. However, when he left the central plains of America, he left behind three Franciscan friars who wanted to spread the gospel. Two of the friars left no traces; but we know that the third, Juan de Padilla, was killed by Indians in what is now southern Kansas in 1542, the first record of a Christian martyr on American soil. This death and others did not dissuade the Catholic church from aggressive plans to evangelize the Indians of the New World. The Society of Jesus took up its cause in Florida and moved as far north as Virginia.

Great success was experienced across the Southwest. As early as 1630 there were 35,000 Christian Indians across New Mexico in 25 Catholic missions. Eusebio Francisco Kino (1645-1711) was an Italian Jesuit missionary who joined the Society of Jesus in Germany and then came to Mexico in

1681. He ministered in Sonora, Mexico, and made 14 major trips into Arizona under the most difficult of conditions.

JUNIPERO SERRA

One of the most impressive Franciscan missionary efforts was the building of a chain of missions from San Diego to San Francisco; but, in particular, it was through the sacrificial love and labor of Father Junipero Serra (1713-1784) that these missions exist. This Spanish Franciscan missionary arrived in Mexico City in 1750. His extensive education included a doctorate in theology, which could have provided him with many university opportunities. Instead, he chose to pursue the difficulties of missionary activity with a vigor that few could match. His establishment of missions, starting in San Diego with San Diego de Alcala mission in 1769, is as remarkable a missionary story as has ever been told. His missionary endeavors are impressive.

- 1769, San Diego
- 1770, San Carlos
- 1771, San Antonio, San Gabriel
- 1772, San Luis Obispo
- 1776, San Francisco de Assisi, San Juan Capistrano
- 1777, Santa Clara
- 1782, San Buenaventura.[16]

His preaching was explosive, and included such bizarre tactics as pounding his chest with a stone, beating himself and sometimes placing a lighted torch next to his chest—all done in order to move people to repentance. By 1784, 5,307 California Indians were listed among his converts.[17] In addition, over 6,000 Indians were baptized.[18] Recent historians have been critical of the Spanish treatment of the Indians. Many were abused and some were even forced to convert to Christianity. Serra was quick to defend the Indians, however. In 1773, he wrote the *Representación,* outlining the proper treatment of Indians, and sent this to the Spanish viceroy in Mexico City.[19] Serra was a gifted administrator, a charismatic preacher, an able executive and an individual of profound piety. Mexico,

California, and the entire southwest to this day are marked by his Catholic influence.

AMAZING GROWTH

As we leave the 1600s and 1700s we realize what an amazing piece of history this period is. In 1600, no Christian church existed in America. By 1800, every European faith had crossed the Atlantic, bringing with it its particular strengths and weaknesses. Thousands of churches were thriving. Christian colleges, none of which had existed a few years earlier, were producing pastors to lead the growing congregations.

The stunning level of growth of churches and Christian academic centers reflects the commitment and devotion of tens of thousands of Christians to spread the good news of Christ throughout the whole world. More importantly, such staggering numbers reflect the resiliency of the gospel and the potency of God's truth in transforming the human heart and mind throughout history.

As a reminder, the Church is God's plan for depositing the gospel in culture. It is how God saves civilization.

To further assist you in understanding the key individuals and events of chapter 12, study questions, charts, diagrams, time lines and links to biographical websites are available on the Internet at www.jimgarlow.com. Please follow the site links to *How God Saved Civilization*, chapter 12 study helps.

AWAKENED AGAIN

THE SECOND GREAT AWAKENING

Dates covered: A.D. 1800-1835
Key persons: Thomas and Alexander Campbell, Timothy Dwight,
Lyman Beecher, Charles Finney

Eric finished sweeping the print shop on his first night of part-time work to pay for his studies at Byerly College. It was strange to be in the deep South after living so long in Virginia. At least Father should be glad he hadn't gone to Oberlin College, like his older brother, Asa. Poor Asa. His brother's politics had greatly angered their father. Now Asa was disowned, leaving Eric as sole inheritor of Father's estate.

Eric made sure the doors and windows were locked securely and went to wash up in the small corner sink. *Strange*, he thought. *Why would Asa care about the slave issue? It had cost him everything—his inheritance.* As he lifted the work apron over his head to hang it in the janitor's closet, the door slammed shut against him. Eric yelled partly from the pain and partly from fear. Who had shut the door behind him? Who was left in the shop this late? Cautiously, he poked his head around the door. Staring straight at him was a young, dark-skinned man with enormous brown eyes. It was the first slave Eric had met so close up! He'd seen a few in the Alabama town nearest the campus, where he'd gone to buy his supplies for the school year.

"Oh, it's you, Mister Eric. I'm Benjamin."

Mr. Benson, the print-shop owner, had warned Eric that Benjamin lived in a room over the business, but Eric hadn't expected him to appear so suddenly and at night!

Benjamin laughed loud and long. "I did give you a fright! You should have seen the look on your face. Sorry to frighten you, Mister Eric. I thought it was maybe a burglar."

Eric half smiled. From that moment, the two men began to develop a strong friendship, but Eric had no idea how costly his affiliation with Benjamin would prove to be.

As the months passed, Eric was more and more intrigued by Benjamin. He would chat with the slave every night as Eric cleaned the shop. Before long, he was tutoring this good-natured, bright young man. Benjamin was adept in learning to read, write and do arithmetic. Yet, when they discussed history, Eric noticed how quickly Benjamin would grow quiet.

Gradually, Eric brought up the issue of slavery with Benjamin. The young man would tell Eric about hardships for a slave in the South, and Eric could easily see how this friendly and seemingly happy man yearned to make a way for himself in life; Benjamin certainly had the gifts to do so.

"What can I do with you, Ben?" Eric asked his friend one night.

"You cain't do nothin' wit' me, Mister Eric. Nothin' but the good ye're already doin'. An' that good is mighty fine."

Benjamin's personal stories and accounts were troubling, but Eric recognized that this was just what Asa described in his letters. Added to Eric's turbulent thoughts was Father's explaining in letters how radical Asa's antislavery stance was. The letters between his father and brother continued to seesaw in his mind. Asa would write how shameful it was that people were being treated like property, like beasts, just because their skin was dark. Father would write how it was wrong to undermine the slavery laws.

Eric's folks had raised him to be honest and kindhearted. He loved his mom dearly and admired his dad, Nathan Edgington, who was a pastor at First Congregational Church near Arlington, Virginia. Reverend Edgington cared for his people; he knew the Bible; he preached with vigor. Eric wanted to be a pastor, too; that's why he had chosen to attend Byerly.

Eric's father taught that the ups and downs of life are to be accepted as coming from the hand of a sovereign God. Slavery was just a social institution. After all, there was no point in undoing the entire structure of the American economy. Besides, many masters treated their slaves kindly. Even in the Bible there was no strict demand to get rid of slavery. Eric's dad believed that slavery might be God's judgment on paganism or God's tool for evangelizing Africa. Anyone who opposed slavery was a rabble-rouser and a troublemaker, even if that person's name was Asa Edgington!

But Asa was persistent in his position that slavery was wrong. Eric wondered how much his brother's ideas were being nurtured by Asa's church, pastored by a man called Finney. Eric knew that Finney believed every true Christian was obliged to do something to free the slaves.

Though Eric wrote to his dad often, he had kept many of his thoughts about the slavery issue to himself. He had not told his father about his teaching sessions with Benjamin and how the tutoring would often go into the early-morning hours. Taking time to teach Ben had even caused Eric's grades to suffer.

This went on for six months, when late one night the shop owner, Oliver Bensen, caught Eric tutoring Benjamin. Though Mr. Benson had always been kind to Benjamin, Eric noticed how irritated his boss became. "Don't ever do that again, Eric. Never!"

"I just think—" Eric tried to answer.

"Don't think!" said Benson as he turned on his heel and walked out.

Eric was confused. As he sat on his bed that night, he picked up a pamphlet written by Charles Finney that Asa had sent through the mail. It read: "We can overthrow slavery, one slave at a time. Will you do your part?" Eric could hardly stand it. His friendship and concern for Ben were growing, and Ben's being a slave increasingly bothered Eric.

Late Tuesday night, Eric and four of his closest friends gathered in their weekly prayer meeting. They had been discussing Benjamin, and the implications of Finney's teaching. "God," one of them prayed, "we believe in You. We want to serve You, but we need Your help. If You want us to do nothing regarding Benjamin, then calm our spirits. But if You want us to help him, stir us up." As he said those words, it was as if electricity ran through the five young men. They opened their eyes and looked at one another. Without saying a word, they all sensed it: "The time is now!"

In a few moments they had pooled their funds, but they only had $7.32—not enough to buy a slave or even to help one escape and start a new life. One of the students sighed and dug deep into his pocket. "Instead of going to school next semester, I'll work." Eric's friend pulled out a staggering sum—$20—a sight Eric had never seen. From there, the friends began to lay out the plan to free Ben. Eric would be the first person to approach Ben, explain the plan and help him to get out of the county.

Eric went home that night happy. He grabbed two shirts from his dresser to give to Ben when he noticed an unopened letter from his father near the nightstand. He paused and opened it slowly. Sweat broke out on his forehead as he read his father's words. "I have heard that you want to follow your brother's example on the slavery issue. I have one thing to say to you, Eric: If you choose to break the laws of this land to help free slaves, I will be forced to disown you, too. This is a warning, son."

Eric was stunned. *Is this what Asa felt?* For several minutes he sat in the darkness, a war raging in his soul. Then, slowly he stood, set his father's letter on the dresser and picked up the shirts. *Every man should have his freedom.*

A DIFFERENT KIND OF AWAKENING

The idea of disestablishment (voluntary private contributions to a church rather than government support) eventually caused numbers of churches and church attendance to flourish, but the results were not immediate. According to Franklin Littell, church membership dropped to between five and seven percent of the population. Not until 1926 did church membership reach a level of 50 percent of the population. What caused this upturn? It was the result of what is known as the Second Great Awakening.

The Second Great Awakening was not a single movement but a convergence of several independent movements whose impact was so significant that they are seen as a whole. The movement contains such divergent streams as prestigious New England university students at Yale, backwoods farmers from Kentucky, sophisticated urbanites from Rochester and members of the underground railroad, who smuggled slaves from South to North. These, and other movements, made the first half of the nineteenth century a vibrant and fascinating time for the Church in the United States.

The First Great Awakening, in contrast to the Second Awakening, seemed to be an unexplainable sovereign move of God. Even Jonathan Edwards's work entitled *A Surprising Narrative* reflected his personal surprise when God's hand moved, and many other leaders of the First Great Awakening seemed to agree. They didn't plan it. They didn't organize it. Revival and renewal just happened.

The Second Great Awakening was not so much an unexplainable move of God as it was a reaction to carefully planned renewal techniques. Does this make it wrong? Of course not. It simply makes it different. God has worked through both. There are times when God's hand moves and revival hits a community, a church or a city, and no one knows how it came or why it left. But other renewal movements are carefully calculated and organized. A Billy Graham Crusade, for example, includes advance teams of people coming to "prepare the soil" for the "sower" (see Mark 4:1-20). These times of renewal are replete with committees and administrative structures. They are planned, prayed for, dreamed for and finally executed. This does not make them wrong. This simply makes them different from the First Great Awakening.

Throughout the Second Great Awakening we will note the administrative structures that helped bring about the desired results. What is unexplainable however, is what caused people to be so inclined to organize so thoroughly with such spiritual vigor. In this inexplicable dedication, we see again what we saw in the First Great Awakening: the mysterious move of God on the human heart.

CAMP MEETINGS

One major phenomenon of the Second Great Awakening was revivalism. By the end of the 1700s, two opposing forms of Protestantism had developed. One extreme favored a rationalistic approach to the Christian faith. Extreme rationalism resulted in Deism, which taught that God exists as the great Architect of Nature, but does not intervene in human affairs. He might be considered the God of nature, for example, but Jesus could not be born of a virgin, God incarnate. Deism so intellectualized God as to exclude anything supernatural. Rationalism of the eighteenth century so overemphasized the intellectual aspects of the faith, that faith was reduced to an intellectual assent to doctrinal statements.

Revivalism emerged along with, and sometimes in response to, the hyper-rationalism of the day. Revivalism emphasized the necessity for the human heart to have an emotional encounter with God. It was not antirational; it was, in fact, clearly grounded in experience. People wanted to *experience* God. They did not want to limit faith to a mere recitation of theological statements.

Such was the mood on the frontiers of Logan County, Kentucky, near the Tennessee border, in 1796 when Presbyterian minister James McGready (ca. 1758-1817) became pastor of three frontier congregations. McGready had vigorously preached repentance in North Carolina, touching off both revival fires and vigorous opposition. One of his most outstanding converts was a man named Barton W. Stone, who went on to become a prominent figure in the Second Great Awakening. In 1800, James McGready and two evangelist colleagues, William Hodges and John Rankin, initiated what would be one of the most profound elements of American religious life through the 1800s: the camp meeting. Camp meetings were outdoor meetings, generally in wooded areas that would provide shade, where people could gather for two or three weeks (or longer) for vigorous gospel singing and preaching. Before the advent of the public-address system, the camp meeting would sometimes feature multiple preaching stations, so the crowd could wander from one preacher to another.

THE CANE RIDGE MEETINGS

In August 1801, Barton Stone led a camp meeting in Bourbon County, Kentucky, near the county seat, Paris. The Cane Ridge camp meeting was named after Stone's Cane Ridge Presbyterian meetinghouse (or church). What happened that hot summer would change the course of Protestant Christianity in America.

Nearly 25,000 people arrived on Friday afternoon. Primitive platforms were hastily constructed to accommodate Presbyterian, Baptist and Methodist preachers, who had set aside their denominational differences for the occasion. The preaching was virtually continuous during the day and would continue through evening by the light of enormous campfires. What occurred is regarded by some as the greatest outpouring of the Holy Spirit since Pentecost.[1]

MANIFESTATIONS

Thousands of people heard the gospel, but physical manifestations of the Spirit's presence occurred as well. Some fell down, some experienced jerking, barking or uncontrollable running. While it is difficult to defend some of the bizarre and even offensive manifestations, one thing is clear—God had come on the scene. His presence was not confirmed by bizarre manifestations. His presence was confirmed by the hundreds, perhaps thousands of lives that were changed. And the camp meetings became a regular tool of Protestants to win back the masses who had left the Church, and to reach those who had never known church life because the frontiers of the country had expanded more quickly than had the number of church congregations.

THE SUCCESS OF THE CAMP MEETING

Why was the camp meeting, which continued to have influence over the next hundred years, so successful? For one thing, the preachers spoke in plain language. Their sermons were not cerebral theological treatises but straightforward emotional appeals. The preachers expected people to make a decision for or against what they were saying. Positive decisions were regarded as conversions. Second, the camp meeting fit the culture in which it was developed. The largely rural population was spread out over large areas. The camp meeting provided a social center. Third, there was clearly spiritual openness, supernaturally affected by the Holy Spirit, which caused the minds and hearts of frontiersmen to respond to the straightforward appeal to repent. Critics have attributed the response to the simplicity and naïveté of the country folk, country bumpkins, who would be easily manipulated by a fiery, conniving Elmer Gantry-type preacher. But such was rarely the case. While it is true that these were simple people, they were also sensitive to the unembellished truth of the gospel. Their hearts were ready and they responded. As a result, community and family life improved vastly. Authentic religion affects the social fabric of the culture, and these camp meeting revivals improved one community after another.

Another feature of the camp meetings was their practicality. The organizers looked for a large, shaded area with adequate space for parking wagons and plenty of surrounding fields where people could pitch their tents. Preachers could erect their preaching stands in the fields, and those in charge of the food could arrange food tables and cooking areas to feed the crowds. Large tents became common, and eventually, permanent buildings were built with fold-up side doors. These were much like a tent, with side flaps that opened to allow the breeze to cool the warm auditorium.

CRITICISM

Not every denomination was thrilled with this response. Although Presbyterians started the first known camp meeting, the Presbyterian church as a denomination immediately split over the camp-meeting techniques. Just as Presbyterians had split into old-school and new-school factions regarding the First Great Awakening, they split once again in their views regarding the Second Great Awakening. The two groups were known as the Old Light and the New Light. New Light Presbyterians eventually formed their own denomination known as the Cumberland Presbyterian Church.

THE RESTORATION MOVEMENT

The unexpected result of the camp meeting successes was the launching of the Restoration movement. Beginning in approximately 1800, this loose connection of submovements set about to restore basic New Testament beliefs and organizational structure to the Church. It was one of several movements throughout history that appealed to primitivism, which is "the impulse to restore the . . . original order of things as revealed in Scripture, free from the accretions of Church history and tradition."[2] The Restoration movement emphasized the authority of the Bible (primarily the New Testament), and the Christian duty of unity. Denominational differences and consistent feuding over trivial theological differences between denominations had taken their toll on the American populace. There was a heart cry for oneness in Christ.

The Restoration movement had four sources:

1. In 1792, James O'Kelly reacted to Bishop Francis Asbury's authoritarian method of appointing preachers. A group of Methodists left Methodism and called themselves Republican Methodists in 1793 but renamed themselves Christian in 1794.
2. In 1801, Baptists split in New England when leaders Abner Jones and Elias Smith disagreed over the issue of predestination (the fact that God predetermines whether or not a person will accept Christ) and the Baptist insistence that new churches belong to an association (I suppose one could argue that that split was pre-destined!).
3. Barton Stone in Kentucky left the Presbyterians in 1803; his associates took upon themselves the name of Christian.
4. Finally, the dynamic driving force of the father-son team of Thomas and Alexander Campbell (by far, the most influential wing of the Restoration movement) greatly expanded the growth of the Restoration movement.

THOMAS AND ALEXANDER CAMPBELL

Thomas Campbell, a Scottish Presbyterian minister, came to western Pennsylvania from Northern Ireland in 1807. He was stunned at the petty denominational jealousies that he encountered and wrote his famous *The*

Declaration and Address. By 1809 he had become famous for the phrase "where the Bible speaks we speak; where it is silent we are silent."[3] But it is his son, Alexander, who became the driving, guiding force for the Restoration movement. Alexander Campbell managed to get significant portions of these four tempestuous streams into one river, sometimes using the name Disciples of Christ and at other times Christian Church. The movement grew rapidly but not due to the normal revivalistic techniques employed by others at the time.

Alexander Campbell was a great debater. He traveled not only in the United States, but overseas, as an articulate and tireless defender of the unity of the Christian body and the authority of Scripture. His skill in debate was matched by his persuasive writing. He produced two monthly journals, *The Christian Baptist* (1823-1830), and *The Millennial Harbinger* (1830-1866). His forceful debating and energetic proselytizing resulted in one of the fastest-growing movements of the century. The Disciples of Christ grew from 22,000 followers in 1832 to almost 200,000 by 1860. In 1827, Alexander Campbell published an English translation of the New Testament, using translation skills he had acquired while studying the Greek New Testament at the University of Glasgow, Scotland. (Alexander and his family had been stranded in Scotland, first in an unsuccessful attempt to come to America and later by an 1808 shipwreck.) By 1834 he had published *Psalms, Hymns and Spiritual Songs,* and in 1839 and 1854, respectively, wrote *The Christian System* and *Christian Baptism.*

USE OF INSTRUMENTS

One would like to believe that any movement founded upon the authority of Scripture and a call to Christian unity would be unified. But, as has been the case throughout all of Church history, division intruded. By 1906, the U.S. Census Bureau listed the noninstrumental Churches of Christ (those who do not believe in using musical instruments) separately from the Christian Churches or Disciples of Christ, showing that the movement had already split into two distinct groups. The debate about whether or not to use instruments in worship developed in 1859 in Midway, Kentucky, when a Christian Church went against Christian Church practice and introduced instrumental music to accompany its congregational singing. In spite of their alleged claim *not* to speak where the Bible was silent, all Restorationists seem to have views on this issue. So intense were those views that the "movement of unity" split into instrumental and noninstrumental groups.

But the use of instruments was not the only issue to split the "movement of unity." By the turn of the century, liberalism had chewed into a portion of the Christian Church, dividing it into the more liberal Disciples of Christ and the more conservative Christian Church. Consequently, what started out as an attempt to unify all believers on very simple principles of the authority of Scripture had failed (if unity was the only test). The four groups that had become one were now three in number.

WHAT WE CAN LEARN

How does one view the Restoration movement? It is easy from our vantage point to look on the meaningless infighting over issues like musical instruments and dismiss the movement's relevance. But such has not been my practice throughout this book. I look for the positive influences brought by each movement, while accepting their respective weaknesses. I believe every movement, every denomination, every local church and every Christian leader is like a two-sided coin. One side reveals strengths and good, positive qualities. The other one shows weaknesses. Every human being since the fall of Adam, with the single exception of Jesus Christ, has been tainted by the impact of original sin. And since movements, denominations and local churches are comprised of people affected by original sin, we should not be surprised to see these movements troubled and divided. Rather than condemn the movements for their obvious and glaring failures, it is good to see what positive contributions a movement makes to the cause of Christ. In reality, God does not accomplish His will *because* of us, our churches or our denominations. Frankly, He accomplishes His will *in spite of* us. There are moments when we seem to be so in tune with God's will that something profoundly significant happens, with His full smile and blessing. But these moments are exceptional. More often, lack of the whole truth seems to dilute the power and purity of God's message. But He doesn't give up on us as quickly as we are inclined to give up on each other; He doesn't seem to find as much fault with us as we find with each other (reader, this is one of the key principles of this book!). It's as though He smiles with a knowing nod and says, "I am going to work with them anyway, in spite of themselves." And that is precisely what He does. That's why you don't find me critical of the so-called unity movement which failed to truly unify. It was a noble attempt that, admittedly, failed. Yet much good was accomplished.

What was that good? Well, even in the rather legalistic, hyperconservative churches that don't believe in musical instruments, tens of thousands of people have come to know Christ. Admittedly, one can find goodness even in a style of worship that seems inhibited (no instruments) or limited. In such environments, people learn to sing *a cappella* and they sing well! In fact, the human voice is the most beautiful instrument ever created. The sound of hundreds, or even thousands of people singing without musical instruments can be a spectacular worship experience.

And what about the Christian Churches that used instruments? They likewise had a profound impact across America, growing at an exceedingly rapid rate. While the original founders of the movement would not like to be known as a denomination, they were, in fact, just that, and a profoundly influential one.

My evaluation of the Disciples of Christ is less charitable. As we will find in later chapters, the move toward theological liberalism contains few authentic Christian advances. Liberalism gutted the Church of Jesus Christ, removing an authentic Jesus, an authentic crucifixion and an authentic resurrection. So the influence of the liberal Disciples of Christ as a "contagious carrier" of the gospel gives fewer reasons for accolades. At the same time, one has to applaud the leadership of Alexander Campbell, Thomas Campbell, Barton Stone, James O'Kelly, Abner Jones and Elias Smith who envisioned that the Church of Jesus Christ could be label free, known only by the name of Christ.

THE YALE UNIVERSITY REVIVAL

The Second Great Awakening was not merely camp meetings on the frontier or vigorous debaters attempting to outline the reasons for Christian unity. One of the earliest evidences of a Second Great Awakening occurred at Yale University in New Haven, Connecticut.

In 1795, Timothy Dwight (1752-1817), grandson of the famous Jonathan Edwards (and great, great grandson of Northampton, Massachusetts, 60-year-tenured preacher, Solomon Stoddard), began to lead students at Yale University to a faith in Christ shortly after he assumed the presidency. Dwight emphasized the important role of logic, but he was quick to point out that reason, unchecked by the vitality of faith, would produce theological distortion. Appealing to the heart as well as to the mind, Timothy Dwight challenged students with the question, Is the Bible the Word of God? The result was that many students were won over to an affirmative "Yes, the Bible *is* the Word of God."

One of the most promising students, Lyman Beecher, was won to this position during President Timothy Dwight's discussions; and Beecher would later become a very significant leader in the Second Great Awakening. Dwight, in the tradition of his grandfather, viewed revivalism as an effective technique for reducing infidelity (lack of faith) among Yale students. So persuasive was this president that in 1802, one-third of the student body were converted under his preaching in the college chapel services!

But President Timothy Dwight produced more than an impressive series of revivals at Yale College. His teaching and teaching style produced some challenges to the basic theology of his well-known grandfather, Jonathan Edwards. Those who followed Jonathan Edwards theologically were known to be a part of the New Divinity movement. Though Timothy Dwight adhered to much that his grandfather, Jonathan Edwards, had believed, he began to question some of the tenets of Calvinism, specifically the issue of a person's capacity to respond to the gospel (remember, Calvin believed that the human heart was incapable of responding to the gospel). According to Calvin, God preselected the individual. Jonathan Edwards adhered to this view. But grandson Timothy Dwight was not so convinced. He believed that the individual could exercise his human will to choose or not to choose to respond to the gospel. If an individual had the capacity to respond positively or negatively to the gospel, then that put even more emphasis upon the necessity of proclaiming the gospel persuasively. Preachers needed to use every tool possible to convince and to persuade.

LYMAN BEECHER

This fervency was picked up by Dwight's disciple, Lyman Beecher (1775-1863). As a young college student, Beecher was "awakened" by Dwight's appeal. They remained very good friends until Dwight passed away in 1817. Beecher was a revivalist, a social reformer and a political observer.

In Connecticut, Congregationalism had been the official established church of the state, complete with state financial support. He fought hard against disestablishment, which occurred in 1817. Beecher felt it was a tragic change and that the "injury done to the cause of Christ . . . [would be] irreparable." Beecher, however, soon realized that disestablishment caused positive developments. He stated "it cut the churches loose from dependence on state support. It threw them wholly on their own resources and on God."[4] While serving as both president of Lane Seminary and pastor of Second Presbyterian Church in Cincinnati, Ohio, in 1832, Beecher discovered what disestablishment really produced: voluntarism (a concept explained in a later chapter).

CHARLES FINNEY

Another major component of the Second Awakening was the revivalist skills of Charles Finney (1792-1875). In 1794, the Finney family moved from Connecticut to Oneida County, New York. Charles received his early education in that community and then eventually returned to Warren Academy in Connecticut in 1812. By 1818 his mother became ill, and he returned to New York to study law. It is uncertain whether Finney was formally admitted to the bar. However, he functioned as an attorney, regularly arguing cases in court. In his courtroom experiences he frequently heard the Bible quoted. Finally, curious about this, he purchased his own copy of the Bible and read it voraciously. He visited a local Presbyterian church where one of the young ladies organized a group to pray for his conversion. Finally, he yielded his will to God. The young woman who organized the prayer meeting began dating him and later became his wife. Once converted he wanted to preach, since elders in his church questioned his conversion.

To settle the matter, Finney went alone into the woods with God on October 10, 1821. While there he was given "a mighty baptism of the Holy Ghost" which went through him "like a wave of electricity." The next morning he exclaimed that he was given a "retainer from the Lord Jesus Christ to plead His cause." Within two years he had left his law practice and had become a licensed evangelist with the Presbyterian church. He went as a missionary to the settlers in upstate New York in 1824. Immediately, revivals broke out in small communities, and by 1825 the word of his crusades had spread. His ministry created similar revivals in Troy, Utica, Rome and Auburn, New York. He immediately became well known for his new measures. These measures included protracted meetings (held night after night) and called for advance teams, primarily comprised of praying women, to go ahead of his crusades and prepare the spiritual climate for his coming. One of the most unusual of his practices was the "anxious bench" in which he invited those who were wrestling with following Christ to move to the front seats of the auditorium. Those seated on the "anxious bench" were treated as if they were a jury, to be persuaded by God's attorney who was arguing a case for Jesus Christ.

Critics of Finney's new evangelistic techniques included Timothy Dwight's student Lyman Beecher, who later met with Finney and began to embrace Finney's methods. Not all were so easily convinced, however. Many denounced his vigorous, exuberant preaching style, feeling it was far too emotional. But that did not deter Charles Finney. His revivals began to be even more influential.

CRUSADES EXPAND

Between the years of 1827 and 1832, revivals swept through New York City, Philadelphia, Boston and Rochester. Revivalism had now shifted from merely frontier rural areas in Kentucky and Tennessee to large metropolitan areas. In this regard, Finney was a precursor of later revivalists such as D. L. Moody and Billy Graham. Although the Finney revivals had few of the emotional excesses of frontier camp meetings, they still included emotional expressions such as shouting, groaning and intense times of struggle, when people were deciding whether or not they would accept the claims of the gospel. All-night prayer meetings in which sinners were prayed for by name were commonplace. And most controversial of all, women were allowed to pray publicly. This and other activities of Finney's crusades would be an indicator of his second career, which we will discuss below.

Finney's famous Rochester crusade, which some claimed saw as many as 100,000 converts (though the number is probably inflated), marked the end of Finney's intense revivalism. By 1832, health concerns forced him to radically curtail his travels. He became the pastor of Second Street Presbyterian Church in New York City, Broadway Tabernacle of New York and finally the First Congregational Church of Oberlin, Ohio (1837-1872), where he was to leave another profound impact on American Christianity.

SOCIAL REFORM: FINNEY'S "SECOND CAREER"

While he served in Oberlin, Finney began to renounce his old-school Calvinism (the view that God preselects those to be saved) and brought out his new-school Calvinism, which was more a Arminian theology (people could choose to accept Christ) than it was Calvinist. In addition, his preaching began to take on a radical confidence in the "perfectibility of human nature and society," which would result in the "establishing [of] the millennial kingdom of God on earth by winning converts . . . [and] social reform. His optimistic view of the maturing of the human character placed him theologically close to the late nineteenth century 'holiness movement.'"[5]

But Finney also believed in social reform where individual converts could make a profound difference in the culture at large. As people came to Christ they shouldn't simply bask in their newfound salvation. They should invest their energies in transforming culture, bringing a halt to those things that violate scriptural principles. It is precisely at this point that Finney's second career had such amazing influence. He found himself heavily involved in the antislavery movement, the women's rights movement, and the temperance movement. Writes Donald Dayton:

> Finney himself made conversions central and was never willing to substitute reform for revival, but he did make the reforms an "appendage" to revival. In discussing the slavery issue, for example, the evangelist wished to make "abolition an appendage, just as he made temperance an appendage to the revival in Rochester." By this connection, Finney preserved the centrality of revivals while still promoting reforms and propelling his converts in the new positions on social issues.[6]

HIS IMPACT

It is impossible to overstate Finney's contribution to the Second Great Awakening. First, he was a brilliant orator, preacher, organizer and debater.

Second, he was a highly skilled administrator. In 1835, in his publication entitled *Lectures on Revivals of Religion*, Finney stated that "revival is not a miracle, or dependent on miracles in any sense. It is the result of the right use of the constituted means."[7] All that has been referred to above bears repeating. Finney, and for that matter the entire Second Great Awakening, was built around the organizational and administrative genius of many human leaders. They planned the renewal. They prayed for revival. And they experienced it.

Another mark of God's blessing on Charles Finney is the fact that whole towns were altered by the revival. In Rochester, New York, it was reported that "the place was shaken to its foundations."[8] Over 1,200 new people joined the churches in Rochester. Every leading lawyer, doctor and businessman was saved. Forty persons entered the ministry at that time. And as a result of what happened in Rochester, revivals broke out in 1,500 other towns and villages.[9] Now that's true revival!

Finally, Finney brought a unique merge of radical revivalism with aggressive social reform. He believed that evil societal institutions could be radically transformed if Christians began to infiltrate the world around them. Thus he and his students at Oberlin College where he served first as theology professor and then as president, continued not only their revivals, but their radical involvement in the antislavery movement, the temperance movement and feminist causes. Finney, like Wesley before him, could affirm that true holiness is *social* holiness.

Finney died in 1875. He proved to be the single most influential evangelist until the time of D. L. Moody (1837-1899). In fact, it is very likely that during the last two years of Finney's life he would have heard reports about the sensational preaching crusades being led by Moody in the British Isles from 1873 to 1875.

This period characterized by disestablishment reflected a Church in discouragement. Financial support had evaporated for many churches; prestige was gone; unbelief was rampant. Attendance was down with church membership plummeting to five percent of the population. Yet the Church, under the guidance of the Holy Spirit, rebounded. Using fresh methodologies while proclaiming a changeless gospel, the Church won back the masses that had fallen aside. How? As always, it was accomplished by the wisdom, grace and power of God working through frail and flawed human beings to bring His gospel to the world. And it was—and still is—through the resilient Church that God saves civilization.

To further assist you in understanding the key individuals and events of chapter 13, study questions, charts, diagrams, time lines and links to biographical websites are available on the Internet at www.jimgarlow.com. Please follow the site links to *How God Saved Civilization*, chapter 13 study helps.

THE RISE OF THE COMMON PERSON

THE SECOND GREAT AWAKENING CONTINUES

Dates covered: A.D. 1830-1860
Key persons: unnamed ordinary people hidden in the
woodwork of history

Della loved to talk as much as she loved to live. And mostly, she loved to talk about God. When she was five, she would stand on a milk crate in her backyard and preach to her little brothers. Her mother always smiled out the window and listened in amazement to the passionate message little Della would deliver. But one day, Della's mother took her in her arms. "Della," she said. "I love to hear you talk about God. But the Bible tells us it is men who preach. So don't stop loving God, but you know you will never be able to be a preacher when you grow up."

One day when Della was 16, she heard B. T. Roberts preach, and life became exciting in a completely new way. He said that God had poured out His Spirit upon men and women. She had never heard the words "and women," before. He said that both men and women would prophesy, even preach. *A woman,* she thought, and her heart skipped a beat. She had never known a woman to prophesy or to preach.

Every night that spring in 1886, Della privately prayed to God. *Dear God, I would love to preach, You know.* She didn't dare ask people at church. It seemed too strange. When the summer arrived, Della's entire family took a wagon and made their annual three-hour journey to a camp meeting in upstate New York. It was a trip she always enjoyed.

When they arrived, hundreds of tents were already going up around them. Camp meetings sometimes could last an entire week. Della was reminded to help set up the family tent, but whenever she would see an old friend, she would stop pounding pegs in the ground and begin a conversation. It wasn't long before her mother gave Della permission to join her friends who were wandering the camp.

As she walked past the main tent, someone handed her a handbill announcing the preachers for the week. Della glanced at it and then stopped in her tracks. One of those preachers was a woman! Suddenly Della's mind raced to her childhood backyard and the orange crate where she would preach. She thought, *Is this possible? Could I possibly preach someday?*

The young people in her own church knew how she loved to talk about God and the Bible. Though she was often the only woman interested, her fellow church members knew that whenever Della spoke, wisdom would come out. Della knew her Bible better than most of the local pastors; her passionate zeal for the Lord was contagious. As she was becoming a woman, she wondered how she could serve God. It was her only real desire in life.

She listened carefully to every preacher, including the woman. Some people seemed offended; indeed, some refused to go to those sessions. But by the end of the week, Della had decided. She announced to her parents, "I'm going to be a preacher!" Dad looked at her with a slight smile and said in an almost inaudible whisper, "I knew it." His sober approval meant a great deal to Della. Her mother, however, looked at her with deep concern and replied, "Don't tell anyone . . . not yet, anyway."

But try as she might, Della could not keep such good news to herself. She promptly blurted the news out as soon as she got home. The five elders in their little country church of about 50 people were immediately divided over the issue. Della could not have imagined the intense discussions that emerged.

The youngest of the elders declared, "Paul clearly stated that no woman should ever teach a man. If she wants to teach so badly, let her teach her own children someday."

Another elder countered, "But Paul also says there is no distinction between a male and a female. And in 1 Corinthians 11, he tells women to wear a covering on their heads when they prophesy. So I think she could preach as long as she wears a hat."

"Even in the Old Testament," a third, soft-spoken elder interjected, "Deborah was obviously used by God. She judged His people."

"Yes," responded the oldest elder, a gentlemen whose voice carried command, "God used Deborah, but the book of Judges shows us just what happens to God's people when they pay no attention to His covenant. I don't think you'd want us copying other behavior in Judges! Besides, the principles run deeper than that. God has placed the husband as the head of his wife, and asks her to submit to him in all things."

"But Della isn't married," the soft-spoken elder continued. "Couldn't she preach if she stays under our authority?"

The fifth elder added, "Everyone is equal in God's eyes, whether slave or free, man or woman. Joel's prophecy clearly states that both men and women will prophesy. And it says it again in the book of Acts. We all know Della's godly heart and desire to serve her Lord. If we deny her the occasion to use her gifts, we are quenching the Spirit."

"Of course," the oldest elder argued, "God works in the hearts of all believers but that doesn't mean we abandon God's ordained structures. I love Della as much as any of you, but Paul appeals to creation structures when he speaks of this issue."

For 18 months, the elders wrestled with this issue; but what began as a polite discussion motivated by a genuine desire to understand the Word of God, soon became an explosive debate characterized by more and more divisive language.

Finally, just a few days before Della's 19th birthday, the little country church split—two elders supported Della's call to ministry and three of them said it was not biblical.

Della felt great pain and guilt over the split. She had known and loved these people for as long as she could remember. Even her brothers who loved her deeply chose to stay with the elders and the church members who opposed Della's call to preach. Now she understood why her mother had said, "Don't tell anyone." However, Della felt compelled to carry on with her plan to be a preacher. Within her own denomination, doors opened readily to her. She was ordained, and she preached for the next 34 years.

VOLUNTARISM

In the previous chapter, we examined the four concurrent streams in the "great river" called the Second Great Awakening:

- the camp meeting,
- the Restoration movement,
- the Yale University Revival under President Timothy Dwight, and
- Charles Finney's urban crusades.

Perhaps the most significant aspect, however, was not the public figures and events but the underside of Church history—the countless individuals who will never be recorded in any dictionary of Church history. They are often called volunteers, but they are so much more than that. They were really conscripted into God's army. Simply stated, they felt God had called them to Kingdom service. One characteristic of the Church throughout the ages is the hope and faith of simple people who believe that their lives count and that their obedience to Christ makes a difference. Although this has always been a gospel principle, such faith was often nearly extinguished in systems that were tightly controlled by a strong hierarchy. But in this period of spiritual vigor, individual believers embraced their role in the Church. Unlike Christians in other centuries who were tempted to think that they could not make a difference, American Christians in the mid to late 1800s were confidently served.

Voluntarism is not so much a movement as it is a loose collection of individuals who joined various causes for the purpose of transforming culture. There were five major voluntaristic appeals:

1. Temperance societies
2. Women's rights issues
3. The antislavery movement
4. The Sunday School movement
5. The Layman Revival

TEMPERANCE

The temperance movement sprang up not so much through the voice of a charismatic leader as through the fact that in northern Europe in the 1700s liquor was cheap. So widespread and pernicious was drunkenness that by 1743, Wesley outspokenly opposed the selling or drinking of liquor. In 1784, Philadelphia's well-known physician, Dr. Benjamin Rush, published a work entitled *An Inquiry into the Effects of Spiritous Liquors on the Human Body and Mind*. By 1800, the temperance movement was under way in America, popularized in the state of Virginia by an abstinence pledge. In 1826, the American Temperance Society was founded in Boston for the purpose of encouraging every person to commit to total abstinence. Seven of the 16 founders of the movement were pastors.

Why such a push for abstinence? Lyman Beecher, the pastor/revivalist who had been trained by Timothy Dwight, preached his *Six Sermons on Intemperance*, which outlined alcohol's threat to a democracy, specifically a Christian democracy. The use of alcohol was ruining lives, destroying families and threatening the very fabric of society.

But the American Temperance Society was not the only such organization. Six reformed alcoholics from Baltimore founded the Washingtonian

movement in 1840, which featured public testimonials of people set free
from alcohol and which sponsored group activities to dissuade individuals
from going to local taverns. Although the organization did not survive long,
by 1850 its counterpart, the Sons of Temperance, had 238,000 members in
the United States, Canada and England. Every member followed a strict personal code of total abstinence.

PROHIBITION

The first prohibition law was proposed in Maine in the 1850s. Several other
states followed suit. So successful was the Abstinence Party that a political
movement known as the Prohibition Party was founded in 1869. In 1874
the Women's Christian Temperance Union was founded. By 1902, every
state required schools to provide temperance instruction. In 1920, the
Eighteenth Amendment officially prohibited the use of intoxicating drinks.
It was repealed, however, in 1933. Most contemporary historians summarize prohibition with the following logic: Prohibition was repealed because
it was a failure. It failed in the sense that so many broke the law. It was simply unenforceable.

But that is very poor logic. Every law, in some measure, is broken.
Murders have been on an increase in most communities for many years, but
that does not cause us to repeal the law against murder. The number of people breaking speed limits is high (and getting higher!), but we don't stop
policemen from having radar guns. In some areas of the nation many illegal
immigrants are entering the country, but we don't disband the Immigration
Service. Laws being widely broken is not why prohibition was repealed. The
laws against drinking changed because of the social climate—among the
clergy and within the Church. In addition, the laws were changed because of
the high profitability of the brewing industry and its lobbying power. In
reality, the consumption of alcohol has brought absolutely no benefit to the
culture. It is, to this day, the single most destructive force in American culture. The effects of heroin and cocaine pale in comparison with the widespread, damaging effects of alcohol. Pastoral ministry would be easier in
every single community in America today, were it not for the rampant consumption of alcohol. Although the majority of Christians today advocate
social drinking, the painful reality is that one out of eight social drinkers
becomes an alcoholic. The economic impact—lost productivity, higher

insurance rates, welfare and homelessness—is catastrophic. But that cost pales when compared to the spiritual and emotional duress caused by drinking.

It takes courage today to stand up against the flow of alcohol in our culture. And it took the same courage for the prohibitionists. They were brilliant, bold and courageous as they addressed the social problems of alcoholism. They were politically incorrect. And it is a shame we don't have more like them today. The failure of the Church to produce more people who are willing to address the socially acceptable ills of our culture is one reason why some wonder if we can make the claim that the Church is really all that alive and well. The Church on this issue (and others!) is conformist, compromised and consumed with a man-pleasing political correctness. The outstanding leaders of the temperance movement have nothing in common with contemporary pastors who are afraid to use the *a* word (abortion), the *h* word (homosexuality) and the *g* word (gambling).

EARLY FEMINISM

When one hears the term "feminism," one may think of the radical feminists of today, with their attacks on the traditional family and their advocacy of gay/lesbian issues. That is *not* the type of feminism I am referring to. Such an approach would be labeled *radical* feminism. What is referred to here is *biblical* feminism; that is, the appropriate treatment of females in a way that honors the name of Christ. Our story begins at Oberlin College in Ohio, which became the first coeducational college in the world. Donald Dayton, in his book *Discovering an Evangelical Heritage*, notes that Asa Mahan, who served as Oberlin's first president, was so proud of his stand on women's rights that he desired the epitaph on his tombstone to include the fact that he was the first to welcome and encourage females, in conjunction with males, to be taken through a full college education.

It seems strange to us to think that women would not be permitted to have a college education, or at least not to follow such an education along with men. But such was the case. The call for women to receive a college education and to be included in the ministry (a more radical cause) was a direct outgrowth of the amazing voluntarism of the Second Great Awakening. The first woman to be ordained as a gospel preacher was Antoinette Brown. Her ordination sermon, entitled "Women's Right to Preach the Gospel," based on Galatians 3:28, was preached by Luther Lee, one of the founders of the Wesleyan Church. This was a radical new teaching.

Although Christian humanist Desiderius Erasmus (ca. 1469-1536) emphasized women's right to education and Bible study in the Reformation period, the Protestant Reformers largely disallowed women any part in public worship. Some Congregationalist women were allowed to vote in their churches in New England, and Baptist females could publicly announce their faith. But few women were allowed to preach. The one exception was the Quakers. One of the early arguments to allow women to preach was written by Quaker Margaret Fell.

In nineteenth-century America, a woman's right to vote and be involved in ministry surfaced with great intensity. Angelina (1805-1879) and Sarah Grimke (1792-1873), daughters of a prominent South Carolina judge, began speaking out against slavery, racism and sexism. In 1837, Sarah Grimke's *Letters on the Equality of the Sexes* attempted to expose the abuse and misuse of Scripture which denied females the expression they desired.

The primary Scripture appealed to was Galatians 3:28, where Paul says "there is neither . . . male nor female, for you are all one in Christ Jesus." Most Holiness and Pentecostal groups would later appeal to Joel 2:28 and Acts 2:17. In Joel the prophesy is stated. In Acts it is fulfilled. In both passages females were used by God. They declared: "your sons *and daughters* will prophesy" (emphasis added).

VOTING AND ORDINATION

Donald Dayton notes the role the Wesleyan denomination (previously called the Wesleyan Methodist church) had in the launching of the women's right to vote movement:

> The Seneca Falls meeting of 1848 that launched the movement and first call for the franchise for women was held in a Wesleyan Methodist church—apparently because only the abolitionist denomination was at all receptive to such radical ideas. (Even here there was some equivocation.) When the women arrived for the meeting, they found the building locked and had to climb in through a window![1]

By the 1860s the Wesleyan Methodists were ordaining women, a full hundred years before the present-day United Methodist church followed that practice. In 1891, B. T. Roberts, founder of the Free Methodist church, a sister denomination of the Wesleyans, wrote a persuasive book entitled *On the Ordaining of Women*. The position was further entrenched in the Free Methodist heritage in 1894 when Bishop W. A. Sellow wrote a work entitled *Why Not?* Even Jonathan Blanchard, the Presbyterian and Congregationalist president of Wheaton College, announced his commitment to Christian feminism in a Cincinnati debate with N. L. Rice; Blanchard proclaimed that "the first alteration which Christianity made in a polity of Judaism was to abdicate this oppressive distinction of sexes," which left women with "almost no rights."[2]

Perhaps the most outstanding example of a female involved in a team ministry was that of Catherine Booth (1829-1890), who in the 1850s founded the Salvation Army in England along with her husband, William (1829-1912). Catherine quickly outshone William. In fact, when they preached at different places on the same day, she drew the bigger crowd. Her defense of being involved in the ministry was recorded in a 32-page pamphlet entitled *Female Ministry*.

Hannah Whitall Smith, author of the classic *The Christian's Secret to a Happy Life*, wrote in one of her Bible studies (entitled the "Open Secret") that in "many . . . ways . . . God is like a mother." She was not advocating a gender-free translation (a controversy today) but was attempting to explain the full spectrum of God's attributes. Her goal was not to radically feminize the Bible. She was simply pointing out that God is gender free, even though we use masculine pronouns such as "He" or "Him." God has the strength traditionally associated with masculinity and the tenderness traditionally associated with femininity. God has merged both qualities into one.

LEADERSHIP AND SPEAKING ROLES

Female leadership was demonstrated in more than issues associated with women's rights issues or women's involvement in ministry. It was evident in other voluntaristic movements which permitted women to rise to high levels of leadership. One example was the Women's Christian Temperance Union (a proabstinence group) that placed persons like Frances Willard (1839-1898) into highly visible roles, including preaching from pulpits. By

1877, Willard was beginning to curtail her temperance work and to encourage women's involvement in the D. L. Moody crusades. When the Methodist church, of which she was a part, refused to ordain her, Willard wrote *Women in the Pulpit*, in 1889. Both the temperance movement and the antislavery movement afforded females opportunities for leadership they had previously been denied.

Perhaps the most impressive involvement of women in high levels of leadership was in the Holiness movement, and then later in the Pentecostal movement. The most influential mover and shaker in New York City and several Christian causes, including the expansion of Holiness teaching, was Phoebe Palmer (1807-1874). Palmer was a tireless revivalist, feminist, humanitarian and editor, and was significantly involved in the revival of 1857-1858 (the Layman Revival) that impacted all of New York City. A prolific writer, Palmer authored a 421-page book in defense of the right of women to preach, *The Promise of the Father*. In addition, she edited a magazine, *Guide to Holiness* (1864-1874), and 10 books, including one entitled *The Way of Holiness* (1845).

Moreover, one Holiness or Pentecostal denomination after another embraced the belief in the right of women to preach. The following are just a few examples:

- The Church of the Nazarene specifically addressed the issue in its founding constitution in 1894 in Los Angeles.
- The Pilgrim Holiness church, founded by Seth Cook Rees, embraced the concept when Rees's wife served as copastor and coevangelist with him.
- The Pillar of Fire denomination founder, Alma White, wife of a Methodist minister, claimed to be the first woman bishop in Christian history.
- The International Church of the Foursquare Gospel, normally known today as simply The Foursquare Church, was founded by a flamboyant woman preacher named Aimee Semple McPherson.

Although still a controversial issue in many denominations today, the right of women to preach in at least some denominations was clearly established. It is an irony that in these same denominations the number of female pastors has decreased. Nonetheless, something had been established—something that was part of a revivalist wave—the *female* voluntarism of the Second Great Awakening.

ANTISLAVERY MOVEMENT

In the pre-Civil War period, churches were divided between gradual emancipation (the gradual releasing of slaves so as not to economically undermine communities) and radical abolitionism (freeing the slaves immediately). One of the early critics of slavery was Jonathan Blanchard, the founding president of Wheaton College in Illinois. Wheaton College was originally founded as a Wesleyan Methodist institution in 1848 and was rechartered in 1860 as a Congregational college. The Wesleyan church learned a hard lesson in the loss of this college and chartered its future schools in a very different way. Charles Finney, president of Oberlin College in 1851, was the first to admit women and he was also the first to admit blacks. This was considered a radical concept. The admission of blacks to a school of whites predates the civil rights movement by over one hundred years. By the 1840s, antislavery sentiment was so strong that Theodore Weld helped organize the American Antislavery Society. Numerous wealthy businessmen joined the cause for reform, along with such well-known businessmen as Arthur and Lewis Tappan. Adding to the antislavery impulse was Orange Scott (1800-1847), who, along with Luther Lee, was effectively forced out of the Methodist Episcopal church (now called the United Methodist church) over his unwillingness to be silent regarding the issue of slavery. Consequently, he formed a denomination called the Wesleyan Methodist (later called the Wesleyan church) in 1843.

ORANGE SCOTT

Born in Brookfield, Vermont, Scott, at age 21, was converted at a camp meeting and became a Methodist preacher with only a year of formal education. As John S. O'Malley noted, Orange Scott was "convinced of the vital relationship between personal and social holiness." He "saw abolition as an inescapable consequence of the Wesleyan doctrine of entire sanctification."[3] Wesleyan "entire sanctification" was a call to holy, righteous living. Orange

Scott properly perceived this doctrine to be a call to change society. Slavery was a despicable evil. No believer, Orange Scott felt, could participate in it. He began to circulate copies of the *Liberator*, an antislavery tract, written by William Lloyd Garrison. In 1836, at the Methodist General Conference, he presented abolitionist legislation. It was defeated. The next year he continued as a lecturer for the American Antislavery Society. Due to his antislavery position, he was kept from expressing his views in several magazines, so in 1838 he formed his own, the *Wesleyan Quarterly Review,* which changed its name the following year to the *American Wesleyan Observer*. After failing to get the General Conference of the Methodist church to agree with him on the slavery issue in 1840, he and Lucius Matlock organized an antislavery convention in New York. In 1842 he withdrew from the Methodist Episcopal church. The following year in Utica, New York, he founded the Wesleyan church and became its president. An 1843 document serves as an omen of a split about to occur in the Methodist church. The fourth principle of this document declares simply that slavery is a sin.

Exhausted and in poor health, Orange Scott died at age 47 in 1847.

DIVISIONS OVER ANTISLAVERY

New England, however, was not the epicenter of the antislavery movement. Lane Seminary in Cincinnati was. By 1833, a student movement led by Theodore Weld was active in the freeing of slaves. When authorities attempted to stop the students they left Lane Seminary and went to Oberlin College. There, under the presidency of Charles Finney, the antislavery movement flourished. One of the most celebrated events occurred in early 1858 when a fugitive named John Price was taken from Oberlin to be shipped back to the South. The ringing of the chapel bell at Oberlin alerted the town that something was wrong. Several hundred Oberlin residents went to Wellington and stormed the hotel where Price was being held until the train came in. The grateful slave was taken back to Oberlin and housed by J. H. Fairchild, the man who had succeeded Finney as president.[4]

The antislavery issue divided more than seminaries and communities; it split entire denominations. In 1845, Southern Baptist Convention was organized due to the opposition to slavery among Northern Baptists. In the same year the Methodist Episcopal church, South, was founded as separate from the North. Presbyterians from both the new-school and the old-school groups split in 1858 and 1851, respectively. Episcopalians also divided. With the exception of the Baptists, these denominations merged again after the Civil War.

It was a tragic scar on the collective Christian conscience that some Church leaders closed their eyes to the evils of slavery. Much of institutional Christianity, for reasons that are embarrassing to mention—economic ease and social acceptance—compromised its values at the altar of expediency. However, God is greater than any social evil or institutional wrong; God always has a remnant of believers in every age who will speak out and struggle against moral and social injustice. Whether it is one person or a thousand who choose to speak His truth, the undying fact remains: God justice can never be dampened or diminished. And even if it's only a small remnant who are unwilling to compromise, they are still the Church. And they (the Church) are God's only strategy for keeping civilization from self-destruction.

It's a tribute to the Church's tenacity for truth that although those who embraced radical abolitionism were disdained at the time, they are heroes to us. Perhaps future historians will feel the same about those who are fighting so valiantly to eradicate abortion. Just as history has been hard on those who were proslavery, it will someday be hard on those who are proabortion. Truth has a way of emerging—eventually.

THE SUNDAY SCHOOL MOVEMENT

The strong voluntarism in the Second Great Awakening was spurred by the belief that the layman could teach the Bible to other Christians. Sunday School seems commonplace, almost passé. It was not so for Robert Raikes (1773-1811). Sunday School was a radical idea that stirred up great controversy. While walking the streets of Gloucester, England, Robert inquired about why the children were playing in the streets. They had nothing else to do, he was told, and thus were getting into trouble. Robert hired a teacher for students between the ages of 6 and 14 and launched a school on Sunday in 1780. Sunday School was not held on Sunday because it coincided with services at church. It was held on Sunday because it was the only day the children were not working, since this predated child labor laws. The subjects covered included not only Bible stories but also reading, writing and religion. The first classes were held in Saint Mary-de-Crypt Church in Gloucester, the same church where George Whitefield first preached a half-century earlier.

The idea was so popular that it crossed the Atlantic. Schools were founded in Virginia as early as 1785; and in 1790 the Sunday School movement spread to Boston, New York and Philadelphia. Since the early schools were designed to help poor families, some Sunday Schools were actually established at the places where the children were employed in factories. With the coming of secularization during the Enlightenment (which began to sweep New England), the Sunday School seemed a practical way of compensating for the loss of Christian values in common educational facilities.

But Sunday School was not readily accepted by all. It was very controversial. What, you ask, was so controversial about something as innocuous as Sunday School? It was controversial because laymen taught in the Sunday Schools. Who would think that a layperson would be allowed to teach the Bible! But the critics were unsuccessful in silencing this exploding movement.

In 1824, the American Sunday School Union was founded. Publishing houses began to produce literature for the burgeoning movement. By 1869, national Sunday School conventions came into prominence. Denominations quickly saw how popular the movement was and began to launch their own Sunday School departments. While one must acknowledge that Sunday Schools have lost some of their prominence since the 1970s, the fact remains that this was a massive movement with equally impressive results. When one considers the fact that Sunday Schools in many of America's approximately 400,000 churches are run by unsalaried laypersons, one sees how much resiliency the movement has demonstrated. As an instructional and evangelistic tool, it is virtually unparalleled in the history of Christianity.

THE LAYMAN REVIVAL

As we near the close of this Second Great Awakening, we must include one more revival. The Layman Revival (1857-1858) is one of the most difficult to explain. Most of the people involved in it are unknown, and historians know little about it, which makes it difficult to research. But what we do know is so unusual that it must be included. Our story starts with Jeremiah Lamphier, who started a prayer meeting in a room in the Dutch Reformed church in Manhattan. Although he advertised it among a population of one million, only six people showed up. The following week, however, he was encouraged when 14 attended. The week after that, 23. At this point, they decided to meet every day. Soon the Dutch Reformed church was filled, so they moved to a Methodist church on John Street. Then they moved to a public building in downtown New York. One newspaper reporter, attempting to get to as many prayer meetings as he could during the noon hour, counted over 6,100 persons in the 12 prayer meetings that he was able to attend during that hour.

The Layman Revival, which lasted for approximately 18 months during 1857 and 1858, accomplished an amazing work of evangelism as well. At one point 10,000 people a week were being converted in New York City alone. As word of the revival spread through New England, it began to be imitated there as well. People were coming to prayer meetings not merely at noon, but at eight in the morning and six in the evening as well. As the Layman Revival spread, it moved across the Atlantic to the British Isles and eventually to South Africa and South India. In one year, it is believed that more than one million people were evangelized; and the revival's effects were felt for the next four decades.[5]

MODERN MISSIONARY MOVEMENT

Those converted and affected by the gospel became concerned for the spiritual condition of other nations. The modern missionary movement traces its roots to a most unusual event in 1806. Students at Williams College in Massachusetts were having a small prayer meeting. When frightened by a thunderstorm, they took shelter under a haystack. This event is known as the famous "haystack prayer meeting" of 1806 in which seven young men pledged their devotion to God to support world missions. From this group came in 1808 an organization known as the Society of the Brethren, whose motto was "We can do it if we will." At Andover Seminary, the group was joined by several other students, the best known being Adoniram Judson. In 1810, Judson and three other students made an appeal for missionary support to the Congregational Ministers Association in Massachusetts. And in that year the American Board of Commissioners for Foreign Missions was formed. The modern missionary movement, which would eventually send tens of thousands of missionaries to every part of the earth, had begun.

CONCLUSION

Walking through 60 years of American history from 1800 to 1860 reveals a vigorous and complex period. How does one explain all the unrest that resulted in such profound changes? It was because God's hand was on His Church. It's a Church with lots of imperfections. It's a Church with an imprecise self-awareness. It's a Church that failed to rid itself immediately of slavery. It's a Church that took advantage of females. It's a Church that didn't take a strong enough stand against alcohol. It's a Church that didn't grasp the role of the missions movement as early as it might have. In those ways and in other ways it was imperfect.

But it's a Church that came to terms with these and many other issues. The impulse of the first 60 years of the 1800s was awesome! All believers ought to hold their heads high as they see how the ways and will of God unfolded, sometimes slowly, but surely nonetheless.

To further assist you in understanding the key individuals and events of chapter 14, study questions, charts, diagrams, time lines and links to biographical websites are available on the Internet at www.jimgarlow.com. Please follow the site links to *How God Saved Civilization*, chapter 14 study helps.

DEALING WITH DIVISIONS

THE POST-CIVIL WAR PERIOD

Dates covered: A.D. 1865-1900
Key persons: D. L. Moody, Russell Conwell,
Washington Gladden, Walter Rauschenbusch

Arlo grabbed an iron rod from the fireplace and screamed at his uncle Lenny. "I hate you! I hate you!"

His uncle lashed out at the 14-year-old with a clenched fist and a mouthful of curses. "You little runt!"

Arlo circled around his uncle and swung the black rod like a baseball bat at Lenny's head. Lenny dodged the blow, and he countered by pushing Arlo against the mantelpiece. He then picked his young nephew up by his collar, walked Arlo to the front door and threw the boy out onto the rain-soaked pavement. In a soft yet frightening voice, he said, "Arlo, if I ever see you again, I'll kill you."

Arlo cried that night. It was cold and wet in the streets of lower Manhattan. If only his father or mother were here. Arlo began to dream of the past. He could remember when he was six and he and his parents had left Italy for the New World. His father had come with a great dream. But the dream had turned into a nightmare. Within 10 days of leaving Italy, Arlo's mother died on board the ship. When he and his father arrived in New York City, they found cousin Lenny's house, but they were hardly welcome. When Arlo's father finally found work at the tanning factory, the low pay forced him to find a second job as an assistant cook in a small restaurant. Combined, both jobs made for long hours, and Arlo watched as his father's health evaporated.

Arlo winced; the memories were painful. Two days before his seventh birthday, his uncle met him at the door with a gruff voice and a stern look. "Your dad's home early. Spitting up blood."

"Let me go see him."

Lenny turned his back and replied, "He's resting!"

"But," Arlo started.

Lenny turned quickly, grabbed Arlo's collar and threw the boy down on the living-room couch, "You rest, too! We're busy lookin' after your old man. I don't want to see you until tomorrow morning. Understood?" After hours of turning and tossing, Arlo finally fell asleep for the night.

The morning that followed was eerie—a gray mist, a pale sun and strange voices by the living-room front door. A man in a black suit and top hat asked, "What time did he die?"

Arlo had crept across the floor and peeked through into the living room. The question struck his heart. He froze and then began howling in a long, loud, empty and angry fashion, "Papaaaaaaaaa!" The cry filled the whole house. "Papaaaaaaaaa!" Before he knew what had come over him, Arlo was banging his head on the fireplace.

He'd gone quiet after that. Over the next seven years he rarely talked to anyone. Only his outbursts of rage flared to the surface. Now at age 14, he found himself alone, in the rain, on the streets. Even his uncle Lenny was fed up.

For three months Arlo survived by working odd jobs or stealing food. With nothing more than an occasional bottle of wine, a stale loaf of bread, an egg or two that he would eat raw, Arlo lived in a world of shadows.

On a cold night in 1892, his hunger was more than even he could take. With no money or possibilities of work, he begged a nice lady at a local bakery for some bread. The woman replied "My boss won't let me. But go to Rauschenbusch."

Arlo wondered, *Rauschenbusch? What kind of a name is that?*

He'd never heard such a name. He wandered down the road where the woman had instructed him to go. For several hours, he watched people walk through a door. *What were they doing in there?* he thought. *What kind of place is it?*

An elderly gentleman exited the building and crossed the street. Arlo was leaning against a brick wall along one of the alleys when the old man caught sight of him. He asked, "Are you hungry?"

Arlo lowered his head.

"Come with me, sir," said the man gently. He reached for Arlo's elbow, but Arlo pulled away.

Arlo stared at the man. *Sir? This man called me "sir?" Does this man know what I am or how I live? Why does he call me sir?*

The elderly man's tone was soft and inviting. "We would love to give you a good meal. There's plenty of food across the street. I have someone to visit in the hospital, so I don't have time to talk with you just now, but I do hope you will have a good meal and stay warm tonight. You are welcome to sleep in our building. We have clean sheets and warm blankets."

The man barely touched Arlo on the shoulder. "You are welcome, sir." The man walked away.

By now, Arlo was so hungry and so cold that he didn't care why the man was so strange. He crossed the street and pushed the door open. A middle-aged woman gave a warm smile that reminded Arlo of his mother.

Arlo could even sense the tears coming. "Glad to have you. Please, come in. We have plenty of food if you're hungry."

He followed her cautiously into a large room. Arlo sat down at a long table, where everyone was eating and drinking. The lady brought him a large bowl of beef soup. Without waiting for the spoon, he lifted the bowl to his lips and drank it down. The lady wasn't shocked at all. "Let me give you more," she said.

Arlo ate more that night than all he had eaten in the last three weeks. An Italian woman showed him where the men's quarters were, and he laid his head on a pillow that night. Arlo barely whispered his disbelief aloud, "Who are these people?"

An older man in the next bed whispered back, "They say they do it because Jesus would do it."

Jesus? Since his mother died, Arlo had only heard the name as a curse word. *Jesus,* he pondered, as he fell to sleep. *Jesus. I wonder who He is? He must be a very good man. I'd like to meet Him. Maybe He'll be here in the morning.*

THE END OF THE WAR

On Palm Sunday, April 9, 1865, General Lee surrendered the army of northern Virginia. Five days later, on Good Friday, President Abraham Lincoln was assassinated; he died the next day. The official close of the rebellion was proclaimed on August 20, 1866, by the newly installed president, Andrew Johnson. The Civil War had finally ended. But what had this war meant? Six hundred thousand had been killed and about one million had been injured.[1] And the immense animosity that tainted relations between North and South would last for over a century. The event called the Civil War had extracted a huge price from American people. And regretfully, the animosity had seeped into the churches.

IMPACT ON DENOMINATIONS

Between 1861 and 1865, church after church had split. Entire denominations—Methodists, Baptists, Episcopalians and Presbyterians—had undergone a North/South split over the issue of slavery! In addition, Christian churches were almost entirely segregated. In 1816, Richard Allen (1760-1831), a brilliant black preacher who had purchased his freedom from a slave owner, founded the African Methodist Episcopal church. Methodist Bishop Francis Asbury, a white, led the formal dedication service for the new denomination in 1794 in Philadelphia. From 1856 to 1876 the A.M.E. church grew 10 times over, from 20,000 to 200,000 members. America's second largest black denomination, the African Methodist Episcopal Zion church, also started with Bishop Asbury's encouragement, due to discrimination in the John Street Methodist Episcopal Zion church in New York City in 1796. The first annual conference was not held until 1821, but this church experienced phenomenal growth.

How do we account for the beginning of the Civil War? The irony is that the Second Great Awakening, with all of its vigor, had actually exacerbated the Civil War (1861-1865). The radical increase of voluntarism, and specifically the abolitionist focus, had caused common people to feel they could make a difference. Many pressed for the immediate release of all slaves (this was advocated by the American Antislavery Society, founded in 1833). Others pressed for gradual emancipation. Others, with more radical ideas, joined the American Colonization Society, which was founded in 1817 with a goal of resettling the freed slaves in Liberia, Africa. Those three positions, all irreconcilable, created increasing friction that finally erupted into war.

Preachers thundered from their pulpits their views of slavery, some fabricating a biblical defense for it. A fascinating study in opposites is provided by the back-to-back sections in Lefferts A. Loetscher's book entitled *American Christianity*. One section begins with the title "Irrepressible Abolitionism," yet the following chapter is entitled "A Biblical Defense of Slavery." "Irrepressible Abolitionism" contains the resolutions passed by a Methodist antislavery convention in Boston on January 18, 1843.

In contrast to those resolutions was the defense of slavery outlined by the articulate bishop, John England (1786-1842), of the Charleston Diocese of the Roman Catholic church. He was an eloquent, colorful and provocative preacher, who argued in a most persuasive style, the legal, moral and religious foundations for slave ownership according to his understanding of the New Testament. His rationale was preserved in Protestant and Roman Catholic churches throughout the South.

The impact of the war was horrendous on every institution in America, including the Church. The war "cost billions of dollars" and it inflicted "more American casualties" than any other war in the history of the United

States.[2] Perhaps equally serious was the racial and sectional distrust that would continue for well over 100 years. The Church fared poorly during this time. Not only did it lose members through death, but its collective conscience also seemed to be damaged by years of bloodshed. During the Civil War years of 1861 to 1865, and also in the years that followed, Church membership and Church attendance seriously declined.[3]

VARIOUS VIEWS OF THE CIVIL WAR

Robert Lewis Dabney (1820-1898) was a Southern Presbyterian professor who had served in the war under Stonewall Jackson. His views were clearly expounded in his preaching and writings, in which he declared that the North had attempted to crush the South out of sheer malice. "I do not forgive . . . those people who have invaded our country, burned our cities, destroyed our homes, slain our young men, and spread desolation and ruin over our land! No, I do not forgive them."[4] Henry Ward Beecher, son of the famous Lyman Beecher (referred to in an earlier chapter), revealed the intense feelings of some Northerners when he stated that "the whole guilt of this war [is] upon the ambitious . . . political leaders of the South. . . . A day will come when God will reveal judgment. . . . And then the guiltiest and most remorseless traitors . . . shall be whirled aloft and plunged downward forever and ever in an endless retribution."[5] Healing was desperately needed!

Famous preacher Horace Bushnell was one of those who regarded the war as a type of national crucifixion where the corporate conscience of America was being punished so that they could somehow experience atonement. In his book *The Vicarious Sacrifice*, Bushnell suggested that the war could be good in the same way that Good Friday was good. It opened the door for something much better. And best of all, after the crucifixion would come a type of national resurrection.[6]

Philip Schaff (1819-1893) viewed the war as a type of divine judgment for the sin of slavery, whose end result could provide a sense of redemption. How else could one make sense out of America's most excruciating moment? How could the dream have gone so far off course? How could America's dream of being the New Israel and the city set on a hill, as the early New England preachers had declared it, have been ripped apart by a five-year cataclysmic struggle that left so many dead, so many wounded, and people in one part of the nation hating those across state and boundary lines?

HEALING

Healing was desperately needed after the Civil War. Sadly, the churches were little prepared to help. The major denominations that had split before the war did not reunite quickly and so could not lead the nation into repentance and forgiveness. Calamities that followed the Civil War also accentuated polarization between the North and the South and various churches: the assassination of President Lincoln, the impeachment of Andrew Johnson, the severe corruption during the Grant administration, the excessive and exploitative greed of expanding corporations and businesses, the failure of national Reconstruction for the South from 1855-1877.[7] How would the Church respond to such a crisis? How would the Church reach the cities' teeming masses?

Critics of the Church could have a heyday concerning this period. The Church appears woefully deficient for the needs of a nation desperately in need of healing. Yet, the common thread we have seen throughout all the centuries of Church history is the grace of God working amid flawed human beings. Once again, at a time when the Church was faced with the daunting task of helping the nation, God was already preparing men and women to face the challenges. The most spectacular response is found in the life and work of a man named Dwight L. Moody.

REVIVALISM: AMERICA'S NEEDED ANSWER

It is not surprising that in this period of radical change, the Church returned to a method of evangelism that she had fine-tuned on previous occasions. Revivalism, aggressively calling people to be serious about God, had worked in New England in the 1600s and early 1700s. It had worked on the frontiers of Kentucky and Tennessee in the early 1800s. And it was about to work again.

If there were such a thing as a Mount Rushmore of Evangelism, one of the four faces would have to be that of Dwight L. Moody (1837-1899). Born

in Northampton, Massachusetts, Moody received very little formal education, and virtually no religious training. As a young man, he was a successful salesman at his uncle's shoe store in Boston in 1854. While visiting
Moody's store one day, his Sunday School teacher, Edward Kimball, led him
to repent of his sins. Two years later, Moody, weary of Boston and eager for
excitement, moved to Chicago where he set the goal of earning $100,000.
That early goal depicted the entrepreneurial spirit of the evangelist
throughout his life.

D. L. MOODY:
REVIVALIST OF BIG DREAMS

Once in Chicago, he started a Sunday School in Chicago's north-side slums.
Soon hundreds of children were coming, and the Sunday School became
the Illinois Street Church. During the Civil War period, he became involved
with the Chicago YMCA. The YMCA had been founded in London in 1844
by George Williams to attempt to combat the sin of city life and provide for
young men a Christian environment. (A fuller discussion of the YMCA will
occur later.) By 1866, Moody was president of the Chicago YMCA and
known around town as "crazy Moody" because of his extreme exuberance
and totally unpredictable preaching style.

Moody dreamed big. He had crowds. He had ministries. Now he needed buildings to house them. On Sunday, September 29, 1867, Moody's
dream of building an enormous multipurpose YMCA building—the first
ever in America—was realized. With a greater-than-capacity crowd present,
Farwell Hall was dedicated. Although named for a primary philanthropist,
John V. Farwell, another man provided much of Moody's funding throughout his ministry—the farm equipment developer, Cyrus H. McCormick.
This building would be a place where the "strongholds of sin" would be broken, declared D. L. Moody that day.[8]

But Moody did not get to enjoy his new building very long. On January
7, 1868, a fire broke out that devastated downtown Chicago, including
Moody's three-month-old Farwell Hall. But "before the embers cooled,
Moody and many friends of the YMCA began knocking on the doors of businessmen, seeking funds to rebuild the partially insured structure. People
responded with extraordinary generosity. . . . on January 19, 1869, doors

opened on Farwell Hall No. 2."[9] But Moody would face another tragedy with his new 2,500-seat auditorium. On Sunday night, October 8, 1871, the great Chicago fire took place, burning over 18,000 buildings and leaving more than 100,000 people homeless. The total loss was conservatively estimated at 200 million dollars—a staggering fortune when one considers that the figure is in 1871 dollars. Fifty-seven insurance companies went bankrupt, along with hundreds of other businesses. At least a thousand people perished, though exact figures were hard to come by, due to the high drifter population of Chicago. When the fire finally burned out on Tuesday night, October 10, "only one house eerily remained standing in a three and a half square mile part of the city."[10] The buildings that D. L. Moody had built were gone: the Illinois Street Church, the second Farwell Hall and his own home on State Street. The Chicago fire of 1871 could not have come at a worse time for Moody. He was severely exhausted and fatigued. He had kept a preaching and teaching schedule that was far too strenuous for him.

MOODY'S LIFE-CHANGING EXPERIENCE

One month after the fire, Moody went to New York and Philadelphia and several other cities for the purpose of raising the funds once again to rebuild his mission. It was while walking in New York City that he wrote, "my heart was not in the work of begging. I could not appeal. I was crying all the time that God would fill me with His Spirit."[11] This profound experience came after four months of agonizing struggle, during which D. L. Moody felt empty and immobilized. An examination of his ministry, he commented, caused him to feel he was preaching and doing good for all the wrong reasons. He regarded himself as miserable. But on that day, on the streets of New York City, God met Moody in such a way that he was never the same. He exclaimed: "Ah, what a day!—I cannot describe it, I seldom refer to it, it is almost too sacred an experience to name—Paul had an experience of which he never spoke for fourteen years—I can only say God revealed Himself to me and I had such an experience of His love that I had to ask Him to stay His hand."[12]

So overpowered was Moody by this experience that he spent much of his time weeping before God. Wrote his good friend, D. W. Whittle, "Moody lost interest in everything except the preaching of Christ and working for souls. He determined to go to England that he might be free from all entanglements in the rebuilding of his church building and [Farwell] Hall."[13]

LARGE CRUSADES AND A MOVEMENT AMONG YOUTH

Moody traveled to England with his spectacular musician friend and chorister, Ira Sankey (1840-1908). After several months, he finally received an official invitation to hold a revival in Edinburgh. The revival services were profoundly successful. As a result, Moody stayed in Great Britain for two more years, 1873-1875, and preached to enormous crowds in Scotland, England and Ireland. With German "higher criticism" (a study of the Bible which eroded the Bible's authority) on the rise, many believers were relieved to see such a profound response to Moody's revival pleas. Having had no theological training, his sermons were theology-free, and appealed in a transdenominational way to the popular mind-set. By the time he returned to the United States, he had become famous and he began conducting crusades from 1875 to 1879 in Brooklyn, Philadelphia, New York City, Chicago and Boston. In 1881, he returned for three years for an equally successful evangelistic tour of Great Britain and then came back for a whirlwind tour of the United States and Canada from 1884 through 1891. He preached to huge crowds at the 1893 Chicago World's Fair.

In addition to beginning two schools in his hometown in Massachusetts (Northfield), Moody established the Northfield Conferences in 1880, which developed into the Student Volunteer Movement in 1886, a precursor to the modern-day Campus Crusade for Christ. Interestingly, both organizations had a similar motto. Moody's Student Volunteer Movement had the motto, "The evangelization of the world in the next generation." In 1889, he helped start a Bible Institute, which after his death was renamed the Moody Bible Institute and continues as a powerful influence in Chicago to the present day.

MOODY—THE MAN

The loveable Moody developed extremely close friends on both sides of the Atlantic among Christians with widely divergent views. Even those who were unsympathetic to his preaching and preaching style seemed to love him as a person. He was modest and congenial. His sermons were straightforward and down-home. He was successful in drawing in the wealthy business community to underwrite his endeavors. And his unlimited energy allowed him to keep ministering, with an indescribably busy schedule, until he died at age 62 while returning from his last revival in Kansas City.

Moody preached during a season of social unrest. Storm clouds on the horizon indicated that labor unrest was imminent. In May of 1886, Chicago's Hay Market Square experienced a riot. Moody remained silent on the social issues that had caused this riot and, instead, spoke only of the spiritual solution. A second eruption occurred in 1894 in numerous cities in addition to Chicago. A nationwide labor strike brought trains to a halt, provoking President Grover Cleveland to send out federal troops. Moody was again silent as he preached continually to the poor (as he always had done) and yet his ministry was funded by the wealthy corporation owners. His critics objected to his silence, but Moody maintained that he was an evangelist and would stay focused. He believed that the only thing that could bring genuine justice to the poor was the gospel of Christ. He argued that righteousness precedes justice. Only then can poverty be addressed adequately or peace return to the cities.

MOODY'S LEGACY

Moody's impact was enormous. His preaching produced parachurch ministries unlike any before. In addition, he left behind independent churches that rose up as a result of his converts. The people who were drawn to his preaching could not tolerate the stuffy traditionalism of mainline churches. They wanted something fresh and powerful, like a Moody-Sankey crusade. In addition, although Moody was not overly concerned with the details of theology, he affected the Church's theology profoundly. Strict Calvinism was largely undercut and replaced by Moody's Arminian understanding of God. Moody's chief concern was getting the message of a loving God to as many people as possible. He was one of the first American revivalists to adopt a premillennialist view, which teaches that Christ will return before a 1,000-year peaceful reign on earth. Moody's view of his work was simple: "I look upon this world as a wretched vessel. God has given me a life-boat and said to me, 'Moody, save all you can.'"[14] That is precisely what he did! And that is why he is the single most influential figure from this time period. Not until the preaching of the baseball-player-turned-evangelist, Billy Sunday (1862-1935), would America see another revivalist of this magnitude.

MOODY'S ENGLISH COUNTERPART

Although our concern is with D. L. Moody and with America, it is important to recognize the preaching of Charles Spurgeon (1843-1892) in Britain. Few preachers in all of Church history command the respect of this English preacher/orator who weekly filled a 6,000-seat London auditorium known as the Metropolitan Tabernacle. His services were much more than an experience. The sermons had rich content. So significant were his sermons that they are still popular reading today. In conjunction with his enormous church building were a college, an orphanage and a social-relief agency. Spurgeon, with his Metropolitan Tabernacle, was way ahead of his time, a precursor of the modern-day megachurches. His preaching style has been a model for the last century, a combination of solid content, expressiveness, enthusiasm and humor.

THE CITIES

On numerous occasions I have stood before students to teach them Church history. As they look at my Church history time line, I point out that in 1844, George Williams began the YMCA in England. In 1878, William Booth started the Salvation Army in England. Both movements quickly came to America. "What does this tell you about what was happening in England and America?" I ask. I always get some blank stares. Then I ask again, "In England, when George Williams started the YMCA and William Booth began the Salvation Army, what does that tell you about conditions within England and the United States?" More blank stares. To help them out, I then ask, "What do these organizations do?"

At that point, I can see the mental wheels turning. "Oh," they say, "there must have been some problems—problems in the cities."

"You are correct," I say.

And problems there were. So significant was the founding of one of these organizations in the overall flow of Church history that when Kenneth Curtis, the former editor of *Church History* magazine, published *Dates with Destiny: The 100 Most Important Dates in Church History*, he included the founding of the Salvation Army. The inclusion of this group has as much to do with the social climate in which the organization was formed as with the organization itself.

PLURALISM

The close of the 1800s was a complex and turbulent time. America no longer looked and acted as if it were united. Unity was gone. It was a time of enormous divergency. The little country churches were beginning to experience the pains of exodus as increasing numbers of people went to the cities for jobs and all the comforts of city life. But the city was not always kind to its inhabitants, especially if they had arrived recently, couldn't speak the language and were economically destitute. If one were reading only the headlines of the newspapers in 1896, one would think that Protestants had reason to rejoice, for both presidential candidates were born-again Christians: Republican William McKinley, a Methodist, and Democrat William Jennings Bryan, a Presbyterian. But in the cities the gap between the middle-class Protestant establishment and the working poor was rapidly growing. And that gap led to a deepening division between those who embraced the "gospel of wealth" and those who advocated applying the "social gospel."

THE GOSPEL OF WEALTH

Intellectuals within the Protestant church reacted to the crisis of the cities in opposite ways. On one side of the issue was Russell H. Conwell (1843-1925). On the other was Walter Rauschenbusch (1861-1918). Conwell became the chief spokesman for what was labeled the gospel of wealth, and advocated this position in a famous sermon entitled "Acres of Diamonds," which he preached 6,000 times! Pastor of one of the largest congregations in America and founder of Temple University in Philadelphia in 1888, Conwell stated that just as Jesus had provided salvation, America provided opportunity and he extolled everyone to reach for the American dream. And he honestly believed that it was within reach of everyone who desired it.

THE SOCIAL GOSPEL

Not everyone was so optimistic, however. By 1900, 10 percent of the American families controlled 90 percent of the nation's wealth. Labor unrest and labor riots quickly became a reality. In an attempt to meet the immediate need, many Christians helped to form rescue missions, the YMCA, the Salvation Army and other organizations. But the most profound theological development to address the inequity of the middle class and the working poor was called the social gospel, later known as social Christianity and on some occasions referred to as Christian socialism.

To men such as Walter Rauschenbusch, proclaiming salvation to an unsaved person was inadequate. The poor had to be lifted out of their deplorable economic conditions by transforming the social structures of the day. The good news was that there were articulate pastors who cared so deeply for the poor. The bad news was that in their concern for the poor, they committed the proverbial error of throwing the baby out with the bathwater, and failed to emphasize the role of personal conversion.

WALTER RAUSCHENBUSCH AND WASHINGTON GLADDEN

When Walter Rauschenbusch pastored in Hell's Kitchen in New York City, he saw that individual conversions and standard Christian discipline failed to solve the hurts and pains of the city. It was then that he turned to the social gospel, and continued refining it as a professor at Rochester Theological Seminary from 1897 to 1918. So powerful was he as a teacher and preacher that he is considered, along with Jonathan Edwards and Horace Bushnell, to be one of the most influential thinkers in American Christianity. He garnered international attention in 1907 when he published *Christianity and the Social Crisis*. Although partially deaf, he traveled to hundreds of locations to give speeches on the topics that would be depicted by the book titles that he left as a legacy:

- *For God and the People: Prayers of the Social Awakening*
- *Christianizing the Social Order*
- *Dare We Be Christians?*
- *The Social Principles of Jesus*
- *A Theology for the Social Gospel*

While he was clearly liberal in his theological perceptions, Rauschenbusch was a genius at analyzing the culture and attempting to make biblical applications. Instead of individual salvation, he preached social salvation. Instead of personal sin, he preached against social sin. Social sin, as defined by Rauschenbusch, were those un-Christlike and antibiblical structures in cultures that deprived people of fundamental and basic needs, such as food, clothing and shelter. He redefined the phrase "kingdom of God." He advocated that God and man somehow work together against the forces of evil to bring in justice, democracy and brotherhood and, thus, bring in the kingdom of God.

Rauschenbusch's ideas were shared by other pastors as well. One of the most articulate spokesmen for the social gospel was Washington Gladden (1856-1918). Gladden pastored some of his most fruitful years in Columbus, Ohio, where he served on the Columbus City Council from 1900 to 1902 as a way of modeling for other Christians his belief that believers should be participants in the issues of city life. Gladden published over 38 books. The titles of these books show the passion of his heart:

- *Applied Christianity* (1886)
- *Social Salvation* (1902)
- *The Christian Pastor and the Working Church* (1907)
- *The Church in Modern Life* (1908)

Gladden was fiercely committed to applying Christian theology to the problems of an industrial and urban culture. The practicality of his concerns was demonstrated in the hymn that he wrote, "O Master, Let Me Walk with Thee," which is found in some Protestant hymnals today. In his sermons and writings, Gladden pleaded with people to integrate their Christian faith in the workplace and to act morally and with justice in all decisions, including business decisions.

Although some of Rauschenbusch's biblical definitions were lacking, it is important to remember that Rauschenbusch's voice, Gladden's concerns and others like them were desperately needed to correct the rampant selfishness of what Mark Twain, in 1873, called the Gilded Age. When evaluating Rauschenbusch's thinking, particularly regarding the coming kingdom of God, it is important to remember that he lived in an age of optimism. The perfectibility of man and culture was considered to be within grasp. According to most thinkers, things were getting better and better. World War I (1914-1917) later crushed that national optimism.

EVALUATING RAUSCHENBUSCH

While I am tempted, as a conservative Evangelical, to attack Rauschenbusch's obvious liberalism, I feel it might be more beneficial to both me and the reader to pause and contemplate what he did and said that we need to heed. His pastoral ministry began in the most revolting portions of New York City. He lived every day with the squalor of a national dream gone awry. As a young pastor and later as a seasoned professor, Rauschenbusch desperately tried to find a way to address the brokenness of humanity. While his biblical interpretation leaves much to be desired, one must respect the bold (though admittedly inadequate) attempts to make biblical application to social issues. When examining the cities and the seeming inability of the gospel to penetrate both the individual hearts of the workers and the structures in which they worked, a solution was desperately needed. Rauschenbusch courageously offered one.

SEARCHING FOR "BOTH/AND" BALANCE

Having said that Rauschenbusch's attempts were noble, I must add that he seems to have refused the fundamental biblical themes of personal sin, personal repentance and personal salvation. The great tragedy of the social gospel was not what it did but what it failed to do. As an amateur Church historian, comfortably removed from this event by 100 years, I find it easy to see the flaws. Here are my questions: Why can't one who advocates the changes of *structural* evils also call for the need for *personal* conversion? Why can't the same person who calls for a slumlord to clean up his building, also call for the landlord and his tenants to come to know Christ in a personal way? Why can't the union organizer who is rallying his workers for a strike also teach them about the appropriate times for biblical submission to authority? Why can't the gospel-of-wealth preachers (such as Russell Conwell) call upon corporation owners to walk with humility, justice and economic fairness? Why does it have to be either/or? Why can't it be both/and?

The answer is *not* found in one side or the other, the gospel of wealth or the social gospel, for if we looked at either side, we would conclude that the Church is not balanced. It is when you put the Church into "one bowl and stir vigorously for 10 minutes" that you have a "mixture" that is truly the Church. Was Walter Rauschenbusch right? Was Washington Gladden right? Was Russell Conwell right? No, because each had imbalances. But when you put them together, along with D. L. Moody, they do a spectacular job of representing the Church. It is in that sense that I enthusiastically say that although civilization itself has no hope, the Church—when reflecting all that Christ is—preserves all that is worth preserving in civilization. Thus God—through His Church—saves civilization.

I concede that this chapter began with division (the Civil War) and ended with division (revivalism versus social gospel). Jesus' prayer, "that we might be one" (John 17:11) was not realized. So, you may ask, "Why don't you give up on the Church?" I can't give up on the Church because God won't give up on the Church. And why doesn't He? Why does He put up with us? Here's the answer. He doesn't give up on His feuding children anymore than an earthly parent gives up on his/her children when they're fighting among themselves. Just like a good earthly parent, God waits. And waits. He waits for full unity and restoration. He doesn't give up on His kids—the Church. Instead, He stands by the Church patiently—trying to reshape it and reform it—so it can be used by Him to save civilization.

To further assist you in understanding the key individuals and events of chapter 15, study questions, charts, diagrams, time lines and links to biographical websites are available on the Internet at www.jimgarlow.com. Please follow the site links to *How God Saved Civilization*, chapter 15 study helps.

Dodging Bullets

CULTS, CITIES AND ATTACKS
ON THE BIBLE

Dates covered: A.D. 1865-1918
Key persons: Joseph Smith, William Miller, Ellen White,
Mary Baker Eddy, Charles Russell, George Williams,
William and Catherine Booth, Julius Wellhausen,
Rudolph Bultmann

In a small corner of the barn loft, sandwiched atop a stack of hay and beneath a large wool blanket, Lindell could be found peeking between the wooden slats of the barn's siding. He was waiting for the sun to rise and burn away the morning mists—a treat he only had time for on his day off when Mr. Elton would milk the cows. Even for a hired hand, the Elton family made no demands of him on a Sunday morning.

Lindell was 12 years old and already knew the predawn ritual of dragging himself half awake from a warm cradle of straw and blanket and stepping down a ladder to where a basin of cold water waited for his hands to make a cup and splash his face. This was his clockwork routine six days of the week, and one he didn't mind given the nature of the Elton house: two tiny bedrooms, six kids and chatter worse than a chicken coop. Lindell was glad for his surroundings—at least the barn belonged to him and to him alone.

Every now and again Lindell would go to church with the Eltons, although he didn't understand much of what was said by the preacher. The people were nice. He liked watching the girls in their fancy hats, giggling and shy. But he couldn't spend enough time to make friends. Besides, he was shy and hadn't had much schooling; and most girls wouldn't even give him a second look, especially Grace Furton.

Still, Lindell was glad when 11-year-old Jenny Elton asked him to come to church with the family. She was the Eltons' oldest, a sweet child who loved to milk the cows with Lindell. Jenny often asked Lindell to take her to church where her best friend's family was attending, and Lindell would often hitch up the wagon and take her.

One Sunday afternoon, they entered the packed church as a local farmer-turned-preacher named William Miller was passionately declaring, "Christ is coming in the clouds."

Lindell carefully listened to the sermon. He had seen the clouds a lot and wondered, *How can anyone move about in the clouds?*

The preacher's voice snagged Lindell's attention again. "Jesus is coming back. He left us, but He will return because He promised, and the Lord has revealed to me just when that coming will be. Are you ready to meet Him?"

Ready? thought Lindell. *How do I do that, exactly?*

Miller pointed to the congregation, "Are you ready to meet the Judge of the earth, who will see right through into your very soul?"

*Look into my soul? I don't want anybody looking right into my soul. Not every-
thing is quite clean or right.*

Lindell was perfectly still as the farmer/preacher continued for nearly
two hours explaining how Jesus Christ was the One who made the world;
how Jesus came once to save people, but they hated Him and killed Him;
how resurrected and went back to His home in heaven and had been waiting for people to love Him. But now, He'd had enough; Jesus was done waiting; Jesus was going to come back and judge everyone. Miller raised his finger and declared confidently, "And He's coming back on October 22, 1844—
in just eight months!"

A gasp went up from the crowd. The farmer/preacher sounded so confident, so sure. Lindell admired the preacher for being bold and self-assured;
why, Miller had even finished high school. After the sermon, Lindell decided he would go to church every Sunday until Jesus came back. Jenny agreed
and soon the entire Elton family was attending.

It was a wonderful time for Lindell. The church folk were kind to him;
Grace Furton smiled at him at least twice. Finally, he was beginning to feel
less lonely. As October approached, Mr. Elton, who had been skeptical at
first, became convinced that he and his family had better be ready for Jesus'
return, too. As the warm September days turned crisp and the leaves fell
from the trees, the Eltons finally sold their farm. Lindell gave what few
things he owned to the church as well. After all, he wouldn't need anything
since Jesus was coming back.

On the evening before Jesus' return, the night was electric with anticipation. Church members met outside in the fields, sang hymns past midnight and prayed fervently. The children ran up the nearby hill to look again
and again into the cold night sky while some spoke quietly among themselves.

Lindell was glad he was with other people. For the first time in his life
he didn't feel afraid or alone. Now that he knew about Jesus, Lindell loved
Him, and he knew Jesus would take him to that perfect home of His. But as
the night wore on Lindell was feeling sleepy. He was usually in bed by 8:00
P.M. It was now 2:00 A.M. How difficult it was to stay awake. But of all
nights, he must stay awake tonight! What would happen if he fell asleep?
Would Jesus forget to take him? He poked himself and drank some more
apple cider. He wandered off on his own for a while to watch the moon and

the stars twinkling. Would Jesus appear at first to be faraway and very small? Would He get bigger and bigger until He filled the whole sky? Would angels come first? He sat on a rock and watched. When Lindell got too cold, he went back to the group and warmed himself by the fire.

Everyone was trying to stay awake as they gathered in small little groups. Then, as the rays of the sun peeked over the hills, the pastor began to preach. "Be patient, people of God. Jesus is coming!"

Lindell's hopes soared, but another voice challenged the preacher. "You're a fraud, William Miller! And I've lost my farm because of you!" Lindell watched with amazement as Mr. Elton shook his fist in anger at Miller. As the new morning passed, some people waited a little longer for Jesus' return, others grumbled with frustration, and a few shouted at the preacher. Lindell waited a few hours more but nothing happened. *Nothing,* he thought. *Nothing happened. The preacher was wrong.*

That morning, Lindell left the church along with the Eltons. As Lindell began to climb into the wagon, Mr. Elton turned to him, "Lindell, I'm terribly sorry, but I have no more work for you. The loss of the farm forces me to move my family in with my parents. I wish you well, young man."

The Eltons all kissed him goodbye and Jenny cried. They drove off into the morning sun. Lindell never forgot the night that Jesus didn't come; he never attended church again either.

CULTS

The last half of the 1800s brought challenges that would have been unimaginable to believers in the first half of the century: (1) the emergence of cult groups, which disturbed the accepted theology of early America; (2) the explosive growth of urban areas; and (3) the attack on the authority of the Bible (the most serious challenge). This unusual season of optimism and disconcerting transition produced four sectarian movements, three of which are labeled cult groups to this day.

SEVENTH-DAY ADVENTISTS

One sectarian group which emerged during this time period was the Seventh-day Adventists. This group, from upstate New York, emphasizes worship on Saturday (in conformity to their interpretation of the fourth commandment of keeping the Sabbath, as described in Exodus 20:8) as opposed to Sunday. The group originated from William Miller's (1782-1849) prediction that Christ would return on October 22, 1844. When Jesus failed to return on Miller's assigned date, Miller and some of his followers simply redefined what the day was supposed to mean. Seventh-day Adventism might not have survived had it not been for the influence of Ellen G. White (1827-1915).

THE TEACHING OF ELLEN WHITE

Although reared in a Methodist family, Ellen and her family embraced the teaching of William Miller. Due to their adherence to Miller's prediction of Christ's 1844 return, they were forced out of the Methodist church. Ellen, although only 17 years of age at the time, received a vision, her first of over 2,000. Her personal ill health led her to a great interest in health issues. By 1863, the emphasis upon health became a significant part of the newly formed Seventh-day Adventist Church. A vegetarian, White emphasized various remedies, including such things as water treatments, and established a hospital and college in Battle Creek, Michigan. This was the beginning of a massive hospital system that would later blanket the globe. Moreover, her emphasis on healthy living was so prevalent that she influenced a certain Seventh-day Adventist, a man named Kellogg, who developed a healthy cereal meal. (Allegedly the recipe was stolen by one his employees, a Mr. Post who developed his own brand of cereals. And thus, both Kellogg and Post cereals come from Battle Creek, Michigan.) Mrs. White's extensive traveling in 1872 to California and then to Europe and Australia charted a course for the Adventist Church's rapid growth.

But what about the Seventh-day Adventist Church today? Are they a sectarian movement outside the historic Christian faith, or are they within the historic truth of Christianity? Are they only different because they worship on Saturday, or are there other differences? One of the major differences between Seventh-day Adventists and historic orthodox Christianity was the issue of salvation by faith. As early as 1888, Ellen White debated the issue of righteousness by faith. Historically, the group has had an intensely legalistic definition of the Christian faith—minimizing any emphasis on the historic teachings of grace and faith that are central to the Protestant understanding of the Christian faith. However, with the passage of time, the emphasis on salvation by faith has become stronger within the movement. While Saturday worship (from sundown Friday night to sundown Saturday night) is still a cardinal principle of Seventh-day Adventism, the emerging and evolving denomination seems to be moving observably closer to the cardinal Christian doctrines of grace and faith. This separates Seventh-day Adventists from the other three sectarian movements mentioned here. There is no such evidence of probiblical movement among the Mormons, Jehovah's Witnesses or Christian Scientists.

MORMONISM

One of the largest of the cult groups was founded about 1830 by Joseph Smith and is known as the Church of Jesus Christ of the Latter-day Saints, or Mormons. According to Mormon history, Joseph Smith discovered and translated the Book of Mormon—which is held on equal standing with the Bible—from special golden plates he allegedly discovered with help from an angel named Moroni.

Smith contended that the golden plates were written in reformed Egyptian and that he translated them by looking through two stones which were regarded by Smith as interpretive devices. Following Smith, the Mormons soon became strong economic communities, a characteristic common to most Mormons today. But criticism of Smith increased when he began to teach and advocate polygamy. As early as 1836, Smith began the practice, and he married as many as 49 women, including some of the wives of several of his disciples. With criticism mounting, Smith and his followers moved from Kirtland, Ohio, to Missouri, and eventually to Nauvoo, Illinois, in 1843—the largest city in the state. The criticism of polygamy resulted in mob action in which Smith was taken to a jail in Carthage, Illinois. A few hours later, on June 17, 1844, he was shot and killed in his jail cell—the work of a group of masked gunmen.

Smith's role became increasingly inflated and embellished after his martyrdom. After Smith's death, Brigham Young emerged to lead the Mormons across the great plains to the Great Salt Basin, where they founded the city of Salt Lake. Although there are five different Mormon groups, the largest one is the one based in Utah. One other major branch of Mormonism is known as the Reorganized Church of Jesus Christ of the Latter-day Saints, with headquarters in Independence, Missouri. This group followed Joseph Smith's legal wife, Emma, and claimed that it alone provided the actual lineal descendants of Joseph Smith.

CHRISTIAN SCIENCE

The third development that flowed out of the radical optimism of the late 1800s was the Christian Science Church. Christian Science developed in 1866 when Mary Baker Eddy (1821-1910) spontaneously recovered from a severe injury. She concluded that reality is totally spiritual. Evil, which includes sickness and death, is only a mental illusion. By teaching that only the mind and spirit are actually real, Christian Science denies the realm of the material, thus negating the doctrines of creation, the fall and redemption. In 1875, Eddy published the first edition of *Science and Health,* a textbook which borrows heavily from the writings of Phineas Parkherst Quimby (1802-1866), a Belfast, Maine, clockmaker, who experimented with mind control that emphasized the application of positive mental attitudes over sicknesses.

At first, the Christian Science Church grew slowly. During these years, Eddy defended herself against charges of plagiarism and immorality. In 1879, she and her followers organized the first Church of Christ, Scientist, in Lynn, Massachusetts, and later moved to Boston, where her church became known as a mother church. In 1908, she founded *The Christian Science Monitor,* which has grown into a respected news journal.

In Boston, she faced challenges regarding the originality of her writing and the authority by which she led. Then from 1890 to 1906, her church experienced a stunning fivefold growth. At that time, according to statistics, 72 percent of the members of the Christian Science group were female. Women, following the pattern of Ellen White, were the practitioners (each comparable to a pastor).

JEHOVAH'S WITNESSES

The last of the four groups that rose out of the radical optimism of the late 1800s was the Jehovah's Witnesses, founded by Charles Taze Russell (1852-1916). Russell was born into a devout Presbyterian family and was exuberant about his faith until approximately age 16, when he experienced the loss of faith. After that, he was renewed and began attending a Congregational church. He later transferred to an Adventist church before finally starting his own Bible study, where he rejected the doctrine of the Trinity and the fact that Jesus was God incarnate. Russell believed that Christ had spiritually returned to earth in 1874, and in this experience Russell was somehow appointed an end-time messenger. In 1884 he founded the Watch Tower Bible and Tract Society, which grew rapidly by his tireless efforts.

After Russell's death, J. F. Weatherford became the leader of the group which changed its name in 1931 to Jehovah's Witnesses. Theologically, Jehovah's Witnesses beliefs are difficult to sort out. One obvious flaw is their unbiblical Christology, which states that Jesus was simply "a god" (note the small *g*) who died on a "torture stake." Their teaching about Jesus is close to Arianism, which emerged in the second century and which advocated that Jesus was merely a perfect man, not divine. They do not accept baptism and the Lord's Supper as sacraments. But they are most known for their means of obtaining salvation by works, which includes their incessant door knocking, probably experienced by every person reading this chapter. However, that incessant door knocking has resulted in enormous evangelistic fruit.[1]

EVALUATION

What do we say about these four groups?

- Seventh-day Adventism has moved consistently toward Christian orthodoxy, from a salvation-by-works stance toward an appropriate biblical salvation-by-faith stance.
- Mormonism has gained great respectability in communities because of its strong moral stands (disciplined lifestyles), its intense emphasis upon family life, its welfare programs for church members (the Bishop's Canneries) and its persistent evangelism (Mormon missionaries on bicycles). However, Mormons are methodologically correct while at the same time being theologically wrong! Their belief system is outside historic Christian orthodoxy.
- Christian Science is a classic example of dangerous spiritual dabbling which results in seriously unbiblical theology. Christian Science is another form of the classical New Age mind over matter, and it is neither Christian nor scientific. The New Age and all of

its precursors are esoteric and historically unverifiable, the result of mental gymnastics performed on doubtful foundations. In contrast, orthodox Christianity is grounded in actual events that are historically verifiable and geographically based.

- The Jehovah's Witnesses continue to reflect intense evangelistic zeal but like the Mormons are outside historic Christian orthodoxy, rejecting cardinal doctrines such as the Trinity.

With the exception of Christian Science, these groups had their roots in upstate New York, which by some has been called the "burned-over district"[2] because of so many revivals that occurred during and since the times of Finney. While much good also came out of upstate New York, one wonders why this area was so prone to cults. The popularity of aberrant groups is always directly traceable to the inadequacy of available, strong, biblical discipleship. In other words, the revivals produced inadequately grounded converts, who were vulnerable to multiple bizarre interpretations, including claims that Jesus was going to return at set places and at set times. Movements such as this discredit the authenticity and integrity of Christianity.

It is hard to improve on the Christian basics: God created and loved this world but man fell; God provided salvation through Jesus, who is both God and man. Once any teacher or group departs, even microscopically, from those biblical basics, they are vulnerable to deception.

URBAN GROWTH AND IMMIGRANTS

In the previous chapter we mentioned the explosive growth of the cities in the mid to late 1800s. America in the post-Civil War period was not the same America as it was in the pre-Civil War period. One writer stated that "the Civil War was a watershed between an old and a new America."[3] Although there would be many more attempts to maintain an American homogeneity, America would become considerably more heterogeneous in religion and outlook.

Several things contributed to this radical change in the American landscape. First, was the move from rural to urban life. People left the farms and flocked to the cities. From 1840 to 1850, the population of the cities increased by 90 percent whereas the country, as a whole, increased only 36 percent. By 1860, the capital that had been invested in industry, railroads, commerce and urban property was greater than the value of all the farms from the Atlantic to the Pacific. Influence had shifted from the farm to the city.[4] Sydney E. Ahlstrom gives this graphic example of America's change:

> When Fort Dearborn was incorporated as the village of Chicago in 1833, it was an ugly, frontier outpost of 17 houses. By 1900, though still ugly, it was a sprawling western metropolis of 1,698,575 people—the fifth largest city in the world. Chicago became the most dramatic symbol of the major social trend of the post-Civil War era: the rise of the city.[5]

But there was a second radical change that occurred after the war—the enormous influx of immigrants, who were never fully acclimated into America's melting pot of religiosity. The numbers are staggering:

- In 1882, over 800,000 immigrants arrived on American shores.
- In 1907, an all-time high of 1,285,349 immigrants arrived—more than the total number of immigrants who had arrived in the 13 colonies in the 169 years between 1706 (the Pilgrims' arrival at Jamestown, Virginia) and 1776 (the signing of the Declaration of Independence).
- Between 1860 and 1900, 14 million immigrants arrived.
- Between 1900 and 1920, an additional 14 million arrived.[6]
- By 1900, one-third of America's population of 75 million were either foreign-born or children of foreign-born parents. Of these 25 million new Americans:

> 8 million were from Germany;
> 5 million from Ireland;
> 2.5 million from Austria, Hungary, Poland and Italy;
> 2.5 million from Scandinavian countries;

850,000 were French Canadian;

774,000 came from Russia.[7]

America's previously successful assimilation techniques were overwhelmed. The melting pot became more of a Mulligan's stew (separate groups which don't naturally assimilate into each other), and America would never look the same.

URBAN MINISTRIES

Our focus is not on the cities themselves, but on the ministries that developed in them in the late 1800s. The great ministries of this time period were not limited to the evangelistic crusades of D. L. Moody, or the reworking of theology of Washington Gladden and Walter Rauschenbusch. There were more pressing concerns, such as "How do I eat today?" And that brings us finally to the stories of the YMCA and the Salvation Army.

YMCA

George Williams (1821-1905) was a 23-year-old clerk in a London drapery store when he began meeting with a group of fellow employees in a Bible study and prayer meeting. Meeting in his small apartment overlooking the churchyard of Saint Paul's Cathedral, Williams and 10 of his colleagues decided on June 6, 1844, to found a group for the purpose of sharing the Christian gospel: the Young Men's Christian Association. In an amazingly short period of time the concept of such an association caught on, and by 1851 had crossed the Atlantic with YMCA's opening in Montreal, Quebec, Canada and in Boston, Massachusetts. By 1894, the YMCA had over 5,000 branches around the world. Its strategy was a simple one: to provide a healthy place for young men to gather in cities where they could be edified in the things of the gospel and cared for personally. The YMCA was blatantly evangelistic, while at the same time it cared for the sick, fed the poor, organized Sunday Schools, worked for temperance and distributed Bibles.[8] Along with spiritual and humanitarian concerns, the YMCA developed recreational facilities for basketball, volleyball and camping as well as inexpensive dormitory rooms in which young men could stay. By 1980, the YMCA was the largest health and social services agency in the United

States, with nearly 2,200 organizations reaching over 12 million people. This global organization now spans 92 nations, serving some 26 million people.

CHANGE (LOSS) OF MISSION

However, the YMCA mission today has been radically altered. To youth in contemporary times, the initials YMCA evoke the strains of a recent rock song advocating homosexuality. George Williams and the 10 men who helped found this organization for purposes of proclaiming the gospel would be horrified that the organization is associated with such a song. But the song is only the tip of the iceberg. As C. V. Anderson correctly notes, those who attend the "Y" today are not necessarily either young, men or Christian.[9] The familiar triangular logo in the original YMCA represented Spirit, Mind and Body, with a reference to John 17:21. Few, if any, users of any local YMCA today are ever taught the foundations of a personal knowledge of Jesus Christ that caused George Williams to give so sacrificially of himself through his entire lifetime. In some cases, the YMCA has embraced a distinctively antibiblical stance.[10]

And what happened at the YMCA is a depiction of what has happened in hundreds, perhaps thousands, of organizations which began with a clear commitment to basic scriptural truths. But within several generations that authenticity waned, and the organization lost sight of its original focus. In a book about the history of the Church's health, it is disappointing to have to analyze once-distinctly Christian groups who have lost their biblical flavor. But it would be less than honest not to acknowledge that such a pattern has repeated itself throughout history. My own children have benefited from the athletic programs at the YMCA. But every time I walk through the doors of our Y, I wonder how George Williams would feel, knowing that it now offers only instruction in soccer and makes no call for a personal relationship with and love of Christ. It is a great tragedy that this massive organization no longer holds up as a beacon the gospel of Jesus Christ. There is only one sense in which one can say the Church is alive and well, when one sees how many organizations have lost their clear Christian focus. It is found in the redeeming fact that for every organization that has spiritually "gone south," new organizations have been formed which fan the flame of the founder's original dream. Although the YMCA (and its sister organization, the YWCA) have little spiritual impact today, in its earlier years it was one of the great forces for Christ in cities around the globe.

THE SALVATION ARMY

William Booth's (1829-1912) birth to extremely poor parents may have been a significant cause in his life's calling to care for the poor. Converted at age 15, he became a Methodist minister in 1852, and continued as a Methodist until 1861. The second most profound influence on his life was his marriage in 1855 to Catherine, who gave birth to eight children. Catherine and William formed a spectacular team, whose boundless energy was demonstrated when they opened a Christian mission in East London in 1865. Somewhat on impulse, William Booth changed the wording on his 1878 annual mission report and listed his work as a salvation army. The concept caught on. William and Catherine as began to formulate an organization in which all eight of their children were eventually given high rank.

The movement exploded and spread rapidly throughout all of Britain, the U.S., Canada, Australia and all of Europe. Referred to as "General" by his children as well as everyone else, Booth and his "army," with Catherine as "Army Mother" began to march. Firmly entrenched within the Wesleyan position of sanctification (a deeper spiritual experience after conversion), General Booth and his profoundly gifted wife set about to transform cities from the inside out. By 1890, he announced his strategy to meet the needs of the poor and disenfranchised in his book *In Darkest England and the Way Out*. Booth's army quickly experienced the success of reaching that segment of the population that traditional Christian churches could not touch. Although deep rifts developed between him and the American branch of the movement, both continued to flourish as a combination social mission and an evangelistic force.

Part of the power of Booth's army came from Catherine's skilled leadership and her prodigious preaching skills. This touches on the role of women in ministry, which we have already discussed. By himself, it is doubtful that Booth could have taken the Salvation Army to the level it reached. Catherine was highly skilled in conflict resolution and possessed extraordinarily strong moral convictions. If one can measure good parenting by whether children follow their parents in ministry, then the Booths must have been among the world's best parents! All eight of their children remained in religious work until old age—five of them as Salvation Army officers, two acting as generals. The study of their family is a most intriguing and profitable activity.

MORE THAN A RESCUE MISSION

The Salvation Army, to the surprise of most who view it as a rescue mission, is a Protestant Evangelical denomination, claiming a global membership of 1.2 million, 117,000 of which are in the United States.[11] It is characterized by holiness doctrine and has its own churches and church membership structure. But it is best known for its widespread social-relief work. It operates in over 86 countries and is everywhere regarded by the general public as one of the most outstanding examples of Christian charity. Its global influence is astounding, since it has only about 1,100 local churches in the United States. The Salvation Army's superb fund-raising for its social work has made it the number one recipient of charitable contributions, receiving 1.2 billion dollars in 1998.[12]

The Salvation Army provides us with a unique example of a blend between individual piety and social relief work. A Salvation Army officer would be puzzled if you asked him to choose between presenting a gospel lesson on how to receive Christ and feeding a hungry person. He would consider preaching a sermon without feeding an empty stomach to be ruthless. And to feed an empty stomach without showing the way to eternal salvation would be just as calloused. The Salvation Army has met both needs superbly.

MAINTAINING FOCUS

Unlike the YMCA, the Salvation Army has stayed the course. The Salvation Army faces "the increasingly complex demands of providing humanitarian assistance . . . while . . . retaining a spiritual emphasis."[13] According to New York University scholar Diane Winston, the group has changed from "rabble-rousing religionists to [a] respected social force."[14] Elected May 15, 1999, Salvation Army General John Gowan stated that his "intention is to remind [the Salvation Army] not to be diverted . . . and not to allow any attractive side paths to divert them."[15] They have veered neither to the right nor to the left but have continued to follow the path envisioned by William and Catherine Booth. They responded courageously to the desperate cries of the city's poor and downtrodden and, to this day, the Salvation Army emblem is a heartwarming sight to anyone who is homeless and hungry. When we read the history of the Salvation Army, we find ourselves saying much more confidently: No matter the circumstances, God is always working to bring His grace to a lost world.

THE WELSH REVIVAL

Both the YMCA and the Salvation Army had their roots in England. Although our concern here is with happenings in America, we cannot ignore the amazing event that was occurring in the British Isles, specifically in Wales. Beginning in 1904, a revival had broken out under the leadership of Evan Roberts (1878-1947), a miner turned blacksmith turned evangelist! Some have claimed that Roberts was not known for his great intellect or his oratorical skills, but these comments do not change the impact of the revival he helped to guide. Churches stayed open 24 hours a day. Within five months, 100,000 had become believers. The revival included "hour-long singing, a de-emphasis on preaching, praying in concert, and interruptions by worshippers."[16]

This outpouring had such an impact that jails were closed, bars were shut down, policemen were laid off, and judges were dismissed. If ever a revival had all the components of social reform, the Welsh Revival did. Accounts of the revival filled hearts in America with expectancy. And hopeful believers didn't have long to wait. Only one year after the end of the Welsh Revival, a renewal broke out at Azusa Street in Los Angeles. But a description of that revival will have to wait for another chapter.

THE EROSION OF
BIBLICAL AUTHORITY

The radical changes that faced America and the Church were not limited to the social upheaval caused by people moving from the farms to the cities or by massive immigration. There was a third major change an intellectual one—which threatened to undo the Church. This attack was multifaceted and insidious; and of the three major causes of change during the last half of the 1800s—urbanization, immigration and intellectualism—it is the last that most muted the Church's impact on culture.

As the 1800s wound to a close, Christianity found itself under intellectual attack "from three directions: from *science* by the theory of evolution, from *philosophy* in the form of alternative world-views intended to make belief in God obsolete, and from *history* in the guise of biblical criticism. If the truth of the Bible could be shown to be doubtful, then there would be nothing left on which Christian faith could stand" (emphasis added).[17]

A THREE-PRONGED ATTACK: BIOLOGY, PHILOSOPHY AND HISTORY

The attack on conservative Christian beliefs began in the field of biology. Herbert Spencer (1820-1903) outlined the doctrine of evolution and applied it to all of life in a series of influential writings:

- *Progress, Its Law and Cause (1857)*
- *First Principle (1862)*
- *Principles of Biology (1864-1867)*
- *Principles of Psychology (1870-1872)*
- *Principles of Sociology (1876-1896)*
- *Principles of Ethics (1892-1893)*

But Charles Darwin, the father of evolution, was yet to make his debut. It was Darwin's (1809-1882) *Origin of the Species* (1859) that became the symbol of the revolution in thinking about biology and about man's place in the world.

The radical change in beliefs was more drastically seen in philosophy, however. Philosopher Friedrich Nietzsche (1844-1900) joined the attack and proclaimed the death of God. He advocated that since God is dead, man must make it on his own. According to Nietzsche, man makes up his own values and his own rules to fit his situation. Christian traditions no longer have any value.

However, this most radical reorientation of thinking occurred not merely in biology and philosophy. It was also occurring in theology. How should we understand and interpret the Scriptures? A movement called "higher criticism" started in Germany, spread to Britain and came to America. This one single intellectual influence would create the major demarcation we see today between liberal and conservative churches.

Before the year 1900 arrived, there were mounting attacks on the Bible. One theory held that Jesus, as we know Him, didn't even exist. Another held that although Jesus lived and died, His disciples simply made up a story that Jesus had been resurrected from the dead. In his *Life of Jesus* (1835-36), D. F. Strauss stated that the Gospels—Matthew, Mark, Luke and John—were myths and that the supernatural stories were conjured up out of the imagination.

JULIUS WELLHAUSEN

The most influential Bible critic was Julius Wellhausen (1844-1918). In his 1878 book entitled *History of Israel*, he indicated that the Old Testament was a collection of primitive stories embellished to justify the ritualism of the Jews. He believed that Moses did not write the first five books of the Bible, which were, he argued, a patchwork collection from a large group of unknown authors. The Bible was not God's supernatural story of His dealings with the nation of Israel, but the human creation of a group of writers who were trying to justify their historical existence by fabricating accounts of unique divine intervention and inserting them into their national history.

Wellhausen did away with any concept of a supernatural God's interacting with His people and revealing Himself to them. Thus Abraham, Isaac and Jacob were mythical individuals who, through the process of time, were portrayed as real by the storytellers, who passed on the account from one generation to another. Julius Wellhausen's thoughts were not well received, causing him to leave his professor position in Griesswald, Germany, in 1882. He went to the University of Halle, then Marburg and finally settled down in Gottingen in 1892. But his popularity was not limited to those who appreciated his teaching at several German universities. Through his book, his views spread to England and to the United States, infiltrating one mainline seminary after another. His impact was felt in denomination after denomination in the decades immediately following his death.

A somewhat parallel approach to Scripture was taught by Rudolph Bultmann (1884-1976), another German. Although we will leave the discussion of Bultmann's "demythologization" of Scripture for a later chapter, the same assessment could be made: Mainline denominations were infected by liberalism in their seminaries, which meant, of course, that the pastors trained there eventually took this thinking into the pulpits of their local churches. Belief in the authority of the Bible, once held so strongly by all

Protestant denominations, had been seriously eroded. This attack, more than any social changes, destroyed the very foundation of the Church. For if belief in the Scriptures as the final authority of faith and practice is abandoned, the Church loses touch with the Word of God and will no longer be reformed by its power.

THE DEEP DIFFERENCES WITHIN DENOMINATIONS

What significance do Julius Wellhausen and Rudolf Bultmann have for contemporary American Christians? These men had such an impact on our churches that we cannot tell the story of most mainline denominations (Presbyterian, Methodist, Baptist, Episcopalian, Disciples of Christ) without noting their influence. New believers must feel confused when they discover that there are so many denominations. Even the mature believer wonders how certain denominations can have both liberal and conservative churches. How do you explain that one Presbyterian church ordains homosexuals while a Presbyterian church down the street adheres closely to the Bible on this issue? Why does one Methodist church advocate abortion while another Methodist church across town is involved in the prolife movement? These conservative/liberal splits were caused when theologians such as Wellhausen advocated a view of Scripture that effectively destroyed biblical authority. Young seminarians who accepted such theories in their years of study took this liberal theology into the Church, where unsuspecting Christians were influenced by it. Gradually, as liberalism made inroads into denominations, some were (and still are) torn divisively, and others have split. Those who loved the Scriptures could not remain in fellowship with those who taught that the Bible was mere myth.

THE RESILIENCY OF TRUTH

That an alleged follower of Jesus Christ would so destroy the foundations of biblical truth is inexcusable. As an admitted conservative and an Evangelical, I find the teaching of these German thinkers and their American counterparts who embraced their teachings to be an abomination. However, it is good to note that there is resiliency in the Church of Jesus Christ.

In many of these divided denominations, Christians have had to become more discerning in order to resist the insidious attacks of liberal theology. Their resistance has kept such antibiblical teaching from having even more impact than it has had already. While I find myself thoroughly annoyed by the rank liberalism that has infiltrated portions of the Presbyterian and Methodist systems, I praise God for the many wonderful Methodist and Presbyterian pastors who stand firmly on biblical truth and uncompromisingly preach the powerful truth of the gospel. The conservatives in denomination after denomination have been ridiculed, mocked and scoffed. Many have been locked out of denominational favor, and yet the Spirit of God is still at work in these denominations and in the hearts of courageous pastors who stand against denominational bureaucracy even though they are attacked as "flaming fundamentalists," due to their deep confidence in the Word of God. As R. D. Linder notes,

> More and more of the energy of the Protestant churches, internally at least, came to be spent on defending orthodoxy and deflecting heresy. For what would prove to be the last time, Protestants joined hands in significant numbers to support America's efforts in World War I; but even as this happened many leaders knew that a major theological confrontation between the forces of the older theologically conservative America, represented by the evangelicals, and the forces of the newer theologically liberal America, represented by the modernists was in the offing.[18]

This enormous split happened and set the stage for the next major challenge of the Christian faith, the Fundamentalist/Modernist controversy. It would test the Church, taking her through the fires of theological debate and internal turmoil. Yet even through controversy or suffering, the truth of Jesus will always emerge triumphant. And as it emerges, His truth creates a people, the people of God—His true Church—without whom civilization would self-destruct. Although the Church is sometimes battered, it is still God's plan for saving civilization.

To further assist you in understanding the key individuals and events of chapter 16, study questions, charts, diagrams, time lines and links to biographical websites are available on the Internet at www.jimgarlow.com. Please follow the site links to *How God Saved Civilization*, chapter 16 study helps.

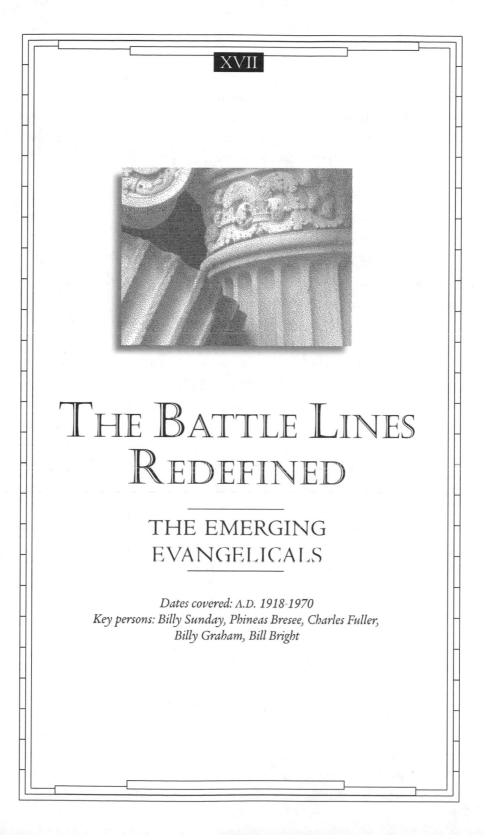

THE BATTLE LINES REDEFINED

THE EMERGING EVANGELICALS

Dates covered: A.D. 1918-1970
Key persons: Billy Sunday, Phineas Bresee, Charles Fuller,
Billy Graham, Bill Bright

Everyone knew Thomas and Bradley would graduate at the top of their class. And they did—co-valedictorians. The year was 1920, only two years after the end of World War I. Everyone knew that the twins would go to college. No one could tell the identical twins apart that graduation day. Everyone knew one more thing: Reverend Matlack's twins would both be Methodist preachers, like their dad.

After all, they had both sat on the front row every Sunday, even though their dad had never required it. He was surprised. *He* had never sat in the front as a boy! Reverend Matlack was delighted. Thomas and Bradley had lots of questions; They loved to sit up late in front of the fire and talk with him about spiritual issues. They both loved the church and went to camp meetings every summer. Reverend Matlack was amazed at their fervency. In contrast, their older brother, David, and their younger sister, Henrietta, showed limited interest in spiritual things.

Four years went by quickly for the twins at the small Methodist college. Their courses only deepened their desire for theology. During their senior year, they began to talk about seminary. Reverend Matlack was hesitant. School was expensive and he had not needed seminary. After all, his training had consisted of a home-study course. Reverend Matlack had been converted at age 23 as a young farmer. He didn't have the educational opportunities his sons were enjoying.

Thomas and Bradley had intended to attend different seminaries. They promised that they would make up their minds alone and they did. What a laugh they had when they discovered they had chosen the same one! Together again. Maybe twins were just destined to stay together forever.

During their first semester at seminary, Thomas was enthralled by the theology professor. What an intense passion for Christ and His Church this man had! Bradley never stopped raving about the New Testament professor. What a terrific scholar he was! He could cite the exact page of anything he had read without even looking at his notes.

Thomas and Bradley ate dinner together every night at first. But gradually they found their own friends and spent less time with each other. Thomas became involved in helping to start a church in the inner city while Bradley would go every Sunday to his New Testament professor's home for his fireside chats. The professor was so thought provoking, so profound. And he challenged Bradley to go beyond his childhood faith. "Don't think of miracles as some kind of magic," he would say. "God used natural means to accomplish His will. Besides, isn't everything a miracle, really?"

Bradley would stay up late even during the week, discussing theology with his friends. They considered the authorship of several New Testament books, and discussed whether Moses had written all of the Pentateuch. Were there not traces of other hands in these books? The Old Testament professor had asked them, "How could Moses have written those books when they describe incidents that happened after his death?" Bradley had never thought about this question.

His New Testament professor would add, "We must not think of the Resurrection the way some primitive peoples would think. Jesus didn't actually resurrect in His body. The Resurrection is a myth, a story with a spiritual purpose. The disciples knew that Jesus didn't really rise from the dead. But His influence was so great that for them it *seemed* that He had risen. Take the feeding of the five thousand. Was it actual food that fed those hungry people? Of course not. The story means to show us that the people were *spiritually* fed. And calming the Sea of Galilee? Was it physically, literally calmed? Certainly not. Like Jesus' parables, this story means that Jesus calms people's turbulent, spiritual lives."

As Bradley walked to the dormitory that night, he was glad he was not rooming with Thomas. It would be difficult to discuss this one. Recently, their discussions had become less frequent and more heated. One day in anger Thomas said, "So what are you going to preach on Easter? That Jesus is still in the grave?"

"No," said Bradley, trying to remember the words his professor had used, that had sounded so convincing. "I will tell them that Christ has arisen." Bradley parroted his professor, "You see, Thomas, there's a difference between the 'Jesus of history' and the 'Christ of faith.'"

"So Jesus is not Christ? Is that what you believe, Bradley?" Thomas asked with great exasperation. Bradley opened his mouth to answer but never had a chance.

"So you get up on Easter," Thomas said, "and you preach that Jesus' body rotted in the grave but that Christ's spirit is with us? Like Jesus is somehow different from Christ?! You know what, Bradley? You have nothing left to preach. Nothing!"

There was a long silence. The twins were no longer identical. In fact, they were opposites.

THE DEMARCATION

What America was before World War I, it was no longer after the war. Everything had changed. So significant was this war in the redefining of America that even American Church history books use World War I as a point of demarcation. The change in America is defined by the title of Henry May's book *The End of American Innocence, 1912-1917*. American Church history professor Robert Handy regarded it as the end of a "Christian America."[1] That scholars argue over whether the technical end of innocence occurred in 1917 or 1918 is immaterial. The point is World War I changed everything.

POST-CHRISTIAN

Dramatizing this vast difference, Sydney Ahlstrom wrote in the opening lines of a chapter entitled "The Little War and the Great War":

> The great war of 1914-1918 left Europe shattered. The best part of its manhood was "missing in action".... the old order was gone.... For Americans, World War I was "over there," in Europe, a long, long way from the United States. On the home front only a very few seemed to comprehend the tragic dimensions of the holocaust. During the 1920s their numbers increased, as participants and observers began to expose the reality and its aftermath. But only with the coming of the Great Depression did a fairly wide range of thinkers begin to see that bourgeois civilization was deep in crisis. And not until a quarter-century after that, did the idea of a "post-Christian" world begin to dawn on the popular consciousness.[2]

What an astounding idea. How could the Puritans have ever envisioned that their city set on a hill, their New Israel, could ever be called post-Christian? What had gone wrong?

OVERVIEW: 1918-1965

The post-World War I period followed a progressive itinerary from 1918 to 1965:

1. The optimism of the late 1800s and early 1900s was forever shattered; the world was not getting better.
2. Due to attacks on biblical authority, a theological war broke out between the Fundamentalists and the Modernists.
3. The Modernists won and became the Protestant establishment.
4. The Modernist victory was short-lived. Protestant liberalism was empty and had no capacity to contribute to the culture. It was soon replaced in a part of the Church by zealous, more conservative, more aggressive evangelical Christianity.

In the above four statements, we have traced the period from 1918 to 1965. Now let's go back and understand this journey better. Can we find God's hand at work in this mess? Two encouraging words at the outset: God's hand is more obvious than one might think; the situation wasn't as messy as one might imagine.

THE FUNDAMENTALIST-MODERNIST CONTROVERSY

The theological controversy that developed following the Great War was waged between two camps. The Fundamentalists were on one side. These were, according to R. D. Linder, the "militantly conservative wings of American Evangelical Christianity" and the "champions of the old Protestant orthodoxy." On the other side were the Modernists, who represented the "militantly liberal wing of the New Theology," and "champions of the new Protestant naturalism."[3] The Fundamentalists were portrayed as a group of people fighting to regain an America that no longer existed. The Modernists were portrayed, in contrast, as the group ushering in the new America. Although our focus here is the period after World War I, the seedbed for this intense division predated the war by several decades. The revolution in America's thinking patterns had been influenced by several developments:

- publication of Charles Darwin's *Origin of the Species* in 1859;
- historical and sociological attacks upon the accuracy of the Bible;

- psychological challenges to absolute religious and moral truth, with an implication that the Christian faith could not claim to be the only true religion in the world.

At the same time, cultural chaos was created by massive immigration, rapid urbanization and rampant industrialization. The Church and her preachers lost influence on society. With the exception of some rural backwaters, American culture had been secularized.

AT THE CROSSROADS

Protestants were at a crossroads. They could choose one of two roads. Liberal theology, the Modernists, chose to accommodate to the culture by developing new theology. This theology emphasized the evolution of thought, and implied that believing in an absolute and timeless revelation from God was an obsolete notion. The Bible, for them, was only a historical record of one nation's *perception* of truth, not necessarily truth itself. The divine Jesus was ousted by a nice Jesus, who stood up for society's underdogs. For Modernists, churches were to transform and improve society, so it could be God's kingdom here and now. With such an emphasis on this life, their interest in heaven, the afterlife or the supernatural quickly vanished.

The other road to take was Fundamentalism. The term "Fundamentalist" was presumably not used before 1920, when Curtis L. Laws coined the term to describe those who were willing "to do battle loyal for the Fundamentals."[4] But the term "fundamentals" was used a full decade before that. *The Fundamentals* was the title of a 12-volume paperback series published between 1910 and 1915, containing the basics of conservative Christianity. The publication project was the idea of a wealthy California oilman named Lyman Stewart, who was assisted by his brother, Milton.[5] The Stewarts sent out 3 million volumes free to religious workers all over the nation! One-third of the 90 articles in the 12 volumes defended the authority of the Bible. Another third were apologetics; that is, defenses of basic doctrines. The final third dealt with practical issues such as missions and evangelism. The 12-volume paperback series was not only a clear statement of where the battle lines were drawn theologically, but it was also a declaration of war sent for use to 3 million Christian leaders. It was not intended to convict liberals but to encourage conservatives to hold firm. As Kenneth Curtis notes, "*The Fundamentals* probably did more to unite and educate those who already agreed with them, rather than convince and convert their intended readers."[6]

And what were the fundamentals of Fundamentalist belief? The doctrinal points included in this series had been decided in the 1895 Niagara Bible Conference. The essentials of the Christian faith were a belief in

- the inerrancy of the Scriptures;
- the virgin birth and the deity of Jesus Christ;
- substitutionary atonement;
- the physical resurrection of Christ;
- His bodily return.[7]

Moreover, the Fundamentalists responded to the heightening theological controversy in one of four distinct ways, depending on which "stream" they were in. They stressed

- an intellectual defense;
- revivalism;
- a call for personal holiness;
- an emphasis on eschatological or end-time doctrines.

INTELLECTUAL DEFENSE

The prime defender of the faith in the intellectual battle was J. Gresham Machen (1881-1937). Machen was a brilliant defender of conservative theology, as depicted in his 1923 classic entitled *Christianity and Liberalism*. In it he claimed that "despite the . . . use of traditional phraseology, modern liberalism not only is a different religion from Christianity, but belongs in a totally different class of religions."[8] But even with the brilliance of Machen and others like him, the battle for the Presbyterian denomination and Princeton Theological Seminary was eventually lost. Conservatives were forced out or walked out and, in 1929, formed Westminster Theological Seminary in Philadelphia. Eventually, these leaders went on in 1936 to form an entirely new denomination, the Orthodox Presbyterian church.

BILLY SUNDAY
AND REVIVALISM

In every time of upheaval, American Christians turned to their faithful methods of revivalism. The revivalist of the hour was Billy Sunday (1862-1935), the retired baseball player, who preached as if he were still in a ball game. His preaching style was flamboyant with theatrical statements and exaggerated gestures which mesmerized his audiences and brought severe criticism from liberal preachers and the press. In his down-home style, complete with a "backwards vocabulary," he attacked the "deodorized and disinfected sermons" of "hireling ministers" in liberal churches. He severely criticized those who concocted a religion but managed to leave Jesus Christ out. He advertised his revivals as "civic cleanups," stating that Christianity was a masculine, "muscular" faith, which called for decency and manliness. Manliness, to Billy Sunday, was "the man who has real, rich, red blood in his veins instead of pink tea and ice water."[9]

Billy Sunday preached to more people than any evangelist ever had, or ever would, until the time of Billy Graham. His success was not merely due to his personality and preaching style. It was also due to the ingenious organizational skills of his wife, Helen Thompson, whom he married in 1888. She organized advance teams that helped prepare each city for the arrival of her husband's confrontational preaching style.

THE HOLINESS MOVEMENT

But the Fundamentalists fought back not only through intellectual defense and revivalism; many chose to emphasize the pursuit of a deeper life, and became involved in what was known as the Holiness movement. The Holiness movement traces its roots to John Wesley in England, who taught that a person could live victoriously, above sin. Early Methodists saw holiness as a part of the reason for the existence of the Methodist church. However, by the end of the nineteenth century, Methodists had become less and less concerned with the Holiness teachings. The theme had been emphasized by Orange Scott and the Wesleyan Methodist church, a group that had broken with the Methodists in 1843, due to their radical abolitionist stance. After the Civil War the Wesleyans were without a cause. They realized, however, that while the sin of slavery had ended, the cause for holiness was far from won; and they reinvigorated the denomination with a fresh call for righteous and holy living.

But the Holiness movement was far greater than the small Wesleyan Methodist denomination. In the 1800s there was a resurgence in Holiness teaching in many denominations (Presbyterian, Methodist, Baptist, Dutch Reformed, Congregationalist and Quaker). The "official experience" was sanctification (an experience after conversion) and the tool that was used to help people experience sanctification[10] was the camp meeting.[11]

- In July 1867, in Vineland, New Jersey, nearly 10,000 people attended a camp meeting, which resulted in the formation of the National Camp Meeting Association for the Promotion of Holiness.
- In 1868, 25,000 attended the camp meeting in Manheim, Pennsylvania.
- In 1869, 20,000 attended the Round Lake, New York, camp meeting.[12]

The Holiness movement was at full steam. By the end of the nineteenth century, most Holiness folk were either forced out or chose to walk out of the denominations that were no longer responsive to the Holiness teachings, thus forming a plethora of small denominations and organizations.

CHURCH OF THE NAZARENE

Though the emphasis on holiness had been around for a long time, the real outbreak of hunger for personal holiness did not occur immediately after the Civil War. It developed at the very end of the 1800s and early in the 1900s. The vigorous pursuit of holiness is most powerfully demonstrated in the formation of a denomination known today as the Church of the Nazarene. Phineas F. Bresee, a Methodist pastor in Los Angeles, was the first to use the name "Church of the Nazarene," in 1895. His break with the Methodists was due not only to his commitment to holiness but also to his commitment to experiential worship and preaching. In addition, he identified with the poor and disenfranchised of society, thus choosing the name "Nazarene" to identify with the poor and insignificant town called Nazareth. The story of the Church of the Nazarene is an amazing tale of amalgamations and mergers. But how was this collection of Holiness churches born?

At the turn of the century there developed a hunger for the things of God, a desire to deepen the Christian walk. All Christians know that God is doing a work of sanctification in them, making them more and more like the image of Christ. In some of the Fundamentalist churches, an emphasis on this process became a primary focus of the church. Some taught that Christians could become perfect (according to a specific definition of perfection) while still here on earth. Testimonials were frequent at the camp meeting gatherings, which revealed that persons had learned to live victorious over sin.

The result was a collection of small Holiness mini-denominations, which eventually began to merge. Phineas Bresee's California-based group merged in 1907 with the Chicago group known as the Association of Pentecostal Churches in America, to form the Pentecostal Church of the Nazarene. In 1908, the Holiness Church of Christ merged with the Nazarene Church at Pilot Point, Texas.[13] The term "Pentecostal" was dropped from the title Pentecostal Church of the Nazarene in 1919, to avoid being confused with Pentecostals who believed in speaking in tongues. The mergers continued at an amazing pace, causing the Church of the Nazarene to eclipse both the Wesleyan Methodists and the Free Methodists and to become the largest of the holiness denominations.

Due to the fact that Nazarene churches were being founded at the turn of the century when urbanization was beginning to occur, many of their churches began near metropolitan areas. In contrast, the Wesleyan, the Free Methodists and groups such as the Pilgrim Holiness were much more rurally based. As the rural Holiness folk moved to the city, they looked for sister Holiness churches and frequently ended up in Nazarene churches. In addition, the Nazarene church carried on an extremely aggressive evangelistic and missionary program which launched it into a worldwide movement with well over a million members today. Headquartered in Kansas City, Missouri, the denomination boasts nine respected universities, a seminary, one of the largest denominational publishing houses and an extremely aggressive missionary program.

ESCHATOLOGY

Many Fundamentalists also developed a strong emphasis on eschatology, the second coming of Christ. The term that is used for these movements is "millennarian," which refers to the millennium, or the 1,000-year reign of peace on earth. Some believed that the 1,000-year period of peace would be brought about through religious revival, which would impact the social structures of culture. These individuals believed that because of the effectiveness of the proclamation of the gospel of Jesus Christ, society would simply get better and better. Then at the end of a 1,000-year season of peace, Christ would return. This is referred to as postmillennialism, meaning that Jesus would come after the 1,000-year period. Not all prophecy groups accepted this viewpoint, however. With urbanization, immigration, attacks on the Bible and the devastation of World War I, many had abandoned any optimism about the state of the world. They shifted their view of the end time to a premillennial position. Premillennialists taught that things were going to get worse until Jesus would suddenly appear and He, not the Church, would usher in the 1,000-year reign of peace.

JOHN NELSON DARBY AND DISPENSATIONALISM

Most pronounced during the late 1800s and the early 1900s was the spread of a type of premillennialism referred to as dispensationalism. Based upon the views of John Nelson Darby of England, dispensationalists taught that following the rapture (taking up) of the Church, the Antichrist would appear and great tribulation would develop. So popular was dispensational premillennialism that massive prophecy conferences were spawned. The primary educational tool of the dispensationalists was the Scofield Reference Bible, published in 1909. While postmillennialists worked hard to improve the world in which they were living, premillennialists were trying to find a way to escape. While postmillennialists could be accused of being naive because things were simply not getting better and better, premillennialists could be rightfully accused of having relatively little confidence in the power of the gospel to transform the society in which they found themselves. The issue here is not to try to decide which crowd was right but, rather, to note the intensity of interest in the second coming of Christ that was stirred up during this time. While we would not for one moment discount the supernatural role of the Holy Spirit in creating this interest, it is important to note from a historical view that in almost every period of Church history when there is enormous turbulence and unsettling change, interest in the Second Coming dramatically increases.

Perhaps a word of caution would be appropriate at this point. To the true lover of Jesus, the Second Coming is a glorious thought. Every follower of Christ looks forward to His return. But a casual study of history reveals that date setting is absolutely fruitless. While one admires the zeal and expectancy of Christians in previous centuries who looked forward to Christ's coming, one wonders how much energy some of them may have wasted speculating about when Christ would return. If history teaches us anything about this issue, it teaches us to be prepared for Him to return today or a million years from today, because, ultimately, it should make no difference to the faithfulness of our Christian walk. Although it is not a bad thing for Christians to analyze the times, they must be obedient to Christ in whatever time they find themselves, ready for Christ to find them faithful were He to return today. The goal is to walk in the spectacular unfolding plan of God.

FUNDAMENTALISM "LOSES"

One might assume, based upon the intellectual and cultural movements of Fundamentalism described above, that the conservatives won the day. Such was not the case. They lost. But not for long. Their day of resurgence was yet to come. But it didn't look very encouraging to them by the end of the 1920s. Notes R. D. Linder:

> By 1930 the old evangelical consensus had been replaced by a new pluralism, the old Protestant Establishment had been replaced by the new Liberal Establishment. . . . the years that followed saw evangelicals in general, and fundamentalists in particular, become a despised sub-culture as the Liberal Establishment held sway in the media and in the universities, theological schools and denominational hierarchies of the land.
>
> The Methodists, Episcopalians, Congregationalists, and Disciples were most heavily influenced by the new theological liberalism, with Presbyterians and Northern Baptists badly divided over the issues. . . . Most important, the institutions of higher education of the leading Protestant denominations . . . became the focal points of liberal dominance of the American Protestant Churches and the period.[14]

It is impossible to overemphasize the importance of the above quote when attempting to understand contemporary Christian churches. The separation caused by the Liberalism versus Fundamentalism battle is the key to understanding the American Church today. Although the terminology and the personalities have altered, the fundamental issues separating conservatives from liberals remain largely intact.

NEO-ORTHODOXY

What lay ahead for the liberal Protestant establishment that had taken control of American religious life? Its glory days were short-lived. The depression of 1929 through 1933 drained the optimism of the advocates of the social gospel. In addition, the hollowness of liberal theology left too great a void for the theologians who would come later. Karl Barth and Emil Brunner of Germany, along with two influential brothers on the American side of the ocean, Reinhold and H. Richard Niebuhr, would usher in an understanding of theology known as Neo-Orthodoxy.

Neo-Orthodoxy abandoned the naive optimism that the human condition could be improved through the social gospel alone. It returned to the more familiar and spiritual themes of Martin Luther and John Calvin, while trying to integrate them with a modern scientific worldview. Liberalism's beliefs that society would improve on its own through an evolutionary process collapsed, and Neo-Orthodoxy's understanding of the brokenness of humanity began to prevail. Neo-Orthodoxy was clearly a reaction to the theological bankruptcy of liberalism. It was not identical to Fundamentalism, however, for although it borrowed seemingly sound principles from Protestant history, it filled them with subtle new meanings which undermined their true source of power, the self-revealed God of Scripture. As an example, the Bible, in its entirety, was not perceived to be the Word of God but "contained" the Word of God or could "become" the Word of God.

FROM FUNDAMENTALISM TO EVANGELICALISM

Meanwhile, Fundamentalism grew up and produced a stepchild known as Evangelicalism. Fundamentalism, by the 1940s and the 1950s, had come to refer more to a sociological than to a theological group. Fundamentalists tended to be isolationistic in their worldview. Evangelicals, while affirming the fundamentals of the faith, were not isolationists. They did not want to retreat from the city, but to evangelize it. Fundamentalists seemed less inclined to infiltrate the cities, which were considered evil places. They put great value on external issues and embraced a legalistic approach to the Christian life (hair style, makeup, length of dresses, etc.). Evangelicals were more concerned with theological conformity, specifically the centrality of the Bible, the Cross, the resurrection of Christ, and personal conversion.[15]

FOUR DIFFERENT READING HABITS

One good way to explain the different approaches during this period is to examine some magazine titles. One magazine, founded in 1884, was renamed the *Christian Century* in the year 1900. The very title shows the profound optimism with which the editors viewed the upcoming century. It was to be truly the Christian century, according to liberals. How disappointing to discover that the century was anything but Christian.

Reacting to that magazine was one founded many years later through the influence of famed evangelist Billy Graham and his father-in-law, L. Nelson Bell—*Christianity Today,* launched in 1956. Guided theologically by editor Carl F. H. Henry (1913–   ), the evangelical magazine quickly eclipsed the *Christian Century* as the single most influential publication of its kind. This magazine's popularity parallels Evangelicalism's rapid rise. One other magazine will help describe the theological climate of the time.

The *Sword of the Lord* was founded in 1934 by the Fundamentalist Baptist evangelist John R. Rice (1895-1980) and published in Murfreesboro, Tennessee. The magazine's title gives a clue to its strident, almost militant viewpoint. Fundamentalist subscribers to the *Sword of the Lord* viewed Evangelicals (*Christianity Today* readers) as having moved too far down the slippery slope toward the liberals (who would have been reading the *Christian Century*). Along with these three magazines, we need to list a fourth group of readers. Those embracing Neo-Orthodoxy would have been reading the writings of Karl Barth. The above four types of reading habits aptly reveal the four theological camps.

WORLD AND NATIONAL COUNCILS OF CHURCHES

If reading habits are considered one indication of theological persuasion, membership in certain organizations certainly qualifies as another.

Throughout the nineteenth and twentieth centuries, interest grew in bringing churches and denominations together. That desire culminated in the founding of the World Council of Churches, which brought together Christians from almost every continent. Although preliminary meetings took place in 1933 and again in 1938, the actual beginning of the organization was to occur in 1939. The outbreak of World War II delayed the first assembly until 1948. The goal was to provide a visible oneness for Christians and to enhance the witness of the Church, which had seen so much divisiveness.

Only two years after the First Assembly of the World Council of Churches, the National Council of Churches was formed on December 1, 1950, in Cleveland, Ohio. It brought together denominations with a collective membership of 33 million. Headquartered in New York City, the NCC became a symbol, considered positive by some and negative by others. Mainline denominations joined in overwhelming numbers, seeing this as an opportunity for Jesus' prayer for unity finally to be evidenced. To them, the word "ecumenical" had a beautiful sound. Evangelicals, however, remained suspicious and did not join in, convinced that the organization represented a theological "dumbing down" which brought the Church in line with the least common denominator. Sacrificed, they felt, were the fundamentals of the faith. Besides, they had already formed the National Association of Evangelicals in 1943. Fundamentalists had a heyday with the founding of the NCC, convinced that it was the "whore of Babylon." While the National Council of Churches had enormous influence in the 1960s, it imploded in the 1980s and by 2000 has minimal influence.

THE FOUR SHEPHERDS

Rob Staples, a former professor at Nazarene Theological Seminary, explains the difference between Fundamentalism, Evangelicalism, Modernism (Liberalism) and Postmodernism in his unique "Shepherd's Story." In his illustration, the manger represents the Bible:

> In my story there are four shepherds—a Modernist, a Fundamentalist, a Postmodernist, and an Evangelical. One by one they come to the manger seeking the Christ.
>
> The Modernist shepherd comes to the manger and says: "This is a weak manger; some of the boards have knotholes in them." So

he sets about to make it better by ripping out the "miracle" board, the "virgin birth" board, the "resurrection" board, and pretty soon he has so weakened the manger that Christ falls into the straw on the stable floor!

Then the Fundamentalist shepherd rushes up. "I will defend the manger," he says, "I will fight anyone who tinkers with it. Let no one lay a hand on it." He spends most of his energy defending the manger, and practically idolizing the boards (the written words), leaving little time to adore the Christ (the Living Word) who lies in it.

The Postmodernist shepherd probably never even bothers to find the manger. He thinks the angel's announcement of a newborn king is a nice story, but only one story among many. It has meaning for some people. Other stories are meaningful to others, and who can say which story is most important? We can each create our own stories, and one is as true as another

Now the Evangelical shepherd differs from them all. Unlike the Postmodernist, he knows he must go to the manger (the Bible) to learn about Christ. There are many mangers (books) in the world, but only this one has the words of eternal life. But, having come to the manger, he differs from the Modernist who wants to reconstruct it. The Evangelical knows that this manger is truly unique. Of all mangers (books) in the world, this is the most important. He respects it, loves it, handles it with care. But he does not worship it. Having come to the manger, he, unlike the Fundamentalist, does not tarry there adoring the manger itself. He does not even defend it, believing its truth is strong enough to defend itself. He quickly turns to worship and adore the Christ who lies there, and then goes and proclaims Him.[16]

When Modernists took over the churches, they created the liberal establishment. But a few years later, Liberalism had played out its course, and Neo-Orthodoxy had replaced it. But Neo-Orthodoxy could never grip the culture the way that Evangelicalism would.

By 1960, Evangelicalism had won the day. Two "Bills" would dominate the Evangelism of the 1960s, 1970s and 1980s: Billy Graham (1918–   ) and

Bill Bright (1921–   ). Both men continue to be God's conduits in leading the Church to spread the gospel throughout all the earth.

BILLY GRAHAM

Billy Graham is clearly the most well-known evangelist in the world today. His crusades are legendary, attracting thousands to various stadiums, arenas, parks and other locations around the world. He is one of the world's most effective Christian leaders in using television and radio in promoting God's gospel of redemption for humankind.

Born near Charlotte, North Carolina, Graham was saved under the evangelistic preaching of Mordecai F. Ham (1877-1961). A few years later he began attending classes at Bob Jones University, and in January 1937 transferred to Florida Bible Institute in Tampa. In March 1938, Graham sensed a call to preaching. Between 1940 and 1943, Graham attended Wheaton College near Chicago, where he married Ruth Bell, whose parents had been missionaries to China. After a period with the burgeoning Youth for Christ organization, Graham conducted a crusade in Los Angeles in 1949 that catapulted him into national fame. At Forest Home Camp in California, he had an experience with God in which he committed himself to the authority of the Bible. Thereafter, his preaching was punctuated with the phrase "the Bible says."

Billy Graham's evangelistic efforts grew throughout the latter half of the twentieth century. Graham, like the immensely popular Los Angeles, California, revivalist Charles Fuller (1887-1969) who preceded him, grasped the power of radio. Moreover, like Fuller, who had broadcast from seven stations in Southern California and would in 1937 build a national audience through his program the "Old-Fashioned Gospel Hour" (a live broadcast from a Long Beach auditorium, which reached 10 million listeners on Sunday evenings), Graham would also launch a successful radio program in 1951, "The Hour of Decision." The Billy Graham Evangelistic Association was also founded in the same year.

From Dwight Eisenhower to the present, every American president has fostered a relationship and sought spiritual counsel and advice from Billy Graham. Today, this evangelist stands without peer as a representative for evangelical Christianity. He has preached the gospel to more people than anyone else in history, having preached in person to over 100 million individuals, not including services preached by radio, television and satellite links. He remains one of the single most influential Christian leaders in the world today, second in influence only to the pope.

BILL BRIGHT

The second Bill of this period is Bill Bright, founder and president of Campus Crusade for Christ, International. Born in a small Oklahoma town, Bright later moved to Los Angeles where he established a company that marketed fancy foods. It was there that he came under the influence of the profoundly gifted Bible teacher, Henrietta Mears, at Hollywood's First Presbyterian Church. (Mears is the world's best-known Sunday School teacher, having had profound influence on some of the world's greatest spiritual leaders.)

In 1945, Bright made a promise to follow Jesus Christ. Although he had previously attended Princeton Theological Seminary for a brief time, he had never completed his theological studies. After his conversion, he decided to go to Fuller Theological Seminary, but never finished his classes there. Instead, he formed a ministry to students at the University of California in Los Angeles, and Campus Crusade was born in 1951. Within a short period of time 250 students had committed their lives to Christ and the movement began to explode. It is now one of the largest student missions movements on the globe.

Headquartered in Orlando, Florida, Campus Crusade has thousands of full-time staff, scattered in virtually every nation on earth. In addition, Campus Crusade has translated the *Jesus* film into 600 languages, with 235 more language translation projects in process. Through the use of small generators, projectors retrofitted to withstand primitive conditions and portable screens, the *Jesus* film has been shown to roughly half of the earth's population. Around 3.4 billion people[17] have seen the film and 90 million have indicated decisions for Christ! The *Jesus* film has been shown in 233 countries with nearly 3,000 film teams operating worldwide. It is not only the world's "most viewed" film, but it is also the most effective evangelistic tool in the history of humanity. Few organizations have so impacted the course of Evangelicalism as Campus Crusade.

Yet even today, as Evangelicalism is making great strides around the world in sharing the redemptive power of God's gospel, another man's legacy—a life that embodied God's gospel message for freedom and human dignity—would rise to challenge injustice everywhere. He is a hero for his courage and wisdom in civil rights: Martin Luther King, Jr. (1929-1968).

MARTIN LUTHER KING, JR.

During the late 1950s and early 1960s, as Christian evangelistic efforts gathered momentum in sharing the gospel with millions in America and abroad, a growing political and spiritual war was raging within the nation. African-Americans were experiencing political and social inequality on a massive scale because of racial discrimination policies.

In the aftermath of the Civil War, the institution of slavery was broken; but the roots of slavery—the mind-set that allows skin color to be the discriminate measure of where a person can eat, what seat on a bus must be used, how a vote should be cast, which schools must be attended and what loans can be secured—this abuse continued. Sadly, the U.S. government's failure after the Civil War to reconstruct a healthy political recovery and economic structure in the South contributed to racial abuses. Even more unfortunate, for nearly 100 years following the Civil War, the Church languished, too, in promoting political and social reforms honoring to God. By the early 1960s, the nation was ripe for a challenge to racial discrimination and the abuses it fostered. Into the cauldron of turmoil walked Martin Luther King, Jr. Although many white Evangelicals regarded King's theology as suspect during the Civil Rights movement, many of those same Evangelicals later repented of their silence regarding civil injustice.

This charismatic leader was the son and grandson of Baptist pastors. Receiving degrees in 1948 and 1951, he complete his Ph.D. in 1955 from the University of Boston. In 1954, he had returned to the South to become the pastor of Dexter Avenue Baptist Church, in Montgomery, Alabama. It was there that Martin Luther King, Jr., mobilized the blacks to stage a bus boycott to end segregation. This launched him into national prominence. The next year he helped organize the Southern Christian Leadership Conference, which took the lead in the civil rights struggle.

Dr. King will always be remembered for his famous "I Have a Dream" speech, which not only mesmerized a crowd of 200,000 in Washington, DC, in August 1963, but which also has held a nation spellbound ever since. By 1964, he saw the Civil Rights Act passed and was awarded the Nobel peace prize. By 1965, Martin Luther King, Jr., would also see the Voting Rights Act passed by Congress. When he was gunned down by an assassin in Nashville on April 4, 1968, some inner-city riots erupted and the nation mourned. In 1986, Martin Luther King, Jr.'s birthday was made a national holiday, celebrated on the third Monday of January.

THE WAR OF VALUES

While our time period began in 1918 with a vigorous battle between Fundamentalists and Modernists (which the Fundamentalists lost), it ends with the rise of Neo-Fundamentalists (Evangelicals) who seized the day. The influence of liberal churches diminished steadily throughout this period. By the mid-1960s the membership in liberal churches had already begun to plateau, indicating that meager days were ahead.

The battle for the Church is not a battle solely over theology. That's far too cerebral. The battle for the Church, that I've outlined in the period between World War I and 1965, is a battle of human passions and values. It's a battle for hearts and minds. Whose values are going to win?

The good news is that as this period closed out, in about 1965, the handwriting was on the wall: nonbiblical Liberalism's influence was in rapid decline. In contrast, Evangelicalism, with its declaration of biblical basics, was noticeably increasing. This is not to say naively that the world was won. Each generation must fight its own battle for the soul of the Church and the truth of the gospel. But the Church—though tested during this period—was alive and well.

To further assist you in understanding the key individuals and events of chapter 17, study questions, charts, diagrams, time lines and links to biographical websites are available on the Internet at www.jimgarlow.com. Please follow the site links to *How God Saved Civilization*, chapter 17 study helps.

AMERICA'S GREATEST EVANGELISTIC FORCE

THE SURGING SOUTHERN BAPTISTS

Dates covered: A.D. 1960-2000
*Key persons: tens of thousands of Baptist laity who have been
contagious carriers of the gospel*

The room was hot, and the air-conditioning was broken. Nearly 50 people were packed into a room designed for 30. In front of the class, one of the church deacons presented David and his wife, Lindy, with a beautiful framed picture of their home on Elm Street.

"Our way of saying thank-you for 10 years of wonderful teaching here at the church," the deacon smiled.

David grinned and turned to the crowd to offer his thanks for the gift and love for the church. As he expressed his heartfelt gratitude, Lindy stood beside him and pondered the picture. *Ten years teaching Sunday School,* she thought, *and 16 years total since we first became members. How time passes.*

The picture opened a flood of old memories. Sixteen years ago, in the summer of '54, on a bright Georgia day, a simple event would change their lives. Lindy recalled she was standing near the window over the kitchen sink; she was watching her two daughters, Sherry and Elly, ride their tricycles outside their two-bedroom home on Elm Street.

Lindy's mental video of the past was in full rewind mode. She could see a couple rounding the corner. They came down the sidewalk where Sherry and Elly were playing. Together, they smiled, leaned down and greeted Sherry first. Lindy could see Elly, being the older of the two girls, pedaling as fast as she could to get closer to where Sherry was. Her younger, three-year-old sister seemed enthralled by the man who was trying to act like a walrus.

Lindy wiped her hands with a kitchen towel and walked outside to see what the strangers wanted, but it didn't take her long to realize these were good, kind folks.

Lindy mused, *Like yesterday. I see it all and still hear their voices.* The gentleman greeted Lindy with a smile. "Good morning, ma'am. Allow me to introduce myself. I'm Bob Turner; this is my wife Elizabeth. We're opening a new Baptist church in the Hoover Elementary School. We will have a fine Sunday School for children on Sunday mornings. If you don't already have a church, we'd love it if you could come and bring your family."

Sherry pleaded, "Oh please, mommy. Let's go. They have a walrus puppet at the church."

Lindy reflected. *That's how it started. That's how we started coming to church, but David wasn't as eager. That, too, was Your doing, Lord.* Lindy's mind flashed to the past again. She could remember asking her husband to come to church with her after Pastor Turner had given their family an invitation to attend. David wasn't interested, though.

Lindy could recall how nervous she was the first Sunday, walking into Hoover Elementary, but recalled how the Turners recognized her, helped the kids get to the right Sunday School class and immediately made her feel at home where she sat with a group of 20 people in the little auditorium. Lindy felt special to be present at what was obviously such a happy moment for everyone. As the pastor began to preach from the Bible, the stories, the words he used, gave her a strange sensation.

On the way home she couldn't stop Elly and Sherry from chattering excitedly about Walter the Walrus and all kinds of other stories, songs and games in Sunday School. The girls were so happy. As she walked home with Sherry and Elly in hand, those few blocks gave Lindy time to know how much she needed, the kids needed and David needed, a church home.

Late that night, as Lindy and David were getting into bed, she broached the topic. "Dave, I think we need to be in church. You were a Presbyterian as a child; I was a Methodist. So maybe we should compromise," she half smiled, "and go to this Baptist church."

"Why?"

"Well, the girls and I had such a good time."

"That's not the only reason though, is it?"

"Yes, you're right, Dave. There's something else. You see, I felt something as the pastor spoke from the Bible. I'm not quite sure what it was. But I want to go back. And I really want all of us to be there, you included."

Dave rolled over and answered sleepily. "Okay, for you."

The next Sunday, David begrudgingly went and, like Lindy, the pastor's words touched his heart. The preacher talked about how one could become a Christian. David listened, but he also whispered his protests to Lindy. "This is strange, honey. What does he mean, 'to become a Christian'? I'm already a Christian. Everybody in America is a Christian, aren't they?"

In perfect sync, the pastor seem to know what David was thinking and he said to the congregation, "Many people think they are Christians, just because they're Americans, but they're not. Jesus died on the cross for our sins. But we must *personally receive* him. That's why I want to give an invitation."

David remarked to Lindy, "Invitation? What's that?"

But the pastor gently elaborated, "If you want to receive Christ, you have to open your heart to him. You must tell Him you are ready for Him to move in and take over. He will clean out the garbage in your mind and make your life far more beautiful than you can imagine. If you don't understand everything, I'll be happy to explain more. Besides, God's Word promises He will come and show Himself to you. I invite anyone here to come up to the front with me and make a decision to follow Jesus. I know it's a little frightening, but believe me, it's worth it!"

Dave's eyes were fixed on the pastor. His heart was beating fast. A strange force, almost outside of himself, had come over him. Lindy sat in amazement as David suddenly stood up and walked to the front. Lindy, exhilarated at her husband's response, was feeling the same thing. She grabbed Sherry and Elly and, walking behind David, went to the front. Together, David, Lindy and the girls professed their faith in Christ that day.

Lindy sighed. The memory of that moment was sweet. *That was the moment we came to know You, Lord. I would never have guessed that You would give David a chance to teach Sunday School six years later or that he would continue to faithfully teach for You over the next 10 years. Oh, Lord, You have been so kind to us.*

A sudden applause from the audience jolted Lindy back to the moment. David was sharing with the class. "And our daughter Sherry just turned 19; she's going on a Mexico youth mission to paint a church. And Elly, of course, is married to a fine young Baptist minister across town."

Lindy was happy inside; but in the corner of her eye, she noticed the one woman whom she wanted to thank most—Elizabeth Turner. She moved graciously and quietly to the side of the room where Elizabeth was listening to David speak.

"I want to thank you and Bob."

A bit startled, the pastor's wife spoke softly, "It's only a picture, Lindy. Besides, it's from the whole class."

Lindy squeezed Elizabeth's hand affectionately, "No, it's not the picture. I want to thank you and Bob for the day you decided to walk down Elm Street."

BAPTIST RESILIENCY: EVANGELISM AND SCRIPTURE

After 1960, two powerful groups came to national prominence at about the same time: the Baptists and the Charismatics. The Baptists (covered in this chapter) started in the 1600s and have steadily grown in numbers. Understanding this amazing journey from 1609 to 1960 is the key in explaining the significant influences of Baptists (particularly the Southern Baptist Convention) from 1960 to the present.

Prior to the Revolutionary War, Congregationalists had the strongest influence on the American Christian experience, followed closely by the Anglican church (also known as the Episcopal church). But after the war of independence, two denominations eclipsed all other denominational groups: the Methodists and the Baptists. Contrast these figures:

- By 1820, Methodists have 2,700 churches; Baptists have an equal number.
- By 1860, the Methodists have nearly 20,000 churches, whereas the Baptists just over 12,000.
- By 1900, Methodists have 54,000 churches; Baptists have 50,000 churches.
- By 1950, there were 77,000 Baptist churches while the Methodists had maintained their 54,000 churches.[1]

It is important to note that the Roman Catholics experienced even more growth than the Baptists over the last 200 years of American history. However, this growth may be attributed to huge influxes of European immigrants who came from Roman Catholic families and backgrounds rather than to evangelistic efforts. At the time of the Revolution there were only 20,000 Roman Catholics out of a total American population of 3.6 million. By 1970, the number of Roman Catholic adherents in the United States had grown to 48 million.[2]

Baptists and Roman Catholics are very different in certain areas of worship, evangelism and theology, but they share an ability to endure setbacks. Over hundreds of years, Roman Catholicism has endured internal strife and external attack. A popular Catholic brochure about Rome says:

Nero burned and crucified Christians here in A.D. 64. Saracen pirates raided and pillaged in 312. Charles V invaded in 1527, and Hitler threatened in World War II. But the Vatican has survived all of its enemies. And after 2,000 years of tumultuous history, it remains the center of the world's largest religious body—the Roman Catholic Church.[3]

In comparison, the Baptists, though a much younger branch of Christianity, also seem to persevere and grow in spite of fierce splits among churches and members. Their growth and resiliency comes from a passionate recognition that each believer must personally know the Scriptures and that personal evangelism (particularly Sunday School) is a priority.

So who are the Baptists, these folks who seem to overcome obstacles?

BAPTIST ROOTS—JOHN SMYTH

The Baptist story is more difficult to tell than the Methodist story, which had a clear beginning in John Wesley. The story of the Baptist movement is not the story of one man's evangelism over a 50-year period and the fruits it brought. The Baptists have a more complex beginning with several facets.

Baptist history begins with an Englishman, John Smyth (ca. 1570-1612), who baptized the first-known Baptists in 1608 or 1609 in a small congregation that had fled to Amsterdam, Holland. Smyth was a Separatist. Unlike the Puritans who tried to cleanse the Anglican church from within, Smyth and Separatists like him, felt such a cause to be hopeless. Therefore, they separated to form their own churches.

In approximately 1606, John Smyth founded a Separatist church in Gainsborough, Lincolnshire, England. To gain religious freedom, his congregation (along with one other) was forced to flee England for Holland. While in Holland, Smyth was influenced by the Mennonites, who were followers of Menno Simons, the German Anabaptist. He became convinced that the only scriptural baptism was adult believers' baptism. Once convinced of this, Smyth rebaptized himself by applying water to his head[4] and then baptized approximately 40 people who embraced the same teaching. Although the thought of believers' baptism is totally normal in American culture today, Smyth's church "was the first English church (which practiced) the principle of baptizing believers only."[5]

CHURCH SPLITS

Kenneth Curtis, in his book *Dates with Destiny*, with tongue in cheek, focuses on Smyth's congregation in Holland and states: "You might consider this the start of the Baptist Church. But it almost didn't happen that way. The birth of the Baptist Church required the start of another Baptist tradition—the church split."[6]

Smyth was so impressed with the Mennonites that he asked them to receive his congregation into their organization. But his friend Thomas Helwys (ca. 1550-ca. 1660) was not in favor of joining the group; and Helwys led the first Baptist church split, taking 10 members back to London where they established the very first Baptist Church in all of England.[7]

John Smyth was finally admitted into the Mennonite church in 1615—three years after he had died of tuberculosis! Meanwhile, Helwys, who might have been known as the founder of the Baptist movement, was arrested and imprisoned in Newgate prison for having had the audacity to inform the king that he was not, in fact, God. Helwys was never heard of again and is believed to have died in 1616. But as Kenneth Curtis says in his book *Dates with Destiny,* "the Baptist movement grew."[8] What an understatement!

Baptists tend to thrive on splits or at least overcome them. Many churches are devastated when difficulties, whether arising from sin or from outside forces, cause a church to split. But Baptists have a certain resiliency, and whenever splits occurred, they simply started more churches. By 2000, the Baptist World Alliance had a staggering 100 million members.[9]

From the founding of their denomination, the Baptist characteristic of the individual being able to interpret Scripture for himself or herself has caused them to divide over various issues. Baptist have or do wrestle over the following:

- How is salvation worked in the life of the unbeliever (1600s-1700s)?
  Split into Regular Baptists (Calvinists) versus General Baptists (Arminians).
- What methods do we use to evangelize (1820s)?
  Split into Pro-Missionary Baptists versus Anti-Missionary Baptists (known as Primitive Baptists).
- What is the role of slavery (1840s)?
  Split into the Northern Baptist Association (later called the American Baptist Convention) and the Southern Baptist Convention.
- How do we understand theology (early 1900s)?
  Split into Fundamentalist Baptists and Modernist Baptists.

· What is meant when we say the Scriptures are inerrant (1980s-'90s)?
Split into Conservatives and Moderates.

There are even variations of Baptist positions after an initial split.
Growing out of the General Baptist, Calvinistic trend, Henry Jessey, William
Kiffin and John Spilsbury founded the Particular Baptist movement in the
late 1630s—so named because Christ, according to their Calvinism, had died
only for particular people.[10]

EVANGELISM AND BAPTISM

Church splits are not unique to Baptists. Plenty of other denominations
have a good reputation for splitting, too. Yet, as we look at the Baptist
movement today, we can clearly see God's hand of blessing. The single,
most potent driving force that has brought Baptists their phenomenal harvests has been their unwavering commitment to proclaiming the gospel and
calling people to respond. Their passion for evangelism has been the key
ingredient in making disciples all over the world. This passion has been the
envy of many other denominations.

On their identifying issue, baptism, they have always been adamant.
They began as a reaction against a formalized church that had baptized its
children without insisting that they believe and be converted. The Anglican,
Lutheran and Roman Catholic state churches had assumed, or seemed to
assume, that just because a religious rite had been performed in a church by
their parents when they were infants, that salvation was assured. Infant baptism runs counter to a fundamental Baptist conviction that people should
not be baptized until they understand the implications of their spiritual
commitment to Christ.

Another aspect of baptism which distinguished Baptists from the state
churches was their practice of immersion. Not only were they concerned
about who should receive baptism, but they were also concerned about the
mode of baptism. They came to believe that baptism should be adminis-
tered by immersion. Baptizing by immersion was certainly not new. It had
been practiced by the Early Church on a rather consistent basis, up through
the Middle Ages. But Baptists argued that the very word for baptism in the
New Testament meant "immersion." The consistent application of this
identifiable public act by which a new believer announces to the world a

faith in Jesus Christ has given the Baptists their spiritual heritage, and many Baptists would argue that this obedience has contributed significantly to their growth.

Their early critics referred to Baptists as coming from German Anabaptists, although it is hotly debated whether the original Baptists had any historical link to Anabaptists. Sometimes Baptists were called the Brethren, the Baptized Churches or the Churches of the Baptized Way. In the 1640s, many were calling them Baptists, and a decade later they accepted the name for themselves. However, it was a hundred years later that the name Baptist would become an official, generally accepted denominational label.[11]

PERSECUTION, THEN TOLERANCE

Throughout the 1640s a battle had raged in England between those who wanted the monarchy and those who wanted a representative government. In 1649, Charles was executed, the monarchy abolished, and Oliver Cromwell ruled England as the Protector of the Commonwealth. For the next eight years religious toleration was encouraged. But in 1658, Oliver Cromwell, leader of the Commonwealth in Britain, died. By 1660, young Charles II had been installed on his father's throne and the royal restoration had taken place. Baptists, along with other independent groups, were blamed for everything that had gone wrong during the short period of time when the monarchy had been abolished, the king beheaded and the Church of England removed from its prominent role. When the king and the monarchy were reinstated, persecution of Baptists, which had grown, became intense. Baptists, however, would not turn from their fundamental principles of religious liberty. They continued to believe, as they did from their inception, that state and Church should be separate and that the government was in no position to dictate the individual conscience of any man. Sufficiently influential were the Baptists in England that by the year 1689 they had helped to bring about the desperately needed Act of Toleration. Finally, Baptists had won the freedoms they had so long desired.

ROGER WILLIAMS

Baptists took root in America through Roger Williams. He started a town he called Providence (Rhode Island), to commemorate God's faithfulness in providing for him during his times of distress. Equally outspoken was Anne Hutchinson, who (like Roger Williams) was ousted from Massachusetts and who became a significant leader in Baptist life in Providence. We see Roger Williams's stamp on the Baptists when we examine his commitments:

1. He was a missionary, specifically to the American Indians. The missions activity of the Baptist church would, years later, become one of their primary characteristics.
2. Williams was a radical advocate of religious liberty and of the right of the individual conscience in all religious matters. This is the hallmark of the Baptist faith, making it very suspicious of anything that smacks of bureaucratic control.
3. He was unbending regarding the separation of Church and state. The civil government, Williams contended, deals with all citizens. But the Church is spiritual and deals only with those who choose to be a part of it.
4. Williams believed in democracy. While this position would fit well in the new America, its rejection of any outside authority's impinging on the congregation made the Baptist churches sometimes susceptible to the whims of its individual members, who could claim freedom of conscience and democratic rights to justify many an expression of carnality.

As R. D. Linder noted, "Williams' Rhode Island experiment was much closer to what America would become than was the strict inflexible Congregational Calvinist of New England."[12]

It should not surprise us to note that Roger Williams, who founded the first Baptist community in America, later left his own movement! He broke with the Baptists and became a Seeker, convinced that since the Baptist church was not the true church, he ought to continue seeking until he found it. Once again, there was a Baptist split. But in this case it was the leader who split from his own movement. The individualism of the Baptists makes it harder to find heroes. However, the lack of heroes has provided the impetus for thousands of ordinary individuals to do the work of the Church.

LACK OF HEROES

If we look for heroes among the Baptists, we find John Smyth in Holland, who left the Baptists to join the Mennonites; Thomas Helwys, who was thrown in prison and never heard from again; and Roger Williams, who left the movement in search of the perfect church!

Of course, my Baptist friends tell me they don't need a hero. Jesus founded their church and He is the only founder they need. But the fact is that Jesus has always used people—like you and me—people who change their minds, who don't always stay with the movements they found. In spite of the abandonments by Smyth and Williams and the disappearance (imprisonment) of Helwys, sufficient biblical foundations were laid that have made this movement what it is today.

EARLY GROWTH

The denomination destined to become the largest Protestant body in America had a sluggish start. It was not until 1684 that a little Baptist church was founded in Philadelphia and the Baptists penetrated the middle colonies. Sometime in the 1680s, the Baptists had their modest beginnings in the southern colonies, where they would eventually dominate.

The enormous colonial-style sanctuary with a tall, cross-crowned steeple was not a luxury enjoyed by Baptists in the early years of colonial America. Most Baptist churches boasted no more than a dozen members, and few congregations owned a building. Many went for years without a pastor. Their worship was informal, but the focal point was the Bible. This dogged determination to remain faithful to God's Word, more than any other factor, may be the key to their incredibly rapid growth.[13] The Baptists did not seem overly worried about the lack of pastors. They realistically and happily allowed their pastors to be bivocational. It was not uncommon for a Baptist preacher to farm Monday through Saturday and to preach on Sunday.

The real turning point for the Baptists was at the beginning of the eighteenth century. In 1700, there were only 24 Baptist churches, with a total membership of 839. So paltry were their churches, that "they had no organized association, sponsored no society for missions or evangelism, and probably had limited awareness of one another."[14] But the First Great Awakening of the 1740s changed all that. Although Baptists did not initiate the revival as other churches did, they gleaned tremendous numbers in membership. Ironically, the First Great Awakening was not originally led by Baptists. The leaders were

- Theodore Freylinghuysen (1691-1747), Dutch Reformed;
- Gilbert Tennent (1703-1764), Presbyterian;
- Jonathan Edwards (1703-1758), a strict five-point Congregational Calvinist; and
- George Whitefield (1714-1770), a British Arminian-turned-Calvinist evangelist.

Baptist democracy fit the rugged individualism of the post-Great Awakening years. This quality in the denomination characterized what America was becoming, and people began flocking to Baptist churches. Over 100 New Light Congregational churches (called New Light because they embraced the revival, as opposed to Old Light, who criticized the revival), left their Congregational ties and became Baptists. By 1790, Baptists numbered 979 churches, with over 67,000 members. In the 20-year span preceding 1795, the number of Baptist congregations went from 494 to over 1,152. As the Baptists entered the 1800s they were poised to become a major influence in America.[15]

Some sociologists argue that the growth of the Baptist church was a purely political and socioeconomic happening. As an unabashed supernaturalist, I see more than political expediency and conformity in the rugged individualism of colonial life. I see God's hand working in the culture to prepare a particular denomination as a profound force for Him. (Since I am not a Baptist, I can't be accused of partisanship.) God was at work, creating a denomination that would become an indescribable force for Christ around the globe.

This influence was not easily won, however. Remember that most of the original colonies had established state churches. This ran counter to a Baptist cardinal doctrine—the separation of Church and state. Although the states gradually disenfranchised established denominations, this process only ended when Massachusetts changed its laws in 1833.

Along with others, Baptists fought for the idea that the state should not limit religious liberty. (This major contribution of the Baptists to

American life has taken a strange twist in our century. The tragic *redefini-*tion of "the separation of Church and state" by historical revisionists in late twentieth-century America has dealt a crushing blow to free expression of Christianity.) Nonetheless, Baptists rightfully took credit for the American practice of separation of Church and state. So significant is their influence that Joseph Dawson concludes that "if the researchers of the world were asked who was most responsible for the American guarantee of religious liberty, their prompt reply would be, 'James Madison.' However, if James Madison might answer, he would as quickly reply, 'John Leland and the Baptists.'"[16]

In spite of disestablishment, the Church flourished. In fact, many Church historians refer to the time period between 1800 and 1900 as "the great century" for the advance of Christianity. That would be true for Baptists as well.[17]

THE MISSIONARY CONTROVERSY

During its unprecedented growth, the Baptist church was plagued by embarrassing divisiveness. The most bizarre of their theological subsets was the Anti-Missionary movement. Baptists today are known for their aggressive missions policies, but such was not the case in certain parts of the Baptist church during the 1820s. The view of some was that conversion was the task of God alone, and that He would do it without any kind of human ingenuity or involvement. Missionary activity was seen as an affront to God's sovereignty. The Anti-Missionary Baptists (Primitive Baptists) and their strict five-point Calvinism resulted their being labeled "hard-shell Baptists."

Within this movement were Baptists influenced by Alexander Campbell and the Restorationists in Kentucky and surrounding states in the 1840s. Given the fluidity with which Baptists and their churches can move in and out of structures and theology, you can guess what happened. One of the prime historians of the movement says it this way: "Hundreds of Baptist Churches left the denomination to line up with Campbell's 'reformers,' who, after 1830 formed a new denomination known as Disciples of Christ or Church of Christ. Historians estimate, for example, that fully half the Baptist Churches of Kentucky switched to the New Disciples Movement."[18]

THE SPLIT OVER SLAVERY

That Christian churches could not stay united, or unite with one another to oppose slavery, has to be one of the most embarrassing moments for the cause of Christ. The following denominations split over the issue and nearly all split North versus South:

- Presbyterians (1837);
- Methodists (1843)—a splinter group formed under the leadership of Orange Scott, calling itself the Wesleyan Methodist church;
- Methodists (1844)—the remaining larger Methodist church;
- Baptists (1845);
- Episcopalians (1861).

While some Baptists would argue that the split between North and South involved, for their church, such issues as organizational structure, Baptist historian James Sullivan says that, "We cannot be honest with our history and minimize the prominence of the problem of slavery."[19] Says McBeth in unusual candor, "Slavery was the main issue that led to the 1845 schism; that is a blunt historical fact. Other issues raised barriers and, in time, might have led to division, if not North/South, possibly East/West. However, slavery did lead to division."[20]

Looking back from our vantage point in history, we wonder how people who love God and His Word could ever defend slavery. How could this happen? It is a tragic note throughout Christian history that believers have frequently been slow to embrace the truth of God's Word, sometimes out of ignorance and other times out of an impure hardness of heart.

Robert Baker states that there were effectively three periods of understanding of American slavery, and the view toward slavery altered significantly from one period to another. Prior to 1830, slavery, according to Baker, was viewed as an economic system. From 1830 to 1840, slavery was seen as a moral issue. After 1840, slavery came to be viewed for its distinct political aspects and, ultimately, led to the Civil War.[21] This three-part description of attitudes to slavery does not excuse Christians, but it at least partially explains the blindness that most seemed to have prior to 1830. While it is inexcusable that Christians participated in such a horrific system, it is a tribute to the resiliency of the truth of God that after 1830 it came to be seen for what it really was—a truly immoral practice.

THE DIVISION AND THE INABILITY TO MERGE

In May of 1845, a delegation of Baptists met in Augusta, Georgia. The result was the formation of what is today called the Southern Baptist Convention. The Northern and Southern Baptists would never again unite. Presbyterians, in contrast, came back together many years later, in 1983. Methodists reunited in 1939. Episcopalians, the last to split, were the first to reunite, only four years later in 1865 immediately following the war. But such was not the case for the Baptists. With other denominations reuniting, it would seem that the Baptists would follow. "But each year of delay made the prospect of success less promising as a result of the steadily increasing Southern Regional self-consciousness."[22]

The Northern Baptists dealt with immigration issues and an industrial economy their southern sister didn't understand. This resulted not only in a different evangelism strategy but also eventually to a difference in theology. The social gospel, which developed as Christians tried to deal with the problems of the cities, began to shape the theology of the Northern Baptists. The Southern Baptists were suspicious of the social gospel. They continued to make extensive use of camp meetings, which worked well in the small towns and rural areas that characterized much of the South.

By the end of the Reconstruction period, the Northern and Southern Baptist denominations had developed culturally and theologically distinct identities. A merger was impossible. In addition, Baptists in the South had 4 million recently freed slaves. Most of the African-Americans who accepted Christianity became Baptists, although they found their own African-American expressions of it.[23] Following the Civil War, African-Americans and Anglo-Americans did not worship together.

Racial prejudice among members of the Anglo-American community combined with the fierce desire within the African-American community to enjoy churches free of whites looking over their shoulders resulted in separate denominations. African-Americans had spent more than a hundred years without their own institutions, restrained in their worship and under the control of whites for theological content. Within 15 years after the Civil War ended nearly one million African-American Baptists worshiped in their own black churches, unaffiliated with whites.[24]

Why can't God's children get along? Why can't they worship together? Our heavenly Father must feel infinitely sad when He looks down on His Church and sees His children separated from each other. However, like a wise father with children who are less than united, our heavenly Father learns to work within our limited parameters. God has chosen to bless His work in spite of us. It is our preference to think He works through us and because of us, but most of the time, God works in spite of our obvious shortcomings. It is not a credit to any group to split. Virtually no issue is worth separating fellowship over, but the fact is that God's kids always have and, regretfully, always will (until heaven) continue to disagree and separate over issues that, in eternity, are really not that significant.

THE SUNDAY SCHOOL

Although Baptist churches grew slowly at first, they later made up for it. In fact, the most powerful wing of America's largest denomination, the Southern Baptist Convention, was not formed until the end of the 1800s. It was not until 1891 that the Sunday School Board of the Southern Baptist Convention was formed. Every Southern Baptist knows that this profoundly successful organization is one of the major components of Southern Baptist life. In the years following the Civil War, most Southern Baptists continued to buy Sunday School materials from the American Baptists in the North. Only a few of the 500 Baptist churches in the South had Sunday Schools by the middle of the 1800s.[25] But that would change. So pervasive was the work of the Sunday School Board of the Southern Baptist Convention that McBeth states, "No Southern Baptist, from the cradle to the grave, escapes the influence of the Sunday School Board."[26] The Sunday School Board is known not only for influencing the key evangelistic tool of the Southern Baptists, the Sunday School, but is responsible for a massive literary output unparalleled in any other denomination.

LANDMARKISM

In spite of the huge strides forward, Baptists were not done with controversy. It struck again, this time in the Landmark movement. Landmarkism, largely stirred by an influential Baptist pastor named James R. Graves (1820-1893), taught, among other things, that:

- Baptist churches are the only true churches in the world;
- there should be no affiliation with non-Baptists;
- only Baptists have an unbroken historical succession to the earliest followers of Jesus.

Most Baptists resisted this movement, which shows that the truth of the gospel had penetrated the hearts of the larger Southern Baptist movement. Had Landmarkism won, the Southern Baptist Convention would have had the arrogance demonstrated by such cult groups as the Jehovah's Witnesses and the Mormons. But Landmarkism was largely defeated, since Baptists see themselves as a part of the larger family of God. Tragically, however, as Baptist historian McBeth notes,

> Southern Baptists absorbed and still retain much of (the) spirit and emphasis (of Landmarkism). The continuing Landmark legacy can be seen in several contemporary Southern Baptist traits and practices. These include an exaggerated emphasis on local church autonomy, continuing tensions over alien immersion (Baptism done outside Baptist churches), and closed communion, a suspicion of other denominations, refusal to participate in organized ecumenical conferences.[27]

Any denomination that views itself as the only true denomination is making an outrageous claim. The family of God extends to *all* who embrace Jesus as the one true Savior and Lord. The Bible implies that at the last day, we will all have a few surprises when we find out exactly who will and who will not be in heaven. Only God knows the heart. Only He will know who are His true children. But we do know that His Church is made up of countless believers, scattered throughout the world in many nations, from many languages, and from many denominations. Any one denomination's claim to have the exclusive truth is evidence of human arrogance at its worst. In reality, each of us, as separate denominations, has a piece of the truth. Frankly, we need one another.

UNIVERSITY ILLUSTRATION

Allow me to illustrate this. Picture a group of Christian students on a state university campus. Where do these believers go for Christian fellowship? It depends on their personality and their makeup. They generally subdivide into four groups: the "know-ers," the "be-ers," the "do-ers, and the "feel-ers" The know-ers will go to the InterVarsity Christian Fellowship and spend the semester reading C. S. Lewis. The be-ers will go to the Navigators and spend the semester memorizing Matthew. The do-ers will join Campus Crusade and try to win the entire student body to Christ. The feel-ers will join whatever Charismatic student organization is on campus and worship God in explosive praise.

Can you guess what happens when these students graduate? The know-ers will go to a conservative, evangelical-type Presbyterian church or a Bible church and carry big notebooks to the worship services. The be-ers will migrate toward Holiness churches, where there is a clarion call to righteous living and integrity of lifestyle. The do-ers will join the Southern Baptist denomination and win their entire state for Christ. The feel-ers will become Charismatics and will continue to do what they do best, throw a party for Jesus every weekend with exuberant praise and worship.

Now let me ask this question: Which group is right? Or better yet: Which group is wrong? Answer: None of them. They divided based upon spiritual temperament, and that isn't necessarily wrong. However, I suspect God would prefer to mix them all together. That might be His ecumenical recipe. I'm sure He would like the feel-ers to know, the know-ers to be, the be-ers to do, and the do-ers to feel. He would like to mix us all up in one church and help us learn from each other. But we stay in our groups, divided over these issues. And God tolerates it, choosing to accomplish His will in spite of our divisiveness. Is God happy with our divisions? Of course not. But is He as critical of us as we are of one another? Not really. In His sovereignty, He is able to nod knowingly and say, "I am going to work with My kids anyway!" And that is precisely what He does.

Fortunately, the Landmarkism movement didn't succeed in the Southern Baptist church. But pockets of people still naively assume that their denomination is the full expression of Christ. The fact is that only the full and complete Church is the full expression of Christ. To be complete, we need one another.

DENOMINATIONS

God tolerates denominations because each group is faithful in responding to part of the whole counsel of God. A denomination preserves its particular grasp of God's truth until other denominations are ready for it. For example, the Baptists—thanks to recording companies like Integrity Incorporated—are learning praise from the Charismatics. The term "holiness," once reserved for Nazarene and Wesleyan types, has become a focus for other denominations who desire to walk in holiness. Many denominations are learning from Pentecostals about the gifts of the Holy Spirit, healing and deliverance. The Baptists are teaching us how to evangelize. And the Episcopalians are instructing us in the value of liturgy. And the mixing up continues. I suspect God is pleased.

BAPTISTS IN THE TWENTIETH CENTURY

The century started with great anticipation.

> Northern Baptists entered the twentieth century on a wave of optimism and growth. The word *forward* shows up on many of their committee and planning reports. The Northern Baptist schools prospered, placing their graduates in leading roles in American life and religion. Perhaps the ultimate in Baptist optimism was expressed in the name given the Northern Baptist fund-raising drive in 1919: "The New World Movement."[28]

The New World movement grew out of the radical American optimism that spread across the nation in World War I, which was considered the war to end all wars. Every denomination and local church shared in this radical optimism. The Northern Baptist Church launched a New World movement with an effort to collect 100 million dollars over a five-year period from 1919-1924. The campaign, though it had all the right motives, immediately met with resistance. Baptists were too independent for a coordinated, denominational fund-raising effort. In addition, the economy was not as robust as some expected. By 1924, the denomination had raised 45 million dollars, an outstanding result, but one that appeared paltry to those who had hoped for more than twice as much. Bitterness and resentment began to develop and the most ominous cloud on the horizon was the Fundamentalist-Modernist controversy that hit the larger American church scene. The result was predictable.

By 1932, a group had left the Northern Baptist Convention and formed the General Association of Regular Baptists. In 1947, another group left to form the Conservative Baptist Association of America. The Northern Baptist Convention, which changed its name in 1950 to the American Baptist Convention, went in an increasingly liberal direction.

Meanwhile, the Southern Baptists, not to be outdone by their Northern neighbors, launched their own financial campaign and intended to raise 75 million dollars over the same time frame, 1919-1924. This was by far the most ambitious fund-raising effort ever attempted. Baptists joyfully pledged 92 million dollars. The entire denomination was ecstatic. However, as is always the case, 75 million dollars "proved easier to pledge than to collect."[29] When the dust had settled, the Southern Baptists had collected nearly 59 million dollars. Instead of rejoicing that they had done so well, the failure to meet the goal engendered criticism that spoiled the occasion to rejoice in what God had done.

This constant delight in finding what went wrong is common to many local churches, Sunday School classes and even home study groups. When a project doesn't measure up to our expectations, we believers tend to turn against one another. This common Christian flaw is illustrated in this incident, when the Northern Baptists and Southern Baptists failed to raise what they intended. Instead of rejoicing at God's blessing, the church members criticized one another for failing to accomplish the specified goals.

PASTORAL STAFFS

The Southern Baptists affected the way churches were run. They began hiring more than one pastor for some of their churches. Prior to World War II,

> most churches regarded themselves as fully staffed if they had a pastor and a janitor (sometimes the same person), but gradually the "educational director," or "minister of education" emerged out of the Sunday School and other educational work of the church. The earliest known paid Sunday School Superintendent was R. H. Coleman, of First Baptist in Dallas in 1910.[30]

To those of us used to multiple staff, the hiring of a Sunday School superintendent seems insignificant. But this emphasis on the Sunday School work, and the Baptists' willingness to invest in it to this extent, was probably one of the reasons they experienced such exceedingly rapid

growth. Baptists led the way in establishing a modern Church phenomenon—churches led by a staff of multiple pastors rather than by a solo
pastor.

AMAZING GROWTH

By 1960, the Southern Baptist Convention has become a major force
nationally. A decade later, one of America's major news magazines had a
cover story entitled "The Surging Southern Baptists."[31] By 1992, both
the president and vice president of the United States were Southern
Baptists.

As of 1998, Southern Baptists alone have almost 41,000 churches in
the U.S., with nearly 10 million members.[32] Overseas, Southern Baptists
have an additional 47,000 churches with 4 million members.[33] The denomination is unashamedly Great Commission driven. No single denomination
has ever experienced such evangelistic fruit.

But the Baptist movement is far more than its largest denomination,
the Southern Baptist Convention. By 1978, the Baptist World Alliance had
in excess of 33 million members, one-third of which were members of the
Southern Baptist Convention.[34] By 2000, approximately 100 million
Baptists are part of the Baptist World Alliance![35] The Baptists have been the
most profound evangelistic force in the last 50 years of American history.

THE SOUTHERN BAPTISTS' SECRET WEAPONS

How is it that one denomination has grown so large? There are, I believe, six
key reasons for their effectiveness.

1. *Strong Leadership*—First, Southern Baptists have strong leadership
   at the helm of their three elected boards: the North American
   Mission Board (Atlanta), the International Mission Board
   (Richmond, VA) and Life Way Christian Resources (formerly
   Sunday School Board-Nashville). While these powerful boards
   wield tremendous influence in providing resources for local
   churches, they do not have denominational control (a concept
   that Baptists soundly reject). The heads of the boards have
   demonstrated profound leadership to what really is a loose connection or series of associations of churches. Only profoundly

strong leadership could hold together a group of autonomous—proudly autonomous—local churches, numbering over 40,000 nationally.

2. *Folk Oratory*—Southern Baptist preachers are folk orators. Folk oratory refers to their capacity to connect with the common person. Generally speaking, Baptist preachers would not win awards in a state-university oratory competition. But when it comes to their ability to draw in the common person, their success is unparalleled. Compare them with the preaching that occurs in Presbyterian, Episcopalian or Methodist pulpits. The preaching there would, generally speaking, reflect strong academic foundations. But Baptists simply resonate with the general populace in ways most others do not. They would not necessarily rank highest in the homiletical or exegetical arenas, but they generate credibility with their audiences that causes people to want to become Baptists.

3. *Activation Among Laity*—Historically, Baptist laity have been profoundly invigorated. As one example, note the number of Sunday School teachers (virtually every Southern Baptist church has an aggressive Sunday School) necessarily to staff 41,000 local churches. Unlike many other denominations, Baptists feel adults, as well as children, should be in Sunday School. And, for the most part, they feel that once a class reaches 20 in attendance, it should divide (multiply) and make two classes, thus requiring another teacher. Meeting the needs of Southern Baptist Sunday Schools alone, not including all the other ministries, requires virtually an army of activated laity.

   Another example of the role of the laity in Baptist churches is demonstrated during pastoral transitions. Many denominations attempt to coordinate pastoral transitions occurring at the same time so that a local congregation will not be without a pastor for a very long time. A one- or two-month period is considered too long for most local churches, with attendance frequently declining during that period. This is not so for many Baptist churches, which may go for many months or even a full year without a pastor, and experience growth during the interim! This is due primarily to the strength of the lay leadership team. Southern Baptists in particular, and Baptists in general, place great value on an activated and invigorated laity. Unlike every other chapter preceding this one, the chapter on the Baptists contains almost no biographies. It is not as though there were no strong leaders. There were, and there are. But there are no Mount Everest personalities among Baptists. They simply put a premium on the role of the common person. Somehow, Baptists, perhaps more successfully than any other group, have trained their laity to be contagious carriers of the gospel.

4. *Singularity of Focus*—I recognize that these paragraphs contain sweeping generalizations; but they are, I believe, sufficiently accurate to explain Baptists' profound growth. Their singularity of focus is salvation. Baptists have historically been unabashedly bold in asking, "Are you saved, brother/sister?" While other denominations have shied away from such an in-your-face approach, Baptists have ended their services with a call to come forward to receive Christ, followed by a trip to the baptismal. The power of this is that Baptists provide for people a defining moment, a time to always point back to as the instance of transformation. Whether Baptists of the future will abandon this secret weapon (as most other denominations have) is yet to be seen. But it has been one of the commanding reasons for their growth.

5. *The Bible*—Until recent Conservative/Modernist controversies plagued the Southern Baptists, the denomination has unbendingly adhered to an intense belief in the Bible. The denomination's best-known evangelist, Billy Graham, has sprinkled his sermons for 50 years with the phrase "the Bible says." This is a strong motto of the Southern Baptists and is a principle for which they have stood courageously.

6. *Zeal*—Baptists have a passion that proves to be contagious. Enthusiasm, which is suspect to many denominations, is a hallmark of

Baptists; and, as a result, millions have been brought to a meaningful relationship with Christ.

Baptist influence has been profound. America is a better place because
of them. In fact, as part of God's great Church, the Baptists continue to be
a major component of God's vehicle for saving civilization.

To further assist you in understanding the key individuals and events of chapter 18,
study questions, charts, diagrams, time lines and links to biographical websites are available
on the Internet at www.jimgarlow.com. Please follow the site links to
How God Saved Civilization, chapter 18 study helps.

An Explosion of the Spirit

PENTECOSTALS, CHARISMATICS AND THE THIRD WAVE

Dates covered: A.D. 1900-2000
Key persons: Charles Parham, William J. Seymour,
Thomas Zimmerman, Aimee Semple McPherson, Jack Hayford,
Oral Roberts, Gordon and Freda Lindsey,
Dennis Bennett, David Du Plessis,
C. Peter Wagner, John Wimber

Laura wished she could stop working. She wasn't educated, so she could only do housework. Not that she minded cleaning. She was good at it. But the work was difficult for her because polio had left her with one leg three inches shorter than the other. Ben would love for her to stop working. The children needed her at home, but there was no way to feed them on his mechanic's salary. Every night on her way home from work, she limped through the rich neighborhood filled with the homes of doctors and lawyers. Now she found herself on Regency Court. It even sounded rich. There were the enormous three-story homes, all lit up as if electricity were free. Laura limped past them and across the railroad tracks. It was about a mile more to her little two-room home. At least they had a tiny garden at the back, where she grew tomatoes. World War II had been over now for five years. Her little Arkansas town hadn't changed much since the war. There were still 750 inhabitants, according to the well-worn sign, which stood on the highway about a block from her house.

Benny came home tired and dirty every night, covered in motor oil and grit. He was a faithful husband and father. Still, it would be nice to have enough money to get a few badly needed items—some clothes for the children, or—oh, what a silly dream—a new pair of legs for herself. She laughed bitterly at her unrealistic thoughts. A new pair of legs. Sure.

"Come get healed!" blared a voice from behind her. Laura jumped with astonishment and nearly fell.

The booming voice seemed to come out of nowhere. Was it God Himself? She turned to look over her shoulder, trying to settle her thumping heart. There she saw a truck with a loudspeaker.

"Come to Reverend Tremble's Healing Crusade. Come and be healed! Come to the big tent out on Old Filmore Road at LaMar's pasture. Seven o'clock tonight."

The truck rumbled along the road and the loudspeaker faded. "LaMar's pasture. Seven o'clock tonight."

Two phrases echoed in Laura's mind all afternoon: "A new pair of legs" and "Come and be healed!" How she wished she could hope for it.

"Why not?" Benny had said, when Laura suggested going to the crusade. "It'll give the kids an outing, and I need some fresh air."

Laura carried one-year-old Lisa, Benny carried three-year-old Joseph on his shoulders, and four-and-a-half-year-old Mandi Lou held her daddy's hand. A car slowed behind them. It was Benny's boss at the station. The ride was a relief to Laura. *Maybe we will own a car, someday*, she thought. *That would be almost as good as a new pair of legs.*

They arrived at the tent a half hour early, but it was already nearly full. It seemed as if half the town had come out to hear Reverend Tremble. A spontaneous choir was being assembled on the platform. Several assistants were running back and forth, setting up the public address system. Benny's boss was there, laughing. "I cain't wait to see 'em all. It's a real circus every year with Reverend Tremble. Thinks he's some apostle, or somethin' like. Ain't nobody gonna get a healed in this lil' ole Arkansas town tonight. But you betcha Mr. Tremble will walk away with his pockets full from them there baskets." He pointed to the rows of baskets set up for the offering.

Laura listened to the boss chatter. But her eyes were fixed on the tattered banner that hung from the tent's roof. It was white with enormous red letters: "God can heal you now."

She squeezed her eyes tight. *God, You used to heal people. Can You still do it?*

Her prayer seemed full of doubt. Would God listen to a prayer like that? Hadn't He let her have polio to start with? Was it wrong to wish to be healed?

The choir began to sing. "Turn your eyes upon Jesus. Look full in His wonderful face. And the things of earth will grow strangely dim in the light of His glory and grace."

Laura felt lost in the music. She didn't notice how much the loudspeakers squealed. She didn't notice the children wiggling. Another hymn started up. "Out of my bondage, sorrow and night, Jesus I come, Jesus I come." She felt that Jesus was calling her to Him, to His peace, to His love. How could she have gone through so much of life without this love? After a while, her legs didn't seem to matter. The music was reaching deep inside, healing her wounded, angry spirit. She'd never felt like this in that snobby church she'd gone to a couple of times.

But the music seemed like nothing when Reverend Tremble began to preach. He told her about the best doctor in the world, Jesus Himself, who could heal not only the body but also the soul. He wanted every person in that tent to be whole.

Laura couldn't take her eyes off the preacher. He reminded her of a football coach, pacing back and forth until he was in a sweat. He urged and cajoled and scolded and encouraged and perspired and yelled. You could tell that his whole being was caught up in this job he had of convincing people to believe. "Jesus wants you whole! Have faith! Expect God's touch tonight."

Quietly, in her heart, she determined to go forward for healing. Even if God didn't want her to have new legs, Laura sensed that somehow, mysteriously, He had already given her a new heart.

Reverend Tremble had finished. He called on those who wished for healing to come forward. Laura looked at Benny. Benny nodded and took Mandi Lou onto his knee. Laura found herself in a line of at least 15 people. She watched Reverend Tremble. She had never seen anything like it. He put his hands on a person's head and prayed for God to heal them. Sometimes nothing happened, or at least she couldn't see anything. A man who came down the aisle on crutches went back up the aisle on crutches. Old man Linder, who couldn't hear, walked back to his chair tilting his head from side to side, still obviously not able to hear.

But then she saw Mildred Letourneau, her neighbor, whose back was bent so much she seemed to see only the ground. Mildred lived four houses away. Reverend Tremble shouted what he had said before, "Faith. Faith. Have faith. Expect it tonight." Something happened that moment inside of Laura. Years later, she would still not be able to describe it. She found herself looking up at the banner, now straight above her. At this closer range she could tell it was extremely well worn as if it had been to a thousand cities. The edges were ragged and torn. A dirty smudge covered one corner and the letter *L* was pulling free from its stitching. But the sign was still very readable: "God can heal you now."

The preacher shouted, "God, heal this woman! Heal her now." Laura looked up the line at Mildred. What Laura saw that moment changed her life. For the first time in the 12 years Laura had known Mildred, the old lady slowly straightened her back and stood tall, at her full 5'8" tall. Laura's heart almost stopped. Mildred seemed a giant. The old woman raised her arms straight in the air, and Laura could see the tears streaming down her cheeks. "Thank you, dear Jesus," whispered Mildred. Her face broke into an enormous smile and Mildred walked right past Laura, still whispering, "Thank you, Jesus. Thank you, Jesus."

Laura was shaking. She felt like pushing the three that were in front of her out of her way to get to Reverend Tremble.

Finally, it was her turn. She felt the Reverend put his hand on her forehead and the other one on the back of her head. Laura's emotions went eerily still. Time stopped. As Reverend Tremble prayed, nothing happened. Absolutely nothing. She had just seen Mildred Letourneau's back straightened, but Laura could tell nothing was happening. Reverend Tremble went on. It was as if he could sense the battle in her soul, the disappointment, the doubt. He asked, "What is your name?"

"Laura."

"What?"

"Laura," she said, softly.

"I can't hear you. What is your name?"

"I said 'Laura.'"

Then suddenly, he shouted as if he were almost angry at God. "God, give this young woman a new heart and a new pair of legs while You're at it!" Softly, he whispered in Laura's ear. "Faith. Have faith. God can heal you now." At that moment Laura felt fire shoot up and down her thighs. Something was happening. She could hardly stand, but she forced herself not to lose her balance. Was God doing something to her legs?

Suddenly, she realized that she was standing straight on both legs—for the first time since she was small. She whooped for joy and went running back up the aisle. "Benny!" she shouted. "God gave me a new heart!" She had meant to say, "new legs," but it was a lot more than that, she knew. The legs were an extra.

DEFINING A NEW MOVEMENT

In the previous chapter, we discussed the Baptist movement. The second forceful movement during the 1900s was the Pentecostal/Charismatic/Third Wave movement. Admittedly, some Pentecostals do not want to be associated with Charismatics, and some Pentecostals and Charismatics are not at all familiar with the phrase "Third Wave." But historically there is enough similarity in these three movements to see them as parts of a larger whole. Whereas Baptists are known for evangelism, Pentecostals are known (along with their Holiness cousins) for their emphasis on a deeper work of the Holy Spirit, something that occurs after conversion.

THE HOLINESS ROOTS

Those who hungered for a deeper life in Christ, known as sanctification, were either forced out of, or chose to leave, the Methodist church during the waning years of the nineteenth century. By the late 1800s, Methodism as a denomination had begun to disassociate from the deeper-life emphasis of its founder, John Wesley. Many of those who left because they wished to maintain the Holiness emphasis, helped found Holiness churches and small Holiness denominations.

PENTECOSTAL BEGINNINGS

A few minutes after midnight on January 1, 1901, a new movement began— the Pentecostal movement. One century later, it would number in the millions. That night in a prayer meeting, Agnes Ozman, a student in Charles F. Parham's Bethel Bible College in Topeka, Kansas, began to speak in tongues. As this experience swept his entire school, Parham became convinced that *glossolalia,* or "unknown tongues," was what he called the Bible evidence of the baptism of the Holy Spirit. This belief became the cardinal doctrine of the emerging Pentecostal movement.

William J. Seymour, an African-American Holiness preacher in Houston, Texas, connected with Charles Parham during Parham's Houston crusade. After that, Seymour moved to Los Angeles where a Mrs. Hutchinson invited him to speak in a Nazarene church on Santa Fe Street. At the time, Los Angeles's population was 228,000[1] and consisted of many who had moved to California from all over America and were sociologically rootless and spiritually open.

THE AZUSA STREET REVIVAL BEGINS

Although Seymour himself did not speak in tongues at the time, he preached what he had learned from Parham: tongues was the Bible evidence of receiving the baptism of the Holy Spirit. Mrs. Hutchinson responded by padlocking the church door to keep Seymour and his message out. But the persistent pastor began to preach in the living room of a house located at 312 Bonnie Brae Street in Los Angeles. When it overflowed, they moved to the porch. The crowd was more than the porch was built to handle, and the floor caved in. Fortunately no one was hurt, but Seymour decided to find larger facilities to continue his preaching.

He and his colleagues located an abandoned Methodist church building at 312 Azusa Street and continued meeting. The old building was in desperate need of repair. No sooner had he begun to preach than the famous Azusa Street Revival began. It continued with three services a day, seven days a week, for the next three and one-half years![2] The Pentecostal movement, which had already claimed over 25,000 believers in the Midwest, was now raised to a higher level of visibility.[3]

The *Los Angeles Times* picked up the story of the Azusa Street Revival on April 18, 1906, with headlines that read "Weird Babble of Tongues; New Sect of Fanatics Is Breaking Loose; Wild Scene Last Night on Azusa Street."[4] The massive San Francisco earthquake the next day displaced coverage of the Azusa Street Revival. The Pentecostals were relieved that God had moved in Los Angeles before needing to wake them up with an earthquake. Years later, in 1972, Yale University scholar Sidney Ahlstrom called William Seymour "the most influential black leader in American religious history."[5] Seymour and Parham are considered the cofounders of Pentecostalism.[6]

DEFENSE OF TONGUES

Pentecostalism's defense for the controversial evidence of tongues was based upon Joel 2:28 and Acts 2. In Acts 2, Peter says that what happened at the first Pentecost, the great inauguration of the Church, was a fulfillment of Joel 2:28. The Spirit would be poured out on all flesh with both "your sons and your daughters" prophesying. In addition, the experiences of the Early Church with tongues speaking (Acts 2:2-4) provided the scriptural anchor for their defense of this phenomenon. Although there is evidence of speaking in tongues, or ecstatic utterances, throughout Church history, most occurrences were regional and short-lived. The Azusa Street Revival changed that. Tongues became global and ongoing. Fully as important to the Pentecostal movement's emphasis upon speaking in unknown tongues was an intense conviction that Christ's second coming was imminent. Another characteristic of the movement's beginnings was faith healing, the praying for the sick.

The Pentecostal movement, like its older sister, the Holiness movement, is an exceedingly complex amalgamation of hundreds of smaller groups that came together. At the helm of these subgroups were some extremely gifted organizers who, seizing the moment, marshaled the forces that helped grow this movement to the enormous importance it has today.

Pentecostals did not originally perceive themselves to be a new denomination, but as a movement that was to function within all denominations.[7] Their goal, however, soon changed. After being severely criticized, especially by Holiness churches, they began to organize their own denominations. So prolific, yet somewhat fragmented, is this massive movement that today, fewer than 100 years after it began, it has produced over 1,500 denominations in the United States alone,[8] and 17,000 different Pentecostal denominations globally.[9]

AN UNCONTROLLABLE FLOW

To some the movement appears fragmented and unmanageable. It is more accurate to view it another way. So powerful was the flow of God's Spirit in inexplicably producing this movement, that sufficient leadership could not be produced fast enough to bring its adherents into one common denomination. When rising flood waters pour over a dam, they create thousands of small tributaries which merge, separate and merge again. Some find their own path and remain separate. The result is still a rushing torrent of water. The Pentecostal movement was like those flood waters. Unlike the Baptist movement that started slowly in 1609, the Pentecostals exploded in 1906!

An intriguing example of this fragmentation, merging and refragmentation was demonstrated by A. J. Tomlinson, leader of one of the denominations using the title Church of God. Tomlinson's church had started as a Holiness church in 1886, but eventually became Pentecostal. By 1943, when he died, it had fragmented into more than two dozen organizations. Tomlinson had served as the first general moderator of the Church of God (Cleveland, Tennessee). In 1923, Tomlinson was relieved of his duties, at which time he moved across town and founded a rival denomination, originally known as the Tomlinson Church of God. At his death, that denomination split into two more groups: the Church of God of Prophecy, and the Church of God of All Nations. In spite of these divisive beginnings, all of these groups still have substantial membership. the Church of God (Cleveland, Tennessee) has experienced enormous growth and exercises significant influence across the nation and around the world. Although other denominations, such as the Baptists and Methodists, have also had numerous splinter groups, the Pentecostals, due to the sheer force of their numbers, make the story of continually emerging new denominations particularly fascinating and complex.

INTEGRATED

It is not insignificant that the Azusa Street Revival was sparked by an African-American preacher. The earliest days of the Azusa Street Revival were clearly multiracial. People of every race traveled from all over the nation and from many other countries to see what was happening at Azusa Street.

Tragically, racism intruded on the spirit of unity in the revival when it was decided that "black hands should not be placed on a white head" during an ordination service. This incident marked a separation of blacks and whites in the Pentecostal movement that would not totally heal until a moving service of reconciliation in the fall of 1994, known as the Memphis Miracle.

The largest African-American Pentecostal group was founded by Charles H. Mason in 1911. Originally a Baptist, he was expelled due to his Holiness experience of entire sanctification. In 1895, Mason and Charles P. Jones founded the Church of Christ (Holiness). In 1907, Mason attended the Azusa Street Revival and began speaking in tongues. When he returned to his church in Mississippi to introduce tongue speaking, a minority of the people withdrew, following Jones and maintaining the name Church of Christ (Holiness). The majority, following Mason, formed the Church of God in Christ, a name that Mason had used as early as 1897. Later Jones rejoined Mason.

But the "father" of all Pentecostal denominations is the Assemblies of God, founded in 1914 in Hot Springs, Arkansas. This enormous denomination has surged from 300 in 1914 to nearly 28 million in 1998 and is by far the largest Pentecostal denomination in the world. The growth rate of the Assemblies of God is virtually unprecedented in Church history. Since they were suspicious of denominational bureaucracy, the delegates originally gathered hoping to accomplish more by working together in limited cooperation. And successful they were! The Assemblies of God was a collection of numerous Pentecostal and former Holiness movements. Like other Pentecostal denominations, the Assemblies of God has historically emphasized tongues as the initial evidence of the baptism of the Holy Spirit. From the mid-1970s on, it has been the fastest-growing American denomination.

One of the marks of the Assemblies of God church during the 1970s, and later, was its ability to relate well to non-Pentecostal bodies. Under the exceptional leadership of Thomas F. Zimmerman, who served as the general superintendent of the Assemblies of God from 1959 until 1985, the denomination joined the National Association of Evangelicals when it was formed in 1942. Superb relationships existed between the distinctively Pentecostal Assemblies of God church and denominations which were not Pentecostal.

PENTECOSTAL-HOLINESS CONFLICT

Early Pentecostals, however, were shocked at the response of the Holiness preachers to their message.[10] It was a common rule of thumb that denominational groups are most vitriolic to those who are closest to them, because they do not want to be confused with them. Such was the case with the early Holiness leaders. Although there should have been a close camaraderie between the two groups, the Holiness churches were intimidated by those who advocated tongues. And the early tongues advocates could be condescending in the way they advocated their gift, some even going so far as to claim that one couldn't truly be saved unless one spoke in tongues. This was particularly offensive to non-Pentecostal denominational groups. Alma White, leader of a Holiness group known by the unusual name of the Pillar of Fire, attacked the Pentecostals with a vengeance, accusing Pentecostals of "leaving spiritual death and devastation everywhere."[11]

She was far from being the only Holiness leader to take such a position. Early followers of the Church of the Nazarene sent representatives to the Azusa Street Revival and felt that what they saw there was clearly not from God. The excesses were more than they could bear, and the result was a generations-long rift between the Church of the Nazarene—the largest Holiness denomination—and any Pentecostal body. But it was never God's plan for such division to occur, for each movement needed the other.

The Pentecostal movement should never have been separated from the Holiness movement. The Holiness movement proclaimed purity. Portions of the Pentecostal movement emphasized power.[12] In the endorsement to a new book entitled *Power, Holiness and Evangelism* by Randy Clark, I wrote that there were two things that were never meant to be separated—purity and power. To have purity without power is like having the spectacular locomotive and train on a sure track but, unfortunately, with no power to move forward. To have power without purity is like having a coal-stoked locomotive, moving forward under a full head of steam, but spinning its wheels in mud because there are no railroad tracks. To have purity and power is to have a locomotive (power) running toward its destination on firmly built tracks (purity). We should affirm Jesus' merger of Spirit—anointing and power—and Truth— integrity and purity (see John 4:24). The great divorce of purity and power should end in a grand remarriage![13]

The Holiness movement produced awesome integrity but much less power. Independent Pentecostal ministries in some measure, and independent Charismatic personalities in greater measure, were tall on power and short on personal righteousness.[14] The two movements could have married and produced terrific offspring!

But it wasn't just Holiness preachers who objected to the Pentecostals. Evangelicals joined in the chorus of criticism. Rubin A. Tory, the dean of Moody Bible Institute and pastor of Moody's Chicago Avenue Church, criticized the "tongues movement" as not being "of God." Evangelicals generally responded to the question, Is the present tongues movement of God?" with a resounding No![15]

Pentecostal bodies and non-Pentecostal bodies were separated for decades.[16] Only a few, such as Thomas Zimmerman, were courageous in reaching across denominational and theological lines to embrace others and to create a climate of mutual trust. Thanks to him and people like David Du Plessis (who will be discussed later in the section on the Charismatic movement), non-Pentecostals and Pentecostals eventually began to learn how to cooperate for the cause of Christ.

AIMEE SEMPLE MCPHERSON AND JACK HAYFORD

The Pentecostal movement produced some of the most flamboyant preachers ever known to Christianity. Few, however, were more spellbinding than the female preacher, Aimee Semple McPherson. Arriving in California in 1918 with two children, this young widow initially associated with the Assemblies of God Church and other denominations, and preached highly successful Pentecostal crusades. In 1927, after attracting thousands to her California crusades, she founded the International Church of the Foursquare Gospel. In 1923, this grand woman of faith built a debt-free 5,300-seat auditorium, known as Angelus Temple, in which she trained pastors and missionaries in a Bible school, while operating the church's radio station. Although McPherson's ministry is slightly tarnished by a sudden disappearance, which was accompanied by rumors of immorality, she led the Foursquare church to become one of the most profound forces for healing in America. Ambulances would line up in front of the church to bring the sick Sunday after Sunday. Hollywood actors and actresses flocked to see the flamboyant and sometimes bizarre preaching antics of McPherson, who could hold a crowd spellbound.

The denomination she founded grew quickly in influence. By the 1990s its best-known church leader, Jack Hayford, founding pastor of The Church On The Way in Van Nuys, California, became somewhat of an "unofficial dean of America's pastors" due to his spiritual and theological acumen. He is the founding president of The King's Seminary and is the general editor of the Spirit-Filled Life series. He has also written dozens of books, is heard nationally on radio and television and has composed over 500 hymns, including the best known "Majesty," which was written in 1978.

HEALING

The Pentecostal movement contributed significantly to a global healing movement. Faith healing did not begin with Pentecostals in the early 1900s, however. Praying for the sick was a common practice with Jesus and His earliest followers. In the third century, Gregory Thaumaturgus (ca. 213-ca. 270) was known as the wonder-worker, because of the number of healings he was instrumental in producing. However, by the ninth century, praying for healing was no longer common.

Waldensians, followers of Peter Waldo, practiced praying for the sick, as did Martin Luther. Through the Middle Ages, the Catholics also maintained the sacrament of anointing for the sick. Healing was emphasized in Europe in the years following the 1850s, and in America after the 1870s. But it was through the Pentecostal movement that healing gained enormous visibility. (One non-Pentecostal, John Alexander Dowie [1847-1907], taught that when people were prayed for, they should not go to a medical doctor. But this view was rarely held by those who prayed for healing.) After World War II, Pentecostal preacher William Branham (1909-1965) stimulated a new emphasis on healing. Although Branham was given to some controversial statements, he did manifest healing gifts. Branham's ministry filled some of the largest auditoriums and stadiums all over the globe.

ORAL ROBERTS

But no healing ministry compared with the highly visible work of Oral Roberts (1918–   ). Converted in 1935, Roberts was supernaturally healed of tuberculosis a few days later. In the post-World War II period he conducted huge tent revivals and then launched a healing ministry with a crusade in Enid, Oklahoma. As his popularity grew, Roberts increased his influence by regular television broadcasts of his crusades. In 1965, he opened Oral Roberts University, a campus filled with futuristic buildings. Although initially criticized, Oral Robert's ministry has long outlived even his most vocal critics. The university, complete with a graduate school, has become respected among academicians in many circles. By the 1970s, Pentecostalism was no longer a movement confined to small white wooden buildings located "across the tracks." Its influence was evident in every socioeconomic group.

GORDON AND FREDA LINDSEY

But the person who gave the healing movement its glue was Gordon Lindsey (1906-1973). He published the influential magazine *Voice of Healing*, from 1940-1967, which served as a connecting point for all the healing evangelists—Branham, Roberts, T. L. Osborne and many others. In 1967, he founded Christ For The Nations Institute in Dallas, Texas. Both the historian and the theologian of the healing movement, Lindsey wrote a staggering 250 books! While preaching at his six-year-old school in Dallas, Lindsey died. It was assumed that the school could not survive. But his wife, Freda (1916–), took the helm and in the years that followed, she not only built an 80-acre debt-free campus but also over the next two decades raised 100 million dollars for global missions! She launched 30 Bible colleges worldwide, and built

11,000 churches! This type of aggressive missions commitment is typical of much of the burgeoning Pentecostal/Charismatic movement.

DIFFERENCES

Although we have referred to Pentecostals/Charismatics as one, the Pentecostal and Charismatic movements are *not* synonymous. They are two distinct sister movements or, in the eyes of some people, stepsisters. In contrast to the Pentecostal movement that grew out of the lower socioeconomic brackets of society, as did the Holiness movement, the Charismatic movement erupted in liturgical denominations among the middle to upper-middle social and economic brackets.

CHARISMATIC BEGINNINGS

As early as 1953, Demos Shakarian had founded the Full Gospel Business Men's Fellowship International as a device to introduce the Pentecostal experience to mainline Christians. Born in 1913, Shakarian was a wealthy California dairyman who, in 1959, successfully launched a worldwide laymen's organization bent on aggressively drawing people into the baptism of the Holy Spirit through well-planned businessmen's luncheons.

There had been charismatic stirrings for a decade: in Harald Bredesen, a Lutheran (1949); in Tommy Tyson, a Methodist in North Carolina (1951); in Episcopalian Agnes Sanford (1956); in James Brown, a Pennsylvania Presbyterian; and finally in Pastor Don Basham (1957). The stirrings increased when, in 1952, Robert Walker wrote a provocative article entitled "Are We Missing Out?" in *Christian Life Magazine*.

The formal "outbreak" of the Charismatic movement's manifestations occurred in Saint Mark's Episcopal Church in Van Nuys, California, in 1959. Dennis Bennett, the pastor of the church, began speaking in tongues, and over the course of the next year, he influenced 100 others in the same experience. On Sunday, April 3, 1960, Bennett decided to speak openly about his experience with tongues in the three Sunday-morning worship services. The reactions after the second worship service were such that Bennett announced his resignation at the third service. *Newsweek* and *Time* ran stories on the event and the Charismatic movement was born, with Dennis Bennett as the unofficial midwife.

Leaving Van Nuys, Dennis Bennett was transferred to Saint Luke's Episcopal Church in Seattle, which became one of the leading Charismatic churches in the United States. During the next two years, the Charismatic experience went from Episcopalians to Catholics, with the first Catholic Charismatics among the faculty at Duquesne University in Pittsburgh, Pennsylvania, and in Notre Dame University in South Bend, Indiana, in February 1967. Unlike the Pentecostal movement, which was a distinctly Protestant phenomenon, the Charismatic movement thrived among liturgical mainline denominations and among Roman Catholics, especially highly educated Catholics. The renewal was so profound that in 1969 it produced a nationwide network known as the Catholic Renewal Services.

In 1963, Russell Hitt, editor of *Eternity* magazine, published an article entitled "The New Pentecostalism." Harald Bredesen and Jean Stone objected to the term "neo-Pentecostalism" and stated that the appropriate phrase was "Charismatic renewal." The term stuck. During the 1970s, the movement produced exploding churches and aggressive media ministries headed by Pat Robertson of the Christian Broadcasting Network, Paul Crouch of the Trinity Broadcasting Network, and Jim Bakker of the PTL Network.

Moreover, a pantheon of Charismatic publishing gained respectability for the movement. The broader culture was profoundly impacted by David Wilkerson's book *The Cross and the Switchblade* (1963) and John Sherrill's *They Speak with Other Tongues* (1964). Charismatic books, magazines and teaching tapes proliferated. Research showed that Charismatics read far more books than did mainline Protestants or non-Charismatic Catholics. Charismatics were aggressive learners. The rising popularity of Stephen Strang's *Charisma* magazine and *Ministries Today* is one more indication of the Charismatic movement's amazing reading appetite.

DENOMINATIONAL REACTIONS

Denomination after denomination began to develop its position toward the Charismatic movement. Some were cautiously open; many were negative; and some were hostile. The American Lutheran church issued a statement against the promotion of speaking in tongues. The Charismatic movement was equally contentious among Presbyterians. Yet the Charismatic Communion of Presbyterian ministers was the first denominational Charismatic organization to be formed. The Southern Baptist Convention took a firm position when their state conventions expelled several Charismatic Baptist congregations. The Church of the Nazarene took an equally firm position, decredentialing any pastor who professed to associate with the movement. With the passage of time, the movement gained footholds in almost every denomination.

Some early Charismatics brought upon themselves much of the initial criticism they received. In their laudable zeal and exuberance, they were sometimes immature and obnoxious, virtually *de*-Christianizing anyone who had not had their particular experience. With time and maturity, the movement noticeably softened and became much more adept at relating to Christians *outside* the Charismatic movement. At the same time, many non-Charismatics overreacted to the excessive zeal of their Charismatic neighbors and unnecessarily criticized and maligned them, in many cases breaking fellowship with them. More recently, most denominations have guardedly lowered the barriers a little and have allowed Charismatic fellowships and pastors to function within numerous denominational structures. The open hostility that characterized the 1970s and early 1980s had essentially vanished by 1990.

DAVID DU PLESSIS

The Charismatic movement owes much of its acceptance to the gracious influence of David Du Plessis (1905-1987), who became known as "Mr. Pentecostal." Unlike many of his colleagues who shied away from mainline or liberal denominational organizations, Du Plessis seemed to thrive on ecumenical contact. He attended the World Council of Churches from its second meeting in 1954 until his death. He was the only Pentecostal invited to attend the third session of Vatican II in 1964. He served as a co-chair in the International Roman Catholic/Pentecostal dialogue from 1977 to 1982. In 1983, Du Plessis received from Pope John Paul II the Good Merit Medal, the first non-Catholic to ever receive the honor. Not surprisingly, his final years were spent at a non-Pentecostal/Charismatic institution—Fuller Theological Seminary in Pasadena, California—where his personal library is housed. He, more than any other, made the term "charismatic" something not to be feared. When asked questions about Pentecostalism, his responses both charmed and disarmed Pentecostalism's critics.

When asked, for example, why Pentecostals fall over ("slain in the Spirit") when prayed for, he answered without emotion, "Because they like it that way!"[17]

INCREASING TENSIONS

As surprising as it may sound, not all Pentecostals were excited about the Charismatic movement. One would expect them to be thrilled to see their prime doctrine of speaking in tongues so frequently practiced. But many Pentecostals were suspicious of the new movement, believing that those receiving the gift of tongues were less than authentic because they often stayed within liberal denominations and did not share the same sociological worship styles as classical Pentecostals.

Other Pentecostals quickly embraced the new movement. Oral Roberts, for example, quickly became a key leader in the burgeoning new Charismatic movement. Ralph Wilkerson, pastor at Melodyland Church in Anaheim, California, was another who quickly crossed over to the Charismatic movement, as did Foursquare pastor Jack Hayford (Van Nuys, California). Assembly of God congregations which embraced the new wave exploded in size and influence. Those that didn't seemed to be caught in a cultural and sociological time warp.

THE DISCIPLING/SHEPHERDING CONTROVERSY

The movement experienced some severe problems, however. In 1969, a team of four men came together to provide encouragement and discipleship for the burgeoning movement. Derek Prince of South Africa, Don Basham from the Disciples of Christ, Charles Simpson from the Southern Baptists, and Bob Mumford, a Pentecostal, were later joined by Vern Baxter to form a five-man team that edited the *New Wine* magazine as a part of their ministry. The movement quickly fell into severe criticism and became known as the Discipling/Shepherding controversy, due to its excessive teaching on authority and submission. By 1975-76, the Charismatics were severely split over this issue. By the late 1980s, the damage from the movement was so significant and so obvious, that the leaders publicly apologized for the harm they had done by their heavy-handed exercise of authority. The Shepherding movement started for all the right reasons and with all the right motives, but it lost a commonsense understanding of Christian balance. All five of these teachers were exceptionally gifted communicators. Their writings are among the finest. Yet the movement is a cautionary example of the danger of otherwise good teaching presented in an unbalanced manner. It is a tribute to the larger Charismatic movement that it had sufficiently strong leadership to confront the Shepherding crisis. And it is a tribute to the current leaders of the Shepherding movement that they openly repented. One major Charismatic magazine carried on its cover these two words in large bold letters from one of the leaders: "I'm sorry."

AND OTHER CONTROVERSIES

The Shepherding movement seemed identifiable and manageable. More difficult to resolve were the excessive claims and extravagant lifestyles manifested in the Word of Faith movement, the wealth and prosperity teachings and what some have called radical faith movements. While each of these movements brought a kernel of biblical truth, they also demonstrated a failure to respect the whole counsel of God and to keep all scriptural teaching in balance. These movements rightly identified God's desire to bring healing and prosperity to His children, an emphasis badly needed in much of American Christianity. However, some of the most prominent advocates of prosperity failed to balance their emphasis with Christ's clear teachings that His Church would suffer and live with persecution for the sake of the gospel. The advocates of faith for healing and of speaking the Word brought important truths, but they failed to contextualize that teaching in the realities of a broken world.

RALLIES

In addition to producing enormous independent churches, constructing Bible colleges and several excellent universities (Oral Roberts University, Evangel, Lee, and Regents University, for example) and establishing three major television networks, the Charismatic movement spawned gargantuan rallies. Fifty thousand people attended the Kansas City Conference in 1977. In 1978, 55,000 people attended the Meadowlands New Jersey Pentecost Sunday "Jesus Rally," only one of many held across the nation. In 1980 over 100 such Jesus Rallies were held. Things were never quite the same after the Kansas City Conference, however. Attendees at the rallies began to dwindle. By 1987, the New Orleans Conference drew only 35,000.

The Charismatic movement, though massive in breadth, was moving to a different phase.

THIRD WAVE

The movement that evolved in the post-1980 era is difficult to label. C. Peter Wagner, a former professor at Fuller Theological Seminary and now head of the World Prayer Center in Colorado Springs, was the first to use the phrase "Third Wave," in contrast to the First Wave (Pentecostal) and the Second Wave (Charismatic). The Third Wave churches were both similar to, yet distinct from, either Pentecostal churches in the first half of the century or Charismatic churches in the 1960s and 1970s.

WAGNER AND WIMBER

The phrase "Third Wave" was introduced partly because of the teachings of John Wimber, founding pastor of the burgeoning network of Vineyard Churches, headquartered in Anaheim, California. Wimber was invited by C. Peter Wagner to teach a course entitled "Signs, Wonders and Church Growth" at Fuller Seminary. Wimber and his congregation had been experiencing an outpouring of signs and wonders in his Vineyard Fellowship in Yorba Linda, California (and later in Anaheim), as early as 1978. In 1983, Wimber began to teach the class at Fuller Seminary and the acceptance of "Signs and Wonders" exploded upon a new young generation of evangelical pastors open to fresh works of the Spirit but not altogether comfortable with the term "charismatic."

CHARACTERISTICS

Third Wave pastors were generally pastoring churches that started after 1980 and commonly stayed within their own denominational churches. Third Wave churches generally had an optional view of the use of tongues; whereas Pentecostals demanded it as the evidence of the baptism of the Holy Spirit and Charismatics insisted on it as a normative expression, Third Wave pastors usually regarded it as simply one of many gifts of the Holy Spirit which may or may not be present in all believers. Third Wave pastors are essentially charismatics (spelled with a small *c*) as opposed to Charismatics (spelled with a capital *C*). The movement is also known for its strong emphasis on basic evangelical doctrine, in contrast with the Charismatic movement, which tended at times to emphasize experience at the expense of doctrine.

Another component of Third Wave churches was present because of Wimber's personal example of a "down-home style and lack of self-promotion," in contrast with some of the more flamboyant (Charismatic) ministries.[18] Third Wavers prayed for the sick as much as Charismatics but without as much hoopla and usually devoid of any faith claims that the healing had been received but not manifested.

A final characteristic of the Third Wave was its emphasis upon academic scholarship, which is found in the fact that the Third Wave largely emerged from classes at Fuller Seminary associated with C. Peter Wagner and John Wimber.

MORAL FAILURES BY INDEPENDENT MINISTRIES

One of the most disappointing aspects of the three movements is a series of moral failures on the part of leaders, whose media fame caused their sins to be broadcast across the country and around the world. Jim and Tammy Bakker of the PTL Network became household names as their network and their marriage collapsed in shame. Jimmy Swaggart, a classical Pentecostal, humiliated himself in two escapades with prostitutes. These two scandals made the nation recoil in the late 1980s, causing many Americans to distrust televangelists altogether.

The history of these three movements reflects fallible, everyday people with clay feet! Yet, they are a people with passion and zeal. This is consistent with the Bible, which is profoundly transparent about the weaknesses of its key figures. In both cases, God's grace works through human shortcomings and failures.

> The Bible is brutally honest about reluctant leaders with stammering tongues (Moses), impulsive tempers (David and Peter), bouts of depression (Elijah), disturbing doubts (Thomas), thorns in the flesh (Paul), and weak stomachs (Timothy). They stumbled along the best they knew how, in all too human form. But in spite of their liabilities, limitations, and failures, God called and used these servants to bless the nations and build His Church. He still does.

Accordingly, we fervently pray for such men and women—not heroes, but people willing to stand in the leadership gap to risk all and serve.[19]

And that is what their history—in fact, all of Church history—is about.

STAGGERING GROWTH

However, in spite of these isolated cases of moral failures and some of the embarrassing excesses by a few, high-profile Pentecostal and Charismatic leaders, the number of believers involved in this movement has continued to explode exponentially. These movements are not essentially about flawed leaders. They're about a profound work of the Holy Spirit.

- By 1945, Pentecostals around the globe were estimated at 16 million;
- 1955, 27 million;
- 1965, 50 million;
- 1975, 96 million;
- 1985, 247 million.

Here are the estimates by waves:

- First Wave (Pentecostalism), 150 million
- Second Wave (Charismatic), 98 million
- Third Wave, another 21 million

In the July/August 1999 issue of *Ministries Today,* David Barrett and Todd Johnson reported that of the two billion persons on the earth today who intentionally or least nominally identify with Christ, one billion are Roman Catholic. Among both Catholics and Protestants, there are 449 million Charismatic and Pentecostal believers! Mainline Protestant denominations number only 321 million. Orthodox (Eastern) churches total around 220 million. The Anglican churches claim 75 million. It is staggering to think that a movement which began in a little Bible college in Topeka, Kansas, in 1901, would have nearly 450 million adherents worldwide in less than 100 years. Even if these numbers are slightly embellished, the statistics are mind-boggling. The world has never witnessed such an explosion as this! As Vinson Synan stated, "Not since the first century has the Holy Spirit moved so mightily as He has in our day."[20]

To further assist you in understanding the key individuals and events of chapter 19, study questions, charts, diagrams, time lines and links to biographical websites are available on the Internet at www.jimgarlow.com. Please follow the site links to *How God Saved Civilization*, chapter 19 study helps.

WHAT A TIME TO BE ALIVE!

THE GOSPEL GOES GLOBAL

Dates covered: A.D. 1980-2000
Key persons: the faithful unknown, missionaries,
first generation Christians in every land,
the persecuted Christians

Eight-year-old Xing Peter Ho loved his name and he always used "Peter" at school, even though his friends made fun of him. Peter was the name his Christian grandma had given him. She had told him of a man called Peter in a wonderful book called the Bible, who had walked on water because Jesus had given him the power.

Peter thought hard about the Bible as he waded through the puddles on his way home from school. Tonight was the special night. The secret visitor would be there with pages from a Bible! He looked over his shoulder as he turned off the street where all the food stalls were. But no one was following him. After the evening meal, he, Mama and Papa, and Aunt Lee-Won would take the secret visitor through the dark streets to Uncle Xwang's house.

He hurried through his schoolwork when he got home, ate his rice and soup and then laid down on his mat to sleep; but Peter couldn't sleep. Instead, in the middle of the night, he heard a muffled noise at the door and footsteps. With curiosity, he got up and went into the other room where his parents were squatting at the table, drinking tea and whispering quietly with the secret visitor. He was surprised to see that it was a beautiful lady, with very long, shiny, black hair. She was not very old. She looked a little older than his big sister, away at university.

He bowed low to greet her.

"What is your name, young Ho?" she asked.

"Peter," he responded proudly. "I am very brave."

The beautiful lady smiled. But it was a sad smile.

"I am Chin-Lu Sang, a daughter of the true God. My Bible name is Judith. Peter, you will need to be very brave."

Yes, brave, Peter repeated in his mind. He understood. Every time Christians met with the other Christians, Peter knew that someone could be arrested and taken away. Every night he prayed for each person in the group. Only last month their pastor had disappeared while he had been out walking along the river. And now Peter's father was leading the little group. Peter turned to look at the calm face of his handsome father and wondered, *What will happen to you, Papa, if you are arrested?*

Chin-Lu whispered, "It is time we begin to leave. The other believers will be there."

So as to not attract attention, each person was to leave the house at a separate time. Peter's father went first; Chin-Lu left 10 minutes later; Peter and his mother would go 15 minutes after her. Peter was not allowed to talk as they walked along the road. When they finally slipped into the butcher's dark shop, they went quietly to the back where a handful of believers from the village were.

Chin-Lu smiled and welcomed each person. Then, from a fold in her clothes, the beautiful lady pulled out a little notebook. In it, Chin-Lu told them, were the first chapters of the Gospel called John. Carefully, tenderly, she opened it; and by the light of a candle she read: "In the beginning was the Word and the Word was with God, and the Word was God." No one wanted her to stop. She read for about 20 minutes. Then she stopped. There were no more pages.

The lady explained that if she had the whole book, it would take her several weeks to read it all to them. The Bible was a very long book. But when she had finished reading the few pages she had, the words lingered in Peter's mind. *Grace. Truth. Love. Believe. Darkness. Light.*

One sentence stood out in his mind. The Bible told him that God loved the world and that He loved it so much, He was willing to let His only, His dearly loved Son, die so that the wicked people in the world could believe in God and live forever. Peter didn't understand. He thought it would have made more sense for God to love His Son and to give the world to His Son as a present. It was very sad that the wonderful Son had to die.

"So, are you happy, little Peter, that you have heard the real words of the Bible?" asked the visitor.

"It is sad that the Son must die."

The lady reached out and touched his thick hair. "Yes, Peter, but that is not the end of the story. The Son lives forever, because death is not strong enough to keep Him. He comes back to life and He lives today in heaven. He watches you and prays for you to the loving Father."

Peter went back to the butcher's shop every night for five nights. The lady read and read the words of the Bible pages, over and over. They would sing together but in a whisper. On Saturday night, the beautiful lady was not there. His parents and their friends prayed together that night, and read the words of the pages out loud, in order to memorize them. The young man Paul Xi was holding the paper and they repeated in unison, "Whoever believes on Him will not perish."

Suddenly there was a crash. Peter's mother screamed and pulled him close. But Peter saw the precious Bible paper fall to the ground. He wiggled away and snatched it up. In the dark corner, he tucked it into his belt and pulled his shirt out over it. Then he ran back to his mother. The police had come through both the back and the front doors at the same time. They wouldn't let anyone out. They kicked his mother and father. As Peter tried to stop one soldier from hitting his mother, the soldier turned on him and struck Peter a hard blow across the face. They took Peter's mother, his father, his aunt and all the adults. When they had all left, the candle was gone; and Peter stood in the black night with a group of four other children, all crying and wailing for their parents.

"We must be brave," said Peter. "Look," he whispered to the children, "God has let me save the Words of Life. Jesus told us that He will always be with us. We will look for our mothers and fathers and aunts and uncles." But from that night, Xing Peter never saw again or heard from his parents or any of the other adults.

NOT JUST NUMBERS

On July 4, 1999, evangelist Greg Laurie gave an invitation at the Harvest Crusade in San Diego's Qualcomm Stadium. A few days later, I received a report sent to Christian leaders in San Diego County, stating that during the three-day crusade a total of 4,513 had made decisions for Christ. Most pastors probably looked at the number of decisions, rejoiced and tossed the paper in the trash. I might have done the same. But this time, I kept mine. Why? Because the number 4,513 is not merely a statistic; one of those 4,513 was my seven-year-old daughter.

That night, as Greg Laurie gave the invitation, Josie turned to me and said, "Daddy, I want to go forward to receive Christ." I asked her a question or two to make sure she understood the decision and then we made our way from the upper level of that stadium onto the playing field to meet with an assigned counselor. (How ironic, how providential, that the counselor assigned to my seven-year-old daughter was my 22-year-old daughter, Janie!).

I tell you this story to remind you that statistics are not merely numbers! They are not numbers *when it's your child*. I am so thankful that the total number of decisions that night was 4,513, instead of 4,512. That one digit is more important than the whole world to me. That digit *was my child!*

This chapter contains hundreds of figures. If you think numbers aren't important, you will find this chapter boring. But if you understand that numbers represent people—somebody's child—then you will rejoice or weep as you make your way through the statistics that crowd the following pages.

GLOBAL EXPANSION

In the years of the gospel's beginnings, the Church was localized in Jerusalem. Within a few years it had spread across Asia Minor and to North Africa. After extremely rapid growth in the first three centuries, it blanketed most of the Roman Empire. A summary of Christianity's growth reads as follows:

- In the first century the gospel spread to Egypt, Sudan, Armenia, France, Italy, Germany, Britain, Iraq, Iran, India, Greece, Yugoslavia, Bosnia, Croatia, Asia Minor, Albania, Algeria, Libya and Tunisia.
- In the 100s Christianity expanded to Morocco, Bulgaria, Portugal, Austria and continued expansion in North Africa.
- In the 200s Christianity moved to Switzerland, Sahara, Belgium, Edessa, Qatar, Bahrain, Hungary and Luxembourg.
- In the 300s Christianity had expanded to Afghanistan and Ethiopia.
- In the 400s it had spread to Western North Africa, the Isle of Man, San Marino, Liechtenstein, The Caucasus, Ireland and Central Asia.
- In the 500s it expanded in North Yemen, Ceylon, Malabar, Nubia, Channel Islands and Andorra.
- In the 600s Christianity reached China, the Netherlands, Indonesia, Niger and Mongolia.
- In the 700s it expanded to Iceland, Pakistan and East Germany.
- The 800s witnessed the expansion of Christianity in Tibet, Burma, Denmark, Czechoslovakia, Sweden and Norway.
- In the 900s the Gospel was carried into Hungary, Kiev (Russia), Greenland, Bohemia and Poland.
- In the 1100s it expanded into Finland.[1]

Although there were periodic setbacks caused primarily by rapid militaristic Islamic advances that slaughtered Christians and burned churches, the list of nations above is most impressive![2]

The passage of 20 centuries has taught us that Christianity is not simply a phenomenon of the Middle East (where it started) or the property of Asiatics (where it grew rapidly in Asia Minor). Nor does it belong only to those who are darker skinned (although it grew extremely rapidly in North Africa in the first three centuries). It is not merely a white man's religion (although it spread explosively across Europe and America). It is not simply a product of Hispanic culture (although it took Spain, South America and Central America with explosive force). The gospel expanded globally. It touches the entire earth.

GLOBAL REVIVAL

The progress of the gospel in today's world is unprecedented. By the most conservative estimates, 70,000 people receive Christ every day.[3] Some claim the figure is over 100,000 a day. From 1600 to 3500 new churches are opening every week![4]

Writer Nate Krupp thinks that this is the Fifth (and final) Awakening.[5] In contrast to the first four awakenings from previous chapters:

- The First Great Awakening (1727-1780 among the Moravians in Germany, and from 1734 to 1760 in the 13 colonies) brought from 10 to 20 percent of the population to Christ.
- The Second Great Awakening (1792-1842) touched much of Europe and North America and led to the explosion of the missionary movement.
- The Third Great Awakening (1857-1859), called the Laymen's Revival, touched not only the United States but Canada, Great Britain, South Africa, New Zealand, Australia and India as well.
- The Fourth Great Awakening (1900-1930) began with the Welsh Revival from 1904 to 1906, and spread to almost every nation, resulting in over five million new converts for Christ.

Krupp goes on to explain four distinct waves of salvation rippling out from the Roman Empire to the rest of the known world over the centuries.

The waves are identified by these dates:

- A.D. 30-500, the gospel overtakes the Roman Empire;
- A.D. 500-1300, Western Europe and Central Asia are evangelized;
- A.D. 1300-1700, Christianity spreads worldwide through Roman Catholic missions;
- A.D. 1700-1960, Christianity continues to spread globally through Protestant missions;
- passing 2000, the fifth wave of evangelism is materializing.[6] By most conservative estimates, 28,000 conversions occur daily in China. In parts of Africa, the daily figure is 20,000 and in South America, over 10,000.[7] Something is happening!

PERCENTAGE OF BELIEVERS

In 1000, the population of the world was 269 million (approximately the number living in the United States today). Christians numbered about 50 million or approximately 19 percent of world population. Before the year 2000, Earth's population crossed the 6 billion mark. The percentage of Christian believers is approximately 32.4 percent. Though it is good news that nearly one-third of the Earth's population identifies with the cause of Christ, the percentage has fallen slightly from its level in 1900. The greatest growth in the history of Christianity came in the nineteenth, or what some have called the great missionary century. In 1900, the percentage of Christians was at an all-time high of 34.2 percent.[8] According to Patrick Johnstone, 30 percent of the earth's population identifies in some way with Christianity. But only nine percent are Protestant, and six percent are Evangelical.[9] Remember, these statistics are somebody's children—in this case, God's.

Currently, the fastest-growing segment of Christianity are the Pentecostals and their related movements. Pentecostalism, which began in the early 1900s, accounts for an annual growth of over 19 million members.[10]

TRACKING THE GROWTH

The Lausanne Statistics Task Force states that Christianity is the world's fastest-growing religion,[11] but its statistics are far more conservative than the figures above. Discrepancies in analyzing Christian growth are partly due to definitions. Some figures include nominal Christians, while others try to identify only born-again, evangelical Christians. The Task Force's figures are percentages of the world's population recognized as Christians during different time periods:

- 2 percent in A.D. 100;
- 45 percent in 1000;
- 1.4 percent in 1500;
- 3.7 percent in 1900;
- 4.8 percent in 1950;
- 9.1 percent in 1980;
- 14.7 percent in 1992.[12]

Remember, *these figures are somebody's children!*

RATIOS

Some statisticians have tracked the growth of Christianity by comparing ratios in particular years. According to Mission Frontiers in November 1990, Christianity has grown in the following manner:

- In 100, there were 360 non-Christians for every Christian
- In 1000, there were 220 non-Christians for every Christian
- In 1500, there were 69 non-Christians for every Christian
- In 1900, there were 29 non-Christians for every Christian
- In 1950, there were 21 non-Christians for every Christian
- In 1980, there were 11 non-Christians for every Christian
- In 1989, there were 7 non-Christians for every Christian[13]

Notice the impressive advance of Christianity!

The same ratio can be expressed by noticing on what date the ratio of Christians to world population increases by one. Below are listed the number of Bible-believing Christians as compared to the total number of people in the world:

1 per 100 in 1430   2 per 100 in 1790
3 per 100 in 1940   4 per 100 in 1960

5 per 100 in 1970   6 per 100 in 1980
7 per 100 in 1983   8 per 100 in 1986
9 per 100 in 1989   10 per 100 in 1993[14]

Notice how rapidly this figure has risen in recent years. To go from one to two took over 300 years, whereas to go from eight to nine took only three! This is a spectacular and encouraging increase. *Remember, these numbers are somebody's children*!

MISSIONARIES

Rapid growth does not come easily, however. According to Patrick Johnstone there are 140,000 Christian missionaries. Their fruitfulness is demonstrated in the fact that Evangelical Christianity now numbers 500 million adherents and is the only major religion in the world growing because of conversions.[15]

By the year 2000, there were more Evangelical Christians outside than within Western Europe and North America. In fact, more Christians speak Spanish than any other language. By the year 2025, 70 percent of all Evangelical Christians will be from less-developed countries. By 2025, 50 percent of the world's full-time missionaries will come from undeveloped countries.[16] This is truly a spectacular time to be alive!

The challenge, however, is great. Two of today's five largest cities are 97-percent non-Christian (Tokyo and Shanghai). By 2050, four of the five largest cities may be hostile to Christianity (Shanghai, Peking, Bombay and Calcutta). It is also estimated that by the year 2050 there may be as many as 160,000 new non-Christians born every day in the world's great cities. By 2050, the world's population is expected to increase to over 14 billion, the overwhelming majority of whom will be poor. Over 50 percent of the world's population will live in megacities.[17]

A PRAYER REVOLUTION

At the heart of this global revival is an explosive prayer movement. As early as 1748, Jonathan Edwards predicted that this force would occur at the year 2000! In a book that wins the award for having the longest title (*An Humble Attempt To Promote Explicit Agreement and Visible Union of All of God's People in Extraordinary Prayer, For the Revival of the Church and the Advancement of Christ's*

Kingdom on the Earth), Jonathan Edwards "predicted that movements of prayer would accelerate in subsequent generations, climaxing with the greatest one around the year 2000."[18] David Bryant, outstanding prayer-movement leader, has stated that "we may be standing in the vortex of the most significant prayer movement in the history of the Church. . . . No generation has ever seen such an acceleration and intensification of prayer worldwide."[19] Regarding Bryant's claim, world-renowned prayer advocate C. Peter Wagner states, "I don't know a single recognized prayer leader who would disagree with Bryant."[20]

This prayer revolution can be seen in the avalanche of prayer books, manuals, tapes and conferences flooding the church scene. Perhaps the most visible symbol of this revolution is the construction of the $5-million, high-tech World Prayer Center, built in Colorado Springs in 1998. In addition to mobilizing millions of people to pray 24 hours a day, 365 days a year, the World Prayer Center is connecting 50 million praying Christians around the globe by linking prayer centers in 120 countries and 5,000 United States churches. The goal of C. Peter Wagner, head of Global Harvest Ministries, is to mobilize as many as 160 million people to pray for the unsaved on the Earth.[21]

Extensive prayer, as almost every Christian knows, is the reason for the explosive growth in the world's largest church—Dr. Yonggi Cho's church, which has over 750,000 members. Intensive prayer, accompanied by a pastoral nurture network of 25,000 cell groups, has caused this church to flourish. Following a similar pattern is a church led by Pastor Dion Robert of Cote d'Ivoire, West Africa, which has over 120,000 members and 8,000 cell groups.[22] It is amazing that in Korea, South America or Africa, churches are 10, 20 and even 50 times larger than the largest church in the United States! The gospel has defied regionalism. It is global, and prayer is the key ingredient in all these churches.

A PRAISE REVOLUTION

In addition to an explosion of prayer, the world has seen an explosion of praise, which seems to have begun with the Jesus movement, and later spread to the burgeoning Charismatic movement. However, it was not until 1980 that this movement began to have a pervasive influence. Hosanna! Music was launched with the dream of introducing praise into American churches and was the basis for Integrity Music. Though no other music company had successfully promoted music tapes without a well-known Christian artist, Integrity Incorporated, founded in 1987 in Mobile, Alabama, featured praise *without* well-known musicians. The response was phenomenal. People from every denomination immediately began buying tapes from Integrity's Hosanna! Music collection. In 1998, Integrity's sales skyrocketed to 48 percent of the market, selling 40 million units in 140 countries. Sixteen of the albums and videos have gone gold. (Gold is a designation given to albums that have sold over 500,000 copies, while a video must sell over 50,000 to be designated gold). The company correctly acknowledges that "this success that we've tapped means an enormous hunger in God's people worldwide for . . . His presence."[23]

In addition to praise music, an avalanche of books was released on the topic, and a wide variety of worship seminars are available.[24] In 1980, worship conferences were almost unheard-of, but 10 years later there were scores to choose from across America.

The transition in music style did not come without controversy. Elmer Towns identified the problem in his book *Putting the End to Worship Wars*.[25] Churches realized that two distinct generations each had its own musical taste: the Builder generation, which preferred more traditional hymns, and the Boomer generation, which tended to prefer contemporary praise music.[26] The Church might have anticipated that the worship wars would soon see a third generation, the Busters, also insisting on their own style of music. Many churches would simply give up trying to keep people in the same worship service and allow for a wide variety of stratified worship to accommodate the various tastes from the different age levels. Even though the great traditional hymns of the church will always have a profound place, the fact is that, as *Christianity Today's* cover story entitled "The Triumph of the Praise Songs: How Guitars Beat Out the Organ in the Worship Wars" stated, contemporary praise music has displaced traditional music in an overwhelming number of American Christian churches.[27]

A RECONCILIATION REVOLUTION

The prayer revival and the praise revival were joined by a reconciliation revival. At the forefront of this movement was Coach Bill McCartney of Promise Keepers, in Boulder, Colorado. Beginning in 1991, the Promise

Keepers movement became a national phenomenon, reaching its peak in 1996. In eight years, 3.2 million men attended 83 stadium events. By 1997, Promise Keepers had begun experiencing economic challenges, and attendance at their rallies dipped. However, Coach McCartney continued to pursue his dream of reconciling the races, specifically whites and blacks in America.

On a broader cultural scale, John Dawson[28] launched a reconciliation ministry intended to teach one culture how to affirm the uniqueness of another. The Reconciliation movement encourages a people group to discern what wrongs it has inflicted on another group and to ask forgiveness for those atrocities, even if they were done many years ago by previous generations. Perhaps the most intriguing example of this approach was the group of believers who, exactly 900 years later, visited the Muslim villages traversed by the Crusaders in 1099, in order to ask forgiveness for their actions. In America, the reconciliation movement often brings Americans of European descent to Native Americans for the purpose of asking for forgiveness. One major reconciliation gathering was the First Nations worship celebration in September 1999 in San Diego. "Christ's Church will not be truly restored until (reconciliation) happens among the peoples who originally inhabited the land where God had placed them," states Richard Twiss, a Lakota/Sioux from Vancouver, Washington.[29] The reconciliation revolution, when genuinely infused by the Holy Spirit, can result in a dramatic easing of tensions among cultural groups that have harbored bitterness for years.

REVIVALS AROUND THE WORLD

Around the globe outbreaks of revivals are occurring. Fortunately, some of these great moves of God are occurring in the United States as well. One unusual work of the Spirit of God began in a daily required chapel service at Asbury College in Wilmore, Kentucky, in February 1970. At the end of the one-hour service in Hughs auditorium, students streamed to the altar for repentance. Classes were canceled by spiritually sensitive administrators who realized that something significant was happening. They canceled classes for the whole day—and the next. In the end, that one chapel service continued unabated for eight days and nights—185 consecutive hours without interruption. Within hours, students from Asbury Theological Seminary across the street began to attend. Word spread to nearby

Lexington. By the second day, people were streaming in from other cities and even other states. As the revival progressed, people even flew in from other countries.

So unusual was the revival that news anchorman Billy Thompson, speaking on the regular evening broadcast of the major network station in Lexington, advised people to lay their newspaper down and listen carefully to this most unusual story. February 1970 was chiseled in the hearts of tens of thousands of people who were affected by this revival, which eventually spread to scores of other Evangelical colleges and to a number of local communities. Truly, Dr. Robert Colman, then professor at Asbury Theological Seminary, was correct when he called it "one divine moment."[30]

While the Asbury Revival touched the Evangelical Christian college campuses, the Jesus movement began in a very different segment of the culture. For inexplicable reasons, the Spirit of God began to woo hippies, hardly the ideal candidates for local churches! Beginning in southern California, the movement spread across America and around the world in the late '60s and early '70s. No single person was at the forefront of the revival that touched thousands of society's dropouts, with their long hair, beards, beads, guitars, drugs and an anti-Establishment attitude.

However, in 1965, Chuck Smith became pastor of two-dozen disheartened Christians in an unknown church called Calvary Chapel. Chuck's exceptional teaching skills attracted larger and larger crowds, and the church had to move repeatedly. During this time of growth, Chuck and his wife had taken in a few of the Jesus-movement converts whom their daughter had met. In May 1968, they rented the first of what would become several homes to Jesus people who were leaving drugs, having recently come to faith. Soon even a 300-seat tent they were using as a facility from which to teach the Bible and to have worship became inadequate to hold the increasing numbers of people who were attending. Today, Calvary Chapel's low-key gentle praise and no-nonsense, in-your-face Bible teaching has established over 600 Calvary Chapels worldwide. Donald Miller, professor of religion at the University of Southern California, makes the claim in a scholarly work that Calvary Chapel, the Vineyard movement and the Hope Chapel movement have "reinvented American Protestantism."[31]

On Saturday, April 24, 1999, 16,000 Jesus people crowded into Arrowhead Pond in Anaheim, California, to celebrate the 30th anniversary of the Jesus movement. This Jesus people reunion included not only Chuck Smith, who was introduced as the "father of the Jesus people movement," but also included his "sons in the Lord," such as Mike McIntosh of the Horizon Chapel movement (San Diego, California) and Greg Laurie of the Harvest Christian Fellowship movement (Riverside, California).[32]

1995 REVIVAL

A lesser-known revival impacted numerous Christian colleges and universities in the spring of 1995. The growth of this revival can be tracked through the biweekly *National and International Religion Report*. The NIRR first noticed the revival on March 20, 1995. By April 3, the revival had spread to multiple campuses in separate states;

- In Kentucky, Moorhead State University and Murray State University
- In Illinois, Wheaton College and Olivet Nazarene University
- In Texas, Howard Payne University in Brownwood; Criswell College in Dallas; Houston Baptist University in Houston; Southwestern Baptist Theological Seminary in Fort Worth (the largest seminary in the world)[33]

By April 17, the revival had spread to more campuses across the nation:

- In Massachusetts, Gordon College and Eastern Nazarene College
- In Kentucky, Asbury College
- In Indiana, Taylor University
- In Illinois, Trinity College/Evangelical Divinity School and Illinois Baptist College
- In Michigan, Cornerstone College
- In Minnesota, Northwest College and Saint Bonifacius College[34]

By May 1, the *National and International Religion Report* reported additional colleges touched by this revival:

- In Massachusetts, Conwell Theological Seminary
- In Kentucky, Southern Baptist Theological Seminary

- In Indiana, Indiana Wesleyan University
- In Illinois, Judson College
- In Iowa, Iowa State University
- In Colorado, Colorado Christian University
- In Oregon, George Fox College and Multnomah School of the Bible[35]

By July 10, the revival had touched at least 50 colleges, including some of the Ivy League Universities: Yale University in Connecticut, Dartmouth College in New Hampshire, and Columbia University in New York City.

A Church historian at Trinity Evangelical Divinity School stated that, "In 25 years of teaching I've never seen anything like this." At various colleges students lined up to confess long-hidden sins such as bitterness, laziness, sexual immorality, pornography, alcohol, drugs, hypocrisy, materialism and past sexual abuse. They were asking for forgiveness and deliverance from the Lord.[36]

Gary Stratton, dean of the chapel at Gordon College in Wenham, Massachusetts, cautioned that "a couple of days of meetings does not an awakening make." He continued, "I'm looking to see a movement of God's Spirit grow and touch millions of students." Some regarded this 1995 outbreak as a renewal rather than a revival, but were encouraged that it may have been "God's warning shot across the bough to say 'get ready,'" according to Stratton.[37]

THE TORONTO BLESSING

In January 1994, a renewal began in the Toronto Vineyard Church and has continued for nearly six years. Most renewal events are controversial, but the Toronto movement has been exceptionally so. Between January 1994 and December 1998, more than two-and-a-half million people had attended meetings at the Airport Vineyard. Many had flown in from Germany, Wales, Japan, Belgium and Hungary. While Charismatic renewals are often accompanied by signs such as being slain in the Spirit, prophecies and tongues, the Toronto Blessing included much more bizarre behavior. Some laughed uproariously for hours on end or barked like dogs, roared like lions and crowed like chickens. In our walk through history, I have tried to walk the "tightrope," affirming what God was doing, even in the most unusual movements whose leaders were obviously flawed. The Toronto Blessing has provoked enormously differing reactions. Some regard it as one of the greatest outpourings of the Spirit ever to be seen in history, while others have sternly condemned it as a tool used by the devil to deceive weak Christians. Whatever you think of the Toronto Blessing, which pastor John Arnott prefers to call the Father's Blessing, two things must be acknowledged: (1) several million people truly believe they have been profoundly touched by God and energized by His Spirit; (2) the revival could have been better managed so that the excesses did not get out of hand. While true moves of God are difficult to direct, it is unfortunate when excesses go unchecked.

By December 1995, John Wimber, the Charismatic leader of the Vineyard Church movement informed John Arnott that his church was excluded from the Vineyard Fellowship due to the excesses. Some Vineyard pastors did not agree with Wimber. Of the approximately 700 affiliated congregations, 31 Vineyard churches pulled out of the Vineyard movement. In November 1997, John Wimber, who had been such a significant global leader in healing and spiritual warfare, died of a massive brain hemorrhage. Three thousand worshipers gathered in the Anaheim Vineyard Church for a three-hour funeral service, which included hours of praise and worship, as well as weeping. The conclusion to the Toronto event has yet to be written.

THE BROWNSVILLE REVIVAL

On Father's Day, June 18, 1995, a similar revival broke out in the Brownsville Assembly of God Church in Pensacola, Florida. While including such charismatic distinctives as slayings in the Spirit and prophecies, this revival was pastored with unusual skill. By its fourth year, millions had attended from six continents. People gather all day, waiting to get in. When doors open, the church fills in 60 seconds. Large overflow areas with TV cameras accommodate crowds numbering 5,000, with 2,000 making commitments to Christ every week.

AMERICA'S SPIRITUAL CONDITION

Along with the good news of revival comes the tragic news of America's decline.[38] The honest reader is asking how I've managed to leave out

America's moral free fall. Our country is on the verge of spiritual bankruptcy. Well-known legal scholar Robert Bork has written a best-selling book about the American decline. He has called it *Slouching Toward Gomorrah*. Bork writes:

> Thirty years ago, (President Bill) Clinton's behavior would have been absolutely disqualifying. Since the 1992 election, the public has learned far more about what is known, euphemistically, as the "character issue." Yet none of this appears to affect Clinton's popularity. It is difficult not to conclude that something about our moral perceptions and reactions has changed profoundly. If that change is permanent, the implications for our future are bleak.[39]

During the late 1980s, televangelist scandals involving Jim Bakker and Jimmy Swaggart splashed across the television screens of our nation. Polls done by the Gallup organization show that the number of Americans who rated clergy as having high ethical standards dropped from 67 percent in 1985 to only 55 percent by 1990.[40] The price of these scandals has been costly to Christian efforts in the nation.

REDUCTION IN MISSIONARIES

From 1996 to 1997 the percentage of Americans who regularly attended church dropped by over 5 percent. In addition, America's role as a primary sending nation for missionaries was put in jeopardy. According to *World Pulse*, "for the first time in five decades, the reported number of people from the United States who became overseas missionaries has fallen from 50,500 in 1988 to 41,142 in 1992."[41]

RISE IN EASTERN RELIGIONS

During this decline in morals and missions, America has seen a dramatic increase of Eastern religions. By the beginning of the 1990s there were more than 3.5 million Muslims in the United States (by 2000, this number is estimated to approach 15 million) and 500,000 Hindus. Moreover, Buddhism is obviously on the rise, if it is only measured by those who travel to see the Dalai Lama. In 1991, 5,000 came to hear him speak in Central Park in New York City. In August 1999, 40,000 crowded into the same park to hear him.

In the midwestern town of Bloomington, Indiana, 5,000 people a day came to hear him lecture in late August of 1999. In the crowds were well-known actors such as Richard Gere, Steven Seagal and Harrison Ford. The day's ritual included creating a mandala, a painting crafted from colors representing a four-faced god with 24 arms.[42]

RISE IN UNCHURCHED INDIVIDUALS

A recent survey found that of 1900 respondents, 70 percent believe the Ten Commandments should not be posted in American schools,[43] the Barna Research Group indicates that although America is awash in the launch of new churches and the growth of megachurches, a new nationwide survey shows that the number of unchurched adults is on the rise. Almost one-third of the nation's adults (31 percent) can be deemed unchurched. This represents 60 to 65 million unchurched adults. To be classified as unchurched, a person had to declare not to have attended church in the past six months.[44]

Commenting on America's rapid decline, popular musician Carman states:

> If you look at a graph on violent crime, rape, abortion, teen homicide, suicide, alcoholism, drug abuse—anything that pertains to national morality, you'll see that in 1962 the statistics began to break. The only thing that happened in 1962 to explain this is that we took prayer out of our public school system. Students weren't allowed to pray in America anymore. It was the first time in the history of America that we took a verbal public stand against God.[45]

RISE IN CRIME, ILLEGITIMATE BIRTHS AND ABORTIONS

Journalist Allan C. Brownfield states, "Since 1960, we have witnessed a 560 percent increase in violent crime and a 400 percent increase in illegitimate births." The U.S. sadly leads the industrialized world in murder and rapes. New York Senator Daniel Moynihan states that "in 1943 only 3 percent of the children were born to single mothers, compared with a citywide average of 45 percent last year. And in some minority neighborhoods the number is as high as 80 percent." Former Education Secretary William Bennett observes that "in many cities abortions outnumber live births."[46]

THE PLIGHT OF CHRISTIAN COLLEGES

Harvard, Yale and Princeton were only a few of the Ivy League Institutions founded for the purpose of teaching students the basics of the Christian gospel. During the First Great Awakening 50 new colleges were founded. How hard-pressed we would be to find *one* of these schools that still desires to exalt the name of Christ. It would shock even the most casual observer to learn that the University of Michigan and the University of California, Berkeley were once Christian colleges. In his groundbreaking work, *The Soul of the American University,* Notre Dame University history professor George M. Marsden tracks the seemingly inevitable sociological move of universities from "Protestant establishment" to "established nonbelief."[47] As if Marsden's 450-page account is not painful enough, James Tunstead Burtchaell released an 850-page book, *The Dying of the Light: Disengagement of Colleges and Universities from Their Christian Churches,*[48] in which he claims that today's Christian colleges continue to lose their Christian distinctives.

I once spoke at a conference for presidents, administrators, key faculty and selected board members from five different colleges and universities. One speaker enthusiastically announced "we will never go the way of those universities who have lost their Christian distinctives." Unfortunately, I was the next speaker and asked, "What makes us think the universities represented here will not be 'liberal' institutions 25 years from now? People like us, sat in rooms like this, representing the very colleges and universities we have just been discussing, and declared, 'It'll never happen to us!' But it did." It seems a cultural inevitability for Christian colleges, denominations and local churches to drift toward a liberal position, losing the purpose for which they were created. I want to shout with my colleagues, "No, it's not inevitable; it can be stopped!"[49] However, history does not support such optimism. It takes tremendous resolve to keep a church, denomination or Christian school from compromising its Christian purpose.

THE GROWTH OF THE MEGACHURCHES

Yet, there are many reasons to rejoice. In the early part of the decade of the 1990s, officials from 30 denominations met to discuss a 10-year strategy to plant 50,000 new churches by 2000. That goal was reached.

A megachurch is a church with a weekend worship attendance of over 2,000 people. As of the turn of the millennium, there were 500 megachurches in America. One new megachurch is born (crosses the 2,000 attendance mark) every two-and-a-half weeks!

In 1990, there were 40 churches in the world with a weekend worship attendance of 10,000 or more. Only three of these were in the United States. One decade later, the United States number had increased fivefold. At the turn of the millennium, there were 75 churches in the United States with an attendance of 10,000 or more![50]

PERSECUTION

The moral bankruptcy of America is only one of the sobering realities of contemporary Christian life at the beginning of a new millennium. The second major challenge is global persecution. Approximately 160,000 Christians are killed every year for their faith in Christ, according to David Barrett, missiologist.[51] Every three minutes, somewhere in the world, a believer is killed for his faith. According to the *World Missions Digest*, there are close to 100 million martyrs in this supposedly humane twentieth century.[52] In a book entitled *By Their Blood*, James and Marti Hefley state that there have been more people martyred for their faith in Jesus Christ in the twentieth century than in all the previous 19 combined.[53] "More people have died in circumstances related to their faith in this century than all the twentieth century wars combined."[54]

Believers may rejoice that Congress passed the Freedom Act in October of 1998. However, it was disappointing to many human-rights activists that economic sanctions were dropped against the 50 or 60 nations that are persecuting some 200 million believers.[55] While it is true that the "blood of the martyrs is the seed of the church,"[56] severe persecution can be devastating to the work of the Kingdom. Christianity has been practically wiped out of several Muslim countries as a result of widespread extermination of believers. One modern-day example of the impact of oppression and persecution is Eastern Germany. It is estimated that 80 percent of the population in the former German Democratic Republic (GDR) is unchurched. In an April 1999 survey, 73 percent of West Germans indicated they believe in God. But in East Germany, where Communism had oppressed Christianity, 65 percent said they did not believe in God. Only 10 percent of them currently attend church each week. In a poll taken by the Emnid Institute, published in May by the *Der Spiegel*, "Forty-three percent of East Germans and 27 percent of West Germans replied that 'Jesus means nothing to me anymore.' Only 10 percent of East Germans and 27 percent of West Germans believed that 'Jesus was God's Son, came as a Savior, and rose from the dead.' In addition, 79 percent of East Germans and 51 percent of West Germans believe there is 'no life after death.'"[57] In East Germany there are nearly 1,500 churches in such poor condition that it would require a minimum of seven million dollars in repairs to make them usable.

The risk of persecution around the globe is enormous. During the 1994 Tutsi/Hutu animosity, "the Catholic Church, which claimed the allegiance of 60 percent of the country's population, lost its archbishop, four of its eight bishops, 103 priests, and 10 percent of its members in the genocide."[58] In China, from 40 to 115 million Christians worship in house churches, which are outside of government control. "Believers know that each time they gather it may be the last time they hear their pastor preach or see the sister beside them raise her hands in praise."[59]

In August of 1998, house-church leaders made an unprecedented and bold appeal to the Chinese government. This daring and high-risk request asked "that the government change repressive religious regulations and release all house-church Christians detained in labor camps."[60] In one propaganda film a New China News Agency journalist explained why it was very important to persecute Christians. He stated that Christianity had played a major role in the changes in Eastern Europe in the late '80s. "If China does not want such a scene to be repeated in its land," he argued, "it must strangle the baby (of Christianity) while it is still in the manger."[61]

In March 1993, the American Coptic Association/Christians of Egypt wrote President Bill Clinton with this amazing statement: "No month during the last twenty years has passed without the murder, beating or torture of Christians, or without their properties or churches being burned. In all cases, without exception, the criminals (who did this) have been set free."[62] One of the more bizarre examples of human-rights violation occurred on August 14, 1998 in Kesk, a village in the Dar As-Salaam region of Egypt. A local bishop reported that two Christians had been killed. Instead of Egyptian authorities arresting the three Muslims who were accused of the murder, they arrested one thousand Christians, including women and children, who were severely tortured. One 11-year-old boy was tied to a ceiling fan. Others were given electric shocks, hung upside down—in some cases all night long—and many were whipped. Although the Egyptian Center for human rights was asked to investigate the case, no action was taken.[63]

In Sudan, persecution has continued under the guise of cultural cleansing, in which soldiers have rounded up children from Christian homes. In the summer of 1994, Sudanese Christians "were sentenced to one hundred lashes *and crucifixion*" (emphasis added). The two men, ages 65 and 43 were spared by a stay of execution.[64] In Peru over 400 pastors and church leaders have died at the hands of Communist guerrillas.[65]

Perhaps we are only discovering persecution that has gone unnoticed before the ease of communication has uncovered it, but there hardly seems an area in the world free from torture and persecution of Christians. Over 60 nations are guilty of serious human-rights atrocities—usually aimed at Evangelical Christians. Over 200 million believers today are persecuted or tortured for their Christian faith. But those who have died have not died in vain. It is still true that the blood of the martyrs is the seed of the church. The Church has flourished under the most difficult circumstances. If space would permit, we would do a roll call of nations on the expanding kingdom of God. But of course, God Himself is the only one able to do such a final roll call. Instead, we will touch briefly on the state of the continents.

AROUND THE WORLD

SOUTH AMERICA

In 1980, Argentina was considered by Evangelicals to be spiritually infertile soil. But shortly thereafter, "It was as if some invisible momentum reached a flash point," says Stephen Wike.[66] From 1980 to 1990, Protestant church-es grew nearly 700 percent! By the early 1990s a claim was made that would have been unthinkable 10 years earlier—that Evangelicals made up nearly 10 percent of the Argentine population.[67] In the city of Resistencia near the Paraguayan border (population over one-third of a million), Evangelicals increased 90 percent in just two years![68] Three key South American leaders have emerged: Hector Gimenez, who serves a 70,000-member congregation in downtown Buenos Aires; Omar Cabrera, whose church has over 90,000; and Carlos Annacondia. One church grew so rapidly through Annacondia's influence that it has 17 services each week in five rented theaters simply to accommodate the growth![69] The Methodist Pentecostal Church of Chili constructs a new church building every three days. The Jotabeche Pentecostal Church in Santiago, pastored by Javier Vasquez, has a membership of 350,000 and may be the second largest church in the world.[70] In Brazil, five new churches are founded every week in the city of Rio de Janeiro, and approximately 90 percent of those are Pentecostal.[71]

Some have suggested that these numbers are highly inflated. When *Time* magazine reported that since the late 1960s the number of Evangelicals in Latin America had increased from 15 to 40 million, many raised questions. Forty million would represent nearly 10 percent of the population. Are these numbers accurate? How are they determined? For example, it was claimed that Costa Rica's Evangelical population is 16 percent. Charles Spicer, Jr., president of the Overseas Council for Theological Education, contends that polling indicates closer to 9 percent. One difficulty in counting believers is that tabulation processes break down in enormous churches. How can one be sure there are 100,000 in attendance, rather than 80,000? Some churches count adult members in a church and multiply by a factor of three or four to account for children, who are otherwise not counted. Some feel that this method and others inflate estimates and result in distorted statistics. However, the figures are strong enough to support the conclusion that Latin America is experiencing explosive growth.[72]

Some have called the explosion of Evangelical Christian churches in South America during the 1980s "the decade of Protestant Reformation," since Evangelical churches grew from 17,000 to more than 59,000. Brazil is the largest Catholic nation in the world but Catholic membership in that same decade dropped from 89 percent to 78 percent. It is believed that non-Catholic churches' memberships have increased to 35 million, with most attending Pentecostal churches.

However, Martin T. Marty, professor at the University of Chicago Divinity School, cautions that the "backdoor losses are not being included in these figures. Thus, they are distorted and often lead to 'over-counting.'"[73] But again, even if we divide the figures by two, three or even five, Church growth remains staggering. Latin American Christians (including all who identify nominally with the cause of Christ) numbered 62 million in 1900, 392 million in 1985 and 571 million in the year 2000.[74]

EUROPE

In Britain only 11 percent of the adult population (4 percent of the entire population) attends church regularly, as compared to 25 percent in America. While Latin America was experiencing explosive growth, England saw church membership decline by 100,000 a year. Anglicans alone lost nearly 4,000 clergy in the 20-year span from 1970 to 1990. Three thousand Methodist, Anglican, Presbyterian and Baptist churches closed in Britain in the decade between 1975 and 1985. However, the number of independent churches has increased dramatically.[75] In a superb analysis of Christianity globally, Peter Brierley charts the demise of a mainline British denomination in the '70s, '80s and '90s, while at the same time demonstrating that the small, new independent churches tripled between the years 1980 and 1985.[76] Perhaps the most sobering analysis of the entire continent is summarized in this phrase: "Europe is the only continent where the Church is declining."[77]

Perhaps the most encouraging statement about Europe's lack of Christian growth comes from Linus Morris, director of Christian Associates International in Thousand Oaks, California. "Europe is not post-Christian," argues Morris, "but *pre*-Christian." There is "little evidence that the present generation of European urbanites have heard enough of the gospel to reject it."[78] While some would argue that Morris's attitude is an "ostrich approach" to Europe's burgeoning paganism, I concur with Morris that Europe is a prime mission field. Whereas Europe's older generation may be apostate (having heard the gospel and rejected it), the younger generation is so thoroughly pagan that it has never understood the essence of the gospel. Yet, there are many encouraging indicators in Europe. For example, in May 1992, more than 250,000 believers "marched for Jesus" in Belfast, Vienna, Prague, Copenhagen and Paris to demonstrate their love of Christ.[79]

Due to the fact that the Soviet Union and several Communist-controlled countries spread across both Europe and Asia, the growth in those countries will be listed under Asia and Eurasia. One country's profound growth that needs to be mentioned now, however, is Bulgaria. In spite of the fact that Pavel Ignatov spent six months in labor camp for refusing to register his denomination, the Church of God denomination in Bulgaria grew from 4,000 to 20,000 members in the five-year span from 1987 to 1993.[80]

In Denmark, Finland, Norway and Sweden nearly 90 percent of the population belongs to the Lutheran church. Sounds like good news! The bad news is that less than 5 percent of them ever attend a Sunday service. However, Mr. Atle Sommerfeldt of the Church of Norway, takes some comfort in the fact that total church attendance (for the year 1987) far exceeded attendance at soccer matches. Six-and-a-half million attended church, while only 800,000 attended soccer matches.[81] Whether this is good news for the Church or bad news for the Norwegian soccer teams, I leave the reader to decide. But the energy of the Christian faith has shifted from Europe to other countries: "In 1900 two-thirds of the world's 558 million Christians lived in Europe and North America. By 2000 two-thirds of the world's two billion Christians will live elsewhere."[82]

MIDDLE EAST

As we shift our focus to the Middle East, we move into the area known as the 10/40 Window, located from West Africa across Asia, extending from 10 degrees north to 40 degrees south of the Equator. Though it includes only one-third of the Earth's total land area, the 64 countries in its boundaries host two-thirds of the world's population.[83] The world can be divided into three segments:

- the Christian world, which has heard the gospel and is influenced by it (slightly less than two billion people);
- the unevangelized non-Christian world, where at least 50 percent of the population have heard the gospel but resist it (2.5 billion people);
- the unevangelized world, where people have never heard the gospel (slightly less than 2 billion people). Ninety-five percent of unevangelized people live in the 10/40 Window.[84]

Because of the cost and local laws that are inhospitable to Christians, the 10/40 Window is a difficult area to evangelize, but the Church of Jesus Christ marches forward.

During the 1991 Persian Gulf War, the Spirit of God set in motion opportunities for ministry in this difficult region. In some ways, Saddam Hussein's 1990 invasion of Kuwait helped open the Muslim world to the gospel of Christ. Iraq's genocidal campaign against the Kurds has given believers the chance to care for this devastated group of people. Christian believers make up 90 percent of the relief force to the Kurds, and have built more than 4,000 homes for Kurdish war victims during 1992.[85] According to *Charisma*, "Kurds are rejecting Islam because they don't want a religion capable of producing a tyrant like Saddam Hussein."[86] According to Greg Livingston, international director of the London-based Frontiers Organization, Muslims have been "converting to Christianity at an unprecedented rate. . . . Thirty years ago nobody knew about Muslims. Today churches are gearing up like never before to reach them."[87]

The number of conversions in Muslim countries is still extremely small, however. In Turkey, for example, where the population numbers 68 million, there are only 500 to 1,000 born-again believers. Though ministry in Turkey is restricted and difficult, believers travel there in their prayers all the time to pull down strongholds, and release the convicting power of the Holy Spirit. In October of 1999, the same Ephesus stadium that was used 2,000 years ago to exalt the goddess Diana was used by believers to lift up the name of Jesus. The worship service continued for four hours, intentionally doubling the two-hour time that Diana was exalted in that same stadium some 2,000 years ago. Five thousand people gathered from 60 nations proclaimed the name of Jesus in that historic gathering.[88]

ASIA

In Asia live more people than in any other continent. The Earth's population is presently distributed as follows: Asia—61 percent; Africa—13 percent; Europe—12 percent; South America—9 percent; North America—5 percent. Although only three to five percent of Asia's population is Christian, the Church's growth there is significant. In his last issue of the century and the millennium, *Ministries Today* editor, Larry Keefauver, stated that while revival fires have swept through America and Latin America in the twentieth century, the Holy Spirit's Fourth Wave in the twenty-first century will be in Asia.[89]

Six new churches are formed every day in South Korea. Many of the world's largest churches are in this country, which only a few years ago had no Evangelical churches. In 1900, Korea did not have a single Protestant church. The country was perceived as being "impossible to penetrate."

However, many faithful Presbyterian missionaries, as well as others, had persisted before having to leave Korea. God blessed their faithfulness, for today Korea's population is over 30-percent Christian, with more than 4,000 churches in Seoul alone. As everyone is aware, the largest church is located there as well.90 Dr. David Cho pastors a congregation of 750,000 members. This church has birthed over 100 daughter churches, two of which had 5,000 attending their first service. One had 10,000 people the first Sunday.[91]

In Indonesia, where it is illegal to follow Christ, the number of Christians is believed to be so high that the government refuses to print statistics. The Christian population may be nearing the 25 percent mark![92]

In the most populated of all nations, China, 28,000 people were coming to Christ every day, as of 1992.[93] That number has increased dramatically since then. But the challenge is still great. In Asia, there are approximately 700 million Hindus, 300 million Muslims, and one billion who espouse Confucianism or Taoism.[94] China was politically closed for over 40 years. No one knew what happened to its one million believers when China experienced its political lockdown. If and when China opened up again, would there be any believers left? When China finally opened up, rumors spoke of nearly 25 million, 50 million, as many as 100 million believers! The Chinese government announced that there were 10 to 12 million Christians (even that lower figure is impressive): a tenfold increase in 40 years! On October 22, 1992, the *South China Morning Post* cited a survey of the state's statistical bureau, which stated that the Chinese Protestant church members numbered 63 million! This means that under the most difficult circumstances, the number of Chinese believers had increased 63 times over in a 40-year span—while Christians were threatened with execution! And that's using the figures of a hostile government. The actual figures may even be higher.[95]

Often major political catastrophes are used by God, in His infinite wisdom for the purposes of His kingdom. Since the Tiananmen Square massacre on June 4, 1989, unprecedented numbers of Chinese intellectuals have come to Christ. According to Lesley Francis of Hong Kong, this spiritual awakening "has no historical parallel in Chinese history."[96] In the Hennan Province, the number of believers grew from 260,000 to 600,000 between 1983 and 1993. One out of every four people on the earth lives in Szechwan Province, where nearly 2,000 new churches were planted between 1990 and

1993, in spite of fierce government resistance.[97] The gospel often thrives in the most hostile environment, such as that in Laos. In a five-year span from 1987 to 1993, the Laotian church grew from 5,000 to 20,000 members.[98]

In India, about 15,000 new believers are baptized every week. Amazingly, 80 percent of new converts come to Christ as a result of a supernatural encounter. A church planted in 1980 among the Gamit people in Gujarat, India, grew from zero to 60,000 in 13 years.[99]

It may be surprising us to see how many believers can be found in countries where they can be killed for their faith. In Indonesia, for example, nearly 20 percent of the population is now following Christ. The number of Christian believers in Mongolia increased from fewer than 15 to 1,000 between 1991 and 1993. Mongolia, the size of the state of Texas, has not had a Christian church for 700 years![100] Of all the Asian nations, the Philippines have been the most receptive to the gospel of Jesus Christ. There are over 32,000 Protestant churches in the Philippines. Of these, 27,000 were planted in the last quarter century. Bishop Efraim Tendero of the Philippine Council for Evangelical Churches demonstrated Philippine fervor when he stated in mid-1999 that they will plant their 50,000th church by December 2000.[101]

As we shift to the former Soviet Union, which spreads across Asia and Eurasia, we find encouraging evidence of the expanding kingdom of God. Protestant churches are sprouting in the Islamic Asian Republics of the former Soviet Union. One church planted in Uzbekistan in 1991 grew to 3,000 members in just four years. By 1995, 800 people were attending each of its four worship services and it had planted 55 other congregations![102]

The fall of Communism seemed to free people to leave their atheism behind, with the old regime. According to the National Option Research Center in Chicago, 22 percent of the 3,000 Russian respondents said they had shifted from atheism to a belief in God. Thirty percent of Russians under age 25 reported converting from atheism.[103] As Communism fell, spiritual revival began in the former Soviet Union. According to Edward E. Plowman, that revival began in approximately 1988 and over the course of the next three years many congregations doubled and tripled in size, with most converts under the age of 30. A large percentage of new believers is made up of public school teachers.[104] After 70 years of oppression in the Soviet Union, Christian believers number about 100 million, or 36 percent of the population (including nominal Christians). The number of people who identify with the name of Jesus is five times greater than those who identified with the Communist party at the height of its popularity.[105]

AFRICA

Some of the most encouraging reports regarding the expansion of the Christian faith come from the continent of Africa. African Christians are five times as many as they were 25 years ago.[106] One Assemblies of God superintendent reported that in Burkina Faso, a church gained 22,000 members in its first half century, while the explosive growth in recent years had increased those numbers to 350,000. On the continent as a whole, the number of Christian believers has increased from about 100,000 to nearly 2.8 million in a 22-year span from 1970 to 1992.[107] If all Christian denominations in Africa are totaled, the numbers are staggering. There were only 10 million believers in 1900. Eighty-five years later there were 236 million, expected to have reached 400 million by the year 2000.[108] Over 20,000 people per day are coming to know Christ. What is even more amazing is that in 1900 Africa was only 3-percent Christian. It is somewhere between 40- and 50-percent Christian today.[109]

AND FINALLY . . .

ATHEISTIC STATION PROCLAIMS THE GOSPEL

Dr. Paul Freed, president of Trans World Radio, reported a powerful and historic event. In 1967, Radio Tirana began broadcasting, declaring Albania to be an officially atheistic nation. In 1992, that same station began to broadcast the gospel of Jesus Christ three hours every night to a potential audience of 100 million people![110] What Satan once claimed, God now uses. As if that news is not enough, observers noted in 1993 that the annual growth rate of the Protestant church in Albania (formerly officially atheistic) had reached the 37 percent mark![111]

RECLAIMED BRICKS

One of the most spectacular accounts of God's plan coming to fruition after being thwarted for years occurred in the Republic of Belarus:

Constantine Jaroshevich, a Russian immigrant to the U.S., met Jesus in New York. He returned to the Soviet Union and Poland where he planted 30 Baptist Churches, until he was imprisoned by Stalinist authorities in the early 1950s, according to *News Network International* (June 26, 1992). In late 1991, the former Soviet Republic of Belarus gave Baptists in the city of Kobryn permission to demolish a Soviet army barracks and missile silo. The Baptists planned to use the salvaged bricks, cement blocks and steel to build their church since the congregation was formed in 1925. While dismantling the silo, the workers found a 42-year-old Russian letter inside an empty World War II artillery shell sealed in a wall. The letter claimed the material used to build the missile silo had actually been taken from the local churches, demolished years ago on orders by their dictator, Joseph Stalin. The letter was signed by several Russian construction workers, apparently of Christian convictions, who almost prophetically asked that if the missile launcher were ever demolished, the bricks be used to build churches. For all those years the Kobryn Baptists met in a frame dwelling seating 200, or accommodating 500 standing. Today they are building a 1,000-seat church (2,000 standing), using the "prophetic" bricks from the missile silo![112]

What the enemy had stolen, God had reclaimed!

WORLD'S LARGEST BAPTISMAL SERVICE

In 1992, South Africa's *Imvo*, a secular newspaper with a circulation of over one million, reported that an extensive revival broke out, in which tens of thousands received Christ. It took Archbishop Mazwi Mboniswa and 21 bishops from Saint John Apostolic Church five hours to baptize a line of new converts five kilometers long. Eyewitnesses reported that physical healings and deliverance from demons occurred as believers came up out of the waters of the Tsomo River (in the Transkei region). The number of people baptized in that November 1992 service totaled 70,000! This is undoubtedly the largest baptismal service ever recorded in Christian history.[113]

AN AMAZING STATISTIC

The single most exhilarating statistic I have ever heard about the expansion of Christianity is related by George Otis, Jr., who says that 70 percent of all evangelization has taken place since 1900! And 70 percent of *that* increase has occurred since World War II! And to demonstrate the explosive growth of Christianity today, 70 percent of the increase since World War II has occurred in the three-year span between 1990 and 1993![114] This is exponential growth!

So beware, all enemies of the Church of Jesus Christ. Contrary to your wishes, the Church of Jesus Christ is alive and well. Nothing will stop God's Church from accomplishing the goal He has set for her. Through the work of the Church of Jesus Christ, civilization will be saved.

Be encouraged, saints of God. Though Christians may yet face great trials and persecutions, though the Church may seem weak and downtrodden, it is alive and well. The Church of Jesus Christ is flourishing; and as Jesus Himself said, the very gates of hell will not stand against His Church. The Church is alive, and it is well! And now you know the story—the story of how God saved civilization.

To further assist you in understanding the key individuals and events of chapter 20, study questions, charts, diagrams, time lines and links to biographical websites are available on the Internet at www.jimgarlow.com. Please follow the site links to *How God Saved Civilization*, chapter 20 study helps.

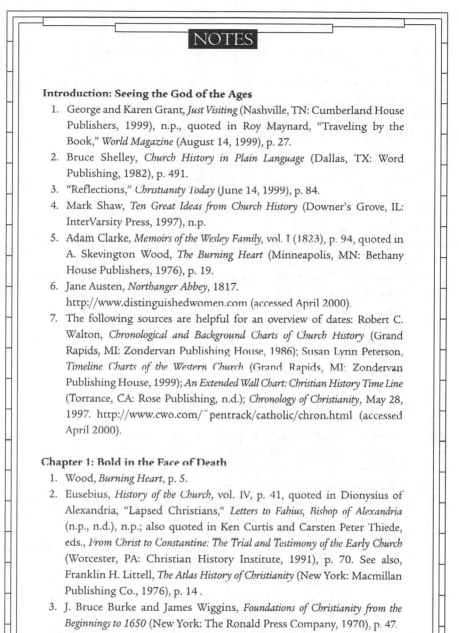

NOTES

Introduction: Seeing the God of the Ages

1. George and Karen Grant, *Just Visiting* (Nashville, TN: Cumberland House Publishers, 1999), n.p., quoted in Roy Maynard, "Traveling by the Book," *World Magazine* (August 14, 1999), p. 27.

2. Bruce Shelley, *Church History in Plain Language* (Dallas, TX: Word Publishing, 1982), p. 491.

3. "Reflections," *Christianity Today* (June 14, 1999), p. 84.

4. Mark Shaw, *Ten Great Ideas from Church History* (Downer's Grove, IL: InterVarsity Press, 1997), n.p.

5. Adam Clarke, *Memoirs of the Wesley Family*, vol. I (1823), p. 94, quoted in A. Skevington Wood, *The Burning Heart* (Minneapolis, MN: Bethany House Publishers, 1976), p. 19.

6. Jane Austen, *Northanger Abbey*, 1817. http://www.distinguishedwomen.com (accessed April 2000).

7. The following sources are helpful for an overview of dates: Robert C. Walton, *Chronological and Background Charts of Church History* (Grand Rapids, MI: Zondervan Publishing House, 1986); Susan Lynn Peterson, *Timeline Charts of the Western Church* (Grand Rapids, MI: Zondervan Publishing House, 1999); *An Extended Wall Chart: Christian History Time Line* (Torrance, CA: Rose Publishing, n.d.); *Chronology of Christianity*, May 28, 1997. http://www.cwo.com/~pentrack/catholic/chron.html (accessed April 2000).

Chapter 1: Bold in the Face of Death

1. Wood, *Burning Heart*, p. 5.

2. Eusebius, *History of the Church*, vol. IV, p. 41, quoted in Dionysius of Alexandria, "Lapsed Christians," *Letters to Fabius, Bishop of Alexandria* (n.p., n.d.), n.p.; also quoted in Ken Curtis and Carsten Peter Thiede, eds., *From Christ to Constantine: The Trial and Testimony of the Early Church* (Worcester, PA: Christian History Institute, 1991), p. 70. See also, Franklin H. Littell, *The Atlas History of Christianity* (New York: Macmillan Publishing Co., 1976), p. 14 .

3. J. Bruce Burke and James Wiggins, *Foundations of Christianity from the Beginnings to 1650* (New York: The Ronald Press Company, 1970), p. 47.

4. William P. Barker, *Who's Who in Church History* (Grand Rapids, MI: Baker Book House, 1969), p. 148.

5. Elmer L. Towns, *The Christian Hall of Fame* (Grand Rapids, MI: Baker Book House, 1971), p. 12.

6. Michael A. Smith, "Ignatius of Antioch," in *Eerdmans Handbook to the History of Christianity*, ed. Tim Dowley (Grand Rapids, MI: Wm. B. Eerdmans Publishing Co., 1977), p. 80.

7. Marie Gentert King, ed., *Foxe's Book of Martyrs*, (Westwood, NJ: Fleming H. Revell Company, 1968), p. 16.

8. Eusebius, *History of the Church*, vol. IV, p. 15, quoted in *Eerdmans Handbook to the History of Christianity*, p. 81.

9. King, *Foxe's Book of Martyrs*, p. 18.

10. Ibid., pp. 19f.

Chapter 2: An Apology Doesn't Always Mean "I'm Sorry"

1. B. K. Kuiper, *The Church in History* (Grand Rapids, MI: Wm. B. Eerdmans Publishing Co., 1979), p. 16.

2. Collin J. Hemmer, "Justin Martyr," in *Eerdmans Handbook to the History of Christianity*, p. 108.

3. King, *Foxe's Book of Martyrs*, p. 18.

4. Jerald C. Brauer, ed., *Westminster Dictionary of Church History* (Philadelphia, PA: Westminster Press, 1971), p. 60.

5. David F. Wright, "What the First Christians Believed," in *Eerdmans Handbook to the History of Christianity*, p. 113.

6. Barker, *Who's Who in Church History*, pp. 272, 273.

7. Brauer, *Westminster Dictionary of Church History*, p. 810.

8. Alan Richardson, ed., *Dictionary of Christian Theology* (Philadelphia, PA: Westminster Press, 1971), p. 334.

9. Brauer, *Westminster Dictionary of Church History*, p. 810.

10. Ibid., p. 811.

11. Tertullian, *Apology*, quoted in *Eerdmans Handbook to the History of Christianity*, p. 112.

12. Barker, *Who's Who in Church History*, p. 212.

13. A. Cabaniss, "Origen," in *Who's Who in Christian History*, eds. J.D. Douglas and Philip W. Comfort (Wheaton, IL: Tyndale House Publishers, 1992), p. 521.

Chapter 3: Troubles Bring Needed Changes

1. For an interesting discussion of Gnostic thinking in today's culture, see Peter Jones, *The Gnostic Empire Strikes Back: An Old Heresy for the New Age* (Phillipsburg, NJ: P & R Publishing Co., 1992).

2. A. Kenneth Curtis, J. Stephen Lane and Randy Petersen, eds., *Dates with Destiny* (Tarrytown, NY: Fleming H. Revell Company, 1991), p. 23.

3. Brauer, *Westminster Dictionary of Church History*, p. 441.

4. David F. Wright, "What the First Christians Believed," in *Eerdmans Handbook to the History of Christianity*, p. 106.

5. The Apostles' Creed: "I believe in God the Father Almighty, Maker of heaven and earth, and in Jesus Christ His only Son our Lord; who was conceived by the Holy Ghost, born of the Virgin Mary, suffered under Pontius Pilate, was crucified, died and buried; He descended into hades; the third day He rose again from the dead; He ascended into heaven, and sitteth on the right hand of God the Father Almighty; from thence He shall come to judge the quick and the dead. I believe in the Holy Spirit; the holy Christian Church; the communion of saints; the forgiveness of sins; the resurrection of the body; and the life everlasting. Amen." *Hymns for the Family of God* (Nashville, TN: Paragon Associates, Inc., 1976), p. 137.

6. Jim Garlow, *Partners in Ministry* (Kansas City, MO: Beacon Hill Publishing, 1981), n.p.

7. For a superb discussion of these and related issues see Burke and Wiggins, *Foundations of Christianity*, pp. 62-65.

8. S. L. Greenslade, *Early Latin Theology* (Philadelphia, PA: Westminster Press, 1956), p. 43.

9. Brauer, *Westminster Dictionary of Church History*, p. 452.

10. Barker, *Who's Who in Church History*, p. 154.

11. Brauer, *Westminster Dictionary of Church History*, p. 453.

12. Richard Todd, "The Fall of the Roman Empire," in *Eerdmans Handbook to the History of Christianity*, p. 179.

Chapter 4: The Grand Detour

1. Martin E. Marty, *A Short History of Christianity* (New York: Living Age Books, 1959), p. 97.

2. George Grant, foreword to *Angels in the Architecture: A Protestant Vision for Middle Earth*, by Douglas Jones and Douglas Wilson (Moscow, ID: Canon Press, 1998), p. 12.

3. Kenneth Scott Latourette, *A History of the Expansion of Christianity: The Thousand Years of Uncertainty*, vol. 2 A.D. 500 to A.D. 1500 (Grand Rapids, MI: Zondervan Publishing House, 1970), p. 22.

4. Stephen Neill, *A History of Christian Missions* (New York: Penguin Books, 1964), p. 61.

5. Ibid., p. 61f.

6. J. D. Douglas, "Columba," in *Who's Who in Christian History* (Wheaton, IL: Tyndale House Publishers, 1992), p. 171.

7. Brauer, *Westminster Dictionary of Church History*, p. 423.

8. Bruce L. Shelley, *Church History in Plain Language* (Dallas, TX: Word Publishing, 1982), p. 493.

9. Timothy Paul Jones, *Christian History Made Easy* (Torrance, CA: Rose Publishing, 1999), pp. 52-56.

10. Brauer, *Westminster Dictionary of Church History*, p. 407.

11. Ibid., p. 408.

12. For an exhaustive, 1500-page, detailed report of the Crusades see: Kenneth M. Setton, ed., *A History of the Crusades*, 2 vols. (Philadelphia, PA: University of Pennsylvania Press, 1958, 1962).

Chapter 5: Growing Conflicts

1. Douglas, "Anselm," in *Who's Who in Christian History*, p. 26.

2. Ibid.

3. T. O. Kay and A. F. Holmes, "Peter Abelard," *Who's Who in Christian History*, p. 2.

4. Ibid.

5. T. O. Kay, "St. Thomas Becket," in *Who's Who in Christian History*, p. 71.

6. Brauer, *Westminster Dictionary of Church History*, p. 434f.

7. Ibid, p. 433.

8. Ibid.

9. Ibid.

10. Barker, *Who's Who in Church History*, p. 114.

11. Ibid., p. 115.

12. Ibid., p. 114.

13. Timothy Paul Jones, *Christian History Made Easy* (Torrance, CA: Rose Publishing, 1999), p. 72.

14. Ibid.

15. Allen Cabaniss, "Joan of Arc," in *Who's Who in Christian History*, p. 370.

16. Brauer, *Westminster Dictionary of Church History*, p. 708f.

17. So significant is John Gutenberg's influence that he is consistently listed as one of the most influential persons in history. The cable TV network A&E in late 1999 aired a series entitled "Biography of the Millenium: 100 People—1,000 Years"; John Gutenberg was selected as the person who most impacted the world in the millennium from 1000 to 2000. "Gutenberg, Johann," http://www.biography.com/features/millennium/topten.html (accessed April 2000). *The Southern California Christian Times,* Nov. 1999, p. 5 reported that the "Religion and Ethics Newsweekly" of the Public Television Series chose the top 10 stories of the millennium; the Gutenberg Bible, published in 1455, was one of those 10 stories.

18. Brauer, *Westminster Dictionary of Church History,* p. 881.

Chapter 6: Intimacy with God

1. Brauer, *Westminster Dictionary of Church History,* p. 124.
2. Burke and Wiggins, *Foundations of Christianity,* p. 235.
3. Barker, *Who's Who in Church History,* p. 269.
4. Brauer, *Westminster Dictionary of Church History,* p. 731.
5. Ibid., p. 809.
6. Ibid.
7. Burke and Wiggins, *Foundations of Christianity,* p. 251.

Chapter 7: Dying for a Change

1. Ronald Finucane, "The Waldensians," in *Eerdmans Handbook of the History of Christianity,* p. 315.
2. Towns, *Christian Hall of Fame,* p. 28.
3. Poggius Bracciolini, *Huss the Heretic* (Poland, ME: Shiloh Publications, May 1977), pp. 65-68.
4. Ibid., pp. 64-68.
5. Ibid., p. 69.
6. Ibid., p. 70.
7. Ibid., p. 72.
8. Ibid.
9. Ibid., p. 74.
10. Ibid., p. 75.
11. Ibid., p. 76.

Chapter 8: The Spiritual Explosion

1. Dowley, *Eerdmans Handbook to the History of Christianity,* p. 364.

Chapter 9: The Chain Reaction

1. William R. Estep, *Renaissance and Reformation* (Grand Rapids, MI: Wm. B. Eerdmans Publishing Co., 1986), p. 186f.
2. Brauer, *Westminster Dictionary of Church History,* pp. 27, 28.
3. Towns, *Christian Hall of Fame,* p. 52.
4. Dowley, *Eerdmans Handbook to the History of Christianity,* p. 381.
5. For a one-volume overview of 43 different Reformers, see Gideon and Hilda Hagstutz, *Heroes of the Reformation* (Reprint, Rapidan, VA: Hartland Publications, 1996).
6. Barker, *Who's Who in Church History,* p. 107f.
7. Brauer, *Westminster Dictionary of Church History,* p. 478.

8. One example of this is the class in "Ignatian Spirituality" at Azusa Pacific University's Graduate School of Theology, Azusa, California.
9. Brauer, *Westminster Dictionary of Church History*, p. 425.
10. Curtis, et al., *Dates with Destiny*, p. 112.

Chapter 10: It'll Never Happen in Britain

1. Edward Halle, *Chronicle*, quoted in F. F. Bruce, in *History of the Bible in English* (New York: Oxford University Press, 1978), p. 38.
2. Estep, *Renaissance and Reformation*, p. 254.
3. Bruce, *History of the Bible in English*, p. 52.
4. King, *Foxe's Book of Martyrs*, p. 233.
5. Estep, *Renaissance and Reformation*, p. 254, footnote 6.
6. A. G. Dickens, *The English Reformation* (n.p., n.d.), quoted in William Estep, *Renaissance and Reformation Reformation* (Grand Rapids, MI: Wm. B. Eerdmans Publishing Co., 1986), p. 256.
7. Source unknown.
8. Franklin H. Littell, *Atlas of the History of Christianity*, p. 73.
9. King, *Foxe's Book of Martyrs*, p. 732.
10. Estep, *Renaissance and Reformation*, p. 264.
11. Ibid.
12. Lewis W. Spitz, *The Protestant Reformation* (Englewood Cliffs, N J: Prentice Hall, 1966), p. 170, quoted in Estep, *Renaissance and Reformation*, p. 265.
13. Estep, *Renaissance and Reformation*, p. 265.

Chapter 11: A Fire in England

1. John Wesley, *The Works of John Wesley*, Journal I (1872; reprint, Salem, OH: Schmul Publishers, n.d.), p. 103.
2. Wesley didn't name his followers Methodists. They were simply labeled Methodists by their critics. Thus Wesley referred to them as "the people called Methodists."
3. S. C. Carpenter, *Eighteenth Century Church and People* (London: John Murray, 1959), p. 216.
4. Francis J. McConnall, *John Wesley* (New York: Abingdon Press, 1938), p. 9.
5. Wesley, *Works of John Wesley*, Journal II, p. 243.
6. Albert Outler, *Evangelism in the Wesleyan Spirit* (Nashville, TN: Tidings, 1971), p. 16f.
7. Ibid., p. 18.
8. Frank Baker, "The People Called Methodists . . . Polity," *Church in Great Britain*, vol. 1, eds. Rupert Davies and Gordon Rupp (London: Epworth Press, 1965), p. 230.
9. Maximim Piette, *John Wesley in the Evolution of Protestantism* (New York: Sheed and Ward, 1937), p. 375.
10. Rupert E. Davies, *Methodism* (London: Epworth Press, 1963), p. 230.
11. Warren A. Candler, *Wesley and His Work* (Nashville, TN: Publishing House of the M. E. Church, South, 1912), p. 55.
12. Wesley, *Works of John Wesley*, Journal 5, p. 360f.
13. Norman W. Mumford, "The Organization of the Methodist Church in the Time of John Wesley," part 1, *London Quarterly & Holborn Review*, vol. 171 (January 1946), pp. 35-40.
14. Henry Bett, *The Early Methodist Preachers* (London: Epworth Press, 1935), p. 9.

15. Robert E., Wearmouth, *Methodism and the Working-Class Movements of England; 1800-1850* (London: Epworth Press, 1937), p. 25.

16. Franz Hildebrandt, *Christianity According to the Wesleys* (London: Epworth Press, 1956), p. 48; also see Stephen Charles Neill, "Britain," *The Layman in Christian History*, eds. Stephen Neill and Hans-Ruedi Webber (Philadelphia, PA: The Westminster Press, 1963), p. 207.

Chapter 12: Fire in the New World

1. Earl Cairns, *Christianity Through the Centuries* (Grand Rapids, MI: Zondervan Publishing House, 1976), p. 391f.

2. Ibid., p. 398f.

3. Edwin Scott Gaustad, *Historical Atlas of Religion in America* (New York: Harper & Row Publishers, 1962), p. 3f.

4. Sydney E. Ahlstrom, *A Religious History of the American People* (New Haven, CT: Yale University Press, 1972), p. 162.

5. DeMoss Foundation, *The Rebirth of America*, ed. Nancy L. DeMoss (Philadelphia, PA: Arthur DeMoss Foundation, n.d.), p. 55.

6. Brauer, *Westminster Dictionary of Church History*, p. 291.

7. Barker, *Who's Who in Church History*, p. 97.

8. DeMoss Foundation, *Rebirth of America*, p. 54.

9. Cairns, *Christianity Through the Centuries*, p. 401f.

10. DeMoss Foundation, *Rebirth of America*, p. 54.

11. Ibid., p. 42.

12. Ahlstrom, *A Religious History of the American People*, p. 286.

13. H. Sheldon Smith, Robert Handy and Lefferts A. Loetscher, *American Christianity, an Historical Interpretation with Representative Documents*, vol. I, 1607-1820 (New York: Charles Scribner's Sons, 1960), p. 315.

14. Ibid.

15. Gaustad, *Historical Atlas of Religion in America*, p. 4.

16. Brauer, *Westminster Dictionary of Church History*, p. 762.

17. Gaustad, *Historical Atlas of Religion in America*, p. 31.

18. Brauer, *Westminster Dictionary of Church History*, p. 762.

19. P. M. Bassett, "Junipero Serra," in *Who's Who in Christian History*, p. 619.

Chapter 13: Awakened Again

1. David D. Eller, "Cane Ridge Revival," in *Dictionary of Christianity in America*, ed. Daniel G. Reid (Downers Grove, IL: InterVarsity Press, 1990), p. 218.

2. Daniel G. Reid, "Primitivism," in *Dictionary of Christianity in America*, p. 940.

3. Curtis, *Dates with Destiny*, p. 145.

4. J. R. Fitzmier, "Lyman Beecher," *Dictionary of Christianity in America*, p. 123.

5. G. M. Rosell, "Charles Grandison Finney," *Dictionary of Christianity in America*, p. 439.

6. Donald W. Dayton, *Discovering an Evangelical Heritage* (Peabody, MA: Hendrickson Publishers, 1976), p.18.

7. Rosell, *Dates with Destiny*, p. 154.

8. Towns, *Christian Hall of Fame*, p. 102.

9. Ibid.

Chapter 14: The Rise of the Common Person

1. Dayton, *Discovering an Evangelical Heritage,* p. 91.
2. Ibid.
3. John S. O'Malley, "Orange Scott," in *Dictionary of Christianity in America,* p. 1059.
4. Dayton, *Discovering an Evangelical Heritage,* p. 48.
5. J. Edwin Orr, "Potent Answers to Persistent Prayer," in *Rebirth of America,* p. 63.

Chapter 15: Dealing with Divisions

1. Ahlstrom, *A Religious History of the American People,* p. 681f.
2. Robert D. Linder, introduction to *Dictionary of Christianity in America,* p. 10.
3. Ibid., p. 10f.
4. *Defense of Virginia* (1867), quoted in William A. Clebsch, "Christian Interpretations of the Civil War," *Church History,* 30 (1961), p. 4, quoted in Ahlstrom, *A Religious History of the American People,* p. 684.
5. Beecher, Henry Ward, address delivered in Charleston on February 14, 1865, when the flag of the Union was restored above Fort Sumter.
6. Ahlstrom, *A Religious History of the American People,* p. 686.
7. Robert D. Linder, *Dictionary of Christianity in America,* p. 11.
8. Lyle W. Dorsett, *A Passion for Souls: The Life of D. L. Moody* (Chicago, IL: Moody Press, 1997), p. 144.
9. Ibid., p. 147.
10. Ibid., p. 152.
11. Ibid., p. 65.
12. Ibid.
13. James F. Findley, Jr., *Dwight L. Moody: American Evangelist, 1837-1899* (Chicago, IL: University of Chicago Press, 1969), p. 132f., quoted in Dorsett, *Passion for Souls,* p. 156.
14. T. P. Weber, "Dwight Lyman Moody," *Dictionary of Christianity in America,* p. 769.

Chapter 16: Dodging Bullets

1. Irving Hexham, "Jehovahs Witnesses," in *Dictionary of Christianity in America,* p. 591.
2. Whitney Cross, *The Burned-Over District: The Social and Intellectual History of Enthusiastic Religion in Western New York, 1800-1850* (out of print).
3. Winthrop S. Hudson, *Religion in America* (New York: Charles Scribner's Sons, 1965), p. 207.
4. Ibid., p. 208f.
5. Ahlstrom, *A Religious History of the American People,* p. 735.
6. Ibid.
7. Hudson, *Religion in America,* p. 207f.
8. C. V. Anderson, "Young Men's Christian Association," in *Dictionary of Christianity in America,* p. 1299.
9. Ibid.
10. An example of this is the San Diego YMCA, which co-sponsors events with the Lesbian and Gay Men's Community Center. Elizabeth Wilberg, "Crowd Rallies Against Hate Crimes with Candlelight Vigil," *San Diego Union Tribune,* October 23, 1999, sec. B, p. 3.
11. Mark Kellner, "Salvation Army Generals Refocus on the Gospel," *Christianity Today,* June 14, 1999, p. 30.
12. *San Diego Union Tribune,* November 1, 1999, sec. A, p. 7.

13. Kellner, "Salvation Army Generals," p. 30.

14. Diane Winston, *Red-Hot and Righteous* (Cambridge, MA: Harvard University Press, 1999), n.p., quoted in Kellner, "Salvation Army Generals," p. 30.

15. Kellner, "Salvation Army Generals," p. 30.

16. C. E. Jones, "Welsh Revival," eds. Stanley M. Burgess and Gary B. McGee, *Dictionary of Pentecostal and Charismatic Movements* (Grand Rapids, MI: Zondervan Publishing House, 1988), p. 881.

17. Colin Brown, "The Ascent of Man," in *Handbook to the History of Christianity*, p. 544.

18. R. D. Linder, introduction to *Dictionary of Christianity in America*, p. 15.

Chapter 17: The Battle Lines Redefined

1. Robert Handy, *A Christian America* (New York: Oxford University Press, 1971), pp. 113-116; 195-197.

2. Ahlstrom, *A Religious History of the American People*, p. 877.

3. G. M. Marsden and B. J. Longfield, *Dictionary of Christianity in America*, ed. Linder, p. 467.

4. Ibid.

5. They were instrumental in founding the Bible Institute of Los Angeles, known today as Biola University.

6. Curtis, et al., *Dates with Destiny*, p. 181.

7. Ibid., p. 182.

8. Ahlstrom, *A Religious History of the American People*, p. 912.

9. Hudson, *Religion in America*, p. 366.

10. Space does not allow a discussion of the profound cultural and social changes that sanctificationist/holiness/revivalist camp meetings brought to the broader culture. See Timothy Smith, *Revivalism and Social Reform* (Nashville, TN: Abingdon Press, 1957).

11. For a fuller understanding of the influence of the camp meeting, see two works by Kenneth O. Brown: *Holy Ground, Too* (Hazelton, PA: Holiness Archive, 1997) and *Inskip, McDonald, Fowler: "Wholly and Forever Thine"* (Hazelton, PA: Holiness Archive, 1999).

12. Melvin E. Deiter, *The Holiness Revival of the Nineteenth Century* (Metuchen, NJ: Scarecrow Press, 1980), pp. 103-109.

13. An example of the extensive number of mergers in the Holiness movement is demonstrated by the antecedent institutions that formed Southern Nazarene University, my alma mater. It was formed by the mergers, or should I say amalgamations, of the following schools during the late 1800s and early 1900s: Texas Holiness University, Peniel College, Arkansas Holiness College, Central Nazarene University, Oklahoma Holiness College, Beulah Heights College, Kansas Holiness College, Southwestern Holiness College, McGee Holiness College, and Holiness Bible College. All of these together now form one University! See *Southern Lights* (Southern Nazarene University, Fall, 1996), p. 5.

14. Linder, introduction to *Dictionary of Christianity in America*, p. 16.

15. "Evangelicals," by definition, are "gospel people" and "Bible people" who share a belief, according to historian David Bebbington, in (1) personal conversion ("being born again"), (2) activism (both evangelistic and social), (3) biblical authority, and (4) the centrality of the Cross." Timothy George, "If I'm an Evangelical, What Am I?" *Christianity Today* (August 9, 1999), p. 62.

16. Rob Staples, "Words of Faith," *Herald of Holiness* (December 1998), p. 11. (Slight alterations in the original wording were made by permission of the author.)

17. Bill Bright, speaking at the National Religious Broadcasters Convention, Anaheim, California, February 7, 2000.

Chapter 18: America's Greatest Evangelistic Force

1. Gaustad, *Historical Atlas of Religion in America*, pp. 43, 44, 54.
2. Littell, *Atlas of the History of Christianity*, p. 134.
3. "Splendors and Secrets of the Vatican," National Geographic Society advertisement.
4. Therefore, he was called a "se-baptist," meaning "self-baptizer." M. A. Noll, "John Smyth," in *Who's Who in Christian History*, p. 630.
5. Brauer, *Westminster Dictionary of Church History*, p. 85.
6. Curtis, et al., *Dates with Destiny*, p. 114.
7. Brauer, *Westminster Dictionary of Church History*, n.p.
8. Curtis, et al., *Dates with Destiny*, n.p.
9. Baptist World Alliance. http://www.bwanet.org/fellowship/member-bodies/index.htm (accessed April 2000).
10. H. Leon McBeth, *Baptist Heritage* (Nashville, TN: Broadman Press, 1987), p. 22.
11. Ibid., p. 48f.
12. Linder, "Roger Williams," in *Dictionary of Christianity in America*, p. 1259.
13. McBeth, *Baptist Heritage*, p. 150.
14. Ibid., p. 200.
15. Bruce Shelley, "Baptist Churches in the U.S.A.," in *Dictionary of Christianity in America*, p. 111.
16. Joseph M. Dawson, *Baptists and the American Republic* (Nashville, TN: Broadman Press, 1956), p. 117, quoted in McBeth, *Baptist Heritage*, p. 283.
17. Ibid., p. 285.
18. Ibid., p. 377.
19. James L. Sullivan, *Baptist Polity As I See It* (Nashville, TN: Broadman Press, 1983), p. 41.
20. McBeth, *Baptist Heritage*, p. 382.
21. Robert A. Baker, *Relations Between Northern and Southern Baptists* (Fort Worth, TX: Evans Press, 1948), pp. 18-25.
22. Hudson, *Religion in America*, p. 217.
23. McBeth, *Baptist Heritage*, p. 392.
24. D. L. Shelley, "Baptist Churches in the U.S.A.," in *Dictionary of Christianity in America*, p. 113.
25. McBeth, *Baptist Heritage*, p. 432f.
26. Ibid., p. 440.
27. Ibid., p. 461.
28. Ibid., p. 563.
29. Ibid., p. 619.
30. Jerry M. Stubblefield, "Creative Advancements in Southern Baptist Sunday School Work," *Baptist History and Heritage* (January 1984), p. 52, quoted in McBeth, *Baptist Heritage*, p. 650.
31. Title taken from *Newsweek's* cover story, July 20, 1970, "Billy Graham and the Surging Southern Baptists."
32. Interview by Jim Garlow, phone, Southern Baptist Statistical Center in Nashville, Tennessee, December 1, 1999.
33. International Mission Board of the Southern Baptist Convention, interview by Jim Garlow, phone, Richmond, Virginia, December 1, 1999.

34. Arthur C. Piepkorn, *Profiles in Beliefs,* vol. II (San Francisco, CA: Harper and Row, 1978), p. 401.

35. Baptist World Alliance. http://www.bwanet.org/fellowship/member-bodies/ index.htm (accessed April 2000).

Chapter 19: An Explosion of the Spirit

1. Edith L. Blumhofer, *The Assemblies of God,* vol. I—to 1941 (Springfield, MS: Gospel Publishing House, 1989), p. 99.

2. Vinson Synan, *The Holiness-Pentecostal Movement in the United States* (Grand Rapids, MI: Wm. B. Eerdmans Publishing Co., 1971), pp. 100-109.

3. For a fuller discussion of the historical roots, see Nils Bloch-Hoell, *The Pentecostal Movement* (New York: Humanities Press, 1964).

4. Blumhofer, *Assemblies of God,* vol. I, p. 99.

5. Vinson Synan, "The Pentecostal 20th Century," *Ministries Today* (November/December, 1999), p. 28.

6. Ibid.

7. Although there are many Pentecostal "denominations," numerous Pentecostal leaders prefer to view these as a movement rather than as a collection of denominations.

8. Paul Chappel, academic dean of The King's Seminary, Van Nuys, California, interview by Jim Garlow, October 1999.

9. Vinson Synan, "The Pentecostal 20th Century," *Ministries Today* (November/December), p. 33.

10. For a treatise on the historical connection between the two movements, see Vinson Synan, *The Holiness-Pentecostal Movement in the United States* (Grand Rapids, MI: Wm. B. Eerdmans Publishing Co., 1971).

11. Blumhofer, *Assemblies of God,* vol. I, p. 181.

12. In some parts of the Pentecostal movement, sanctification and holy living were strongly emphasized. In some parts, the emphasis tended to be on speaking in tongues or the power of the Holy Spirit.

13. Endorsement by Jim Garlow in Randy Clark *Power, Holiness and Evangelism* (Shippensburg, PA: Destiny Image Publishers, 1999).

14. "Short on personal righteousness" does not refer to denominations but to selected high-profile independent ministries and personalities.

15. Blumhofer, *Assemblies of God,* vol. I, n.p.

16. So intense was the tension that even the mainline Evangelical magazine *Christianity Today* proposed a truce. At about the same time, David Shibley wrote *A Charismatic Truce* (Nashville, TN: Thomas Nelson, 1978).

17. Reverend Henry Poteet, who heard Dr. David Du Plessis speak at a gathering of Charismatic Episcopalians at the Sheraton Hotel, San Antonio, Texas, 1977; inteview by Jim Garlow, April 2000.

18. P. D. Hocken, "Charismatic Movement," eds. Stanley M. Burgess and Gary B. McGee, *Dictionary of Pentecostal and Charismatic Movements* (Grand Rapids, MI: Zondervan Publishing House, 1988), p. 143.

19. Mark McCloskey, "Nehemiah, Leader of Leaders," *Heart and Mind* (St. Paul, MN: Bethel Seminary, Spring, 1999), p. 4.

20. For a spectacular analysis of Pentecostal/Charismatic growth, see Vinson Synan, "The Pentecostal 20th Century," *Ministries Today* (November/December 1991), pp. 26-35.

Chapter 20: What a Time to Be Alive

1. Bruce Shelley, Mark Galli, Gary Burge, Timothy Paul Jones and Fritz Runge, "Christian History Time Line," (Torrance, CA: Rose Publishing, 1998), n.p.
2. Stephen Neill, *The Expansion of Christianity* (New York: Penguin Books, 1964).
3. Steve Buris, The U.S. Center for World Mission, Pasadena, California, quoted in the A.C.S.I. *Christian School Comment*, vol. 22, no. 7 (n.d.), n.p. Grant McClung, Jr., says that number is at least 78,000 per day. See *Ministries Today*, (July/August 1987), p. 60.
4. Ibid.
5. Nate Krupp, *Fulfilling the Great Commission by A.D. 2000* (Salem, OR: Preparing The Way Publishers, n.d.), p. 45.
6. Ibid., p. 7.
7. H. B. London, Jr., *The Pastors Weekly Briefing*, vol. II, no. 39 (September 30, 1994), p. 1.
8. Vinson Synan, "A Vision for the Year 2000," *Charisma* (n.d.), n.p.
9. Patrick Johnstone, *Operation World* (Grand Rapids, MI: Zondervan Publishing House, 1993), p. 21.
10. Pentecostals and Charismatics alone, without the Third Wave, account for 13 million of these, or 35,000 per day. Statistics are taken from *Christian History* (n.d.), quoted in *Ministries Today* (November/December 1998), p. 14.
11. According to *Church Around the World* (February 1993), n.p.
12. Freda Lindsay, "Christianity Tops World Religions," *Christ For The Nations Institute Newsletter* (May 1993), p. 15.
13. *Mission Frontiers* (November 1990), quoted in "Global Glimpses," *Quarterly Missions News*, ed. Helen Temple, no. 3 (January 1991), n.p.
14. These figures are from the Lausanne Statistic Task Force. See "Milestone Dates in the Growth of True Christianity," *The Wesleyan Advocate* (October 1993), p. 5.
15. "Christianity's Growth," *The Pastor's Weekly Briefing*, vol. 3, no. 7 (February 17, 1995), p. 2.
16. Samuel Dunn, *The Futurist Magazine* (April/May, 1989), quoted in John A. Knight, "This Same Jesus," *World Missions Magazine*, vol. 15, no. 6 (June 1989), p. 7.
17. *World Missions Magazine*, vol. 15, no. 6 (June 1989), p. 4.
18. David Bryant, "Today's Growing Prayer Movement Signals Hope for the World," *National and International Religion Report*, vol. 9, no. 6 (March 6, 1995), p. 4.
19. David Bryant, *The Hope at Hand* (Grand Rapids, MI: Baker Book House, 1995), p. 130.
20. C. Peter Wagner and Pablo Deiros, eds., *The Rising Revival* (Ventura, CA: Gospel Light, Renew Books, 1998), p. 8.
21. "World Prayer Center," (Colorado Springs, CO), brochure.
22. Larry Stockstill, *The Cell Church* (Ventura, CA: Regal Books), 1998, p. 27.
23. Integrity Incorporated. http://www.integinc.com (accessed April 2000).
24. For example, the "Discover the Future of Worship" seminar, led by LaMar Boschman (800-627-0923). http://www.lamarboschman.org (accessed April 2000).
25. Elmer L. Towns, *Putting an End to Worship Wars* (Nashville, TN: Broadman & Holman Publishers, 1997), n.p.
26. For a superb detailed discussion of the growth of contemporary Christian music see Charlie Peacock, *At the Crossroads* (Nashville, TN: Broadman-Holman Publishers,

1999), p. 59ff. For an interesting Reformed treatment of this subject, see John M. Frame, *Contemporary Worship Music: A Biblical Defense* (Phillipsburg, NJ: P & R, Publishing, Co., 1997).

27. Michael S. Hamilton, "The Triumph of Praise Songs: How Guitars Beat out the Organ in the Worship Wars," *Christianity Today*, vol. 43, no. 8, (July 12, 1999), p. 28.

28. Founder of International Reconciliation Coalition (P.O. Box 3278, Ventura, CA 93006).

29. Keat and Judy Wade, "First Nations' Worship Celebration Marks New Era in the History of the Church," *Body of Christ News*, (November 13, 1999), n.p.

30. Robert Colman, *One Divine Moment* (Old Tappan, N J: Revell, 1970); see also the account of this moment in Robert E. Colman, *The Coming World Revival* (Wheaton, IL: Crossway Books, a division of Good News Publishers, n.d.), pp. 26-28.

31. Donald Miller, *Reinventing Protestantism: Christianity in the New Millennium* (Berkeley, CA: University of California Press, 1997), especially note p. 32ff.

32. Dan Wooding, "Jesus People Reunion Celebrates Hippie Revival that Began Thirty Years Ago," *Horizon International Magazine*, vol. 1, issue 3 (July 1999), p. 20f.

33. *National and International Religion Report*, vol. 9, no. 8 (April 3, 1995), p. 1.

34. *National and International Religion Report*, vol. 9, no. 9 (April 17, 1995), p. 13.

35. *National and International Religion Report*, vol. 9, no. 10 (May 1, 1995), p. 3.

36. *National and International Religion Report*, vol. 9, no. 9 (April 17, 1995), p. 1.

37. *National and International Religion Report*, vol. 9, no. 15 (July 10, 1995), n.p.

38. For one Christian scholar's recent analysis, see the well-documented book by Peter Jones, *Spirit Wars: Pagan Revival in Christian America* (Mukilteo, WA: Winepress Publishing Co., 1997).

39. Robert H. Bork, *Slouching Toward Gomorrah* (New York: HarperCollins Publishers, Regan Books, 1996), flyleaf.

40. *Insights*, vol. 3, no. 6 (June 1990), p. 1.

41. *World Pulse* (April 23, 1993), n.p.

42. *San Diego Union Tribune*, August 23, 1999, sec. A, p. 8.

43. *Ministries Today* (September/October 1999), p. 20.

44. *The Wesleyan Advocate* (July/August 1999), p. 27.

45. Freda Lindsay, *Christ For The Nations Institute* (March 1994), p. 14.

46. Ibid.

47. George M. Marsden, *The Soul of the American University* (New York: Oxford University Press, 1994), n.p.

48. James Tunstead Burtchaell, *The Dying of the Light: Disengagement of Colleges and Universities from Their Christian Churches* (Grand Rapids, MI: Wm. B. Eerdmans Publishing Co., 1998), n.p.

49. "Generation to Generation" conference, hosted by Indiana University, Marion, Indiana, June 1, 1999.

50. John Vaughn, interview by Jim Garlow, Megachurch Research Center, December 1, 1999.

51. David C. Barrett, "Annual Statistical Table on Global Missions," *International Bulletin of Missionary Research* (January 1997), p. 25.

52. H. B. London, "The Persecuted Church Fact Sheet," *Pastor to Pastor* (1997), p. 1.

53. James and Marti Hefley, *By Their Blood* (Minneapolis, MN: Bethany House Publishers, 1991), n.p.

54. London, "The Persecuted Church Fact Sheet," p. 1.

55. David Aikman, "Persecutors, Beware," *Charisma* (December 1998), p. 110.

56. Curtis, *Dates with Destiny*, p. 24.

57. Richard J. Nyberg, "East German Churches Lag Behind the West," *Christianity Today* (August 9, 1999), p. 24.

58. Odhiambo Okite, "Bishop Faces Genocide Accusation," *Christianity Today* (June 14, 1999), p. 23.

59. "Our Extended, Persecuted Family," *Christianity Today* (April 29, 1996), p. 14.

60. "News Briefs," *Charisma* (December 1998), p. 46.

61. "China's Stranglehold Getting Tighter," *Send!* vol. 12, no. 5 (September/October 1992), p. 2.

62. Stephen M. Wike, *National and International Religion Report*, vol. 7, no. 6 (March 8, 1993), p. 8.

63. "News Briefs," *Charisma* (December 1998), p. 46.

64. "Two Sudanese Christians" *Charisma* (November 1994), p. 105.

65. Randy Frame, "Peru, Binding the Strong Man: For Better or Worse?" *Christianity Today* (October 26, 1992), p. 80.

66. Stephen Wike, *National and International Religion Report*, vol. 5, no. 14 (July 1, 1991), p. 1.

67. Ibid.

68. Ibid.

69. Ibid., p. 2.

70. *National and International Religion Report*, vol. 5, no. 16 (July 29, 1991), p. 5.

71. *National and International Religion Report*, vol. 7, no. 16 (July 26, 1993), n.p.

72. Thomas S. Giles "Forty Million and Counting," *Christianity Today* (April 6, 1992), p. 32.

73. Martin T. Marty, "A Protestant Reformation in Latin American?" *Ministries Today* (September/October, 1993), p. 79f.

74. "New Christendom," *The Economist* (December 24, 1988), p. 61.

75. Freda Lindsay, "Here and There," *World Prayer and Share Letter* (November/December 1990), n.p.

76. Peter Brierley, *Future Church* (London, UK: Christian Research, Monarch Books, 1998), pp. 14-16.

77. Ibid., back cover.

78. *National and International Religious Report*, vol. 8, no. 8 (April 4, 1994), p. 3.

79. "Rekindling the Fires of Faith," *Charisma* (January 1993), p. 56.

80. Ibid., p. 56.

81. "New Christendom," *The Economist* (December 24, 1988), p. 61.

82. Ibid.

83. C. Peter Wagner, Stephen Peters and Mark Wilson, eds., *Praying Through the 100 Gateways of the 10/40 Window* (Seattle, WA: YWAM Publishing, 1995), p. 12.

84. Ibid., p. 17.

85. "Penetrating the Arab World," *Charisma* (January 1993), pp. 21-23.

86. Ibid., p. 24.

87. *National and International Religion Report*, vol. 6, no. 22 (October 19, 1992), n.p.

88. Ted Haggard, "Celebrating in Ephesus," *Ministries Today* (September/October 1999), p. 27.

89. Larry Keefauver, "God's Next *Chairos*?" *Ministries Today* (November/December 1999), p. 7.

90. *Christian School Comment*, vol. 22, no. 7, p. 1.

91. John Vaughn, interview by Jim Garlow, Megachurch Research Center, December 1, 1999.

92. Buris, *Christian School Comment*, p. 1.

93. Freda Lindsay, "Revival in China and Russia," *World Prayer and Share Letter* (November 1992), p. 14.

94. E. LeBron Fairbanks, "Who Really Is Our Enemy?" *World Mission Magazine* (June 1990), p. 5.

95. "In the News," *The Wesleyan Advocate* (January 1993), p. 15.

96. *National and International Religion Report*, vol. 5, no. 16 (July 29, 1999), n.p.

97. "Revival Fires in the Dragon's Lair," *Charisma* (January 1993), p. 38.

98. Ibid., p. 35.

99. "Into the Heart of Darkness," *Charisma* (January 1993), p. 27.

100. *National and International Religion Report*, vol. 7, no. 8 (April 5, 1993), p. 1.

101. "Harvest Season," *Christianity Today* (June 14, 1999), p. 18.

102. *National and International Religion Report*, vol. 9, no. 16 (July 24, 1995), p.1.

103. "Religion on Upswing in Russia," *Herald of Holiness* (February 1994), p. 45.

104. Edward E. Plowman, "Reporters Notebook: The New Soviet Christians," *National and International Religion Report*, vol. 5, no. 16, (July 29, 1991), p. 1.

105. Bill and Amy Stearns, *Catch the Vision 2000* (Minneapolis, MN: Bethany House Publishers, 1991), n.p.

106. *National and International Religion Report*, vol. 5, no. 15 (July 15, 1991), n.p.

107. *National and International Religion Report*, vol. 6, no. 23 (November, 2, 1992), n.p.

108. "New Christendom," *The Economist* (December 24, 1988), p. 61.

109. Steve Buris, *Christian School Comment*, p. 1.

110. *Insights*, vol. 2, no. 6 (December 1992), p. 2.

111. *National and International Religion Report*, vol. 7, no. 21 (October 4, 1993), n.p.

112. Freda Lindsay, *Christ For The Nations Institute* (November 1992), p. 15.

113. *National and International Religion Report*, vol. 7, no. 2 (January 11, 1993), p. 1.

114. Ibid.

INDEX

More Great Books from Regal

How the New Apostolic Reformation
Is Shaking Up the Church As
We Know It
C. Peter Wagner
Hardcover
ISBN 08307.19156

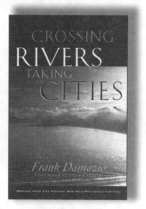

Moving into the Future God
Has Prepared for You
Frank Damazio
Paperback
ISBN 08307.23927

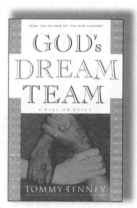

A Call to Unity
Tommy Tenney
Paperback
ISBN 08307.23846

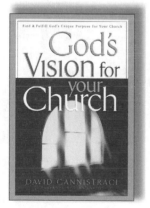

How to Find and Fulfill Your
Corporate Gifting
David Cannistraci
Paperback
ISBN 08307.25156

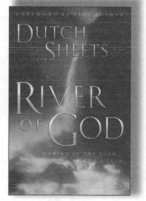

Moving in the Flow of God's
Plan for Revival
Dutch Sheets
Paperback
ISBN 08307.20758

He Was Sent to Save the World
E. L. Towns
Paperback
ISBN 08307.24281

Available at your local Christian bookstore.
www.regalbooks.com

Regal
FROM GOSPEL LIGHT

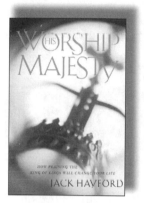
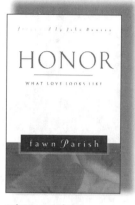

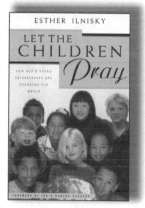

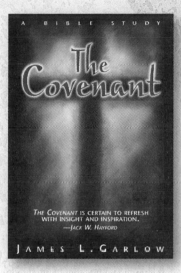
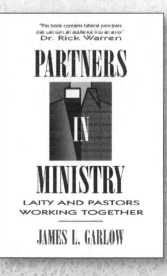